A Manual of

International Dispute Resolution

By Anthony Connerty

Commonwealth Secretariat
Marlborough House
Pall Mall, London SW1Y 5HX
United Kingdom

Published by the Commonwealth Secretariat
Publication editor: Tina Johnson
Designed by kc gan designs
Printed and bound by CPI Group (UK) Ltd, Croydon, CR0 4YY
Wherever possible, the Commonwealth Secretariat uses paper sourced from sustainable forests or from sources that minimise a destructive impact on the environment.

Copies of this publication may be ordered direct from:
The Publications Manager
Communications and Public Affairs Division
Commonwealth Secretariat
Marlborough House
Pall Mall, London SW1Y 5HX
United Kingdom

Tel: +44 (0) 20 7747 6342
Fax: +44 (0) 20 7839 9081

E-mail: publications@commonwealth.int
Websites: www.thecommonwealth.org/law
www.thecommonwealth.org/publications

ISBN 13: 978-8-0-85092-837-2

A Manual of

International Dispute Resolution

By Anthony Connerty

Acknowledgments

I would like to thank Sandra Day O'Connor, the first woman to serve as an Associate Justice of the United States Supreme Court, for graciously agreeing to write the Foreword to the Manual. Justice O'Connor served for over 24 years on the Supreme Court Bench. It is a measure of her greatness that she was prepared to take the time out of her busy schedule to write the Foreword.

The original proposal for the Manual was put to me by Dr Emmanuel Awuku of the Commonwealth Secretariat in London. I am indebted to him for that proposal, as well as for his support – and for the support of his colleague at the Secretariat, Katalaina Sapolu – whilst writing the book.

Following the completion of the manuscript I have been greatly helped by the Secretariat's Publications Manager in London, Guy Bentham, and by the publications editor in New York, Tina Johnson.

I am grateful to Don McKinnon, Secretary-General of the Commonwealth Secretariat, for writing the Preface.

I would also like to thank the following, who have read, commented on and made suggestions in relation to various chapters and sections of the Manual. I am very grateful to them all for their time and their help.

Dame Rosalyn Higgins, CBE, a Judge of the International Court of Justice (ICJ), The Hague, The Netherlands. Judge Higgins, the UK Judge at the ICJ, was the first woman Judge at the Court and was elected as its first woman President in February 2006.

Tjaco van den Hout, Secretary-General, and Brooks Daly, Senior Legal Counsel, Permanent Court of Arbitration, The Hague, The Netherlands.

Philippe Gautier, Registrar, International Tribunal for the Law of the Sea, Hamburg, Germany.

Christoph H Schreuer, Professor of International Law at the University of Vienna, and author of *The ICSID Convention: a Commentary*.

Adrian Winstanley, Director General, London Court of International Arbitration, London, UK.

Mark E Appel, Senior Vice-President, International Centre for Dispute Resolution of the American Arbitration Association, Dublin, Ireland.

Eric P Tuchmann, General Counsel and Corporate Secretary, American Arbitration Association, New York, USA.

Emmanuel Jolivet, General Counsel, and Melanie Meilhac, Jurist, International Chamber of Commerce, Paris, France.

F D von Hombracht-Brinkman, Managing Director, Netherlands Arbitration Institute, Rotterdam, The Netherlands.

Allan Connarty, Director of Operations, Chartered Institute of Arbitrators, London, UK.

Eun-Joo Min, Senior Legal Officer, United Nations World Intellectual Property Organization, Geneva, Switzerland.

Colin Rule, Director, Online Dispute Resolution, eBay, San Jose, California, USA.

Emilia Onyema, barrister and solicitor of the Supreme Court of Nigeria, and solicitor of the Supreme Court of England and Wales; PhD Researcher at Queen Mary College, University of London.

Sophie Nappert, Arbitration Group Leader, Denton Wilde Sapte, London – particular thanks to her for bravely agreeing to read an early draft of the Manual.

The mistakes are mine – but I quote from the 1852 Preface by Peter Mark Roget to his Thesaurus: *"...trusting to the indulgence of those for whose benefit it is intended, and to the candour of critics who, while they find it easy to detect faults, can, at the same time, duly appreciate difficulties"*.

Anthony Connerty

Contents

Foreword

This Manual addresses a topic at the confluence of several powerful trends in contemporary law, commerce and international relations. The reader will find within it reverberations of many forces. The rising globalisation of trade has demanded common dispute resolution platforms for parties engaged in international commerce. The last six decades have witnessed a renewed commitment to the peaceful resolution of international disputes among States. Private investment needs the confidence of arbitral recourse to make it willing to supply capital to developing States and state-run industries. The rule of law is on the rise in countries around the world. The explosive growth of the Internet as a new medium of commerce has created the challenge of devising mechanisms for dispute resolution among contracting parties who have never met. For years there has been a steady adoption of alternative dispute resolution on the local level. And the list goes on.

These trends intersect in so many ways that any treatment of international dispute settlement will, in a sense, be the product of an arbitrary classification of larger trends, amalgamated with concrete illustrations and practical applications. One might divide the topic into commercial dispute resolution and governmental dispute resolution. Or one could view it through a historical lens, tracing the development of modern international dispute resolution from its roots in treaties and local dispute resolution practices. The genius of the Manual's plan is that it is entirely practical, laying out the foundations and mechanics of various dispute-resolution frameworks, explaining the relevant tribunals and arbitration organisations, and illustrating the application of these to specific types of disputes. This is a very sound approach: International dispute resolution, in one or another form, is the practical concern of innumerable businessmen, public servants, lawyers and leaders. The Manual will be a useful tool.

Of necessity, this work can only offer a survey of this wide and fast-evolving field. Mr Connerty is candid, and perhaps a bit too humble, in admitting the limitations of the Manual, but his references to further reading give the reader a path to more detailed knowledge. Throughout, the Manual demonstrates, in a concrete and surefooted fashion, the importance of its topic – and, by extension, the relevance of the work done by its readers. It is a timely and useful publication.

Sandra Day O'Connor
Associate Justice of the Supreme Court of the United States, 1981-2006

Preface

In 2003 at their meeting in Abuja, Nigeria, Commonwealth Heads of Government recognised that globalisation has significant potential benefits for all. However, the world is characterised by uneven development, and Heads stressed that globalisation must provide real opportunities for developing countries to transform their economies and societies through diversification. This, they said, would require a legal order that is fair, efficient, predictable and accessible. It would also need properly functioning courts and other legal institutions that could bring about a favourable business climate by protecting investments and by enforcing contracts and property rights.

Globalisation inevitably leads to an increase in disputes in the field of trade and commerce. Such disputes arise in the commercial sphere, and also in inter-State relations. The Commonwealth Secretariat therefore decided that it would be useful to produce a Manual dealing with international disputes, dispute resolution and the organisations dealing with such disputes. To be of benefit, the topics covered would have to be of particular interest to Commonwealth countries.

We believe that the resulting ***Manual of International Dispute Resolution*** achieves this in three ways.

First, it concentrates on areas of inter-State disagreement such as territorial and maritime boundaries, as well as trading and commercial, investment and intellectual property disputes. The Manual also examines the various methods of resolving these disputes, such as arbitration and alternative dispute resolution.

Second, the Manual examines the different courts and tribunals that handle these international disputes, such as the International Court of Justice, the Permanent Court of Arbitration, the International Tribunal on the Law of the Sea and the International Centre for the Settlement of Investment Disputes.

Third, it focuses on various international dispute resolution institutions in the area of trade and commerce, such as the International Chamber of Commerce and the World Intellectual Property Organization. Use of the Internet has had a significant impact on world trade, and the Manual looks also at developments in online dispute resolution, especially regarding documentary credits and domain names.

We would like to thank the author, Anthony Connerty, for preparing this Manual. We sincerely hope that it will be a valuable resource for Commonwealth legal officers and for all those interested in the settlement of international disputes.

Don McKinnon
Commonwealth Secretary-General

Author's Note

When I was asked to write a book for the Commonwealth Secretariat on the subject of international dispute resolution, my first concern was "Where do I start?" The problem is not so much what to put in but rather what to leave out. What are the particular topics that, say, Commonwealth law officers are likely to face?

There are traditional areas of dispute: for example, inter-State disputes concerning territorial boundaries and maritime delimitation, and disputes in the area of international trade and commerce. But in addition there are new types of dispute that have emerged: arbitrations concerning investment treaty disputes, and disputes arising out of the increasing use of the Internet. One example is the problem of cybersquatting: domain name disputes.

If those types of dispute would be of potential interest to Commonwealth countries, then so also might the methods of resolving such disputes – arbitration, for example – and, similarly, the courts and tribunals handling those disputes, such as the Permanent Court of Arbitration (PCA).

I have therefore chosen five topics in the field of international dispute settlement and resolution, and have sought to provide an overview of each.

The first topic is what might be termed supranational disputes – disputes where one or more of the parties is likely to be a State. The areas chosen are territorial disputes, maritime delimitation disputes and investor-State disputes.

The second topic is the supranational dispute resolution bodies dealing with such disputes. There are four that may be of particular interest to Commonwealth Governments: the International Court of Justice (ICJ), the PCA, the International Tribunal for the Law of the Sea (ITLOS) and the World Bank's International Centre for Settlement of Investment Disputes (ICSID).

The dispute resolution methods considered in relation to supranational disputes and the supranational dispute resolution bodies are litigation, arbitration and mediation/conciliation.

The third topic is dispute resolution in the area of international trade and commerce. Four methods of dispute resolution are considered: litigation again (but this time in the national courts), arbitration, various forms of alternative dispute resolution (in particular mediation/conciliation) and expert determination.

The fourth topic deals with institutions and other bodies concerned with dispute resolution in international trade and commerce. These are international commercial arbitral institutions – the International Chamber of Commerce (ICC), the London Court of International Arbitration (LCIA), the China International Economic and Trade Arbitration Commission (CIETAC), the American Arbitration Association (AAA) and so on – and a major organisation concerned with international trade and commerce: the United Nations.

The fifth topic is a rapidly developing area: online dispute resolution (ODR). After a general introduction, two particular areas have been chosen that are of great significance in the field of international trade and commerce and international intellectual property:

documentary credits and domain name disputes. The two systems considered are the ICC's DOCDEX scheme and the World Intellectual Property Organization's Domain Name Dispute Resolution system.

The topics are illustrated by decisions of the supranational dispute resolution bodies – the ICJ, PCA, ITLOS and ICSID – and by decisions of national courts, including those relating to the New York Convention and the United Nations Commission on International Trade Law's (UNCITRAL) Model Arbitration Law.

Each of the topics covers an enormous field. The Manual can do no more than provide an overview and seek to highlight matters of particular importance. Leading textbooks are available on areas that could be covered only briefly. These include, for example, in the field of international law, Ian Brownlie's *Principles of Public International Law* and Malcolm Shaw's *International Law*; in the area of international commercial arbitration, works such as Redfern and Hunter's *Law and Practice of International Commercial Arbitration* and Gary Born's *International Commercial Arbitration – Commentary and Materials*; and in the specific field of ICC arbitration, *International Chamber of Commerce Arbitration* by Craig, Park and Paulsson. *Bernstein's Handbook of Arbitration and Dispute Resolution Practice* (by John Tackaberry QC and Arthur Marriott QC) also contains chapters on domestic and international arbitration. An entire library could be filled with works dealing with arbitration.

Because of the number of investor-State disputes that have arisen in recent years, investment treaty arbitration has increased enormously. Reference is made in Chapter 9 to *International Investment Law and Arbitration: Leading Cases from the ICSID, NAFTA, Bilateral Treaties and Customary International Law*, edited by Todd Weiler. The volume contains essays by a number of leading experts in the field. Specific reference is made to an essay by Professor Christoph Schreuer on the *Vivendi I* case. Professor Schreuer is also the author of the 1,500-page work, *The ICSID Convention: A Commentary*.[1]

Advocacy is only touched on in the Manual, although it is one of the strands that run through the subject of international dispute settlement – particularly in relation to the areas covered. Chapter 7 deals briefly with advocacy in the context of the need to prove the indirect methods of showing title in territorial disputes. One work of particular significance given the topics dealt with in the Manual is The *Art of Advocacy in International Arbitration*, edited by R Doak Bishop. The book contains essays by Mr Bishop and other leading international arbitration practitioners.

A useful work on the comparatively new area of ODR, dealt with in Part V of the Manual, is *Online Dispute Resolution* by Etan Katsh and Janet Rifkin, both of the University of Massachusetts.

The Manual tries to look – through the eyes of Commonwealth countries – at the world beyond the Commonwealth: the world of international dispute resolution in the area of inter-State disputes and in the fields of international trade and commerce, investment and intellectual property.

Anthony Connerty
Berkhamsted, England
March 2006

1 In the Acknowledgments I have recorded my thanks to Professor Schreuer for his comments and assistance in relation to the chapter on investor-State disputes and investment treaty arbitration and the chapter on the ICSID Centre.

Acronyms and Abbreviations

AAA	American Arbitration Association
AALCO	Asian-African Legal Consultative Organisation
ADR	Alternative Dispute Resolution
BIT	Bilateral Investment Treaty
BOC	Bureau of Customs
CEDR	Centre for Effective Dispute Resolution
CCOIC	China Chamber of International Commerce
CCPIT	China Council for the Promotion of International Trade
ccTLD	Country Code Top Level Domain
CDP	City Disputes Panel
CIETAC	China International Economic and Trade Arbitration Commission
CISS	Comprehensive Import Supervision Scheme
CLOUT	Case Law on UNCITRAL Texts
DAC	Departmental Advisory Committee on Arbitration Law
DB	Dispute Board
DOCDEX	Documentary Instruments Dispute Resolution Expertise
ECT	Energy Charter Treaty
EEZ	Exclusive Economic Zone
FOB	Free on Board
gTLD	Generic Top Level Domain
ICANN	Internet Corporation for Assigned Names and Numbers
ICC	International Chamber of Commerce
ICDR	International Centre for Dispute Resolution
ICJ	International Court of Justice
ICSID	International Convention on the Settlement of Investment Disputes or International Centre for Settlement of Investment Disputes
ICT	Information and Communications Technology
IT	Information Technology
ITLOS	International Tribunal for the Law of the Sea
LCIA	London Court of International Arbitration
MAL	Model Arbitration Law
Mercosur	Southern Common Market
MFN	Most Favoured Nation
MIT	Multilateral Investment Treaty
MOX	Mixed Oxide
NAFTA	North American Free Trade Agreement
NAF	National Arbitration Forum
NAI	Netherlands Arbitration Institute

OAU	Organisation of African Unity
ODR	Online Dispute Resolution
OECD	Organisation for Economic Co-operation and Development
PCA	Permanent Court of Arbitration
PSI	Pre-Shipment Inspection
SCC	Stockholm Chamber of Commerce
SGS	Société Générale de Surveillance
UCP	Uniform Customs and Practice for Documentary Credits
UDRP	Uniform Domain Name Dispute Resolution Policy
UN/CEFACT	United Nations Centre for Trade Facilitation and Electronic Business
UNCITRAL	United Nations Commission on International Trade Law
UNCLOS	United Nations Convention on the Law of the Sea
UNCTAD	United Nations Conference on Trade and Development
UNECE	United Nations Economic Commission for Europe
URC	Uniform Rules for Collections
URDG	Uniform Rules for Demand Guarantees
URR	Uniform Rules for Bank-to-Bank Reimbursement under Documentary Credits
WIPO	World Intellectual Property Organization

Part I: Overview of Dispute Avoidance and Resolution

"Arbitration is a valuable lubricant in international trade and businessmen are entitled to such help as Governments can reasonably give them in making it effective."

Sir Michael Kerr [2]

2 Sir Michael Kerr, "Concord and Conflict in International Arbitration", *Arbitration International* 13, p 143. That "memorable sentence" was quoted by Sir Michael, former Lord Justice of Appeal and distinguished international arbitrator, in reference to the Report of the Private International Law Committee in which it advocated the enactment by the British Government of the New York Convention.

1 Introduction

This Manual seeks to give an outline of five broad areas of international dispute settlement and resolution:

- supranational disputes;
- supranational dispute resolution bodies;
- international commercial dispute resolution;
- institutions and other bodies concerned with the resolution of disputes in the field of international commerce;
- online dispute resolution.

Within these areas, it looks at territorial and maritime delimitation disputes as well as at disputes in the fields of investment, international trade and intellectual property. It is divided into six parts:

Part I contains an overview of dispute avoidance and dispute resolution.
Part II deals with supranational dispute resolution.
Part III looks at supranational dispute resolution bodies.
Part IV considers international commercial dispute resolution and the bodies dealing with such disputes.
Part V moves into the electronic era and looks at online dispute resolution.
Part VI seeks to provide a summary of the Manual and to take a look into the future.

Part I

The chapters in Part I contain introductory matters and seek to give an overview of material that appears in Parts II-V of the Manual.

Although the focus here is mainly on dispute resolution and settlement, it goes without saying that – if at all possible – disputes should be avoided. Chapter 2 therefore looks at some methods in use around the world that are aimed at stopping disputes from arising in the first place.

Chapter 3 gives a brief introduction to the four dispute resolution processes that are considered in detail later in the Manual: litigation, arbitration, alternative dispute resolution (ADR) and expert determination. It also mentions some of the organisations involved in the resolution of international disputes. First, there are what might be described as supranational courts and tribunals: the International Court of Justice (ICJ), the Permanent Court of Arbitration (PCA), the International Tribunal for the Law of the Sea (ITLOS) and the International Centre for Settlement of Investment Disputes (ICSID Centre). All of these are considered in more detail in later chapters.

Second, these organisations include some of the international bodies concerned with international commercial dispute resolution: the London Court of International Arbitration; the International Court of Arbitration of the International Chamber of Commerce (ICC); the

American Arbitration Association's International Centre for Dispute Resolution in Dublin; the China International Economic and Trade Arbitration Commission; the Arbitration Institute of the Stockholm Chamber of Commerce; the Netherlands Arbitration Institute; and a specialist intellectual property body – the United Nations' World Intellectual Property Organization (WIPO). Similarly, a more detailed look is taken at these various organisations later in the Manual.

Chapter 4 refers to a number of international treaties and conventions that are of particular relevance to international trade and investment and to the resolution of international disputes: the Washington Convention (the Convention on the Settlement of Investment Disputes between States and Nationals of Other States, also known as the ICSID Convention); the 1982 Law of the Sea Convention (UNCLOS III); and the New York Convention (the Convention on the Recognition and Enforcement of Foreign Arbitral Awards).

Part II

The Chapters in Part II deal with supranational dispute resolution: areas of dispute where one or more of the parties is likely to be a State.

Following introductory material in Chapter 5, Chapter 6 looks at international law and a convention of great significance in this field: the Vienna Convention on the Law of Treaties.

Chapters 7, 8 and 9 consider three areas of considerable importance in international dispute resolution: territorial disputes, maritime delimitation disputes and investor-State disputes. The growing importance of these three areas is demonstrated by the increasing number of disputes that are being dealt with by supranational dispute resolution bodies.

Part III

Chapters 10 to 14 of Part III deal with supranational dispute resolution bodies.

Chapter 10 contains introductory matters. Chapter 11 provides an historical overview of the ICJ and looks at the United Nations Charter, the Charter of the International Court itself and the ICJ Rules of Court and Practice Directions. The PCA is considered in Chapter 12: its history (including the Hague Peace Conventions) and some of the present-day Arbitration and Conciliation Rules.

Chapter 13 looks at ITLOS, a creation of UNCLOS III. In particular, it looks at the complex provisions for dispute resolution contained in the 1982 Convention and its Annexes.

The World Bank's ICSID Centre in Washington is considered in Chapter 14. The considerable increase in the number of cases being dealt with by the Centre shows the growing importance of international investment. The chapter looks at the history of the Centre, at various sets of ICSID Rules and at a number of problems that have arisen in the field of investor-State disputes.

Part IV

Part IV of the Manual is concerned with international commercial dispute resolution.

Following introductory matters in Chapter 15, litigation in national courts is considered in Chapter 16, including a consideration of national courts as a forum for the enforcement of – and challenge to – arbitral awards.

Chapter 17 considers international commercial arbitration. It starts by seeking to compare arbitration and litigation, and goes on to look at the United Nations Commission on International Trade Law (UNCITRAL) Model Arbitration Law and the New York Convention, arguably the most important convention in the field of international commercial arbitration.

Chapter 18 looks at some of the international commercial arbitral institutions and their various Rules. There are many such institutions worldwide, and space permits only some of them to be considered in the Manual. This chapter also looks at another area where the UN has contributed to the smooth running of world trade: the UNCITRAL Arbitration Rules.

Chapter 19 is concerned with a third method of dispute resolution in the international commercial field: ADR – its development, the different types of ADR used and some of the institutions worldwide that offer various types of ADR services. This is again an area in which the UN has played a major role, and the chapter considers the UNCITRAL Model Law on International Commercial Conciliation and the UNCITRAL Conciliation Rules.

A fourth method of dispute resolution is considered in Chapter 20: expert determination. The chapter makes some comparisons between expert determination and arbitration, and looks at cases in the area and at some of the institutions around the world that offer expert determination facilities.

Part V

Part V of the Manual is concerned with a comparatively new and exciting area of dispute resolution: online dispute resolution (ODR). This seems certain to increase in importance in the electronic era.

Chapters 21 to 25 look first at the emergence of ODR and then at two specific systems of ODR that are of particular relevance in the field of international trade and international intellectual property: the ICC's procedure for dealing with documentary credit disputes – the Documentary Credit Dispute Resolution Expertise (DOCDEX) System – and WIPO's Domain Name Dispute Resolution system.

Part VI

Chapter 26 provides a summary of the Manual and takes a look into the future.

Dispute Resolution Chart

The Dispute Resolution Chart is intended to give a broad view of the types of disputes covered in the Manual and the types of tribunal dealing with those disputes. The relevant chapter numbers are indicated on the Chart. Also indicated is any relevant international convention.

For example, international commercial disputes (Chapters 15 to 18) might be dealt with by national courts (Chapter 16) or by international commercial arbitration tribunals such as those administered by the American Arbitration Association (Chapter 18). The relevant international treaty is the New York Convention (Chapters 4 and 17).

Online disputes of the kind considered in Part V of the Manual – which looks at the Electronic Era – might be dealt with under WIPO's Domain Name Dispute Resolution scheme or the ICC's DOCDEX system. These two systems are dealt with in Chapters 23 and 24.

The Chart is not intended to be exhaustive. For example, virtually all of the disputes listed in the first column of the Chart could also be dealt with by alternative dispute resolution (Chapter 19), and a limited number of such disputes might be dealt with by way of expert determination (Chapter 20).

Types of Dispute	Tribunals Dealing with Disputes						International Conventions Applicable (Chap. 4)		
	International Court of Justice (ICJ) (Chap. 11)	Permanent Court of Arbitration (PCA) (Chap. 12)	International Tribunal for the Law of the Sea (ITLOS) (Chap. 13)	International Centre for Settlement of Investment Disputes (ICSID Centre) (Chap. 14)	National Courts (Chap. 16)	International Tribunals (Chaps. 18, 23 and 24)	United Nations Convention on the Law of the Sea (UNCLOS III) (Chap. 8)	International Convention on the Settlement of Investment Disputes (ICSED) (Chap. 9)	New York Convention (Chap. 17)
Territorial Disputes (Chap. 7)	✓	✓							
Maritime Delimitation Disputes (Chap. 8)	✓	✓	✓				✓		
Investor-State Disputes (Chap. 9)				✓				✓	
International Commercial Disputes (Chaps. 15, 16, 17 and 18)					✓	✓			✓
Online Disputes (Chaps. 21-25)						✓			

2 Dispute Avoidance

It is obviously preferable to avoid disputes arising in the first place. This chapter looks briefly at three areas of dispute avoidance:

1) Negotiation
2) Schemes aimed at minimising and managing risk
3) Alternative dispute resolution (ADR) filter mechanisms

1) Negotiation

The parties to a potential dispute can seek to avoid their disagreement becoming a full-blown dispute by negotiating. Discussions aimed at resolving differences are perhaps one of the most obvious methods of dispute avoidance.

2) Schemes Aimed at Minimising and Managing Risk

A common thread can be seen in steps taken in various industries around the world aimed at avoiding disputes arising, i.e., schemes aimed at minimising and managing risk. These steps include the following.

Planning

- ensuring that contractual documents are clear, precise and fair;
- maintaining accurate records;
- anticipating potential problem areas;
- defining problems when they arise.

Schemes to lessen the risk of disputes arising

One example of schemes to reduce the risk of disputes is partnering. This is a concept used originally in the construction industry. The aim is to establish a working relationship between the contracting parties involved in a project: through co-operation and teamwork the parties should achieve their mutual goals. Good faith is obviously a vital component.

Resolving disputes before they escalate

Contracts can include provisions for dealing with disputes as they arise, in an effort to stop them escalating:

- *Dispute Review Boards (DRB).* A number of respected professionals are nominated prior to the commencement of the project. These professionals familiarise themselves with the project and keep abreast of developments as work proceeds. Disputes are referred to the DRB for a non-binding ruling. If that does not resolve the dispute, the matter is referred to a further dispute resolution process.

- *A Standing or On-Site Neutral.* This is a similar concept involving an industry professional / expert in whom both parties have confidence and who will serve in an informal capacity to resolve disputes by, for example, conducting neutral fact-finding exercises.
- *Multi-step ADR.* One example of this is the 'wise men' procedure used in the oil and gas industry. The wise men will be respected executives in the companies concerned (but who are not involved in the particular project). They investigate the dispute. If they are unable to resolve the matter, it proceeds to the next stage. This might be arbitration.

Dispute avoidance schemes can be used for all aspects of a project. For example, an Oil and Gas Industry Bulk Liquid Terminal Scheme for the avoidance of industrial disputes provides for a step-by-step process for settling labour grievances. Work is to continue during the period of negotiations.

3) ADR Filter Mechanisms

These mechanisms are considered in Chapter 19, which deals with ADR. It may be arguable whether such mechanisms are a form of dispute resolution or whether they are actually an example of dispute avoidance. Whatever label is put on them, they are certainly aimed at avoiding the full-scale conflict involved in both litigation and arbitration. An example of ADR filter mechanisms in action is given in Box 1.

Box 1: ADR Filter Mechanisms in the Boston Central Artery / Tunnel Project

Provision for ADR 'filters' was made in the Boston Central Artery / Tunnel Project. The Boston Project was one of the largest and most complex highway projects ever undertaken. The original estimate for the Project was for a duration of 10 years and a cost in excess of US$6 billion. The Project was located in the middle of downtown Boston in a tight circle of land about one mile in diameter known as the 'Hub'. The area was bounded on three sides by waterways: the Charles River Basin to the North, Boston's Inner Harbour to the East and Fort Point Channel to the South. Downtown Boston was full of skyscrapers, narrow streets and many 19th century buildings. The Project included a four-lane tunnel under Boston Harbour, three complex major highway interchanges within the city of Boston limits, a new highway to be constructed under 10 active railroad tracks, a depressed multi-layered artery through the centre of Boston and a billion-dollar bridge located in the centre of a multiple highway interchange.

It was expected that about 100 construction contracts would be involved in the Project. Some of the larger of these were in the range of US$200-300 million. In addition, there were several hundred sub-contracts, together with contracts for construction management and geotechnical services.

Clearly the potential for disputes in a project of such complexity was considerable: however careful the managers of the Project might be, disputes were bound to arise. Any one dispute might bring the entire Project to a standstill. A scheme for avoiding disputes, or at least ensuring that disputes did not escalate into full-scale litigation or arbitration battles, was therefore vital.

An ADR scheme was devised aimed at dealing with potential problems. This involved the following series of 'filters' designed to resolve disputes before they escalated:

- partnering;
- the presentation of a dispute to an 'authorised representative';
- a Dispute Review Board (DRB);
- a mediation or ADR programme, which might be triggered during the DRB process.

Under the first filter – the partnering scheme – contractors were invited to enter into a process that consisted of efforts by trained facilitators to educate all participants in the Project in the mutual benefits of working towards common goals. The programme comprised off-site conferences that were to be repeated throughout the course of the Project.

Under the second filter, disputes were put to an 'authorised representative' to make a decision on the claim in question.

The third filter involved the establishment of a DRB. Three panellists, technically qualified in the type of construction work involved in that particular contract, were selected for the DRB at the outset of each contract. They were to be familiar with the scope of the contract and able to begin the dispute resolution process immediately a claim was put to the Board. The standard procedure to be followed at a meeting of the DRB did not involve the usual trial practices such as cross-examination of witnesses. The process required the DRB panellists to keep abreast of construction developments during the progress of works in question.

The fourth filter involved a provision for mediation or some other form of ADR. This might be triggered during the period of the DRB. Again, the filter was designed to resolve disputes before they reached the stage of formal arbitration or litigation.

Source: Anthony Connerty, 'The Role of ADR in the Resolution of International Disputes' [1996] 13 Arbitration International 121.

In an ideal world, disputes would be avoided. But experience shows that, despite all the precautions taken by the parties to contracts (and similar arrangements), disputes will nevertheless arise. It is therefore worthwhile to provide efficient mechanisms for resolving them.

The following chapters look at dispute resolution and at some of the international bodies involved in resolving such disputes.

3 Dispute Resolution

1) Introduction

This chapter briefly describes two areas that are dealt with in more detail in later chapters. First, it looks at some of the methods of dispute resolution used internationally, both in the context of inter-State disputes and in the context of international trade and commerce. Second, it reviews some of the organisations involved in international dispute resolution – again, in both inter-State and commercial dispute resolution.

2) Some Methods of Dispute Resolution Used Internationally

There is probably little doubt that the two major methods of dispute resolution in use are litigation and arbitration, both in the inter-State area and in the pure commercial area. However, it is clear that other dispute resolution processes are also being used, among them alternative dispute resolution (ADR) and – in fairly restricted areas – expert determination. One example of the use of expert determination is in the oil and gas industry in relation to measurement disputes.

Which type of dispute mechanism is to be used in a particular case will depend on the precise nature of the dispute. For example, a jurisdiction dispute arising out of an international contract is more likely to be settled by litigation (or arbitration) than by, say, expert determination.

There are certain areas where disputes between States and disputes between States and non-State bodies (such as corporations) may be resolved by way of methods specified in international conventions. Areas of particular importance globally are investor-State disputes and maritime and land boundary disputes. Such disputes are likely to be resolved by what may be described as supranational dispute resolution bodies such as the International Court of Justice (ICJ), the Permanent Court of Arbitration (PCA), the International Tribunal for the Law of the Sea (ITLOS) and the World Bank's International Centre for Settlement of Investment Disputes (the ICSID Centre).

In the case of the ICJ, the method of dispute resolution is litigation. In the case of the PCA and the ICSID Centre, the process used is international arbitration, administered under the rules prescribed by these organisations. The 1982 UN Convention on the Law of the Sea (UNCLOS III) contains provisions for a mixture of dispute resolution processes, some to be administered by ITLOS and some to be administered by other organisations (including the ICJ): litigation, arbitration and conciliation.

3) Organisations Providing Dispute Resolution Facilities

Dispute resolution bodies can be divided into what may be described as the supranational and the international commercial dispute resolution organisations.

i) Inter-State Courts and Tribunals

Among the supranational bodies are inter-State Courts and Tribunals such as those mentioned earlier: the ICJ, the PCA, ITLOS and the ICSID Centre. These are considered in Part III of the Manual.

ii) International commercial organisations

There are many international organisations concerned with commercial dispute resolution. It is not possible to consider them all, but they include the International Chamber of Commerce in Paris, the London Court of International Arbitration, the American Arbitration Association, the CPR Institute of Dispute Resolution, the China International Economic and Trade Arbitration Commission, the Arbitration Institute of the Stockholm Chamber of Commerce, the Netherlands Arbitration Institute and the UN's specialist intellectual property organisation, the World Intellectual Property Organization. The Chartered Institute of Arbitrators, in its role as a teaching organisation, plays a prominent part in commercial dispute resolution.

International commercial dispute resolution – together with the various international commercial arbitral institutions and other international bodies dealing with disputes in these areas – is considered in Part IV of the Manual.

4 International Conventions Dealing with Dispute Resolution

There are various international conventions that deal with – or that include provision for – dispute resolution. Three of these are of particular relevance in the context of maritime disputes, investment disputes and international trade disputes generally:

1) The 1982 United Nations Convention on the Law of the Sea (UNCLOS III);
2) The International Convention on the Settlement of Investment Disputes (the ICSID/ Washington Convention);
3) The Convention on the Recognition and Enforcement of Foreign Arbitral Awards (the New York Convention).

A fourth Convention – the Vienna Convention on the Law of Treaties – is of significance in the context of public international law and is therefore of general importance in relation to supranational dispute resolution and the supranational bodies dealing with such disputes. The Vienna Convention is considered in Part II of the Manual in the chapter dealing with international law.

1) UNCLOS III

The third UN Convention on the Law of the Sea (commonly known as UNCLOS III) states in Article 2 that:

> *"(1) The sovereignty of a coastal State extends beyond its land, territory and internal waters… to an adjacent belt of sea, described as the territorial sea.*
>
> *(2) This sovereignty extends to the air space over the territorial sea as well as to its bed and subsoil.*
>
> *(3) The sovereignty over the territorial sea is exercised subject to this Convention and to other rules of international law."*

Articles 3 and 5 deal with the breadth of the territorial sea and the 'normal baseline'. Article 3 provides that:

> *"Every State has the right to establish the breadth of its territorial sea up to a limit not exceeding 12 nautical miles, measured from baselines determined in accordance with this Convention."*

Article 5 states that: *"The normal baseline for measuring the breadth of the territorial sea is the low water-line along the coast…."*

In addition to dealing with the territorial seas, the Convention also deals with contiguous zones, exclusive economic zones and continental shelves, and maritime delimitation.

Given the complexity of the subject matter of UNCLOS III, it is unsurprising that the dispute resolution processes contained within the Convention are themselves complex. Part XV contains provision for the settlement of disputes. Article 279 provides that States that are parties to the Convention *"shall settle any disputes between them concerning the interpretation or application of this Convention by peaceful means…"*. Article 287 provides that States shall be free to choose one of the methods of dispute settlement set out in the Convention. These include Conciliation in Annex V, Arbitration in Annex VII and 'Special Arbitration' in Annex VIII.

UNCLOS III is considered in more detail in Part II of the Manual in the chapters dealing with supranational dispute resolution.

2) The ICSID / Washington Convention

The 1995 International Convention on the Settlement of Investment Disputes (ISCID) (also known as the Washington Convention) was formulated by executive directors of the World Bank.

The preamble to the Convention refers to the need for international cooperation in relation to economic development and investment. Such investment may give rise to disputes, which should be settled on the basis of international methods of dispute settlement. The Washington Convention established the International Centre for Settlement of Investment Disputes (ICSID Centre) for the purposes of dealing with such investment disputes.

The provisions of the ICSID Convention and the services of the ICSID Centre are now being widely used, particularly in relation to bilateral investment treaties.

An obvious difference between the resolution of investor-State disputes and the resolution of pure commercial disputes is that investor-State disputes must be decided in accordance with the provisions of the relevant treaty and in accordance with principles of public international law.

The ICSID Convention is discussed further in Part II of the Manual in the chapters dealing with supranational dispute resolution.

3) The New York Convention

The ultimate object of referring a dispute to international commercial arbitration is the enforcement of the award made by the Arbitral Tribunal. The United Nations Convention on the Recognition and Enforcement of Foreign Arbitral Awards of 1958 (commonly referred to as the New York Convention) is intended to provide for the mutual recognition and enforcement of arbitral awards made in countries that are parties to the Convention.

Most of the world's trading nations have ratified the New York Convention. This means, for example, that if there is a dispute between companies based in England and Germany, an award made against the English company could be enforced by the German company in England through the English courts. And if the English company had assets in, say, France and Italy, the German company could likewise enforce the award through the French and Italian courts since both France and Italy have ratified the Convention.

The New York Convention is considered in Part IV in the chapters dealing with international commercial dispute resolution.

Part II: Supranational Dispute Resolution

"The greatest contribution from the legal systems of Great Britain and the United States toward peace in the world has been the principle that all nations should live under the Rule of Law. The concept of the Rule of Law – that laws should be enacted by democratically elected legislative bodies and enforced by independent judiciaries – is fundamental to a free society. The knowledge that there are certain basic rights of the individual that are enforceable even against the state has been the hallmark of our system of governance.

"Our constitutional heritage has been influenced significantly by Magna Carta, the document signed by King John of England in 1215 limiting his own monarchical powers as a settlement with his own warring barons. Its importance is acknowledged in the Supreme Court building itself, where the two bronze doors through which most people enter the Court depict a scene of King John sealing Magna Carta. In the courtroom itself, as I sit on the bench, I can see a marble frieze portraying the great lawmakers of history. There, amongst Chief Justice John Marshall, Napoleon, and Justinian, stands King John – clothed in chain-mail armour and clutching a copy of Magna Carta."

Sandra Day O'Connor[3]

3 Sandra Day O'Connor, *The Majesty of the Law: Reflections of a Supreme Court Justice*, Random House, 2004, p 33. Justice O'Connor was nominated by President Reagan as Associate Justice of the Supreme Court of the United States, the first woman to hold that high judicial office.

5 Introduction

Disputes that involve States or in which one of the parties is a State may conveniently be labelled 'supranational' so as to distinguish them from pure commercial disputes. As suggested earlier, there are three particular types of supranational dispute that are of considerable significance in today's world: disputes involving land, disputes involving maritime boundaries and investor-State disputes (or investment treaty disputes, as they are often described). These are considered in later chapters of this part of the Manual.

One significant factor that distinguishes these supranational disputes from pure commercial disputes is the type of Tribunal that deals with them. They are likely to be dealt with by one of the supranational bodies considered in Part III of the Manual: the International Court of Justice (ICJ), the Permanent Court of Arbitration (PCA), the International Tribunal for the Law of the Sea (ITLOS) or the International Centre for Settlement of Investment Disputes (ICSID Centre). Pure commercial disputes, on the other hand, are likely to be dealt with in national courts or by one of the international commercial arbitral bodies considered in Part IV of the Manual.

Another distinguishing factor between supranational disputes and pure commercial disputes is that the former are likely to arise out of a treaty: a maritime delimitation dispute may be governed by the 1982 Law of the Sea Convention (UNCLOS III), for example, and an investor-State dispute by the ICSID Convention.

A further broad distinction is that supranational disputes may be subject to international – as opposed to national – law. The function of the ICJ, for example, is to decide *"in accordance with international law such disputes as are submitted to it"*. The Court is to apply international conventions, international customs and the general principles of law recognised by civilised nations (Article 38 of the Statute of the ICJ).

Another distinction lies in the area of enforcement. An international commercial arbitral award is enforceable – provided the relevant criteria are satisfied – in accordance with the provisions of the Convention on the Recognition and Enforcement of Foreign Arbitral Awards (the New York Convention). Enforcement may be radically different in the case of a supranational dispute. In the area of investor-State disputes, for example, an ICSID award does not depend for enforcement on the New York Convention. The ICSID Convention contains a self-enforcing mechanism.

Supranational disputes, therefore, differ from pure commercial disputes in a number of significant ways: they are likely to involve a State; they are likely to be heard by one of the supranational dispute resolution bodies such as the ICJ; the issues may require to be decided in accordance with the provisions of a treaty; the principles of international law are likely to be applied; and, in the case of an ICSID award, the provisions of the New York Convention are not relevant to enforcement.[4]

---

4 Major textbooks dealing with international law, territorial boundary disputes and maritime delimitation disputes – some of the topics covered in this Part of the Manual – include Ian Brownlie, *Principles of Public International Law*, Oxford University Press, 2003 (6th edition) and Malcolm Shaw, *International Law*, Cambridge University Press, 2003 (5th edition).

6 International Law and the Vienna Convention on the Law of Treaties

This chapter deals with two separate but related matters: First, it gives an overview of international law, a significant part of which is concerned with treaties; and second, it looks at the Vienna Convention on the Law of Treaties.

1) International Law

International law is important both to the areas that give rise to supranational disputes (territorial and maritime boundary disputes and investor-State disputes) and to the supranational bodies that deal with these disputes.

Systems of law can be divided into three types:

i) municipal law;

ii) private international law;

iii) public international law.

i) Municipal law

Municipal law, or national law, is the domestic system of law that operates within a State. This law regulates the relationships between the State and its citizens and between citizen and citizen within that State.

English law, for example, comprises a complex and extensive framework of law based on both the Common Law and Statute. This framework covers criminal and civil matters. In the civil field, for example, statutes such as the Sale of Goods Act govern the relationships between buyers and sellers. In the field of dispute resolution, the Arbitration Act 1996 deals primarily with arbitration in the domestic sphere but in addition contains provisions dealing with the recognition and enforcement of *"certain foreign awards"* – namely, Geneva Convention awards and New York Convention awards.[5]

Written law in England dates back to the Anglo-Saxons (see Box 2). The Laws of King Alfred the Great (about AD 886) contained a series of 77 laws. While including the 'tariff' of compensation payable for wrongs and injuries caused, his laws also included other provisions: for example, provisions dealing with traders. The first of King Alfred's list of Laws is of particular interest:

> *"First we insist that there is particular need that each person keep his oath and his pledge carefully. If anyone be compelled to give either of these wrongly, either to support treachery to his lord or to provide any unlawful aid, then it is better to forswear than to fulfil. But if he pledge himself to that which it is right for him to fulfil*

5 The Geneva Convention of 1927 was the predecessor of the New York Convention.

> *and fails, let him submissively hand over his weapons and his possessions to his friends to keep, and stay 40 days in prison in a property of the King. Let him undergo there whatever the bishop prescribes as penance...."* [6]

A sanctity of contracts rule? An Anglo-Saxon law on *pacta sunt servanda* (Latin: pacts must be respected / promises must be kept)?[7] Compare this to the Vienna Convention on the Law of Treaties, which came into force over a thousand years later. Article 26 provides that: *"Every treaty in force is binding upon the parties to it and must be performed by them in good faith."*

Box 2: Early English Law

Following the migration to Britain in the middle of the fifth century of the Germanic peoples – the Angles, the Saxons and the Jutes – the first written English laws were those of the Anglo-Saxon King Aethelbirht of Kent. Dated about the year 600, these were concerned with what might broadly be described as criminal matters. For example, they included a 'tariff' of compensation to be paid for crimes or injuries caused to others. The compensation for slaying a man was 100 shillings. The compensation to be paid for stabbing through the thigh was six shillings.

In the ninth century Alfred the Great, King of the West Saxons, collated earlier laws. The Preface or Introduction to his Laws is based on biblical material, especially Mosaic Law. The intention seems to have been to associate the concept of human law with divine law. The Preface refers twice to *'foreigners'*. The West-Saxons were warned not to *"harass visitors from abroad, and foreigners, for you were formerly strangers in the land of the Egyptians"*. And later: *"Do not behave unkindly to foreigners and visitors from abroad; do not harass them with unjust acts."*

Winston Churchill, in his *History of the English-Speaking Peoples*, states that King Alfred's Book of Laws set out the existing laws of Kent, Wessex and Mercia and *"attempted to blend the Mosaic code with Christian principles and old Germanic customs"*.[a] Later Churchill says that the Laws of Alfred *"continually amplified by his successors grew into that body of customary law, administered by the shire and hundred courts which, under the name of the Laws of St Edward (the Confessor), the Norman kings undertook to respect, and out of which, with much manipulation by feudal lawyers, the Common Law was founded"*.

Note: a Generally on the Anglo-Saxon Dooms, AD 560-975: see *The Medieval Source Book*: www.fordham.edu/halsall/source/560-975dooms.html.

6 Bill Griffiths, *An Introduction to Early English Law*, Anglo-Saxon Books, 2000.

7 The Preamble to the Vienna Convention notes that " the principles of free consent and of good faith and the *pacta sunt servanda* rule are universally recognized..."

ii) Private international law

Private international law relates to the law within a State where there is a 'foreign' element. A trading contract made between two Englishmen in England is governed by English municipal law, but a trading contract between an Englishman and a Frenchman made in England and to be performed in France involves a foreign element. Unless the parties have made express provisions stating which law is to apply and which country's courts are to have jurisdiction, disputes may arise as to whether the contract is governed by English or French law, and whether the courts of England or France have jurisdiction over the contract and any dispute relating to it. Proceedings instituted in the English courts might, for example, involve an English judge applying French law for the purpose of resolving a dispute between the parties.

Many such 'foreign' cases are heard in the English courts. For example, it is estimated that approximately 80 per cent of the cases heard in the Commercial Court in London (part of the Queen's Bench Division of the High Court of Justice) involve a foreign element and/or foreign parties.

One of the functions of the Commercial Court is to deal with the enforcement of New York Convention arbitration awards.[8] In this context the English Court is operating in a ' foreign' as opposed to municipal or domestic sphere, i.e., the enforcement in England of a foreign arbitral award.

The New York Convention is one of the three conventions mentioned earlier in the Manual as being of particular significance to international dispute resolution – and therefore to international trade generally. It is considered later in the Manual in the context of pure international commercial disputes (as opposed to supranational disputes).

iii) Public international law

Public international law is concerned with the relationship between States. It is a separate system of law. Unlike municipal law, public international law has no central law-making process and no system of courts.

Public international law – which will from now on be referred to simply as international law – derives from a number of sources. It is generally accepted that the Statute of the International Court of Justice (ICJ) sets out in Article 38 what can be regarded as the sources of international law (the Statute will be considered in more detail in Chapter 11 in the context of the ICJ itself).

Article 38 (1) provides that the Court:

> "... *whose function is to decide in accordance with international law such disputes as are submitted to it" is to apply:*
>
> *"a. international conventions, whether general or particular, establishing rules expressly recognized by the contesting states;*

---

8 As mentioned earlier, the provisions of the New York Convention were implemented into English law by the Arbitration Act 1996.

b. *international custom, as evidence of a general practice accepted as law;*
c. *the general principles of law recognized by civilized nations;*
d. *subject to the provisions of Article 59, judicial decisions and the teachings of the most highly qualified publicists of the various nations, as subsidiary means for the determination of rules of law."* [9]

For the purposes of this brief overview of international law, it may be convenient to take each of these sources in turn.

a) International conventions

The first of the four categories referred to in Article 38 is concerned with conventions, also referred to by a number of different terms including treaties and agreements.

Article 38 (1) (a) refers to general and particular conventions. These can be broadly divided into:
(i) 'law-making' treaties, which are intended to have a general application to many States, and
(ii) 'treaty-contracts', which apply only to the limited number of States that are the parties to that particular treaty.

Treaty-contracts will involve only a small number of States and will be concerned with a specific, limited area. One example is bilateral investment treaties (BITs), which are considered in Chapter 11 in relation to investor-State disputes. These treaties involve two States and are concerned with attracting inward investment. Another example is the Agreement between Britain and Norway relating to the laying of submarine pipes under the sea between the British and Norwegian coasts (see Chapter 8).

Examples of general law-making treaties are the Hague Conventions of 1899 and 1907, considered later in relation to the Permanent Court of Arbitration (PCA), and the various Geneva Conventions dealing with the treatment of prisoners and the protection of civilians. A further example is the New York Convention of 1958 dealing with the recognition and enforcement of foreign arbitral awards. Law-making treaties involve a large number of States and seek to set out general principles of international law in a certain field – over 130 countries are parties to the New York Convention, for example.[10]

Treaties may have a relevance in relation to international custom, the second of the sources of international law referred to in Article 38 of the Statute of the ICJ. It may be that a treaty will be evidence of customary law. An early example is a commercial treaty made between King Offa and the Emperor Charlemagne (see Box 3) where reference is made to reciprocity of royal protection "according to the ancient custom of trading".

---

9 When quoting from Statutes, Arbitration Rules and the like, I have retained the spelling used in the original. This results at times in both the English and American spellings of a word appearing in the Manual.

10 While the United Kingdom ratified the New York Convention in 1975, the Arbitration Act 1996 that implements it into domestic law applies in England, Wales and Northern Ireland, but not in Scotland. For the sake of brevity, reference will be made to 'English' and 'England'.

Box 3: The First Commercial Treaty in English History

The first commercial treaty in English history was made over 1,000 years before the New York Convention. In AD 796 a treaty was made between the Anglo-Saxon King Offa and the Holy Roman Emperor Charlemagne. Sir Frank Stenton in his *Anglo-Saxon England* stated that King Offa *"was the only ruler in western Europe who could attempt to deal on equal terms with Charlemagne. The materials for English diplomatic history begin with the letters which passed between the two kings."*[a]

Relations were not always easy between them. A dispute that arose following a proposal by Charlemagne that his son should marry one of Offa's daughters led to the closure to English traders of ports in Charlemagne's territory. This suggests that *"in normal times there was regular trade between England and the Frankish kingdom".* When friendly relations between King Offa and Charlemagne were restored some years later *"the two kings proceeded to conclude the first commercial treaty in English history. In 796, they agreed that traders entering Gaul from England or England from Gaul should have the protection of the public authorities in the country which they were visiting, and the right of access to the King in case of trouble."*

Winston Churchill refers to Charlemagne's marriage proposals, noting that Offa stipulated that his son must simultaneously marry the daughter of Charlemagne: *"the founder of the Holy Roman Empire appeared at first incensed at this assumption of a equality, but after a while he found it expedient to renew his friendship with Offa. It seems that 'the King of the English' had placed an embargo upon Continental merchandise, and the inconvenience of this retaliation speedily overcame all points of pride and sentiment. Very soon Offa was again the Emperor's 'dearest brother', and Charlemagne is seen agreeing to arrange that there should be reciprocity of royal protection in both countries for merchants 'according to the ancient custom of trading'. Apparently the commodities in question were 'black stones', presumably coal, from France, in return for English cloaks. There were also questions of refugees and extradition."*[b]

Notes: a Frank M Stenton, *Anglo-Saxon England*, Oxford University Press, 1971.
b Winston Churchill, *A History of The English-Speaking Peoples*, Abridgment, Cassell & Co, 1957.

A treaty evidencing general principles accepted by many States (the third of the sources cited to in Article 38) can be seen in sections of the 1982 UN Convention on the Law of the Sea (UNCLOS III) – referred to later in this part of the Manual in connection with disputes relating to the territorial sea and the continental shelf.

In the *Gulf of Maine* case the Chamber of the ICJ looked at the relationship between international customary law and international treaty law. A Special Agreement between Canada and the United States requested the Chamber "... *to decide, in accordance with the principles and rules of international law applicable in the matter as between the*

Parties, the following question: What is the course of the single maritime boundary that divides the continental shelf and fisheries zones of Canada and the United States of America...."

The Chamber described the background to the dispute:

> *"Beginning with a reference to the Truman Proclamations of 1945, the Chamber summarizes the origins and development of the dispute, which first materialized in the 1960s in relation to the continental shelf, as soon as petroleum exploration had begun on either side, more particularly in certain locations on Georges Bank. In 1976-1977 certain events occurred which added to the continental shelf dimension that of the waters and their living resources, for both States proceeded to institute an exclusive 200 mile fishery zone off their coasts and adopted regulations specifying the limits of the zone and continental shelf they claimed. In its account of the negotiations which eventually led to the reference of the dispute to the Court, the Chamber notes that in 1976 the United States adopted a line limiting both the continental shelf and the fishing zones and the adoption by Canada of a first line in 1976 (Map No. 2)."*

The Chamber referred to applicable principles and rules of international law:

> *"After observing that the terms 'principles and rules' really convey one and the same idea, the Chamber stresses that a distinction has to be made between such principles or rules and what, rather, are equitable criteria or practical methods for ensuring that a particular situation is dealt with in accordance with those principles and rules. Of its nature, customary international law can only provide a few basic legal principles serving as guidelines and cannot be expected also to specify the equitable criteria to be applied or the practical methods to be followed. The same may however not be true of international treaty law.*
>
> *"To determine the principles and rules of international law governing maritime delimitation, the Chamber begins by examining the Geneva Convention of 29 April 1958 on the Continental Shelf, which has been ratified by both the Parties to the case, who both also recognize that it is in force between them. In particular the Chamber examines Article 6, paragraphs 1 and 2, from which a principle of international law may be deduced to the effect that any delimitation of a continental shelf effected unilaterally by one State regardless of the views of the other State or States concerned is not opposable by those States. To this principle may conceivably be added a latent rule that any agreement or other equivalent solution should involve the application of equitable criteria. The Chamber goes on to consider the bearing on the problem of various judicial decisions and to comment upon the work of the Third United Nations Conference on the Law of the Sea, noting that certain provisions concerning the continental shelf and the exclusive economic zone were, in the Convention of 1982, adopted without any objections and may be regarded as consonant at present with general international law on the question."*[11]

The Gulf of Maine case demonstrates the relationship between treaty law and principles of international law.

---

11 The ICJ Case Summary of the *Gulf of Maine* case is available at www.icj-cij.org/icjwww/idecisions/isummaries/icpsummary501120.htm.

b) International custom

Custom relates to a practice that has general recognition among States. By their very nature customary rules have no written source. The ICJ has stated that a degree of uniformity among States is required to demonstrate the existence of custom.

An example of the application of international custom is the Asylum Case (Columbia v Peru). The origin of the dispute lay in

> *"... the asylum granted on January 3rd, 1949, by the Colombian Ambassador in Lima to M. Victor Raúl Haya de la Torre, head of a political party in Peru, the American People's Revolutionary Alliance. On October 3rd, 1948, a military rebellion broke out in Peru and proceedings were instituted against Haya de la Torre for the instigation and direction of that rebellion. He was sought out by the Peruvian authorities, but without success, and after asylum had been granted to the refugee, the Colombian Ambassador in Lima requested a safe-conduct to enable Haya de la Torre, whom he qualified as a political offender, to leave the country. The Government of Peru refused, claiming that Haya de la Torre had committed common crimes and was not entitled to enjoy the benefits of asylum. Being unable to reach an agreement, the two Governments submitted to the Court certain questions concerning their dispute; these questions were set out in an Application submitted by Colombia and in a Counter-Claim submitted by Peru."*

Colombia maintained before the Court that

> *"... according to the Convention in force – the Bolivarian Agreement of 1911 on Extradition, the Havana Convention of 1928 on Asylum, the Montevideo Convention of 1933 on Political Asylum – and according to American International Law, she was entitled to qualify the nature of the offence for the purposes of the asylum. In this connection, the Court considered that, if the qualification in question were provisional, there could be no doubt on that point: the diplomatic representative would consider whether the required conditions had been satisfied, he would pronounce his opinion and if that opinion were contested, a controversy would then arise which might be settled according to the methods provided by the Parties."*

The Court referred to the various treaties that had been invoked and finally dealt with the contention based on American international law. In relation to that the Court stated that *"as regarded American international law, Colombia had not proved the existence, either regionally or locally, of a constant and uniform practice of unilateral qualification as a right of the State of refuge and an obligation upon the territorial State. The facts submitted to the Court disclosed too much contradiction and fluctuation to make it possible to discern therein a usage peculiar to Latin America and accepted as law."*[12]

The decision in the *Asylum Case* shows some of the difficulties faced by a party seeking to rely on international custom.

---

12 The ICJ Case Summary of Judgment of 20 November 1950 in the *Asylum Case (Columbia v Peru)* is available at www.icj-cij.org/icjwww/idecisions/isummaries/icpsummary501120.htm.

c) General principles of law recognised by civilised nations

Where no direct authority from some other source is available, resort may be had to what can be described as general principles: rules of law that have long been accepted nationally and internationally. One example is the principle concerning the sanctity of contracts, *pacta sunt servanda*, or that breaches of agreements involve an obligation to make compensation. This is demonstrated by a case that came before the predecessor of the ICJ, the Permanent Court of International Justice, in 1928. The *Chorzow Factory* case involved a dispute between the German and Polish Governments in connection with the seizure by Poland of a factory in Upper Silesia.[13]

On receipt of the German Government's case in the suit in March 1927, the Polish Government raised a preliminary objection denying the Court's jurisdiction to hear the suit brought before it, and submitting that the Court should, *"without entering into the merits, declare that it had no jurisdiction"*.

In the application the Court was asked:

> *"(1) to declare that the Polish Government, by reason of its attitude in respect of the Oberschlesische and Bayerische Companies, which attitude the Court had declared not to be in conformity with the Geneva Convention, is under an obligation to make good the consequent damage sustained by those Companies;*
>
> *(2) to award compensation, the amount of which is indicated in the application, for the damage caused to each of the respective Companies;*
>
> *(3) to fix the method of payment, and among other things to order the payments to be made by the Polish Government to be effected to the account of the two Companies with the Deutsche Bank at Berlin."*

The Court stated that:

> *"It is a principle of international law that the reparation of a wrong may consist in an indemnity corresponding to the damage which the nationals of the injured State have suffered as a result of the act which is contrary to international law. This is even the most usual form of reparation; it is the form selected by Germany in this case and the admissibility of it has not been disputed. The reparation due by one State to another does not however change its character by reason of the fact that it takes the form of an indemnity for the calculation of which the damage suffered by a private person is taken as the measure. The rules of law governing the reparation are the rules of international law in force between the two States concerned, and not the law governing relations between the State which has committed a wrongful act and the individual who has suffered damage. Rights or interests of an individual the violation of which rights causes damage are always in a different plane to rights belonging to a State, which rights may also be infringed by the same act. The damage suffered by an individual is never therefore identical in kind with that which will be suffered by a State; it can only afford a convenient scale."*

13 Available at www.icj-ij.org/cijwww/cdecisions/ccpij/serie_A/A_09/28_Usine_de_Chorzow_Competence_Arret.pdf.

The *Chorzow Factory Case* illustrates the way in which general principles of law may have an impact on the decisions of international tribunals.

(d) Judicial decisions

The fourth and final category set out in Article 38 is concerned with *"judicial decisions and the teachings of the most highly qualified publicists of the various nations"*. The Statute of the ICJ states that this category is to be used only as a subsidiary means of determining the rules of law.

However, it can reasonably be argued that some of the decisions of the ICJ itself – and of other supranational dispute resolution bodies such as the PCA and the International Tribunal for the Law of the Sea (ITLOS) – are likely to have an influence on the development of public international law. Decisions of the ICJ, the PCA and ITLOS are referred to in various parts of the Manual.[14]

The increasing number of bilateral investment treaties (BITs) and the rapid increase in recent years of awards made under the auspices of the International Centre for Settlement of Investment Disputes (ICSID Centre) are other factors likely to have an influence on the development of international public law. Again, ICSID decisions are referred to in the Manual.

To give one example of an influential decision, the PCA *Island of Palmas* case has had considerable significance in the field of territorial sovereignty (and is discussed further in Chapter 7). It concerned a territorial dispute between the Netherlands and the United States in relation to the Island of Palmas. During the course of his award, Max Huber, the sole arbitrator, made a number of observations concerning territorial sovereignty. He said:

> *"If a dispute arises as to the sovereignty over a portion of territory, it is customary to examine which of the States claiming sovereignty possesses a title – cession, conquest, occupation, etc. – superior to that which the other State might possibly bring forward against it. However, if the contestation is based on the fact that the other Party has actually displayed sovereignty, it cannot be sufficient to establish the title by which territorial sovereignty was validly acquired at a certain moment; it must also be shown that the territorial sovereignty has continued to exist and did exist at the moment which for the decision of the dispute must be considered as critical. This demonstration consists in the actual display of State activities, such as belongs only to the territorial sovereign. Titles of acquisition of territorial sovereignty in present-day international law are either based on an act of effective apprehension, such as occupation or conquest, or, like cession, presuppose the ceding and the cessionary Powers or at least one of them, have the faculty of effectively disposing of the ceded territory.... It seems therefore natural that an element which is essential for the constitution of sovereignty should not be lacking in its continuation. So true is this, that practice, as well as doctrine, recognizes... that the continuous and peaceful display of territorial sovereignty (peaceful in relation to other States) is as good as a title. The growing insistence with which international law, ever since the middle of the 18th century, has demanded that the occupation shall be effective would be*

---

14 The President of ITLOS, Dolliver Nelson, when addressing the UN General Assembly in November 2004 said that the Tribunal *"has already made some contribution to the development of international law"* in a number of areas (see Box 8).

inconceivable, if effectiveness were required only for the act of acquisition and not equally for the maintenance of the right. If the effectiveness has above all been insisted on in regard to occupation, this is because the question rarely arises in connection with territories in which there is already an established order of things." [15]

Conclusions on public international law

Public international law plays a major role in the areas of supranational disputes considered in this part of the Manual, and it is of great significance to the supranational dispute resolution bodies dealing with those disputes.

With the expansion of world trade, and with the increasing need of many countries to encourage inward investment, the role of public international law is perhaps now of greater importance than ever.

2) The 1969 Vienna Convention on the Law of Treaties

The provisions in the Vienna Convention that are of particular relevance to the area of supranational disputes are those in Articles 31 and 32 that deal with the interpretation of treaties. In addition, the Convention in Article 66 contains provisions dealing with judicial settlement, arbitration and conciliation in relation to disputes concerning the invalidity, determination, withdrawal from or suspension of the operation of the treaty. The Annex to the Convention contains provisions dealing with the conciliation process.

The Preamble refers to the *"fundamental role of treaties in the history of international relations as a source of international law"* and to the ever-increasing importance of treaties *"as a source of international law"*.

It notes that the principles of free consent and of good faith and the *pacta sunt servanda* rule are universally recognised, and affirms that disputes concerning treaties, like other international disputes, should be settled by peaceful means and in conformity with the principles of justice and international law. It also states the belief that *"the codification and progressive development of the law of treaties"* achieved in the Convention will promote the purposes of the United Nations – set out in the UN Charter – for the maintenance of international peace and security.

The Preamble concludes by affirming that *"the rules of customary international law will continue to govern questions not regulated by the provisions of the present Convention"*.

Part 1 of the Convention comprises an introduction, which includes definitions. Part II contains provisions dealing with the conclusion and entry into force of treaties. Means of expressing consent to be bound by a treaty include signature; an exchange of instruments constituting a treaty; ratification, acceptance or approval; and accession. Part III deals with the observance, application and interpretation of treaties. Article 26 contains the *pacta sunt servanda* provision: *"Every treaty in force is binding upon the parties to it and must be performed by them in good faith"*.

---

15 The decision of the PCA in the *Island of Palmas* case (1928) is available at www.pca-cpa.org/ENGLISH/RPC/EY/2ch1ER-YE.htm.

Articles 31 and 32 contain the significant provisions relating to interpretation of treaties (see Box 4). The primary approach to interpretation is textual: in construing a treaty, the words of the treaty are to be given their natural and ordinary meaning. The treaty should be construed as a whole. If there is ambiguity in the text, the object and purpose of the treaty can be considered in an effort to resolve the ambiguity. The 'context' of the treaty for the purposes of interpretation includes not only the treaty and its preamble and annexes, but also any agreement or instrument made between the parties in connection with the conclusion of the treaty. Additionally, the context is to include, for interpretation purposes, any subsequent agreement regarding the interpretation or application of the treaty, any subsequent practice in the application of the treaty and any relevant rules of international law.

Box 4: Articles 31 and 32 of the Vienna Convention on the Law of Treaties

Article 31 – The general rules of interpretation

"1. A treaty shall be interpreted in good faith in accordance with the ordinary meaning to be given to the terms of the treaty in their context and in the light of its object and purpose.

2. The context for the purpose of the interpretation of a treaty shall comprise, in addition to the text, including its preamble and annexes:

(a) any agreement relating to the treaty which was made between all the parties in connection with the conclusion of the treaty;

(b) any instrument which was made by one or more parties in connection with the conclusion of the treaty and accepted by the other parties as an instrument related to the treaty.

3. There shall be taken into account, together with the context:

(a) any subsequent agreement between the parties regarding the interpretation of the treaty or the application of its provisions;

(b) any subsequent practice in the application of the treaty which establishes the agreement of the parties regarding its interpretation;

(c) any relevant rules of international law applicable in the relations between the parties.

4. A special meaning shall be given to a term if it is established that the parties so intended."

Article 32 – The supplementary means of interpretation

"Recourse may be had to supplementary means of interpretation, including the preparatory work of the treaty and the circumstances of its conclusion, in order to confirm the meaning resulting from the application of article 31, or to determine the meaning when the interpretation according to article 31:

(a) leaves the meaning ambiguous or obscure; or

(b) leads to a result which is manifestly absurd or unreasonable."

"Supplementary means" of interpretation can be applied either to confirm the interpretation obtained by applying the general rules, or to determine the meaning when interpretation in accordance with those general rules either still leaves the meaning of the treaty ambiguous or obscure, or alternatively leads to a result that is *"manifestly absurd or unreasonable"*. The supplementary means include the preparatory work of the treaty and the circumstances of its conclusion.

Interpretation of treaties may be of considerable importance in the context of supranational disputes, particularly because of the growing number of BITs and the increasing number of investment treaty arbitrations.

Part IV deals with amendment and modification of treaties.

Part V contains provisions dealing with invalidity, determination and suspension of the operation of treaties. Article 65 sets out procedures to be followed in relation to challenges to a treaty. Article 66 states that, if no solution is reached within 12 months following the date on which an objection was raised, any of the parties may apply to the ICJ in relation to disputes concerning Article 53 of the Convention (treaties conflicting with a peremptory norm of general international law – *jus cogens*) or Article 64 (the emergence of a new peremptory norm of general international law). In relation to a dispute concerning any of the other Articles in Part V of the Convention, the application is to be submitted to the UN Secretary-General (such applications are dealt with in the Convention's Annex).

Part VI contains miscellaneous provisions. Part VII deals with depositaries, notifications, corrections and registration. Part VIII contains the Final Provisions.

The Annex contains provisions dealing with conciliation in relation to Article 66. A list of conciliators consisting of qualified jurists is to be drawn up and maintained by the UN Secretary-General. When a request to the Secretary-General is made under Article 66, it is to be brought before a Conciliation Commission consisting of five conciliators, one acting as chairman.

The Commission may invite any party to the treaty to submit its views orally or in writing. Decisions or recommendations of the Commission are to be by a majority vote of the five members. Paragraph 4 states that the Commission *"may draw the attention of the parties to the dispute to any measures which might facilitate an amicable settlement"*. It is to hear the parties, *"... examine the claims and objections, and make proposals to the parties with a view to reaching an amicable settlement of the dispute"*.

The Commission is to report within 12 months of its constitution. The report is deposited with the Secretary-General and is transmitted to the parties to the dispute. It is not binding: *"The report of the Commission, including any conclusions stated therein regarding the facts or questions of law, shall not be binding upon the parties and it shall have no other character than that of recommendations submitted for the consideration of the parties in order to facilitate an amicable settlement of the dispute"* (paragraph 6).

The Secretary-General is to provide the Commission with such assistance and facilities as it may require, and the expenses of the Commission are to be borne by the United Nations.

Conclusions on the Vienna Convention

Treaties play an important part in public international law, and the Vienna Convention on the Law of Treaties plays a significant role in relation to the operation and development of trade and investment on a global basis: for example, in the field of investor-State disputes.

The Vienna Convention may additionally be relevant in the area of territorial disputes. Two of the cases considered in the next chapter involved arguments based on treaties: the *Island of Palmas* case and the *Temple of Preah Vihear* case.

7 Territorial Disputes

1) Introduction

This chapter deals with boundary disputes relating to land. The following chapter deals with maritime boundary disputes.

Territorial disputes are concerned with sovereignty and involve the concept of title. A supranational court or tribunal faced with conflicting claims over rights to a territory will be presented with arguments and evidence aimed at showing that title to the disputed territory is vested in the contending party and not the opposing party.

There are two main methods of demonstrating the right to territory. The first method involves roots of title and is concerned with circumstances where a fairly direct and clear-cut right to territorial sovereignty can be demonstrated. The direct methods considered here are:

i) treaties;

ii) *uti possidetis;*[16]

iii) decisions of international courts and tribunals;

iv) agreements concluded with local rulers.

Second, where such direct claims cannot be demonstrated, there are various indirect methods of showing title. These include:

i) effective occupation;

ii) prescription;

iii) discovery;

iv) symbolic annexation.

2) Intertemporal Law and Critical Dates

Before looking at the direct and indirect methods of demonstrating the right to territory, however, it may be useful to consider two preliminary matters: intertemporal law and critical dates.

Intertemporal law

In considering the claims of the parties in a dispute concerning territorial sovereignty, it may be necessary for the Court or Tribunal to apply principles of international law in force at an earlier date.

---

16 *Uti possidetis* is the doctrine that has been used to establish the frontiers of newly independent States after decolonisation by following the existing boundaries. In the African context, it was seen as preventing the stability of new States being endangered by territorial border disputes following the withdrawal of the administering power.

One example can be found in the *Island of Palmas* case,[17] a decision of significance that is considered in various parts of the Manual. As mentioned in Chapter 6, the case came before the Permanent Court of Arbitration (PCA) in 1928 and the sole arbitrator was Max Huber.

The Netherlands and the United States agreed that the only duty of the arbitrator was to determine whether the Island of Palmas formed part of territory belonging to one or the other party. Their respective claims had to be tested on the basis of international legal principles ruling in the 16th century, the period when the island was discovered.

The report of the case sets out the arbitrator's statement in the Award on the matter of intertemporal law. He said that it was admitted by both sides that international law underwent profound modifications between the end of the Middle Ages and the end of the 19th century as regards the rights of discovery and acquisition of uninhabited regions:

> *"Both Parties are also agreed that a juridical fact must be appreciated in the light of the law contemporary with it, and not of the law in force at the time when a dispute in regard to it rises or falls to be settled. The effect of discovery by Spain is therefore to be determined by the rules of international law in force in the first half of the 16th century – or (to take the earliest date) in the first quarter of it, i.e., at the time when the Portuguese or Spaniards made their appearance in the Sea of Celebes.*
>
> *"If the view most favourable to the American arguments is adopted – with every reservation as to the soundness of such view – that is to say, if we consider as positive law at the period in question the rule that discovery as such, i.e. the mere fact of seeing land, without any act, even symbolical, of taking possession, involved ipso jure territorial sovereignty and not merely an 'inchoate title', a jus ad rem, to be completed eventually by an actual and durable taking of possession within a reasonable time, the question arises whether sovereignty yet existed at the critical date, i.e. the moment of conclusion and coming into force of the Treaty of Paris."*

The arbitrator then went on to deal with what he described as *"so-called intertemporal law"*:

> *"As regards the question which of different legal systems prevailing at successive periods is to be applied in a particular case (the so-called intertemporal law), a distinction must be made between the creation of rights and the existence of rights. The same principle which subjects the act creative of a right to the law in force at the time the right arises, demands that the existence of the right, in other words its continued manifestation, shall follow the conditions required by the evolution of law. International law in the 19th century, having regard to the fact that most parts of the globe were under the sovereignty of states members of the community of nations, and that territories without a master had become relatively few, took account of a tendency already existing and especially developed since the middle of the 18th century, and laid down the principle that occupation, to constitute a claim to territorial sovereignty, must be effective, that is, offer certain guarantees to other States and their nationals. It seems therefore incompatible with this rule of positive law that there should be regions which are neither under the effective sovereignty of a State, nor without a master, but which are reserved for the exclusive influence of one State, in virtue solely of a title of acquisition which is no longer recognized by existing law,*

17 *Supra.* The case can be viewed on the PCA website: www.pca-cpa.org/.

even if such a title ever conferred territorial sovereignty. For these reasons, discovery alone, without any subsequent act, cannot at the present time suffice to prove sovereignty over the Island of Palmas (or Miangas); and in so far as there is no sovereignty, the question of an abandonment properly speaking of sovereignty by one State in order that the sovereignty of another may take its place does not arise.

"If on the other hand the view is adopted that discovery does not create a definitive title of sovereignty, but only an 'inchoate' title, such a title exists, it is true, without external manifestation. However, according to the view that has prevailed at any rate since the 19th century, an inchoate title of discovery must be completed within a reasonable period by the effective occupation of the region claimed to be discovered. This principle must be applied in the present case, for the reasons given above in regard to the rules determining which of successive legal systems is to be applied (the so-called intertemporal law). Now, no act of occupation nor, except as to a recent period, any exercise of sovereignty at Palmas by Spain has been alleged. But even admitting that the Spanish title still existed as inchoate in 1898 and must be considered as included in the cession under Article III of the Treaty of Paris, an inchoate title could not prevail over the continuous and peaceful display of authority by another State; for such display may prevail even over a prior, definitive title put forward by another State. This point will be considered, when the Netherlands argument has been examined and the allegations of either Party as to the display of their authority can be compared."

Another example can be seen in the Western Sahara case, mentioned later in this chapter, where the ICJ considered the law relating to terra nullius in the period beginning 1884.

Critical dates

A specific date may be relevant in a territorial dispute. For example, the 1898 date of the treaty of cession was relevant to the United States' claim in the *Island of Palmas* case.

The concept of critical dates is especially important in relation to the doctrine of *uti possediti*s, under which a new State retains the earlier colonial boundaries following independence. The date of independence may therefore be of particular significance in a territorial dispute.

3) Direct Methods of Acquisition of Title – Roots of Title

This section looks at the direct methods of acquisition of title.

i) Treaties

One of the direct methods of proving title is by reliance on the provisions of a treaty. In the *Island of Palmas* case the United States relied on a treaty of December 1898 under which Spain transferred the Philippines to the United States. The report of the Award of Max Huber dealing with the US claim states:

"The United States, as successor to the rights of Spain over the Philippines, bases its title in the first place on discovery. The existence of sovereignty thus acquired is, in the American view, confirmed not merely by the most reliable cartographers and authors, but also by treaty, in particular by the Treaty of Munster, of 1648, to which Spain and the Netherlands are themselves Contracting Parties. As, according to the same argument, nothing has occurred of a nature, in international law, to cause the acquired title to disappear, this latter title was intact at the moment when, by the Treaty of December 10th, 1898, Spain ceded the Philippines to the United States. In these circumstances, it is, in the American view, unnecessary to establish facts showing the actual display of sovereignty precisely over the Island of Palmas (or Miangas). The United States Government finally maintains that Palmas (or Miangas) forms a geographical part of the Philippine group and in virtue of the principle of contiguity belongs to the Power having the sovereignty over the Philippines."

Another case involving a territorial claim based on a treaty that came before the International Court of Justice (ICJ) involved a frontier dispute. The subject of the dispute related to the sovereignty over a region in which a temple was situated. The treaty in question was made in 1904 between France and Siam.

The proceedings in the case of the *Temple of Preah Vihear* concerned a dispute between Cambodia and Thailand. They were instituted in October 1959 by an Application of the Government of Cambodia. The Government of Thailand raised two preliminary objections. The ICJ Case Summary of 15 June 1962 shows that the Court by its Judgment of 26 May 1961 found that it had jurisdiction. The Court referred to the boundary treaties:

"In its Judgment, the Court found that the subject of the dispute was sovereignty over the region of the Temple of Preah Vihear. This ancient sanctuary, partially in ruins, stood on a promontory of the Dangrek range of mountains which constituted the boundary between Cambodia and Thailand. The dispute had its fons et origo in the boundary settlements made in the period 1904-1908 between France, then conducting the foreign relations of Indo-China, and Siam. The application of the Treaty of 13 February 1904 was, in particular, involved. That Treaty established the general character of the frontier, the exact boundary of which was to be delimited by a Franco-Siamese Mixed Commission.

"In the eastern sector of the Dangrek range, in which Preah Vihear was situated, the frontier was to follow the watershed line. For the purpose of delimiting that frontier, it was agreed, at a meeting held on 2 December 1906, that the Mixed Commission should travel along the Dangrek range carrying out all the necessary reconnaissance, and that a survey officer of the French section of the Commission should survey the whole of the eastern part of the range. It had not been contested that the Presidents of the French and Siamese sections duly made this journey, in the course of which they visited the Temple of Preah Vihear. In January-February 1907, the President of the French section had reported to his Government that the frontier-line had been definitely established. It therefore seemed clear that a frontier had been surveyed and fixed, although there was no record of any decision and no reference to the Dangrek region in any minutes of the meetings of the Commission after 2 December 1906. Moreover, at the time when the Commission might have met for the purpose of winding up its work, attention was directed towards the conclusion of a further

Franco-Siamese boundary treaty, the Treaty of 23 March 1907. The final stage of the delimitation was the preparation of maps...."

The Court upheld the submissions of Cambodia concerning sovereignty over Preah Vihear. [18]

ii) Uti possidetis

The operation of the doctrine of *uti possidetis* can be seen in Latin America, where the administrative boundaries of the Spanish empire were taken to be the boundaries for the newly independent states. It can also be seen in Africa. A resolution of the Organisation of African Unity (OAU) in 1964 stated that colonial frontiers existing at the date of independence should be respected.

In the *Case Concerning the Frontier Dispute (Burkina Faso / Republic of Mali)* the Chamber constituted by the ICJ considered the principle of *uti posseditis juris*. The ICJ Case Summary of the Judgment of 22 December 1986 shows that the task of the Chamber was:

> *"... to indicate the line of the frontier between Burkina Faso and the Republic of Mali in the disputed area which is defined by Article I of the Special Agreement as consisting of 'a band of territory extending from the sector Koro (Mali) Djibo (Upper Volta) up to and including the region of the Béli'. Both States have indicated, in their submissions to the Chamber, the frontier line which each of them considers to be well-founded in law."*

The Chamber considered two principles:

> *"1. The principle of the intangibility of frontiers inherited from colonization (para. 19)*
>
> *The Judgment considers the question of the rules applicable to the case, and seeks to ascertain the source of the rights claimed by the Parties. It begins by noting that the characteristic feature of the legal context of the frontier determination to be undertaken by the Chamber is that both States involved derive their existence from the process of decolonization which has been unfolding in Africa during the past 30 years: it can be said that Burkina Faso corresponds to the colony of Upper Volta and the Republic of Mali to the colony of Sudan (formerly French Sudan). In the preamble to their Special Agreement, the Parties stated that the settlement of the dispute should be 'based in particular on respect for the principle of the intangibility of frontiers inherited from colonization', which recalls the principle expressly stated in resolution AGH/Res. 16 (I) adopted in Cairo in July 1964 at the first summit conference following the creation of the Organization of African Unity, whereby all member States 'solemnly... pledge themselves to respect the frontiers existing on their achievement of national Independence'...*
>
> *"2. The principle of uti possidetis juris (paras. 20-26).*
>
> *In these circumstances, the Chamber cannot disregard the principle of uti possidetis juris, the application of which gives rise to this respect for intangibility of frontiers. It emphasizes the general scope of the principle in matters of*

18 The ICJ Case Summary in the *Temple of Preah Vihear* case is available at www.icj-cij.org/icjwww/idecisions/isummaries/ictsummary620615.htm.

decolonization and its exceptional importance for the African continent, including the two Parties to this case. Although this principle was invoked for the first time in Spanish America, it is not a rule pertaining solely to one specific system of international law. It is a principle of general scope, logically connected with the phenomenon of the obtaining of independence, wherever it occurs. Its obvious purpose is to prevent the independence and stability of new States being endangered by fratricidal struggles provoked by the challenging of frontiers following the withdrawal of the administering power. The fact that the new African States have respected the territorial status quo which existed when they obtained independence must therefore be seen not as a mere practice but as the application in Africa of a rule of general scope which is firmly established in matters of decolonization; and the Chamber does not find it necessary to demonstrate this for the purposes of the case."

The Chamber went on to consider the significance of the principle in a dispute concerning sovereignty.

"The principle of uti possidetis juris accords pre-eminence to legal title over effective possession as a basis of sovereignty. Its primary aim is to secure respect for the territorial boundaries which existed at the time when independence was achieved. When those boundaries were no more than delimitations between different administrative divisions or colonies all subject to the same sovereign, the application of this principle resulted in their being transformed into international frontiers, and this is what occurred with the States Parties to the present case, which both took shape within the territories of French West Africa. Where such boundaries already had the status of international frontiers at the time of decolonization, the obligation to respect pre-existing international frontiers derives from a general rule of international law relating to State succession. The many solemn affirmations of the intangibility of frontiers, made by African statesmen or by organs of the OAU, should therefore be taken as references to a principle already in existence, not as affirmations seeking to consecrate a new principle or to extend to Africa a rule previously applicable only in another continent.

"This principle of uti possidetis appears to conflict outright with the right of peoples to self-determination. In fact, however, the maintenance of the territorial status quo in Africa is often seen as the wisest course. The essential requirement of stability in order to survive, to develop and gradually to consolidate their independence in all fields has induced African States to consent to the maintenance of colonial boundaries or frontiers, and to take account of this when interpreting the principle of self-determination of peoples. If the principle of uti possidetis has kept its place among the most important legal principles, this is by a deliberate choice on the part of African States." [19]

The *Temple of Preah Vihear* case considered earlier is another example of consideration being given to pre-independence boundaries.

---

19 The ICJ Case Summary in the *Case Concerning the Frontier Dispute (Burkina Faso/Republic of Mali)* is available at www.icj-cij.org/icjwww/icases/iHVM/ihvmframe.htm.

iii) Decisions of international Courts and Tribunals

The award of a Tribunal and the decision of an international Court may be said to create title, or at any rate to demonstrate the existence of that title. The award of the arbitrator in the *Island of Palmas* case and the decision of the Court in the *Temple of Preah Vihear* case are examples of this method of acquisition of title. Further examples can be seen in the *Eastern Greenland* case and in the *Minquiers and Ecrehos* case, both considered later.

Yet another example is the *Clipperton Island* case. Clipperton Island is a remote and barren atoll 600 miles south of Mexico in the Pacific Ocean that was claimed by France for its guano in 1858, but then ignored for decades because the guano was not commercially exploitable. After Mexico asserted jurisdiction over the atoll in the 1890s (claiming historic links traced back to earlier Spanish explorers), France and Mexico agreed to submit the ownership dispute to arbitration, selecting as arbitrator Victor Emmanuel, the Italian Emperor.

The Emperor's decision, finally announced many years later in 1931, stated that something more than mere discovery is normally needed to establish ownership: effective occupation is also required. And 'effective occupation' usually requires a presence in the territory and some governmental structure capable of enforcing laws. But for uninhabited islets, these requirements are apparently reduced. All that is necessary is that *"from the first moment when the occupying State makes its appearance there,"* the territory is *"at the absolute and undisputed disposition of that State"*.

Thus, based primarily on its 'discovery' of the atoll – and despite the fact that US citizens had explored Clipperton and Mexico had established a garrison there – the Emperor awarded title to France.[20]

iv) Agreements concluded with local rulers

An example of the acquisition of sovereignty through an agreement concluded with a local ruler can be seen in the *Western Sahara* case. The ICJ Case Summary of the Advisory Opinion of the ICJ, 16 October 1975, states that the UN General Assembly had posed two questions concerning the Western Sahara, the first of which was: "Was Western Sahara (Rio de Oro and Sakiet El Hamra) at the time of colonisation by Spain a territory belonging to no one (*terra nullius*)?"

The Court in its Advisory Opinion stated that:

> *"For the purposes of the Advisory Opinion, the 'time of colonization by Spain' may be considered as the period beginning in 1884, when Spain proclaimed its protectorate over the Rio de Oro. It is therefore by reference to the law in force at that period that the legal concept of terra nullius must be interpreted. In law, 'occupation' was a means of peaceably acquiring sovereignty over territory otherwise than by cession or succession; it was a cardinal condition of a valid 'occupation' that the territory should be terra nullius. According to the State practice of that period, territories inhabited by*

20 [1932] 26 AJIL 390.

tribes or peoples having a social and political organization were not regarded as terrae nullius: in their case sovereignty was not generally considered as effected through occupation, but through agreements concluded with local rulers. The information furnished to the Court shows (a) that at the time of colonization Western Sahara was inhabited by peoples which, if nomadic, were socially and politically organized in tribes and under chiefs competent to represent them; (b) that Spain did not proceed upon the basis that it was establishing its sovereignty over terrae nullius: thus in his Order of 26 December 1884 the King of Spain proclaimed that he was taking the Rio de Oro under his protection on the basis of agreements entered into with the chiefs of local tribes." [21]

4) Advocacy – Proof and Indirect Methods of Showing Title [22]

The previous section considered the acquisition of territorial sovereignty by demonstrating the right to a root of title through a relatively clear-cut process: by way of reference to a treaty, for example. Such proof is comparatively straightforward. Direct methods of proof may not always be available, however. What is to be done in those circumstances?

Say the dispute involves State A and State B. Looking at the matter from the point of view of an advocate acting for State A, the case is to be approached in much the same way as any other case (but subject, needless to say, to the specific Rules applicable to the procedure in question). This is likely to involve consideration of the following matters, which can be divided into two broad stages: the pre-hearing preparatory stage and the hearing stage.

The precise ways in which those stages are dealt with will be dictated by whatever Rules are in force for the relevant tribunal, whether it be a Court or an Arbitral Tribunal. However, what is set out below is a general guide to the procedure likely to be adopted. The advocacy process described approaches the matter from the common law adversarial viewpoint, with its emphasis on the need for discovery of documents, the cross-examination of witnesses (and experts) and the importance of oral advocacy, and the outcome decided by an impartial tribunal. That may be described as the Anglo-Saxon approach to advocacy.[23]

However, it is fair to say that the influence of the civil law countries is seen in the increasing use – particularly in international commercial arbitration – of the written testimony of witnesses and the written submissions of advocates.

---

21 The ICJ Case Summary in the *Western Sahara* case is available at www.icj-cij.org/icjwww/idecisions/isummaries/isasummary751016.htm.

22 A particularly important book in the context of indirect methods of showing title is R Doak Bishop (ed.), *The Art of Advocacy in International Arbitration*, Juris Publishing, 2004.

23 In an article in *The Sunday Times* in early 2005, Clive Anderson said that the adversarial approach "...pitching one side against the other, the winner chosen by an impartial court, is the norm throughout the Anglo-Saxon world, America, the Commonwealth and beyond. It allows for the interests of one person to be balanced against those of another and the interests of the state to be weighed against the rights of the individual." 'The jury is out on Rumpole of the Elysée', 13 February 2005.

i) Pre-hearing preparatory stage

What is to be proved?

The factual and legal aspects of the case need to be analysed in order to discover what issues will be faced by the international Tribunal. Put shortly, this will involve the broad question of whether territorial sovereignty is vested in State A or State B.

How is it to be proved?

How will the party prove its case?[24] What evidence will be required to satisfy the Tribunal on the issues to be decided? For example, what documents are needed by State A? Does State B have documents that will assist State A in proving its case (or in disproving the case of State B)? The process of discovery and inspection of documents may play a vital role in the dispute.

Is evidence required from factual witnesses? Is evidence required from expert witnesses? How is the factual and expert evidence to be presented to the international body dealing with the dispute? Normally, the testimony of witnesses as to fact will be set out in witness statements or affidavits and the opinion evidence of experts will be set out in expert reports. The Rules of the particular Court or Tribunal will invariably deal with the exchange between the parties of their factual and expert testimony, and with the way in which such factual and expert testimony is to be presented.

For example, the PCA's Rules for Arbitrating Disputes between Two States contain provisions in Article 25 relating to evidence. Where witnesses are to be heard, at least 30 days prior to the hearing date each party is to communicate to the Tribunal and the other party the names and addresses of the witnesses it intends to call, the subject matter of their testimony and the language in which such testimony will be given. Where appropriate, arrangements will be made for the translation of oral statements. Hearings are held in camera unless the parties agree otherwise. The Tribunal is entitled to require the retirement of any witnesses during the testimony of other witnesses and is also entitled to determine the manner in which witnesses are to be examined. The evidence of witnesses may be in the form of written statements. The Tribunal determines the admissibility, relevance, materiality and weight of the evidence.

Pleadings

Once the advocate has marshalled the facts and considered the relevant law, and has decided how the issues involved are to be proved by way of documentary and other evidence (together with the evidence of witnesses and experts), the next vital stage of the advocacy process is the pleadings.

The importance of written pleadings cannot be over-emphasised. They are a vital part of the advocacy process as they are likely to be the first statement of the parties' case that the Tribunal will see. They should set out clearly and concisely the nature of the case being put by the parties to the dispute. Pleadings cannot be properly drafted by the advocate

---

24 It is for the party bringing the claim to prove its case: the burden of proof is on the Claimant.

who is to present the case at the hearing until he or she has a clear understanding of the case: the facts, the law, the issues, the evidence.

The rules in force for the particular Tribunal will set out what written pleadings are required from the parties. However, they are likely to involve:

- a claim by the Claimant (probably described as a Statement of Claim or a Memorial);
- a defence by the Respondent (probably described as a Statement of Defence or a Counter-Memorial) – this may well include a counter-claim by the Respondent;
- further written pleadings responding to the defence and any counterclaim. For example, the London Court of International Arbitration (LCIA) Rules specifically require the service of a Reply. And the International Convention on the Settlement of Investment Disputes (ICSID) Arbitration Rules, in addition to requiring a Memorial and a Counter-Memorial, make provision for the service of a Reply and a Response.

To take a further example, the Rules of Court of the ICJ deal with the 'written proceedings' in Articles 44 to 53. In the case of proceedings begun by an application, the pleadings are to consist of a Memorial and Counter-Memorial. The Court may also direct service of a Reply and a Rejoinder.

The pleadings will usually be accompanied by (and cross-referenced to) the relevant documents to which they refer. Those documents will normally be contained in separate paginated and indexed files (or 'bundles' as some lawyers call them).

The success of the hearing stage – and therefore of the case itself – is likely to depend on how well and how competently the preparatory work was carried out.

ii) The hearing

The second major stage of the advocacy process involves the oral hearing. Arguably, this is the most important stage of the entire process. Common law judges and arbitrators set great store on the 'dialogue' between the tribunal and counsel: the opportunity for the Tribunal to put questions to the advocates.

It is assumed that in an international dispute the complexities of fact and law will inevitably require an oral hearing at which each party can present its case to the Tribunal and can test the other party's case.

This is likely to involve the advocate for each party making opening oral submissions to the Tribunal. Next will follow the examination, cross-examination and re-examination of the factual witnesses and experts. Again, to take the ICJ Rules as an example, Articles 54 to 72 deal with the oral proceedings. They contain detailed provisions covering the production of documents, evidence, witnesses and experts. Finally, closing oral submissions are made to the Tribunal on the issues, the evidence and the law.

In addition to the oral submissions, the advocates are likely to have prepared written submissions for the Tribunal. Indeed, either the Tribunal is likely to have directed that such submissions be prepared, or the procedural rules in question may require the service of opening and/or closing submissions.

Such written submissions are of benefit both to the advocates and to the members of the Tribunal. The advocates are likely to feel that the Tribunal will have a better understanding of the nature of the case that they are putting forward if the Tribunal has read beforehand the points that will be made at the oral hearing. For its part, the Tribunal should be better able to follow the oral submissions of the advocates if it has had the opportunity of pre-reading the written submissions.

Further, it is likely to be of great benefit to the Tribunal – when drafting its judgment or award – to be able to look back at the written witness statements and expert reports, the pleadings and the written submissions of the advocates. It is at that stage that the Tribunal has to decide (if it has not already done so) which of the competing claims of the parties has been proved. As the Permanent Court of International Justice stated in the *Eastern Greenland Case* (considered in the next section):

> *"In most of the cases involving claims to territorial sovereignty which have come before an international tribunal, there have been two competing claims to the sovereignty, and the tribunal has had to decide which of the two is the stronger."*

The International Court in the *Minquiers and Ecrehos* case (again considered in the next section) referred specifically to "convincing proof of title":

> *"Under the Special Agreement, the Court was asked to determine which of the Parties had produced the more convincing proof of title... each Party therefore had to prove its alleged title and the facts upon which it relied."*

The importance of written and oral advocacy – both of which involve the careful preparation of the case in accordance with the relevant Rules – cannot be stressed too strongly. The Rules of various supranational Courts and Tribunals, and of a selection of international arbitral bodies, are considered in Parts III and IV of the Manual.

5) Indirect Methods of Acquisition of Title

There are also a number of indirect methods of demonstrating the right to territorial sovereignty where more direct methods, such as treaty rights, are not available. Some examples are:

- i) effective occupation;
- ii) prescription;
- iii) discovery;
- iv) symbolic annexation.

i) Effective occupation

This method of acquisition of territorial sovereignty tends to relate to *terra nullius*: that is, land possessed by no one. This issue arose in the *Western Sahara* case considered earlier. It will be remembered that the Court said that the *"time of colonization by Spain"* might be considered as the period beginning in 1884, when Spain proclaimed its protectorate over the Rio de Oro: *"According to the State practice of that period, territories inhabited by tribes or peoples having a social and political organization were not regarded as terrae nullius: in their case sovereignty was not generally considered as effected through occupation, but through agreements concluded with local rulers...."*

The question of effective occupation arose as well in the *Island of Palmas* case. The arbitrator stated that effective occupation involved not simply possession of territory but – in relation to that possession – the exercise by a State of activities of sovereignty in respect of the territory.[25] This issue was also considered by the Permanent Court of International Justice in the *Eastern Greenland Case: Denmark v Norway*. The Permanent Court described the background:

> *"According to the information supplied to the Court by the Parties, it was about the year 900 A.D. that Greenland was discovered. The country was colonized about a century later. The best known of the colonists was Eric the Red, who was an inhabitant of Iceland of Norwegian origin; it was at that time that two settlements called Eystribygd and Vestribygd were founded towards the southern end of the western coast. These settlements appear to have existed as an independent State for some time, but became tributary to the kingdom of Norway in the XIIIth century. These settlements had disappeared before 1500.*
>
> *"Information as to these early Nordic settlements and as to the extent to which the settlers dominated the remainder of the country is very scanty. It seems clear that the settlers made hunting journeys far to the North on the western coast, and records exist of at least one expedition to places on the East coast.*
>
> *"In 1380, the kingdoms of Norway and Denmark were united under the same Crown; the character of this union, which lasted until 1814, changed to some extent in the course of time, more particularly as a result of the centralization at Copenhagen of the administration of the various countries which were under the sovereignty of the Dano-Norwegian Crown. This evolution seems to have obliterated to some extent the separation which had existed between them from a constitutional standpoint. On the other hand, there is nothing to show that during this period Greenland, in so far as it constituted a dependency of the Crown, should not be regarded as a Norwegian possession."*

The Permanent Court went on to consider the question of effective occupation, and referred to the phrase used in the *Palmas Island* decision, namely, a title that was founded *"on the peaceful and continuous display of State authority..."*. The Court said:

> *"The Danish claim is not founded upon any particular act of occupation but alleges – to use the phrase employed in the Palmas Island decision of the Permanent Court of Arbitration April 4th, 1928 – a title 'founded on the peaceful and continuous display of State authority over the island'. It is based upon the view that Denmark now enjoys all the rights which the King of Denmark and Norway enjoyed over Greenland up till 1814. Both the existence and the extent of these rights must therefore be considered, as well as the Danish claim to sovereignty since that date.*

25 See the remarks by Max Huber quoted in Chapter 6.

"It must be borne in mind, however, that as the critical date is July l0th, 1931, it is not necessary that sovereignty over Greenland should have existed throughout the period during which the Danish Government maintains that it was in being. Even if the material submitted to the Court might be thought insufficient to establish the existence of that sovereignty during the earlier periods, this would not exclude a finding that it is sufficient to establish a valid title in the period immediately preceding the occupation.

"Before proceeding to consider in detail the evidence submitted to the Court, it may be well to state that a claim to sovereignty based not upon some particular act or title such as a treaty of cession but merely upon continued display of authority, involves two elements each of which must be shown to exist: the intention and will to act as sovereign, and some actual exercise or display of such authority.

"Another circumstance which must be taken into account by any tribunal which has to adjudicate upon a claim to sovereignty over a particular territory, is the extent to which the sovereignty is also claimed by some other Power. In most of the cases involving claims to territorial sovereignty which have come before an international tribunal, there have been two competing claims to the sovereignty, and the tribunal has had to decide which of the two is the stronger. One of the peculiar features of the present case is that up to 1931 there was no claim by any Power other than Denmark to the sovereignty over Greenland. Indeed, up till 1921, no Power disputed the Danish claim to sovereignty.

"It is impossible to read the records of the decisions in cases as to territorial sovereignty without observing that in many cases the tribunal has been satisfied with very little in the way of the actual exercise of sovereign rights, provided that the other State could not make out a superior claim. This is particularly true in the case of claims to sovereignty over areas in thinly populated or unsettled countries." [26]

ii) ***Prescription***

Prescription, to the extent that it exists as a separate method of acquiring territorial sovereignty, differs from the taking of possession of *terra nullius* in that it involves the occupation of territory that in the past has been – or may have been – under the sovereignty of another State.

The ICJ delivered a judgement in November 1953 in a dispute between the United Kingdom and France over a group of islets lying between the island of Jersey and the coast of France. *The Minquiers and Ecrehos (France / United Kingdom)* case could be regarded as falling under the category of occupation or prescription. It was submitted to the Court by virtue of a Special Agreement concluded between the United Kingdom and France on 29 December 1950.

The Court began by defining the task laid before it by the Parties:

" The two groups of islets in question lie between the British Channel Island of Jersey and the coast of France. The Ecrehos lie 3.9 sea miles from the former and 6.6 sea

---

26 A report of the decision in the *Eastern Greenland Case: Denmark v Norway* is available on the ICJ website, Series A/B 53, Judgment April 1953.

miles from the latter. The Minquiers group lie 9.8 sea miles from Jersey and 16.2 sea miles from the French mainland and 8 miles away from the Chausey islands which belong to France. Under the Special Agreement, the Court was asked to determine which of the Parties had produced the more convincing proof of title to these groups and any possibility of applying to them the status of terra nullius was set aside. In addition, the question of burden of proof was reserved: each Party therefore had to prove its alleged title and the facts upon which it relied. Finally, when the Special Agreement refers to islets and rocks, in so far as they are capable of appropriation, it must be considered that these terms relate to islets and rocks physically capable of appropriation. The Court did not have to determine in detail the facts relating to the particular units of the two groups."

In a unanimous decision, the Court found that sovereignty over the islets and rocks of the Minquiers and Ecrehos groups, in so far as these islets and rocks were capable of appropriation, belonged to the United Kingdom.[27]

iii) Discovery

Again, it may be arguable to what extent discovery can stand alone as a separate head of acquisition of territorial sovereignty as it is closely linked to effective occupation. Indeed mere discovery, unless linked to – and followed by – occupation, would be unlikely to lead to success in a dispute before an international Court or Tribunal.

Discovery was one of the bases of claim put forward by the United States in the *Island of Palmas* case. Again, it is perhaps worth looking at what was said by the arbitrator:

"As pointed out above, the United States bases its claim, as successor of Spain, in the first place on discovery. In this connection a distinction must be made between the discovery of the Island of Palmas (or Miangas) as such, or as a part of the Philippines, which, beyond doubt, were discovered and even occupied and colonized by the Spaniards. This latter point, however, will be considered with the argument relating to contiguity; the problem of discovery is considered only in relation to the island itself which forms the subject of the dispute.

"The documents supplied to the Arbitrator with regard to the discovery of the island in question consist in the first place of a communication made by the Spanish Government to the United States Government as to researches in the archives concerning expeditions and discoveries in the Moluccas, the 'Talaos' Islands, the Palos Islands and the Marianes.

"The above mentioned communication of the Spanish Government does not give any details as to the date of the expedition, the navigators or the circumstances in which the observations were made; it is not supported by extracts from the original reports on which it is based, nor accompanied by reproductions of the maps therein mentioned.

27 A report of the decision in the *Minquiers and Ecrehos (France / United Kingdom)* case is available at www.icj-cij.org/icjwww/idecisions/isummaries/ifuksummary531117.htm.

"In any case for the purpose of the present affair it may be admitted that the original title derived from discovery belonged to Spain." [28]

iv) Symbolic annexation

In the *Clipperton Island* case considered earlier, France claimed sovereignty by virtue of a proclamation of French sovereignty in the 1850s by a lieutenant in the French Navy. That proclamation was subsequently published in Honolulu. On the particular facts of the case, namely the uninhabited and inhospitable nature of the island, the arbitrator considered that the taking of possession, albeit symbolic, was sufficient to give sovereignty to France.

6) Territorial Border Disputes

So far this chapter on territorial disputes has primarily concentrated on the right to the possession of an entire territory. Disputes also arise, however, concerning the extent of territory: what line does the border follow between State A and State B?

Such territorial disputes have a long history. For example, the English Privy Council in London dealt with border disputes in the American colonies in the 1600s and 1700s:

"During the pre-revolutionary period in America, the colonies developed their own judicial systems. Despite the enormous influence of the English common-law legal system, each colony had its local variations and customs to which strong attachments developed. This preference for local institutions and local law meant that authority in the American colonies was badly fragmented, which posed a problem for the colonies in their relations with one another and also in their relations with the Crown. There was a need for some overriding judicial authority to deal with legal issues arising in the colonies. Ever practical, the English revived an old institution – the Royal Privy Council – and sowed the seeds that resulted in the establishment of the judiciary as a separate and coequal branch of government under the Constitution of 1787.

"...[An] important function of the Privy Council was the resolution of border disputes that often raged with great intensity between the colonies. These disputes seldom could be resolved except through the offices of a judicial body superior to the colonial courts, because those courts were both ill suited to task and frequently disinclined to perform it impartially." [29]

A more recent example of a border dispute is the *Temple of Preah Vihear* case, mentioned earlier, concerning the disputed frontier line on the boundary between Cambodia and Thailand.

The line of a frontier may change as a result of accretion, erosion or avulsion. One State may acquire or lose territory as a result of accretion or erosion. The line of a frontier fixed by reference to a river may give rise to a dispute where a significant change in the course of the river – avulsion – has occurred. That argument arose in a dispute between El Salvador and Honduras that was heard by the ICJ.

---

28 Supra.

29 Sandra Day O'Connor, *The Majesty of the Law*, Random House, 2004, p 206.

On 10 September 2002 the Republic of El Salvador submitted a request to the Court for revision of the Judgment delivered on 11 September 1992 by the Chamber of the Court formed to deal with the case concerning the *Land, Island and Maritime Frontier Dispute (El Salvador / Honduras: Nicaragua intervening).*

The revision was sought on the basis of new facts alleged by El Salvador. These concern on the one hand the avulsion of the river Goascorán and on the other the 'Carta Esférica' and the report of the 1794 El Activo expedition. In relation to the river Goascorán, the Court said:

> *"Turning to consideration of El Salvador's submissions concerning the avulsion of the Goascorán, the Chamber recalls that an application for revision is admissible only if each of the conditions laid down in Article 61 is satisfied, and that if any one of them is not met, the application must be dismissed; in the present case, the Chamber begins by ascertaining whether the alleged facts, supposing them to be new facts, are of such a nature as to be decisive factors in respect of the 1992 Judgment.*
>
> *"In this regard, the Chamber first recalls the considerations of principle on which the Chamber hearing the original case relied for its ruling on the disputes between the two States in six sectors of their land boundary. According to that Chamber, the boundary was to be determined 'by the application of the principle generally accepted in Spanish America of the* uti possidetis juris, *whereby the boundaries were to follow the colonial administrative boundaries' (para. 28 of the 1992 Judgment). The Chamber did however note that 'the* uti possidetis juris *position can be qualified by adjudication and by treaty'. It reasoned from this that 'the question then arises whether it can be qualified in other ways, for example, by acquiescence or recognition'. It concluded that 'There seems to be no reason in principle why these factors should not operate, where there is sufficient evidence to show that the parties have in effect clearly accepted a variation, or at least an interpretation, of the* uti possidetis juris *position' (para. 67 of the 1992 Judgment).*
>
> *"The Chamber then considered 'The contention of El Salvador that a former bed of the river Goascorán forms the* uti possidetis juris *boundary. In this respect, it observed that:*
>
>> *'[this contention] depends, as a question of fact, on the assertion that the Goascorán formerly was running in that bed, and that at some date it abruptly changed its course to its present position. On this basis El Salvador's argument of law is that where a boundary is formed by the course of a river, and the stream suddenly leaves its old bed and forms a new one, this process of 'avulsion' does not bring about a change in the boundary, which continues to follow the old channel.' (Para. 308 of the 1992 Judgment.)*
>
> *"The Chamber added that:*
>
>> *'No record of such an abrupt change of course having occurred has been brought to the Chamber's attention, but were the Chamber satisfied that the river's course was earlier so radically different from its present one, then an avulsion might reasonably be inferred.' (Ibid.)*
>
> *"Pursuing its consideration of El Salvador's argument, the Chamber did however note:*
>
>> *'There is no scientific evidence that the previous course of the Goascorán was such that it debouched in the Estero La Cutú... rather than in any of the other*

neighbouring inlets in the coastline, such as the Estero El Coyol' (para. 309 of the 1992 Judgment).

"Turning to consideration as a matter of law of El Salvador's proposition concerning the avulsion of the Goascorán, the Chamber observed that El Salvador 'suggests... that the change in fact took place in the 17th century' (para. 311 of the 1992 Judgment). It concluded that ' On this basis, what international law may have to say, on the question of the shifting of rivers which form frontiers, becomes irrelevant: the problem is mainly one of Spanish colonial law.' (Para. 311 of the 1992 Judgment.)

"Beginning in paragraph 312 of the 1992 Judgment, the Chamber turned to a consideration of a different ground. At the outset, it tersely stated the conclusions which it had reached and then set out the reasoning supporting them. In the view of the Chamber, 'any claim by El Salvador that the boundary follows an old course of the river abandoned at some time before 1821 must be rejected. It is a new claim and inconsistent with the previous history of the dispute.' (Para. 312 of the 1992 Judgment.)

"In the present case, the Chamber observes that, whilst in 1992 the Chamber rejected El Salvador's claims that the 1821 boundary did not follow the course of the river at that date, it did so on the basis of that State's conduct during the nineteenth century.

"The Chamber concludes that, in short, it does not matter whether or not there was an avulsion of the Goascorán. Even if avulsion were now proved, and even if its legal consequences were those inferred by El Salvador, findings to that effect would provide no basis for calling into question the decision taken by the Chamber in 1992 on wholly different grounds. The facts asserted in this connection by El Salvador are not 'decisive factors' in respect of the Judgment which it seeks to have revised." [30]

Disputes concerning territorial sovereignty, both in relation to entire territories and in relation to frontiers between territories, are likely to be heard by bodies such as the ICJ and the PCA.

30 The ICJ website carries a report of the *Land, Island and Maritime Frontier Dispute (El Salvador / Honduras: Nicaragua* intervening case at www.icj-cij.org/icjwww/idocket/iesh/ieshframe.htm.

8 Maritime Delimitation Disputes and the 1982 Law of the Sea Convention

1) Introduction

For the purposes of the Manual, maritime delimitation disputes can be divided into three areas: those concerning

- the territorial sea and the contiguous zone;
- the exclusive economic zone;
- the continental shelf.

These areas are dealt with in the 1982 United Nations Convention on the Law of the Sea (UNCLOS III). It will be recalled that in an earlier chapter it was suggested that there were three international treaties that have a particular relevance to maritime disputes, international investment disputes and international trade disputes generally: UNCLOS III, the International Convention on the Settlement of Investment Disputes (ICSID Convention) and the Convention on the Recognition and Enforcement of Foreign Arbitral Awards (New York Convention).

As in the case of territorial boundary disputes, the international dispute settlement bodies dealing with maritime boundary disputes are likely to include the International Court of Justice (ICJ) and the Permanent Court of Arbitration (PCA), both in The Hague. In addition, UNLCOS III set up a third international body dealing specifically with maritime disputes: the International Tribunal for the Law of the Sea (ITLOS).

While the concept of the freedom of the high seas is accepted internationally, it is similarly accepted that coastal states have rights in relation to the seas off their coasts and that the resources in the seas and on the seabed need to be exploited. This can lead to disputes concerning the delimitation of the territorial sea between States with opposite or adjacent coasts, disputes concerning the delimitation of the continental shelf and disputes concerning exclusive economic zones. What may well lie behind a maritime delimitation dispute, as with a land dispute, is the existence – or suspected existence – of an oil and/or gas field.

Various conferences have been held that sought to deal with these potentially conflicting areas of interest. These conferences led to the 1958 Conventions on the territorial sea and contiguous zone; the high seas; the continental shelf; and fishing and conservation of the living resources of the high seas, and then subsequently to UNCLOS III. The Preamble to the 1982 Convention sets the scene (see Box 5).

Box 5: Preamble to the 1982 United Nations Convention on the Law of the Sea

The States Parties to this Convention:

"***Prompted*** *by the desire to settle, in a spirit of mutual understanding and cooperation, all issues relating to the law of the sea and aware of the historic significance of this Convention as an important contribution to the maintenance of peace, justice and progress for all peoples of the world,*

Noting *that developments since the United Nations Conferences on the Law of the Sea held at Geneva in 1958 and 1960 have accentuated the need for a new and generally acceptable Convention on the law of the sea,*

Conscious *that the problems of ocean space are closely interrelated and need to be considered as a whole,*

Recognizing *the desirability of establishing through this Convention, with due regard for the sovereignty of all States, a legal order for the seas and oceans which will facilitate international communication, and will promote the peaceful uses of the seas and oceans, the equitable and efficient utilization of their resources, the conservation of their living resources, and the study, protection and preservation of the marine environment,*

Bearing in mind *that the achievement of these goals will contribute to the realization of a just and equitable international economic order which takes into account the interests and needs of mankind as a whole and, in particular, the special interests and needs of developing countries, whether coastal or land-locked,*

Desiring *by this Convention to develop the principles embodied in resolution 2749 (XXV) of 17 December 1970 in which the General Assembly of the United Nations solemnly declared inter alia that the area of the seabed and ocean floor and the subsoil thereof, beyond the limits of national jurisdiction, as well as its resources, are the common heritage of mankind, the exploration and exploitation of which shall be carried out for the benefit of mankind as a whole, irrespective of the geographical location of States,*

Believing *that the codification and progressive development of the law of the sea achieved in this Convention will contribute to the strengthening of peace, security, cooperation and friendly relations among all nations in conformity with the principles of justice and equal rights and will promote the economic and social advancement of all peoples of the world, in accordance with the Purposes and Principles of the United Nations as set forth in the Charter,*

Affirming *that matters not regulated by this Convention continue to be governed by the rules and principles of general international law,*

Have agreed as follows...."

UNCLOS III deals with, among other things, the rights over – and the methods of prescribing the limits of – the three areas mentioned above: the territorial sea and contiguous zone, the exclusive economic zone and the continental shelf (and other areas such as islands, bays and archipelagic States). It provides various methods for settling disputes, with detailed and complex dispute resolution provisions contained in Part XV and various Annexes of the Convention.

The development of claims

While it has long been accepted that coastal States have a right to regard an 'adjacent belt of sea' as part of their territorial waters, a less certain question was how far that belt of sea around the coastline extended into the high seas.

At one time the breadth of a coastal State's territorial waters was taken to be 3 miles: the distance of a cannon-shot. The limit is now accepted as 12 miles, measured from a baseline, which is the State's low-water mark (inland waters sited on the landward side of the baseline are deemed to be part of the internal waters of a State). When the coastline of a State is deeply indented, or where there are bays or where islands run parallel to the coast, the positioning of the baseline may raise difficulties. In the case of a bay, for example, should the baseline be taken from the low-water mark on the coast or should a 'straight baseline' drawn across the mouth of the bay be used?

Islands are capable of having a territorial sea (and an exclusive economic zone and a continental shelf). Attempts have sometimes been made in the case of archipelagic States comprising a number of islands to argue that the straight baseline method can be used to define their outer limits.

A coastal State may be entitled to exercise rights beyond the 12-mile limit of its territorial sea. For example, in a zone of the high seas contiguous to its territorial sea, a coastal State may lay claim to exercise control for the purposes of preventing the infringement of its customs regulations or in order to protect its immigration or sanitary laws and regulations. Additionally, a coastal State may be entitled to enjoy rights in relation to continental shelves and exclusive economic zones. Both are considered in the following sections and both may extend jurisdiction beyond the limit of the territorial sea.

The scheme of the 1982 Convention on the Law of the Sea (UNCLOS III)

UNCLOS III comprises 320 Articles and is divided into 17 Parts.

Part I: Introduction

Part II: Territorial Sea and Contiguous Zone

Part III: Straits used for International Navigation

Part IV: Archipelagic States

Part V: Exclusive Economic Zone

Part VI: Continental Shelf

Part VII: High Seas

Part VIII: Regime of Islands

Part IX: Enclosed or Semi-Enclosed Seas

Part X: Right of Access of Land-Locked States to and from the Sea and Freedom of Transit

Part XI: The Area (this Part of the Convention is concerned with the 'common heritage of mankind' and with seabed resources and contains provisions relating to the Seabed Disputes Chamber of ITLOS)

Part XII: Protection and Preservation of the Marine Environment

Part XIII: Marine Scientific Research

Part XIV: Development and Transfer of Marine Technology

Part XV: Settlement of Disputes

Part XVI: General Provisions

Part XVII: Final Provisions

There are nine Annexes, which include:

Annex V – Conciliation

Annex VI – Statute of ITLOS

Annex VII – Arbitration

Annex VIII – Special Arbitration

Part XV of the Convention, dealing with the settlement of disputes – and Annexes V, VI, VII and VIII containing provisions dealing with methods and processes of dispute resolution – are relevant to the later part of the Manual dealing with supranational dispute resolution bodies.

The remainder of this chapter considers Part II: Territorial Sea and the Contiguous Zone (section 2), Part V: Exclusive Economic Zone (section 3) and Part VI: Continental Shelf (section 4). Since delimitation disputes are likely to arise in relation to all three areas, it also looks at delimitation (section 5) and considers some of the cases concerning delimitation that have come before supranational dispute resolution bodies such as the ICJ and the PCA (section 6).

2) Territorial Sea and Contiguous Zone

Territorial sea

A baseline divides the inland territories of a coastal State from its territorial sea. The inland territories may include rivers and other inland waters, and *"internal waters"* are dealt with in Article 8 of the Convention. As noted above, the baseline is generally measured from the low-water mark of the coastal State, although a different baseline may apply. Article 2 of the Law of the Sea Convention defines the territorial sea as a coastal State's *"adjacent belt of sea"*. It deals with the legal status of the territorial sea, the air space over that sea, and the seabed and its subsoil:

"1. The sovereignty of a coastal State extends, beyond its land territory and internal waters and, in the case of an archipelagic State, its archipelagic waters, to an adjacent belt of sea, described as the territorial sea.

2. *This sovereignty extends to the air space over the territorial sea as well as to its bed and subsoil.*
3. *The sovereignty over the territorial sea is exercised subject to this Convention and to other rules of international law."*

Articles 3, 4 and 5 deal with the breadth of the territorial sea. Article 3 provides: *"Every State has the right to establish the breadth of its territorial sea up to a limit not exceeding 12 nautical miles, measured from baselines determined in accordance with this Convention."* Article 4 states that: *"The outer limit of the territorial sea is the line every point of which is at a distance from the nearest point of the baseline equal to the breadth of the territorial sea."* Article 5 provides that the normal baseline for measuring the breadth of territorial sea is *"the low-water line along the coast as marked on large-scale charts officially recognized by the coastal State"*.

Different baseline provisions apply in the case of reefs. Article 6 states that: *"In the case of islands situated on atolls or of islands having fringing reefs, the baseline for measuring the breadth of the territorial sea is the seaward low-water line of the reef, as shown by the appropriate symbol on charts officially recognized by the coastal State."*

Article 7 of the Convention deals with 'straight baselines' and the problem of deltas and other unstable coastlines: *"In localities where the coastline is deeply indented and cut into, or if there is a fringe of islands along the coast in its immediate vicinity, the method of straight baselines joining appropriate points may be employed in drawing the baseline from which the breadth of the territorial sea is measured..."*.

Waters on the landward side of the baseline of the territorial sea *"form part of the internal waters of the State"* (Article 8). Article 9 states that if a river flows directly into the sea *"the baseline shall be a straight line across the mouth of the river between points on the low-water line of its banks"*.

In the case of bays, the coast of which belongs to a single State, Article 10 contains provisions that determine whether the waters of a bay are internal waters. Article 10 (4) states that *"If the distance between the low-water marks of the natural entrance points of a bay does not exceed 24 nautical miles, a closing line may be drawn between these two low-water marks, and the waters enclosed thereby shall be considered as internal waters."* However, where the distance exceeds 24 nautical miles, *"a straight baseline of 24 nautical miles shall be drawn within the bay in such a manner as to enclose the maximum area of water that is possible with a line of that length"* (Article 10 (5)).

Provisions are set out in Articles 11 and 12 that deal with ports and roadsteads. Article 13 contains provisions dealing with low-tide elevations:

"1. *A low-tide elevation is a naturally formed area of land which is surrounded by and above water at low tide but submerged at high tide. Where a low-tide elevation is situated wholly or partly at a distance not exceeding the breadth of the territorial sea from the mainland or an island, the low-water line on that elevation may be used as the baseline for measuring the breadth of the territorial sea.*

2. *Where a low-tide elevation is wholly situated at a distance exceeding the breadth of the territorial sea from the mainland or an island, it has no territorial sea of its own."*

Article 14 states that a combination of methods may be used for determining baselines: *"The coastal State may determine baselines in turn by any of the methods provided for in the foregoing articles to suit different conditions."* Article 15 contains provisions dealing with the delimitation of the territorial sea between States with opposite or adjacent coasts. Those provisions are considered later.

Article 16 deals with charts and lists of geographical coordinates for the purposes of lines of delimitation:

"1. *The baselines for measuring the breadth of the territorial sea determined in accordance with articles 7, 9 and 10, or the limits derived therefrom, and the lines of delimitation drawn in accordance with articles 12 and 15 shall be shown on charts of a scale or scales adequate for ascertaining their position. Alternatively, a list of geographical coordinates of points, specifying the geodetic datum, may be substituted.*

2. *The coastal State shall give due publicity to such charts or lists of geographical coordinates and shall deposit a copy of each such chart or list with the Secretary-General of the United Nations."*

Articles 17 to 32 of Part II of the 1982 Convention contain provisions dealing with the right of innocent passage in the territorial sea and provisions relating to merchant ships, government ships operating for commercial purposes, and warships and other government ships operating for non-commercial purposes.

Contiguous zone

Article 33 contains provisions relating to the contiguous zone:

"1. *In a zone contiguous to its territorial sea, described as the contiguous zone, the coastal State may exercise the control necessary to:*

   (a) *prevent infringement of its customs, fiscal, immigration or sanitary laws and regulations within its territory or territorial sea;*

   (b) *punish infringement of the above laws and regulations committed within its territory or territorial sea.*

2. *The contiguous zone may not extend beyond 24 nautical miles from the baselines from which the breadth of the territorial sea is measured."*

Part IV of the Convention in Articles 47 to 54 contains provisions relating to archipelagic States, including provisions dealing with the measurement of the breadth of the territorial sea, the contiguous zone, the exclusive economic zone and the continental shelf.

3) Exclusive Economic Zone

As seen in the last section, the contiguous zone – a zone bordering on the territorial sea – extends the jurisdiction of a coastal State to 24 miles. Some coastal states have sought to extend the limit of their jurisdiction yet further. Where an exclusive economic zone can be claimed by a coastal State, that jurisdiction reaches a limit of 200 miles. Many of the claims have been based on exclusive rights in relation to fisheries. Claims may now be based on rights in relation to natural resources in the 200-mile zone.

The right to claim an exclusive economic zone may exist in customary international law, and is in any event a right recognised by UNCLOS III. Part V (articles 55 to 75) contains detailed provisions.

Article 55 defines an exclusive economic zone as *"an area beyond and adjacent to the territorial sea, subject to the specific legal regime established in this Part, under which the rights and jurisdiction of the coastal State and the rights and freedoms of other States are governed by the relevant provisions of this Convention".*

Article 56 deals with the rights, jurisdiction and duties of the coastal State in relation to the exclusive economic zone. The coastal state has the following rights and duties:

1. *"(a) sovereign rights for the purpose of exploring and exploiting, conserving and managing the natural resources, whether living or non-living, of the waters superjacent to the seabed and of the seabed and its subsoil, and with regard to other activities for the economic exploitation and exploration of the zone, such as the production of energy from the water, currents and winds;*

   (b) jurisdiction as provided for in the relevant provisions of this Convention with regard to:

   (i) the establishment and use of artificial islands, installations and structures;

   (ii) marine scientific research;

   (iii) the protection and preservation of the marine environment;

   (c) other rights and duties provided for in this Convention.
2. *In exercising its rights and performing its duties under this Convention in the exclusive economic zone, the coastal State shall have due regard to the rights and duties of other States and shall act in a manner compatible with the provisions of this Convention.*
3. *The rights set out in this article with respect to the seabed and subsoil shall be exercised in accordance with Part VI."*

Article 57 provides that the breadth of the exclusive economic zone *"shall not extend beyond 200 hundred nautical miles from the baselines from which the breadth of territorial sea is measured".* Article 58 deals with the rights and duties of other States in the exclusive economic zone.

Article 59 sets out provisions for the resolution of conflicts in relation to the attribution of rights and jurisdiction in and use of the exclusive economic zone. The article provides that, in cases where the Convention does not attribute rights or jurisdiction to the coastal State or to other States within the zone, and *"... a conflict arises between the interests of the coastal State and any other State or States, the conflict should be resolved on the basis of equity and in the light of all the relevant circumstances, taking into account the respective importance of the interests involved to the parties as well as to the international community as a whole".*

Article 60 deals with the rights referred to in Article 56 in relation to the coastal State's rights in the exclusive economic zone to construct artificial islands and other installations and structures. Article 60 (1) and (2) provides that the coastal State shall have the exclusive right *"... to construct and to authorize and regulate the construction, operation and use of:*

(a) artificial islands;

(b) installations and structures for the purposes provided for in article 56 and other economic purposes;

(c) installations and structures which may interfere with the exercise of the rights of the coastal State in the zone."

Article 60 (2) states that *"The coastal State shall have exclusive jurisdiction over such artificial islands, installations and structures, including jurisdiction with regard to customs, fiscal, health, safety and immigration laws and regulations."* Article 60 (8) makes it clear that *"Artificial islands, installations and structures do not possess the status of islands. They have no territorial sea of their own, and their presence does not affect the delimitation of the territorial sea, the exclusive economic zone or the continental shelf."*

Articles 61-72 make provisions in relation to living resources, including the rights of land-locked States (Article 69) and of geographically disadvantaged States (Article 70).

Article 73 provides for the enforcement in the exclusive economic zone of the coastal State's sovereign rights to explore, exploit and conserve and manage the living resources in the zone. The measures taken may include boarding, inspection, arrest and judicial proceedings.

Articles 74 and 75 deal with the delimitation of the exclusive economic zone and the settlement of disputes. The dispute resolution provisions of the Convention are considered in Part III of the Manual.

Article 74 provides that:

"1. The delimitation of the exclusive economic zone between States with opposite or adjacent coasts shall be effected by agreement on the basis of international law, as referred to in Article 38 of the Statute of the International Court of Justice, in order to achieve an equitable solution.

2. If no agreement can be reached within a reasonable period of time, the States concerned shall resort to the procedures provided for in Part XV.

3. Pending agreement as provided for in paragraph 1, the States concerned, in a spirit of understanding and cooperation, shall make every effort to enter into provisional arrangements of a practical nature and, during this transitional period, not to jeopardize or hamper the reaching of the final agreement. Such arrangements shall be without prejudice to the final delimitation.

4. *Where there is an agreement in force between the States concerned, questions relating to the delimitation of the exclusive economic zone shall be determined in accordance with the provisions of that agreement."*

The outer limit lines of the exclusive economic zone and the lines of delimitation drawn in accordance with Article 74 *"... shall be shown on charts of a scale or scales adequate for ascertaining their position. Where appropriate, lists of geographical coordinates of points, specifying the geodetic datum, may be substituted for such outer limit lines or lines of delimitation."* The coastal State is to give due publicity to those charts or lists of geographical coordinates, and is to deposit a copy of each with the UN Secretary-General.

The rights given to coastal States by Part V of the 1982 Convention in relation to the exploitation of natural resources in an exclusive economic zone are of great significance. Article 56 (3) of Part V provides that rights in relation to the seabed and subsoil are to be exercised in accordance with Part VI of the Convention. That Part deals with the continental shelf and governs rights concerning the seabed and the subsoil. Much may be at stake in delimitation disputes concerning continental shelves and exclusive economic zones.

4) Continental Shelf

i) The US Submerged Lands Act

'Continental shelf' is a geological term referring to a ledge or shelf that projects from the landmass of a coastal State and that is covered by only a shallow layer of water. For example, the United States Submerged Lands Act [43 USC s. 1301-1315] refers to *"lands beneath navigable waters"*, which the Act defines as meaning:

"(1) all lands within the boundaries of each of the respective States which are covered by nontidal waters that were navigable under the laws of the United States at the time such State became a member of the Union, or acquired sovereignty over such lands and water thereafter, up to the ordinary high water mark as heretofore or hereafter modified by accretion, erosion, and reliction;

(2) all lands permanently or periodically covered by tidal waters up to but not above the line of mean high tide and seaward to a line three geographical miles distant from the coast line of each such State and to the boundary line of each such State where in any case such boundary as it existed at the time such State became a member of the Union, or as heretofore approved by Congress, extends seaward (or into the Gulf of Mexico) beyond three geographical miles...."

Continental shelves may carry deposits of oil and gas (for the purposes of the Submerged Lands Act, the term 'natural resources' includes oil, gas and all other minerals). To state the obvious, a coastal State will be anxious to secure control of such valuable resources.

ii) The Truman Declaration

The Truman Declaration – Presidential Proclamation No. 2667 issued on 20 September 1945 – set out the policy of the United States with respect to the natural resources of the subsoil and sea bed of the continental shelf.

A preamble to the Proclamation stated that:

> *"Whereas the Government of the United States of America, aware of the long range world-wide need for new sources of petroleum and other minerals, holds the view that efforts to discover and make available new supplies of these resources should be encouraged; and*
>
> *"Whereas its competent experts are of the opinion that such resources underlie many parts of the continental shelf off the coasts of the United States of America, and that with modern technological progress their utilization is already practicable or will become so at any early date; and*
>
> *"Whereas recognized jurisdiction over these resources is required in the interest of their conservation and prudent utilization when and as development is undertaken; and*
>
> *"Whereas it is the view of the Government of the United States that the exercise of jurisdiction over the natural resources of the subsoil and sea bed of the continental shelf by the contiguous nation is reasonable and just, since the effectiveness of measures to utilize or conserve these resources would be contingent upon cooperation and protection from shore, since the continental shelf may be regarded as an extension of the land mass of the coastal nation and thus naturally appurtenant to it, since these resources frequently form a seaward extension of a pool or deposit lying within the territory, and since self-protection compels the coastal nation to keep close watch over activities off its shores which are of their nature necessary for utilization of these resources...."*

The proclamation then went on to set out the US policy:

> *"Having concern for the urgency of conserving and prudently utilizing its natural resources, the Government of the United States regards the natural resources of the subsoil and sea bed of the continental shelf beneath the high seas but contiguous to the coasts of the United States as appertaining to the United States, subject to its jurisdiction and control. In cases where the continental shelf extends to the shores of another State, or is shared with an adjacent State, the boundary shall be determined by the United States and the State concerned in accordance with equitable principles. The character as high seas of the waters above the continental shelf and the right to their free and unimpeded navigation are in no way thus affected."*

The approach taken by the United States has been followed by other countries. Part VI of UNCLOS III contains provisions along the lines of the Truman Declaration, and customary international law follows a similar line – as demonstrated by various decisions of the ICJ.[31]

---

31 The Truman Declaration is referred to by the ICJ in the *North Sea Continental Shelf Cases*, mentioned later in this chapter.

iii) Provisions of UNCLOS III

Article 76 of UNCLOS III contains significant provisions defining *"continental shelf"*:

"1. The continental shelf of a coastal State comprises the seabed and subsoil of the submarine areas that extend beyond its territorial sea throughout the natural prolongation of its land territory to the outer edge of the continental margin, or to a distance of 200 nautical miles from the baselines from which the breadth of the territorial sea is measured where the outer edge of the continental margin does not extend up to that distance.

2. The continental shelf of a coastal State shall not extend beyond the limits provided for in paragraphs 4 to 6.

3. The continental margin comprises the submerged prolongation of the land mass of the coastal State, and consists of the seabed and subsoil of the shelf, the slope and the rise. It does not include the deep ocean floor with its oceanic ridges or the subsoil thereof.

4. (a) For the purposes of this Convention, the coastal State shall establish the outer edge of the continental margin wherever the margin extends beyond 200 nautical miles from the baselines from which the breadth of the territorial sea is measured, by either:

(i) a line delineated in accordance with paragraph 7 by reference to the outermost fixed points at each of which the thickness of sedimentary rocks is at least 1 per cent of the shortest distance from such point to the foot of the continental slope; or

(ii) a line delineated in accordance with paragraph 7 by reference to fixed points not more than 60 nautical miles from the foot of the continental slope.

(b) In the absence of evidence to the contrary, the foot of the continental slope shall be determined as the point of maximum change in the gradient at its base.

5. The fixed points comprising the line of the outer limits of the continental shelf on the seabed, drawn in accordance with paragraph 4 (a)(i) and (ii), either shall not exceed 350 nautical miles from the baselines from which the breadth of the territorial sea is measured or shall not exceed 100 nautical miles from the 2,500 metre isobath, which is a line connecting the depth of 2,500 metres.

6. Notwithstanding the provisions of paragraph 5, on submarine ridges, the outer limit of the continental shelf shall not exceed 350 nautical miles from the baselines from which the breadth of the territorial sea is measured. This paragraph does not apply to submarine elevations that are natural components of the continental margin, such as its plateaux, rises, caps, banks and spurs.

7. The coastal State shall delineate the outer limits of its continental shelf, where that shelf extends beyond 200 nautical miles from the baselines from which the breadth of the territorial sea is measured, by straight lines not exceeding 60 nautical miles in length, connecting fixed points, defined by coordinates of latitude and longitude."

Article 76 (10) states that the provisions of the article"... *are without prejudice to the question of delimitation of the continental shelf between States with opposite or adjacent coasts*".

Article 77 contains important provisions dealing with the rights of a coastal State over the continental shelf:

> "1. *The coastal State exercises over the continental shelf sovereign rights for the purpose of exploring it and exploiting its natural resources.*
>
> 2. *The rights referred to in paragraph 1 are exclusive in the sense that if the coastal State does not explore the continental shelf or exploit its natural resources, no one may undertake these activities without the express consent of the coastal State.*
>
> 3. *The rights of the coastal State over the continental shelf do not depend on occupation, effective or notional, or on any express proclamation.*
>
> 4. *The natural resources referred to in this Part consist of the mineral and other non-living resources of the seabed and subsoil together with living organisms belonging to sedentary species, that is to say, organisms which, at the harvestable stage, either are immobile on or under the seabed or are unable to move except in constant physical contact with the seabed or the subsoil.*"

Article 78 deals with the legal status of the superjacent waters and air space and with the rights and freedoms of other States. The rights of other States to lay submarine cables and pipelines are dealt with in Article 79. (An example of an agreement between coastal states in relation to the laying of submarine pipelines – the Framework Agreement between Britain and Norway – is given later in this chapter.) Article 80 applies the Article 60 provisions in relation to artificial islands, installations and structures on the continental shelf: the coastal State is therefore to have the right to construct, etc, artificial islands and the like.

Significant provisions are contained in Article 81 in relation to oil and gas deposits. The coastal State is to have the exclusive right to authorise and regulate drilling on the continental shelf for all purposes. Article 82 makes provisions in relation to payments and contributions with respect to the exploitation of the continental shelf beyond 200 nautical miles.

Given the number of disputes relating to delimitation of continental shelves, the provisions of Article 83 of the 1982 Convention are of great importance. The Article deals with the delimitation of the continental shelf between States with opposite or adjacent coasts and makes provision for the resolution of any disputes by use of the dispute resolution procedures contained in Part XV of the Convention. Article 83 will be considered in the next section of this chapter.

Article 84 states that the outer limit lines of the continental shelf, and the lines of delimitation drawn in accordance with Article 83, are to be shown on charts of adequate scale. Those charts, and any lists of geographical coordinates of points, are to be given due publicity and copies are to be deposited with the UN Secretary-General. Finally, Article 85 states that Part VI is not to prejudice the right of the coastal State to exploit the subsoil by means of tunnelling "... *irrespective of the depth of water above the subsoil*".

5) Delimitation

UNCLOS III contains various provisions dealing with methods of prescribing the limits of the different maritime areas over which coastal and other States may lay claim: territorial seas and contiguous zones, exclusive economic zones and continental shelves. Provisions are made for the width and extent of these. Basic rules are laid down for delimitation based on measurement from low-water baselines and for measurement using straight baselines. Rules provide for difficulties that arise in relation to bays, islands, reefs and archipelagic States.

Specific provisions are made in relation to problems that arise in relation to delimitation of the territorial sea between States with opposite or adjacent coasts. Problems may also arise in relation to delimitation of the continental shelves and exclusive economic zones between adjacent or opposite States.

Two broad maritime delimitation principles can be said to have emerged from a combination of sources, including customary international law and treaties (in particular the provisions of UNCLOS III) and decisions of international dispute settlement tribunals. One is based on, or at any rate is evidenced by, the provisions of Article 15 of the Convention: the *"equidistance / special circumstances rule"*. Delimitation should be based on the drawing of an equidistance line, which is regarded as likely to provide an equitable resolution to maritime delimitation disputes. However, special circumstances may indicate any change that should be made to this line.

The second principle is the *"equitable principles / relevant circumstances method"*. This method is very similar to the first rule and involves drawing the equidistance line and then considering whether there are circumstances that need to be taken into account that may result in redrawing it so as to produce an 'equitable' result.

The specific provisions of UNCLOS III are set out below.

Article 15

Article 15 of Part II of the Convention deals with the delimitation of the territorial sea between States with opposite or adjacent coasts:

> *"Where the coasts of two States are opposite or adjacent to each other, neither of the two States is entitled, failing agreement between them to the contrary, to extend its territorial sea beyond the median line every point of which is equidistant from the nearest points on the baselines from which the breadth of the territorial seas of each of the two States is measured. The above provision does not apply, however, where it is necessary by reason of historic title or other special circumstances to delimit the territorial seas of the two States in a way which is at variance therewith."*

Article 74

Article 74 in Part V contains provisions covering delimitation of the exclusive economic zone between States with opposite or adjacent coasts:

> *"1. The delimitation of the exclusive economic zone between States with opposite or adjacent coasts shall be effected by agreement on the basis of international law,*

as referred to in Article 38 of the Statute of the International Court of Justice, in order to achieve an equitable solution.

2. *If no agreement can be reached within a reasonable period of time, the States concerned shall resort to the procedures provided for in Part XV.*
3. *Pending agreement as provided for in paragraph 1, the States concerned, in a spirit of understanding and cooperation, shall make every effort to enter into provisional arrangements of a practical nature and, during this transitional period, not to jeopardize or hamper the reaching of the final agreement. Such arrangements shall be without prejudice to the final delimitation.*
4. *Where there is an agreement in force between the States concerned, questions relating to the delimitation of the exclusive economic zone shall be determined in accordance with the provisions of that agreement."*

The provisions of Article 74 (1) require agreement "*on the basis of international law*" as set out in Article 38 of the Statute of the ICJ. This Article, which is of significance to the Convention, was referred to earlier in the chapter on international law.

Where no agreement is reached, Article 74 (2) requires the parties to use the dispute settlement provisions contained in Part XV of the Convention. These are considered in detail in the later section of the Manual dealing with supranational dispute resolution bodies. Put shortly, the parties are required to seek to agree, failing which detailed provisions are made for disputes to be resolved by ITLOS, by the ICJ or by arbitration or special arbitration under the systems set out in Annexes VII and VIII of the Convention.

Article 83

Article 83 in Part VI sets out the provisions for delimitation in the case of a continental shelf between States with opposite or adjacent coasts. The provisions are similar to those contained in Article 74 dealing with exclusive economic zones. References are again made to agreement on the basis of international law, as set out in Article 38 of the ICJ Statute, and to the dispute resolution provisions contained in Part XV of the 1982 Convention.

6) Two Cases Illustrating Maritime Delimitation

By way of illustration, this section contains brief references to two maritime delimitation decisions: one by the ICJ and the other by the PCA. One predates the 1982 Convention; the other is dated some 15 years after the Convention was open for signature.

North Sea Continental Shelf Cases

The first example is a judgement given by the ICJ in February 1969 in the *North Sea Continental Shelf Cases*. The dispute related to the delimitation of the continental shelf (i) between the Federal Republic of Germany and Denmark and (ii) between the Federal Republic of Germany and the Netherlands. The Parties asked the Court to state the principles and rules of international law applicable, undertaking to carry out the delimitations on that basis.

The Court rejected the contention of Denmark and the Netherlands to the effect that the delimitations in question had to be carried out in accordance with the principle of equidistance as defined in Article 6 of the 1958 Geneva Convention on the Continental Shelf. The Court held:

- that the Federal Republic, which had not ratified the Convention, was not legally bound by the provisions of Article 6;
- that the equidistance principle was not a necessary consequence of the general concept of continental shelf rights and was not a rule of customary international law.

The Court also rejected the contentions of the Federal Republic seeking acceptance of the principle of an apportionment of the continental shelf into just and equitable shares. It held that each Party had an original right to those areas of the continental shelf that constituted the natural prolongation of its land territory into and under the sea. It was not a question of apportioning or sharing out those areas, but of delimiting them.

The Court found that the boundary lines in question were to be drawn by agreement between the Parties and in accordance with equitable principles, and it indicated certain factors to be taken into consideration for that purpose. It was now for the Parties to negotiate on the basis of such principles, as they had agreed. The Court stated that:

> *"... the basic principles in the matter of delimitation, deriving from the Truman Proclamation, were that it must be the object of agreement between the States concerned and that such agreement must be arrived at in accordance with equitable principles. The Parties were under an obligation to enter into negotiations with a view to arriving at an agreement and not merely to go through a formal process of negotiation as a sort of prior condition for the automatic application of a certain method of delimitation in the absence of agreement; they were so to conduct themselves that the negotiations were meaningful, which would not be the case when one of them insisted upon its own position without contemplating any modification of it. This obligation was merely a special application of a principle underlying all international relations, which was moreover recognized in Article 33 of the Charter of the United Nations as one of the methods for the peaceful settlement of international disputes."*

The Court found in each case that;

> *"The use of the equidistance method of delimitation was not obligatory as between the Parties; that no other single method of delimitation was in all circumstances obligatory; that delimitation was to be effected by agreement in accordance with equitable principles and taking account of all relevant circumstances, in such a way as to leave as much as possible to each Party all those parts of the continental shelf that constituted a natural prolongation of its land territory, without encroachment on the natural prolongation of the land territory of the other; and that, if such delimitation produced overlapping areas, they were to be divided between the Parties in agreed proportions, or, failing agreement, equally, unless they decided on a régime of joint jurisdiction, user, or exploitation."*

The Court stated that, in the course of negotiations that would take place between the parties, the factors to be taken into account by them in those negotiations were to include:

"the general configuration of the coasts of the Parties, as well as the presence of any special or unusual features; so far as known or readily ascertainable, the physical and geological structure and natural resources of the continental shelf areas involved, the element of a reasonable degree of proportionality between the extent of the continental shelf areas appertaining to each State and the length of its coast measured in the general direction of the coastline, taking into account the effects, actual or prospective, of any other continental shelf delimitations in the same region." [32]

Arbitration between the Governments of Eritrea and Yemen

The second case is an award of the PCA given in October 1996 in the maritime delimitation phase of an arbitration between *the Government of the State of Eritrea and the Government of the Republic of Yemen.* The members of the Arbitral Tribunal were Professor Sir Robert Y Jennings (President), Judge Stephen M Schwebel, Dr Ahmed Sadek El-Kosheri, Mr Keith Highet and Judge Rosalyn Higgins.

Article 2 of the relevant Arbitration Agreement provided that:

"1. *The Tribunal is requested to provide rulings in accordance with international law, in two stages.*

2. *The first stage shall result in an award on territorial sovereignty and on the definition of the scope of the dispute between Eritrea and Yemen....*

3. *The second stage shall result in an award delimiting maritime boundaries. The Tribunal shall decide taking into account the opinion that it will have formed on questions of territorial sovereignty, the United Nations Convention on the Law of the Sea, and any other pertinent factor."*

In the course of its award dealing with delimitation, the Arbitral Tribunal stated at paragraphs 131-133 that:

"131. *It is a generally accepted view, as is evidenced in both the writings of commentators and in the jurisprudence, that between coasts that are opposite to each other the median or equidistance line normally provides an equitable boundary in accordance with the requirements of the Convention, and in particular those of its Articles 74 and 83 which respectively provide for the equitable delimitation of the EEZ and of the continental shelf between States with opposite or adjacent coasts. Indeed both Parties to the present case have claimed a boundary constructed on the equidistance method, although based on different points of departure and resulting in very different lines.*

"132. *The Tribunal has decided, after careful consideration of all the cogent and skilful arguments put before them by both Parties, that the international boundary shall be a single all-purpose boundary which is a median line and that it should, as far as practicable, be a median line between the opposite mainland coastlines. This solution is not only in accord with practice and precedent in the like situations but*

32 A report of the *North Sea Continental Shelf Cases* is available at www.icj-cij.org/icjwww/idecisions/isummaries/icssummary690220.htm.

is also one that is already familiar to both Parties. As the Tribunal had occasion to observe in its Award on Sovereignty (paragraph 438), the offshore petroleum contracts entered into by Yemen, and by Ethiopia and by Eritrea, 'lend a measure of support to a median line between the opposite coasts of Eritrea and Yemen, drawn without regard to the islands, dividing the respective jurisdiction of the Parties'. In the present stage the Tribunal has to determine a boundary not merely for the purposes of petroleum concessions and agreements, but a single international boundary for all purposes. For such a boundary the presence of islands requires careful consideration of their possible effect upon the boundary line; and this is done in the explanation which follows. Even so it will be found that the final solution is that the international maritime boundary line remains for the greater part a median line between the mainland coasts of the Parties.

"133. The median line is in any event some sort of coastal line by its very definition, for it is defined as a line 'every point of which is equidistant from the nearest points on the baselines from which the breadth of the territorial seas of the two States is measured' (Article 15 of the Convention), although the same definition will be found in many maritime boundary treaties and also in expert writings. The 'normal' baseline of the territorial sea as stated in Article 5 of the Convention – and this again accords with long practice and with the well established customary rule of the law of the sea – is 'the low-water line along the coast as marked on large scale charts officially recognized by the coastal State'. There do arise some questions about what is to be regarded as the 'coast' for these purposes, especially where islands are involved; and these questions, on which the Parties differ markedly, require decisions by the Tribunal." [33]

7) The Framework Agreement between Britain and Norway Relating to the Laying of Inter-Connecting Submarine Pipelines

An example of co-operation between coastal States under UNCLOS III is the Agreement made between the Governments of Britain and Norway in relation to the laying of submarine pipelines under the seas between the British and Norwegian coasts.

The rights of other States to lay submarine cables and pipelines are dealt with in Article 79 of the Convention, which provides that:

"1. All States are entitled to lay submarine cables and pipelines on the continental shelf, in accordance with the provisions of this article.

2. Subject to its right to take reasonable measures for the exploration of the continental shelf, the exploitation of its natural resources and the prevention, reduction and control of pollution from pipelines, the coastal State may not impede the laying or maintenance of such cables or pipelines.

3. The delineation of the course for the laying of such pipelines on the continental shelf is subject to the consent of the coastal State.

---

33 A report of the decision in *Government of the State of Eritrea and the Government of the Republic of Yemen* case is on the PCA website.

4. *Nothing in this Part affects the right of the coastal State to establish conditions for cables or pipelines entering its territory or territorial sea, or its jurisdiction over cables and pipelines constructed or used in connection with the exploration of its continental shelf or exploitation of its resources or the operations of artificial islands, installations and structures under its jurisdiction.*
5. *When laying submarine cables or pipelines, States shall have due regard to cables or pipelines already in position. In particular, possibilities of repairing existing cables or pipelines shall not be prejudiced."*

The Framework Agreement between the Governments of the United Kingdom of Great Britain and the Kingdom of Norway relating to the Laying of Inter-connecting Submarine Pipelines, in force in June 2000, recites that the Governments are:

> *"Mindful of the High Seas Convention of 1958, the Continental Shelf Convention of 1958 and the United Nations Convention on the Law of the Sea of 1982;*
>
> *Recalling that Articles 58, 79, 86 and 87 of the United Nations Convention on the Law of the Sea of 1982 define the legal regime of submarine pipelines in the context of that Convention as a whole, and that Article 79 of that Convention is at the core of the existing regime covering pipelines on the continental shelf...."*

Article 17 of the Framework Agreement deals with arbitration:

"1. *Any dispute about the interpretation or application of this Agreement, or any other matter referred to the Governments for settlement under the agreements between the owner of an inter-connecting pipeline and between such owner and the owner of an infrastructure, shall be resolved by negotiation between the two Governments.*

2. *If any dispute cannot be resolved in this manner or by any other procedure agreed to by the two Governments, the dispute shall be submitted, at the request of either Government, to an Arbitral Tribunal composed as follows:*

   Each Government shall designate one arbitrator, and the two arbitrators so designated shall elect a third, who shall be the Chairman and who shall not be a national of or habitually reside in the United Kingdom or in the Kingdom of Norway. If either Government fails to designate an arbitrator within three months of a request to do so, either Government may request the President of the International Court of Justice to appoint an arbitrator. The same procedure shall apply if, within one month of the designation or appointment of the second arbitrator, the third arbitrator has not been elected. The Tribunal shall determine its own procedure, save that all decisions shall be taken, in the absence of unanimity, by a majority vote of the members of the Tribunal. The decisions of the Tribunal shall be binding upon the two Governments and shall, for the purpose of this Agreement, be regarded as agreements between the two Governments."

The effect of that last sentence is evidently intended to elevate any arbitral award to an international obligation between the Governments of the United Kingdom and Norway.

9 Investor-State Disputes and Investment Treaty Arbitration

1) Introduction

The encouragement of investment, particularly investment into developing countries, is clearly a desirable objective. Investment treaties are designed to achieve two separate but related purposes, one for the benefit of a State and the other for the benefit of an investor. First, there is a need to attract inward investment into a 'host' State. Second, there is a need to protect the investment of the investor in the host State, in particular against uncompensated expropriation by that State.

Those two objectives – the promotion and the protection of investments – have been successfully achieved through the medium of bilateral investment treaties (BITs). BITs have tended to be made between developed capital-exporting countries and developing capital-importing countries, but there is also an increasing trend towards BITs between developing countries.

The first BIT was entered into over 40 years ago between Germany and Pakistan (in 1959). The number of such treaties now exceeds 2,000, and BITs are seen as instruments both for encouraging foreign investment and for protecting the interests of foreign investors.

> *"The first BITs were made in the period 1959-1969. Much of the inspiration for these and the later treaties came from the 1959 Abs-Shawcross Draft Convention on Investments Abroad and the 1967 OECD Draft Convention on the Protection of Foreign Property…."* [34]

The resolution of disputes between investors and States was seen to require special machinery. This need was supplied the 1965 Convention on the Settlement of Investment Disputes Between States and Nationals of Other States, commonly referred to as the ICSID Convention or the Washington Convention. The Convention created an organisation whose purpose is to deal with investment treaty disputes – the International Centre for Settlement of Investment Disputes (the ICSID Centre) in Washington.

An understanding of investor-State disputes – and investment treaty arbitration – requires a consideration of two matters: BITs and the ICSID Convention. These are considered in sections 2 and 3 of this chapter. Section 4 sets out some of the problems that have arisen in investor-State arbitrations.

The ICSID Arbitration Rules are dealt with in Chapter 14, which also looks at the ICSID Centre. The United Nations Commission on International Trade Law (UNCITRAL) Arbitration Rules (which may be used as an alternative to the ICSID Arbitration Rules) are

34 Antonio Parra, 'Applicable Substantive Law in ICSID Arbitrations', *ICSID News 2000*, 17(2). The paper delivered by Mr Parra, Deputy Secretary-General of ICSID, at the 17th ICSID/AAA/ICC Colloquium in Washington DC in November 2000 can be found on the ICSID website.

dealt with in Chapter 18, which looks at international commercial arbitral institutions and other international bodies.

Because ICSID – both the Convention and the Centre – are dealt with in some detail, only comparatively brief reference can be made in the Manual to two other investment dispute resolution processes: Chapter 11 of the North American Free Trade Association (NAFTA) and Article 26 of the Energy Charter Treaty (ECT) (see sections 6 and 7 of this chapter).

The NAFTA is concerned with trade generally and the ECT with energy disputes specifically. Both are, needless to say, of considerable international importance, and further information about them can be found on their websites.[35]

2) Bilateral Investment Treaties: the Japan-Vietnam Agreement

Perhaps the simplest way to see how BITs work is to look at the details of one such treaty. A comparatively current example is the agreement made between Japan and the Socialist Republic of Vietnam, entered into in November 2003.[36]

The agreement between Japan and Vietnam contains the type of provisions that are likely to be found in many BITS:

i) provisions to encourage investment;

ii) fair and equitable treatment provisions and provisions relating to expropriation and compensation;

iii) provisions relating to the free transfer of capital, profits and so on;

iv) investor-State dispute resolution provisions that provide for attempts at amicable settlement, followed if necessary by either ICSID arbitration or arbitration under the UNCITRAL Arbitration Rules.

The Agreement states that Japan and Vietnam wish to promote investment *"in order to strengthen the economic relationship between the two countries"*, intending to *"further create favourable conditions for greater investment by investors of one country in the Area of the other country"*. It contains 23 Articles.

Introductory matters

Article 1 sets out a series of definitions, including *"investments"*. That term covers *"every kind of asset owned or controlled… by any investor"*, including enterprises, shares, bonds, debentures, loans, rights under contracts, claims to money, intellectual property rights and concessions (*"including those for exploration and exploitation of natural resources"*), and tangible and intangible, movable and immovable property.

---

35 www.nafta-sec-alena.org/DefaultSite/index.html and www.encharter.org/index.jsp.

36 The Japan-Vietnam Investment Agreement can be found on the UNCTAD website: www.unctad.org/sections/dite/iia/docs/bits/japan_vietnam.pdf.

Article 2 requires each Contracting Party to accord *"no less favourable treatment"* to investors of the other Contracting Party than it accords to its own investors. Article 3 requires no less favourable treatment for investment in relation to access to the courts and tribunals of the host State.

Requirements are not to be imposed, as a condition of investment activity, in connection with matters such as the appointment of managers, etc, of any particular nationality, or in relation to the location of an investor's headquarters in the host country (Article 4). However, Article 5 permits each Contracting Party to maintain *"exceptional measures"* in relation to the matters set out in Annex 1. For example, in relation to Japan, these are matters relating to fisheries, the space industry and the electricity and gas industries. For Vietnam, the matters covered include oil and gas exploration, precious mineral mining and the exploitation of timber.

Article 6 permits the maintenance of the *"exceptional measures"* listed in Annex 11 that existed at the date of the Agreement. For Japan, these include the mining and oil industries. For Vietnam, they cover legal, accounting, insurance and banking services.

Article 7 requires each Contracting Party to publish *"its laws, regulations, administrative provisions and administrative rulings and judicial decisions of general application as well as international agreements"* that pertain to or affect investment activities. *"Sympathetic consideration"* is to be given by each Contracting Party to applications for entry and residence of natural persons of the nationality of the other Contracting Party (Article 8).

Fair and equitable treatment / no expropriation clause

Article 9 sets out essential provisions relating to fair and equitable treatment:

> *"Each Contracting Party shall accord to investments in its Area of investors of the other Contracting Party fair and equitable treatment and full and constant protection and security."*

Article 9 (2) (3) and (4) contain the *"no expropriation without fair compensation"* provisions. Article 9 (2) states that neither Contracting Party shall *"expropriate or nationalize investments in its Area of investors of the other Contracting Party or take any measure tantamount to expropriation or nationalization... except: (a) for a public purpose; (b) in a non-discriminatory manner; (c) upon payment of prompt, adequate and effective compensation; and (d) in accordance with due process of law"*.

Article 9 (3) provides that compensation shall be equivalent to the *"fair market value of the expropriated investments immediately before the expropriation occurred. The fair market value shall not reflect any change in value because the expropriation had become publicly known earlier. The compensation shall be paid without delay and shall carry an appropriate interest, taking into account the length of time until the time of payment. It shall be effectively realizable and freely transferable and shall be freely convertible into the currency of the Contracting Party of the investors concerned, and into freely usable currencies as defined in the Articles of Agreement of the International Monetary Fund, at the market exchange rate prevailing on the date of expropriation."*

Article 9 (4) states that, without prejudice to Article 14 (dealing with investment dispute resolution), the investor affected is to have the right of access to the courts of justice or administrative tribunals or agencies of the Contracting Party making the expropriation *"for a prompt review of the investors' case, and the amount of the compensation"*.

Article 10 contains provisions dealing with compensation for losses suffered to investment activities due to armed conflict, civil disturbances and similar events. Article 11 deals with subrogation and insurance.

Free transfer of capital, etc

Article 12 deals with a matter of considerable importance to the investor: the freedom to transfer monies out of the host State. Each Contracting Party is to ensure that all payments relating to investments in its Area of an investor of the other Contracting Party:

> *"may be freely transferred into and out of its Area without delay. Such transfers shall include, in particular, though not exclusively:*
>
> *(a) the initial capital and additional amounts to maintain or increase investments;*
>
> *(b) profits, interest, capital gains, dividends, royalties and fees…."*

Various other types of payments are listed in Article 12 (1)

Neither of the Contracting Parties is to prevent transfers being made without delay and in freely convertible currencies at the market rate of exchange existing as at the date of the transfer. However, transfers may be delayed or prevented in circumstances involving bankruptcy, insolvency, criminal offences or in order to comply with orders or judgments made in adjudicatory proceedings (Article 12 (2) and (3)).

Dispute resolution provisions: ICSID and UNCITRAL

Articles 13 and 14 contain the dispute resolution provisions. Article 13 (1) states that each Contracting Party shall accord *"sympathetic consideration"* to representations made by the other Contracting Party in relation to any matter affecting the operation of the Agreement.

Any dispute between the Contracting Parties as to the interpretation or application of the Agreement that cannot be satisfactorily dealt with by *"diplomacy"* is to be referred to an arbitration board. This board is to be composed of three arbitrators. One is to be appointed by each of the Contracting Parties within a period of 30 days from the date of receipt of a note requesting arbitration. The third arbitrator is to be appointed as President by the other two arbitrators within a further period of 30 days. He or she is not to be a national of either Contracting Party. In the event that the party-appointed arbitrators cannot agree on the appointment of a third arbitrator, the Contracting Parties must ask the President of the ICJ to make the appointment.

The arbitration board is to reach its decision within a reasonable time. The decision may be by a majority vote and is final and binding (Article 13 (2) and (4)). Article 13 (5) deals with the cost of the arbitral proceedings.

Article 14 (1) defines an *"investment dispute"* as a dispute between a Contracting Party and an investor of the other Contracting Party *"that has incurred loss or damage by reason of, or arising out of, an alleged breach of any rights conferred by this Agreement with respect to investments of investors of that other Contracting Party"*.

Article 14 (2) requires that, as far as possible, an investment dispute is to be settled amicably through consultation. However, if there is no settlement within three months from the date on which the investor requested the consultation, the dispute – at the request of the investor concerned – is to be submitted to either:

"(1) conciliation or arbitration in accordance with the provisions of the Convention on the Settlement of Investment Disputes between States and Nationals of Other States done at Washington, March 18, 1965... or conciliation or arbitration under the Additional Facility Rules of the International Centre of Settlement of Investment Disputes...; or

(2) arbitration under the Arbitration Rules of the United Nations Commission on International Trade Law, adopted by the United Nations Commission on International Trade Law on April 28, 1976."

These provisions, providing for either ICSID arbitration or arbitration under the UNCITRAL Rules, are common in BITs.

The arbitration decision shall be final and binding and is to be executed in accordance with the applicable laws and regulations in force in the country in whose Area such execution is sought (Article 14 (5)).

Article 14 (6) states that a dispute is not to be submitted to arbitration where an investor of either Contracting Party is seeking *"judicial or administrative settlement in the Area of the other Contracting Party or arbitral decision in accordance with any applicable previously agreed dispute-settlement procedures, concerning an investment dispute, or in the event that a final judicial settlement on such dispute has been made...."*

Article 14 (7) deals with *"legal persons"* for the purposes of investment disputes. Finally, Article 14 (8) provides that the provisions of Article 14 are not to be construed so as to prevent an investor from seeking judicial or administrative settlement in the Area of the Contracting Party that is a party to such a dispute.

Protective measures

Articles 15 and 16 deal with the right of the Contracting States to take measures for their protection in time of war, armed conflict or other emergencies, and to adopt measures dealing with *"serious balance-of-payments and external financial difficulties."* Article 17 states that the Contracting Parties may adopt measures in relation to financial services, including measures for the protection of investors.

Intellectual property

Intellectual property rights are dealt with in Article 18: *"nothing in this Agreement shall be construed so as to derogate from the rights and obligations under multilateral agreements in respect of protection of intellectual property rights, to which the Contracting Parties are parties".*

Other provisions

Article 19 deals with taxation.

Article 20 provides for the setting up of a Joint Committee whose function is to discuss and review the operation of the Agreement, to discuss and review any exceptional measures relating to Articles 5 and 6, to discuss other investment-related matters and where necessary to make appropriate recommendations to the Contracting Parties *"for the more effective functioning or the attainment of the objectives of this Agreement".* The Committee is to be composed of representatives of the Contracting Parties. It is entitled to determine its own rules of procedure for the purposes of carrying out its functions. It is also entitled to establish sub-committees and to delegate specific tasks to them. Unless the Contracting Parties decide otherwise, the Committee is to meet once a year *"and otherwise at the request of either Contracting Party".*

Article 21 deals with environmental matters. The Contracting Parties recognise that it is *"inappropriate to encourage investment by investors of the other Contracting Party by relaxing environmental measures. To this effect, each Contracting Party should not waive or otherwise derogate from such environmental measures as an encouragement for the establishment, acquisition or expansion in its Area of investment by investors of the other Contracting Party."*

Article 22 (1) requires each Contracting Party to take reasonable measures to ensure the observance of the agreement by *"local governments in its Area".* Article 22 (2) deals with the situation where investors in a third country own or control an *"investor".* Article 22 (3) provides that preferential treatment need not be extended in relation to membership of free trade areas, customs unions, or international agreements for economic integration or similar international agreements.

The final article, Article 23, deals with the entry into force, duration and termination of the Agreement. The Agreement is to remain in effect for a period of 10 years following its entry into force, and it is to continue until terminated by one Contracting Party giving one year's advance notice in writing to the other Contracting party *"at the end of the initial 10-year period or at any time thereafter".*

Article 23 (3) states that, in respect of investments acquired prior to the date of termination of the Agreement, the provisions of the Agreement are to continue in effect for a period of 10 years from its date of termination. However, the Agreement is not to apply to claims arising out of events that occurred prior to its entry into force.

The Agreement was made in Japanese, Vietnamese and English. In the event of disputes concerning interpretation, the English text is to prevail.

3) The ICSID Convention

i) Introduction

The Convention on the Settlement of Investment Disputes between States and Nationals of Other States – commonly known as the ICSID Convention or the Washington Convention – was mentioned earlier in the Manual as one of the conventions that are of particular relevance in the context of international trade and investment.[37]

The Convention was formulated by the Executive Directors of the World Bank and was submitted by them to member States of the Bank in March 1965 for their consideration and with a view to signature and ratification. The Convention entered into force on 14 October 1966.

The Convention established the International Centre for Settlement of Investment Disputes, based in Washington DC (considered in more detail in Chapter 14). The ICSID Centre is a public international organisation that provides facilities for the conciliation and arbitration of investment disputes between Contracting States and nationals of other Contracting States. The objective of the Centre in making such facilities available is to "*promote an atmosphere of mutual confidence between States and foreign investors conducive to increasing the flow of private international investment*".

The Centre does not itself take part in the conciliation or arbitration process. That task is undertaken by conciliators and arbitrators appointed either by the parties or as provided for in the ICSID Convention. The Centre assists the parties in the commencement and the conduct of the conciliation or arbitration proceedings, performing various administrative functions in connection with those proceedings.

Conciliation and arbitration under the ICSID Convention is voluntary:

> *"No Contracting State or national of such a State is obliged to resort to such conciliation or arbitration without having consented to do so. However, once the parties have consented, they are bound to carry out the undertaking and, in the case of arbitration, to abide by the award. Moreover, all Contracting States, whether or not parties to the dispute, are required to recognise awards rendered pursuant to the Convention as binding and to enforce the pecuniary obligations imposed thereby. Such awards are not subject to any appeal or to any other remedy except those which, like the remedy of annulment, are provided for in the Convention itself."*

In addition to the conciliation and arbitration facilities set out in the ICSID Convention, the ICSID Centre has provided an Additional Facility that allows it to administer certain proceedings between States and nationals of other States that fall outside the scope of the Convention itself, i.e., where one of the parties is not a Contracting State or a national of such a State.

As of January 2006, 155 States had signed the Convention and 143 have ratified it.

---

37 Detailed information about the Convention can be found in Christoph Schreuer, *The ICSID Convention: A Commentary*, Cambridge University Press, 2001.

ii) The Convention

The Convention is divided into 10 Chapters.

The Centre

Chapter I is concerned with the Centre. Article 1 states that the Centre *"is hereby established"* and that its purpose is to provide facilities for conciliation and arbitration of investment disputes between Contracting States and nationals of other Contracting States *"... in accordance with the provisions of this Convention"*. Article 2 provides that the seat of the Centre is to be the principal office of the International Bank for Reconstruction and Development. The Centre is to have an Administrative Council and a Secretariat and is to maintain a Panel of Conciliators and a Panel of Arbitrators.

Articles 4 to 11 of the Convention deal with the Administrative Council and the Secretariat. Articles 12 to 16 are concerned with the Panels. Each Contracting State may designate four persons to the Panel of Conciliators and the Panel of Arbitrators. Persons designated to serve on the Panels *"... shall be persons of high moral character and recognised competence in the fields of law, commerce, industry or finance, who may be relied upon to exercise independent judgement. Competence in the field of law shall be of particular importance in the case of persons on the Panel of Arbitrators."*

The Chairman of the Administrative Council, when designating persons to serve on the Panels, is to pay due regard to *"the importance of assuring representation on the Panels of the principal legal systems of the world and of the main forms of economic activity"*.

Articles 17 to 24 deal with the financing, status, immunities and privileges of the Centre, the Chairman, the members of the Administrative Council and persons acting as conciliators and arbitrators. They are to enjoy immunity from legal process in relation to acts performed by them in the exercise of their functions.

Jurisdiction of the Centre

Chapter II deals with the jurisdiction of the Centre. This is to extend to *"any legal dispute arising directly out of an investment, between a Contracting State... and a national of another Contracting State, which the parties to the dispute consent in writing to submit to the Centre. When the parties have given their consent, nobody may withdraw its consent unilaterally"* (Article 25).

Article 26 provides that the consent of the parties to arbitration under the Convention shall, unless otherwise stated, be deemed to be consent to such arbitration to the exclusion of any other remedy. However, a Contracting State may require the exhaustion of local administrative or judicial remedies as a condition to its consent to arbitration under the Convention.

Conciliation

Chapter III (Articles 28 to 35) deals with Conciliation.

A Contracting State (or a national of a Contracting State) that wishes to institute conciliation proceedings is to send a written request to the Secretary-General of the Centre, who is to send copy of that request to the other party. The request is to contain information relating to the issues in dispute, the identity of the parties and their consent to the conciliation process. The Secretary-General is to register the request *"unless he finds, on the basis of the information contained in the request, that the dispute is manifestly outside the jurisdiction of the Centre"* (Article 28).

A Conciliation Commission is to be constituted as soon as possible after the registration of the request. This may consist of either a sole conciliator or any uneven number of conciliators. The Commission is to be the judge of its own competence, and any objection by a party to the dispute to the effect that the dispute is not within the jurisdiction of the Centre is to be considered by the Commission, *"which shall determine whether to deal with it as a preliminary question or to join it to the merits of the dispute"*.

The conciliation proceedings are to be conducted in accordance with the provisions of Articles 32 to 35, and in accordance with the Conciliation Rules in effect on the date on which the parties consented to conciliation. Any question of procedure not covered by either the Convention or the Conciliation Rules is to be decided by the Commission.

The Commission is to clarify the issues in dispute between the parties and is to endeavour to bring about agreement between them on mutually acceptable terms. For that purpose it may at any stage of the proceedings and from time to time *"recommend terms of settlement to the parties"*. The parties are to cooperate in good faith with the Commission in order to enable it *"to carry out its functions, and shall give the most serious consideration to its recommendations"*. If the parties reach agreement, the Commission is to draw up a report *"noting the issues in dispute, and recording that the parties have reached agreement"*. However, if at any stage of the proceedings the Commission considers that there is no likelihood of agreement being reached between the parties, it is to close the proceedings and draw up a report recording the failure of the parties to reach agreement. The Commission is also to close the proceedings if one party fails to participate in them (Article 34).

The conciliation process is confidential. Unless the parties agree otherwise, neither of them is entitled to rely on – in other proceedings – any views expressed or statements or offers of settlement made by the other party in the conciliation proceedings (Article 35).

Arbitration

Chapter IV (Articles 36 to 55) deals with Arbitration.

Article 36 provides for a Request for Arbitration. As in the case of Conciliation, a written request is to be addressed to the Secretary-General, who is to send a copy to the other party. The request is to contain information relating to the issues in dispute, the identity of the parties and their consent to arbitration. The Secretary-General is to register the request, unless he or she finds that the dispute is outside the jurisdiction of the Centre.

Articles 37 to 40 deal with the appointment of the Arbitral Tribunal. Again, as in the case of Conciliation, the Tribunal is to be constituted as soon as possible after registration of the request. It is to consist of either a sole arbitrator or any uneven number of arbitrators. Where the parties do not agree on the number of arbitrators, or the method of their appointment, the Tribunal is to consist of three arbitrators: one appointed by each party and the third, who is to be its President, to be appointed by agreement between the parties (Article 38).

Articles 41 to 47 deal with the powers and functions of the Tribunal. It is to be the judge of its own competence, and any objection by one of the parties in relation to the jurisdiction of the Centre is to be considered by the Tribunal, which may either deal with the challenge as a preliminary question or may join it to the merits of the dispute (Article 41).

Article 42 provides that the Tribunal is to decided the dispute *"in accordance with such rules of law as may be agreed by the parties. In the absence of such agreement, the Tribunal shall apply the law of the Contracting Party to the dispute (including its rules on the conflict of laws), and such rules of international law as may be applicable."* The Tribunal may not bring in a finding of *non liquet*[38] on the ground of silence or "obscurity of the law". Provided the parties agree, the Tribunal is entitled to decide a dispute *ex aequo et bono.*[39]

Unless the parties agree otherwise, the Tribunal may, if it considers it necessary, call on the parties to produce documents or other evidence and may in addition visit the scene connected with the dispute and *"conduct such enquiries there as it may deem appropriate"* (Article 43).

The arbitration proceedings are to be conducted in accordance with the provisions of Articles 41 to 47 of the Convention (unless the parties agree otherwise) and also in accordance with the ICSID Arbitration Rules in effect on the date on which the parties consented to arbitration. Any procedural question not covered either by the relevant provisions of the Convention or by the Arbitration Rules (or any rules agreed by the parties) is to be decided by the Tribunal (Article 44).

Failure by a party to appear or to present its case is not deemed an admission of the other party's assertions. However, where a party fails to do so, the other party may request that the Tribunal deal with the questions submitted to it and render an award. Before rendering such an award the Tribunal shall notify – and grant a period of grace to – the party failing to appear or to present its case *"unless it is satisfied that that party does not intend to do so"* (Article 45).

---

38 *Non liquet* refers to a situation where, for want of legal rules, a court is unable (or unwilling) to give a decision based on law.

39 According to what is just and good.

Article 46 gives power to the Tribunal to determine any incidental or additional claims or counterclaims that arise directly out of the subject matter of the dispute. Unless the parties agree otherwise, the Tribunal may recommend any provisional measures needed to preserve the respective rights of either of the parties (Article 47).

The Arbitration Award

The Award is dealt with in Articles 48 to 55. Article 48 deals with the basic requirements of an award made under the ICSID Convention:

i) the Tribunal may decide questions by a majority vote;
ii) the award is to be in writing and is to be signed by the members of the Tribunal who voted for it;
iii) the award is to deal with every question submitted to the Tribunal and is to give the reasons on which the award is based;
iv) any member of the Tribunal is entitled to attach his/her individual opinion to the award, whether or not he or she dissents from the majority – similarly, any member of the Tribunal may attach a statement of dissent;
v) the Centre is not to publish the award without the consent of the parties.

Article 49 provides that the Secretary-General is to dispatch certified copies of the award to the parties. The award is deemed to have been rendered on the date on which the certified copies were dispatched. That Article also contains provisions enabling the Tribunal to decide any question that it had omitted to decide in the award, and to rectify any clerical, arithmetical or similar errors.

Articles 50 and 51 deal with interpretation and revision of the award. The parties may apply to the Secretary-General requesting an interpretation of the award in the event of a dispute as to the meaning or scope of the award. If possible, the request is to be submitted to the Tribunal that rendered the award. If for any reason that is not possible, a new Tribunal is to be constituted. The Tribunal may stay enforcement of the award pending its decision on interpretation.

An application requesting a revision of the award is to be made in writing to the Secretary-General. Such an application may be made on the ground of discovery of some fact *"of such a nature as decisively to affect the award, provided that when the award was rendered that fact was unknown to the Tribunal and to the applicant, and that the applicant's ignorance of that fact was not due to negligence"*. The application is to be made within 90 days of discovery of the fact in question, and in any event within three years of the date on which the award was rendered. If possible, the request for revision is to be submitted to the Tribunal that rendered the award, failing which a new Tribunal is to be constituted. If the Tribunal considers it necessary, enforcement of the award may be stayed pending decision.

Annulment of the arbitration award

Article 52 contains important and significant provisions relating to the annulment of an ICSID award.

Either party may request an annulment of the award. Such application is to be made in writing to the Secretary-General on one or more of the following grounds set out in Article 52 (1):

(a) that the Tribunal was not properly constituted;

(b) that the Tribunal has manifestly exceeded its powers;

(c) that there was corruption on the part of a member of the Tribunal;

(d) that there has been a serious departure from a fundamental rule of procedure;

(e) that the award has failed to state the reasons on which it is based.

The annulment application is to be made within 120 days after the date on which the award was rendered, except in circumstances where the annulment is requested on the ground of corruption. In that case the application is to be made within 120 days after discovery of the corruption, and in any event within three years after the date on which the award was rendered.

An ad hoc Committee of three persons is to be appointed from the Panel of Arbitrators. No member of the Committee is to have been a member of the Tribunal that rendered the award. The Committee is to have authority to annul the award or any part of that award on any of the grounds set out in Article 52 (1). The Committee may stay enforcement of the award pending its decision. If the Committee annuls the award, either party may request that the dispute be submitted to a new Tribunal (Article 52 (6)).

Recognition and enforcement of ICSID arbitration awards

Articles 53 to 55 deal with the recognition and enforcement of the award. It is of considerable importance to note that an ICSID award is self-enforcing. Unlike an award made by an international commercial arbitration tribunal in a pure commercial dispute – whose enforcement relies on the provisions of the New York Convention – an ICSID award is enforceable pursuant to the provisions contained within the ICSID Convention itself.

Article 53 provides that the award is binding on the parties and is not to be subject to any appeal or to any other remedy save as provided for in the Convention.

Article 54 (1) states that each Contracting State is to recognise an award rendered pursuant to the Convention *"as binding and enforce the pecuniary obligations imposed by that award within its territories as if it were a final judgement of a court in that State. A Contracting State with a federal constitution may enforce such an award in or through its federal courts and may provide that such courts shall treat the award as if it were a final judgement of the courts of a constituent state."*

A party seeking recognition or enforcement of the award is to furnish to a competent court (or other authority designated for the purpose) a copy of the award certified by the Secretary-General. Execution of the award is governed by the laws concerning execution of judgements in force in the State in whose territories the execution is sought (Article 54 (3)). Article 55 states that nothing in Article 54 is to be construed as derogating from the law in force in any Contracting State relating to immunity of that State (or of any foreign State) from execution.

Other chapters of the Convention

Chapter V contains provisions in Articles 56, 57 and 58 relating to the replacement and disqualification of conciliators and arbitrators, Chapter VI deals with the cost of proceedings and Chapter VII deals with the place of proceedings.

Chapter VIII in Article 64 deals with disputes between Contracting States concerning the interpretation or application of the Convention. If such a dispute is not settled by negotiation, it is to be referred to the ICJ on the application of any party to the dispute, unless the States concerned have agreed on another method of settlement. Chapters IX and X contain provisions on amendment and the final provisions.

4) Some Problems Arising in Investor-State Disputes

There are a number of problems that have arisen in investor-State disputes that, taken together, are peculiar to such disputes. First, there are jurisdiction issues. Second, there is the problem of different decisions being reached by different international tribunals on similar facts / similar issues.

i) Jurisdiction issues

There are a group of issues that can be broadly classified as issues relating to the jurisdiction of a Tribunal appointed under the provisions of a BIT:

- 'umbrella' / *pacta sunt servanda* clauses;
- causes of action;
- forum selection clauses;
- 'fork in the road' provisions.

Specifically, does such a Tribunal have jurisdiction to deal only with claims under the treaty ('treaty claims', to which international law will apply), or may that Tribunal also deal with claims under an investment contract ('contract claims', to which the local law of the relevant State will apply)?

'Umbrella' / pacta sunt servanda clauses

There are circumstances in which a Tribunal may have jurisdiction to deal also with contractual claims. One example is where the treaty contains a so-called 'umbrella' clause – also referred to as a *pacta sunt servanda* clause or a 'sanctity of contract' clause.

Professor Christoph Schreuer describes an umbrella clause as *"a provision in a treaty for the protection of investments under which the State parties undertake to observe any obligations they may have entered into with respect to investments. In other words, contractual obligations are put under the treaty's protective umbrella. It is widely accepted that under the regime of an umbrella clause violations of the contract become treaty violations."*

Later he says that the object and purpose of an umbrella clause is to *"add extra protection to the investor. It dispenses with the often difficult proof that there has been an indirect expropriation or a violation of the fair and equitable standard under the treaty."* [40]

The consequence of an umbrella / *pacta sunt servanda* clause in a BIT may therefore be to convert a breach of an investment contract into a treaty breach. Take, for example, the umbrella clause in Article X (2) of the BIT in the *SGS v Philippines* case (discussed below):

> *"Each Contracting Party shall observe any obligation it has assumed with regard to specific investments in its territory by investors of the other Contracting Party."*

And compare that provision with the umbrella clause in the *SGS v Pakistan* case (again mentioned below). Clause 11 of the Swiss-Pakistan BIT provided that: *"Either Contracting Party shall constantly guarantee the observance of the commitments it has entered into with respect to the investments of the investors of the other Contracting Party."*

It will be recalled that Article 26 of the Vienna Convention on the Law of Treaties (referred to in Chapter 6 of the Manual) provides that *"Every treaty in force is binding upon the parties to it and must be performed by them in good faith"*.

Antonio Parra of ICSID was quoted earlier as saying that much of the inspiration for the first BITs made in the period 1959-1969 – and for later treaties – came from the 1959 Abs-Shawcross Draft Convention on Investments Abroad (and the 1967 OECD Draft Convention on the Protection of Foreign Property). Sir Hartley Shawcross had been a British Attorney-General and Dr Herman Abs was the Chairman of Deutsche Bank. Article II of their Draft Convention provided that: *"Each Party shall at all times ensure the observance of any undertakings which it may have given in relation to investments made by nationals of any other Party."*

Whether an umbrella clause in an investment treaty achieves its objective of elevating a breach of an investment agreement into an international breach may be open to argument. The *SGS* cases discussed later were concerned with that problem. A more recent decision than the *SGS* cases is the Partial Award in *Eureko B.V. v Poland* of 19 August 2005 at paras. 244-260.[41]

Causes of action and forum selection clauses

The issue of jurisdiction is also concerned with causes of action: does the claim or cause of action arise under the treaty or under the investment contract?

The jurisdiction question may also involve consideration of a forum selection clause in a contract that confers exclusive jurisdiction on the courts of a specific State. For example, the forum selection clause in the *SGS v Philippines* case provided in Article 12 of the Comprehensive Import Supervision Scheme (CISS) Agreement that contractual disputes be submitted to specific courts in the Philippines and be decided in accordance with that country's laws.

---

40 'Overlapping Contract & Treaty Claims - the Vivendi I Case' in Todd Weiler (ed.), *International Investment Law and Arbitration: Leading Cases from the ICSID, NAFTA, Bilateral Treaties and Customary International Law,* Cameron May, 2005, pp 299 and 301.

41 http://ita.law.uvic.ca/documents/Eureko-PartialAwardandDissentingOpinion.pdf.

'Fork in the road' provisions

Jurisdiction issues may also arise in relation to 'fork in the road ' provisions. These are provisions in BITs that give the investor the choice of commencing a claim in the domestic courts of the host State or of bringing a claim before an international tribunal.

An example of a 'fork in the road' clause is contained in the BIT in the *SGS v Philippines* case. That provision states that, if a dispute is not resolved by consultations between the parties pursuant to Article VIII (1) of the treaty, the investor may submit the dispute *"either to the national jurisdiction of the Contracting Party in whose territory the investment has been made or to international arbitration"*, and in the latter case, at the investor's option, to ICSID or UNCITRAL arbitration.

ii) Different decisions by different tribunals

Similar facts and similar issues in investor-State disputes have given rise to different decisions by different tribunals. This raises the question of the extent to which the problems created by such conflicting decisions could be dealt with by way of consolidation or similar measures – such as similar fact disputes being dealt with by the same tribunal.

In addition, to what extent could the problem of different / conflicting decisions being reached by different tribunals faced with similar facts / similar issues be resolved by an appellate system being introduced into investor-State arbitrations? The ICSID system has its annulment provisions, but is something more than that needed?

5) An Example: *SGS v Philippines*

These problems, in particular the 'umbrella' clause and 'fork in the road' difficulties, are illustrated by the decisions in two ICSID cases that involved the same Claimant: Société Générale de Surveillance S.A. The cases – *SGS v Pakistan* and *SGS v Philippines* – may both be found on the ICSID website.[42]

The extent of the problem can be seen by considering the later decision, namely that of the ICSID Tribunal in the *SGS v Philippines* case.

Background

The background to the case is set out in paragraphs 1-4 of the Tribunal's Decision. The first paragraph states that:

> "1. *On 26 April 2002, the International Centre for Settlement of Investment Disputes (ICSID) received from Société Générale de Surveillance S.A. (SGS) a request for arbitration dated 24 April 2002 against the Republic of the Philippines (hereafter the Philippines or the Respondent, as the context requires). SGS is a large Swiss corporation providing verification, testing, monitoring and certification services in respect of various products, to the private sector as well as to governments and international institutions. On 23 August 1991, SGS concluded an agreement with the Philippines regarding the provision of comprehensive import supervision*

42 www.worldbank.org/icsid.

services (the CISS Agreement), under which SGS would provide specialized services to assist in improving the customs clearance and control processes of the Philippines. A dispute having arisen between the parties concerning alleged breaches of the CISS Agreement, SGS invoked in the request for arbitration the provisions of a bilateral Agreement of 1997 between the Swiss Confederation and the Republic of the Philippines on the Promotion and Reciprocal Protection of Investments (the BIT).

Paragraphs 2-4 deal with the registering of the request for arbitration on 6 June 2002 by the ISCID Secretary-General and the agreement on 24 June 2002 that the Tribunal should consist of three arbitrators, one appointed by the Claimant and the second by the Respondent. The President of the Tribunal would be appointed by agreement between the two parties or, failing agreement within 30 days of the appointment of the second arbitrator, by the ISCID Secretary-General.

The contract

The relevant provisions of the contract – the CISS Agreement – are set out in paragraphs 19-25 of the Decision:

"19. ... SGS accepted to carry out, on an exclusive basis, pre-shipment inspection in any country of export to the Philippines. Inspections would cover quality, quantity and price comparisons. Article 5 required SGS to maintain a liaison office in the Philippines. Under Article 16, SGS also agreed to provide the Philippines with the assistance set out in Schedule II. This assistance was to be provided free of cost; on the other hand it was stated to be a 'special condition' which 'shall govern the other services to be conducted by SGS'. The assistance to be provided included:

- *training courses to be conducted by SGS for various Philippines agencies, in particular the BOC [Bureau of Customs];*
- *the provision to the BOC of customs equipment and the maintenance of that equipment;*
- *the provision of customs consultants to carry out feasibility studies and evaluation of the BOC's computerisation needs;*
- *the provision of a customs specialist to investigate the practicability of an 'open' bonded warehouse system for the BOC;*
- *the provision of a customs intelligence / investigative consultant for a stipulated period to conduct an in-depth review of the coordination between various Philippines intelligence units, the provision of computer hardware and software to support the coordination process, and thereafter to provide technical support; and*
- *setting up a BOC library, stocked with the most comprehensive trade publications from the twenty leading exporting countries to the Philippines, as well as other price data and basic customs texts on administration and procedure.*

"20. In exchange for the performance of SGS's obligations, according to Article 6 and Schedule I, the Philippines agreed to pay SGS, in Swiss francs, a fee amounting

to 0.6% of the FOB [Free on Board] value declared on the exporter's final settlement invoice covering each shipment inspected. A minimum of USD225 (convertible into Swiss francs at the prevailing exchange rate) per shipment or part shipment would be applicable where the rate of 0.6% would produce a smaller amount. For inspections of shipments invoiced at less than USD2,500 the minimum fee was USD150.

"21. *Under Articles 7 and 10.1.4, the Philippines had to maintain a letter of credit in the amount of CHF7,500,000 against which SGS could present for payment invoices for fees due under the CISS Agreement.*

"22. *Article 12 of the CISS Agreement provided that:*

'The provisions of this Agreement shall be governed in all respects by and construed in accordance with the laws of the Philippines. All actions concerning disputes in connection with the obligations of either party to this Agreement shall be filed at the Regional Trial Courts of Makati or Manila.'

Thus contractual disputes were required to be submitted to specified courts in the Philippines to be decided in accordance with Philippines law.

"23. *Under the terms of the First Addendum, executed on 14 December 1994, in consideration of the extension of the CISS Agreement for a period of three years from 15 March 1995, SGS agreed to carry out the 'Exit Program' as set out in Schedule A of the Addendum. The Exit Program consisted of a number of 'projects' to be undertaken jointly by the BOC and SGS in addition to the regular pre-shipment inspection programme. The objectives of these projects were stated to be:*

(i) to set in place on or before 16 March 1998 or at the end of the CISS Agreement between the Philippines and SGS the various systems that would enable the Philippines to value imported goods, identify high risk shipments that would be subjected to careful verification, conduct examinations on such shipments following the same procedure and level of scrutiny as SGS, and maintain a data bank of various files / control tables needed for the proper determination of dutiable values;

(ii) to identify leakages in customs revenue generation and set in place systems to plug such leaks, manage and monitor their occurrence; and

(iii) to extend to BOC information on the latest available hardware, systems and technology utilized by other customs and port administrations in facilitating trade and preventing smuggling and other frauds on customs.

"24. *The Second Addendum to the CISS Agreement, executed on 29 January 1998, extended the duration of the CISS Agreement to the end of 1999; it also made certain changes to the terms of the CISS Agreement intended to enhance the efficiency of pre-shipment inspection operations and to provide relevant electronic infrastructure.*

"25. *The provisions of Article 12 of the CISS Agreement concerning governing law and the settlement of disputes continued to apply to the Agreement as amended by the First and Second Addenda, as well as to the further extension of the Agreement to 31 March 2000."*

The BIT and the ICSID Convention

The relevant provisions of the BIT – the 1997 Swiss-Philippines Bilateral Agreement – are set out in paragraphs 26-34 of the Decision. The Tribunal also referred to provisions of the ICSID Convention:

"26. *The Tribunal's jurisdiction, if it exists, must arise by virtue of the ICSID Convention associated with the BIT. It was not disputed by the parties that at the jurisdictional stage the Tribunal may deal with all issues of law that are necessary in order to determine its jurisdiction. It is not enough that the Claimant raises an issue under one or more provisions of the BIT which the Respondent disputes. To adapt the words of the International Court in the Oil Platforms case, the Tribunal 'must ascertain whether the violations of the [BIT] pleaded by [SGS] do or do not fall within the provisions of the Treaty and whether, as a consequence, the dispute is one which the [Tribunal] has jurisdiction ratione materiae*[43] *to entertain' pursuant to Article VIII (2) of the BIT.*

"27. *With regard to the ICSID Convention, the relevant provisions are Article 25(1) and 26.*

"28. *Article 25(1) sets out the criteria to be met in order for ICSID to have jurisdiction over a dispute. It provides that:*

'The jurisdiction of the Centre shall extend to any legal dispute arising directly out of an investment, between a Contracting State (or any constituent subdivision or agency of a Contracting State designated to the Centre by that State) and a national of another Contracting State, which the parties to the dispute consent in writing to submit to the Centre. When the parties have given their consent, no party may withdraw its consent unilaterally.'

This has to be read in conjunction with Article 42(1) of the Convention, which provides that:

'The Tribunal shall decide a dispute in accordance with such rules of law as may be agreed by the parties. In the absence of such agreement, the Tribunal shall apply the law of the Contracting State party to the dispute (including its rules on the conflict of laws) and such rules of international law as may be applicable.'

"29. *It is clear from the general language of Article 25(1) that ICSID jurisdiction may extend to disputes which are purely contractual in character. For example a dispute arising out of an investment contract between a State or constituent subdivision or agency could be covered, and this could be the case even though the dispute exclusively concerns issues arising under the proper law of the contract. There is no distinction drawn in Article 25, or in Article 42(1), between purely contractual and other disputes (e.g. claims for breach of treaty).*

"30. *In accordance with Article 25, ICSID jurisdiction is based on the written consent of the parties to the dispute. This raises the question of the relation between consent given for the purposes of the ICSID Convention and any dispute resolution provisions specifically included in investment contracts. In this regard, Article 26 of the ICSID Convention provides that:*

---

43 Subject matter jurisdiction.

'Consent of the Parties to arbitration under this Convention shall, unless otherwise stated, be deemed consent to such arbitration to the exclusion of any other remedy.'

"31. *In the present case, the Claimant relies upon the consent to ICSID arbitration given by the Philippines in the BIT, combined with its own written consent contained in the Request for Arbitration. It is well established that the combination of these forms of consent can constitute 'consent in writing' within the meaning of Article 25(1), provided that the dispute falls within the scope of the BIT.*

"32. *Article II of the BIT provides that:*

'The present Agreement shall apply to investments in the territory of one Contracting Party made in accordance with its laws and regulations by investors of the other Contracting Party, whether prior to or after the entry into force of the Agreement.'

"33. *It is not disputed that SGS is potentially an investor of the other Contracting Party under the BIT: no issue of SGS's nationality or effective control is raised. Furthermore it is not denied by the Respondent that the services provided by SGS, itself or through its wholly owned Swiss affiliates, and the resulting rights to payment are capable of constituting an investment. Under Article I (2) of the BIT, the term 'investments' is defined to include 'every kind of asset' including '(c) claims to money or to any performance having an economic value'. But the Respondent denies that SGS made any investment in the territory of the Philippines, on the basis that all or substantially all the services for which SGS now claims payment were performed abroad, and were indeed stipulated to have been so performed in the CISS Agreement.*

"34. *As to the basis of claim and Respondent's consent to jurisdiction, SGS relies on the following provisions of the BIT:*

"ARTICLE IV: PROTECTION, TREATMENT

1. *Investments and returns of investors of each Contracting Party shall at all times be accorded fair and equitable treatment and shall enjoy full protection and security in the territory of the other Contracting Party. Neither Contracting Party shall in any way impair by unreasonable or discriminatory measures the management, maintenance, use, enjoyment, extension or disposal of such investments.*

2. *Each Contracting Party shall in its territory accord investments or returns of investors of the other Contracting Party treatment not less favourable than that which it accords to investments or returns of its own investors or to investments or returns of investors of any third State, whichever is more favourable to the investor concerned.*

"ARTICLE VI: DISPOSSESSION, COMPENSATION

Neither of the Contracting Parties shall take, either directly or indirectly, measures of expropriation, nationalization, or any other measures having the same nature or the same effect against investments of investors of the other Contracting Party, unless the measures are taken in the public interest, on a non-discriminatory basis, and under due process of law, and provided that provisions be made for effective and adequate compensation. Such compensation shall amount to the market value of the investment expropriated immediately before the expropriatory action was taken or became public knowledge, whichever is earlier. The amount of compensation shall include interest, from the date of dispossession until payment, shall be settled in a freely convertible currency and paid without delay to the person entitled thereto without regard to its residence or domicile.

"ARTICLE VIII: SETTLEMENT OF DISPUTES BETWEEN A CONTRACTING PARTY AND AN INVESTOR OF THE OTHER CONTRACTING PARTY

1. *For the purpose of solving disputes with respect to investments between a Contracting Party and an investor of the other Contracting Party and without prejudice to Article IX of this Agreement (Disputes between Contracting Parties), consultations will take place between the parties concerned.*

2. *If these consultations do not result in a solution within six months from the date of request for consultations, the investor may submit the dispute either to the national jurisdiction of the Contracting Party in whose territory the investment has been made or to international arbitration. In the latter event the investor has the choice between*

   (a) the International Center for the Settlement of Investment Disputes (I.C.S.I.D.) instituted by the Convention on the settlement of investment disputes between states and nationals of other States, opened for signature at Washington, on 18 March 1965;

   (b) an ad hoc arbitral tribunal which unless otherwise agreed upon by the parties to the dispute shall be established under the arbitration rules of the United Nations Commission on International Trade Law....

"ARTICLE X: OTHER COMMITMENTS

1. *If the provisions in the legislation of either Contracting Party or rules of international law entitle investments by investors of the other Contracting Party to treatment more favourable than is provided for by this Agreement, such provisions shall to the extent that they are more favourable prevail over this Agreement.*

2. *Each Contracting Party shall observe any obligation it has assumed with regard to specific investments in its territory by investors of the other Contracting Party.'"*

The umbrella clause

We move now to the first of the problems concerning investor-State disputes that were raised earlier: the 'umbrella' clause. The Tribunal dealt in paragraphs 113-129 of their Decision with the problems concerning the umbrella clause – Article X (2) of the BIT, quoted above:

"113. On the footing that it had made an investment in the territory of the Philippines, the principal jurisdictional submission of SGS is that, having failed to pay for services due under the CISS Agreement, the Philippines is in breach of Article X (2) of the BIT, and that the Tribunal's jurisdiction is attracted by Article VIII (2) in respect of such breaches. The Philippines for its part denies that Article X (2) has such an effect, relying inter alia on the decision of the SGS v Pakistan Tribunal on the equivalent BIT provision in that case.

"114. One must begin with the actual text of Article X. It is headed 'Other Commitments'. Article X (1) is a kind of 'without prejudice' clause, providing that legislative provisions or international law rules more favourable to an investor shall to that extent 'prevail over this Agreement'. It deals with the relation between commitments under the BIT and distinct commitments under host State law or under other rules of international law. It does not appear to impose any additional obligation on the host State in the framework of the BIT.

"115. Article X (2) is different. It reads:

> *'Each Contracting Party shall observe any obligation it has assumed with regard to specific investments in its territory by investors of the other Contracting Party.'*

This is not expressed as a without prejudice clause, unlike Article X (1). It uses the mandatory term 'shall', in the same way as substantive Articles III-VI. The term 'any obligation' is capable of applying to obligations arising under national law, e.g. those arising from a contract; indeed, it would normally be under its own law that a host State would assume obligations 'with regard to specific investments in its territory by investors of the other Contracting Party'. Interpreting the actual text of Article X (2), it would appear to say, and to say clearly, that each Contracting Party shall observe any legal obligation it has assumed, or will in the future assume, with regard to specific investments covered by the BIT. Article X (2) was adopted within the framework of the BIT, and has to be construed as intended to be effective within that framework.

"116. The object and purpose of the BIT supports an effective interpretation of Article X (2). The BIT is a treaty for the promotion and reciprocal protection of investments. According to the preamble it is intended 'to create and maintain favourable conditions for investments by investors of one Contracting Party in the territory of the other'. It is legitimate to resolve uncertainties in its interpretation so as to favour the protection of covered investments.

"117. Moreover it will often be the case that a host State assumes obligations with regard to specific investments at the time of entry, including investments entered into on the basis of contracts with separate entities. Whether collateral guarantees, warranties or letters of comfort given by a host State to induce the entry of foreign investments are binding or not, i.e. whether they constitute genuine obligations or mere advertisements, will be a matter for determination under the applicable law, normally the law of the host State. But if commitments made by the State towards specific investments do involve binding obligations or commitments under the applicable law, it seems entirely consistent with the object and purpose of the BIT to hold that they are incorporated and brought within the framework of the BIT by Article X (2).

"118. The Respondent argued that, if Article X (2) does have substantive effect, it should be interpreted as being limited to obligations under other international law instruments. But such a limitation could readily have been expressed. The argument accepted that Article X (2) may have operative effect, but read into that provision words of limitation which are simply not there.

"119. This provisional conclusion – that Article X (2) means what is says – is however contradicted by the decision of the Tribunal in SGS v Pakistan, the only ICSID case which has so far directly ruled on the question. It should be noted that the 'umbrella clause' in the Swiss-Pakistan BIT was formulated in different and rather vaguer terms than Article X (2) of the Swiss-Philippines BIT. Article 11 of the Swiss-Pakistan BIT provides that:

> *'Either Contracting Party shall constantly guarantee the observance of the commitments it has entered into with respect to the investments of the investors of the other Contracting Party.'*

Apart from the phrase 'shall constantly guarantee' (what could an inconstant guarantee amount to?), the phrase 'the commitments it has entered into with respect to the investments' is likewise less clear and categorical than the phrase 'any obligation it has assumed with regard to specific investments in its territory' in Article X (2) of the Swiss-Philippines BIT.

"120. Nonetheless it is relevant to consider the reasons given by the Tribunal in SGS v Pakistan for giving a highly restrictive interpretation to the 'umbrella clause', in the context of the more specific language of Article X (2), the provision the present Tribunal has to apply. Essentially there were four such reasons.

"121. The first reason was textual. As the Tribunal noted, Article 11 could cover a wide range of commitments including legislative commitments; it went on to say that the interpretation favoured by SGS was 'susceptible of almost indefinite expansion'. It is true that Article X (2) of the Swiss-Philippines BIT likewise is not limited to contractual obligations. But it is limited to 'obligations… assumed with regard to specific investments'. For Article X (2) to be applicable, the host State must have assumed a legal obligation, and it must have been assumed vis-à-vis the specific investment – not as a matter of the application of some legal obligation of a general character. This is very far from elevating to the international level all 'the municipal legislative or administrative or other unilateral measures of a Contracting Party'.

"122. Secondly, the Tribunal applied general principles of international law to generate a presumption against the broad interpretation of Article 11. The principle relied on was that 'a violation of a contract entered into by a State with an investor of another State, is not, by itself, a violation of international law'. This principle is well established. It was affirmed by the ad hoc Committee in the Vivendi case, cited by the Tribunal. But the Franco-Argentine BIT considered in the Vivendi case did not contain any equivalent to Article 11 of the Swiss-Pakistan BIT, and the ad hoc Committee therefore did not need to consider whether a clause in a treaty requiring a State to observe specific domestic commitments has effect in international law. Certainly it might do so, as the International Law Commission observed in its commentary to Article 3 of the ILC Articles on Responsibility of

States for Internationally Wrongful Acts. The question is essentially one of interpretation, and does not seem to be determined by any presumption.

"123. Thirdly, the Tribunal was concerned that the effect of a broad interpretation would be, inter alia, to override dispute settlement clauses negotiated in particular contracts. The present Tribunal agrees with this concern, but – as will be seen – it does not accept that this follows from the broad interpretation of Article X (2).

"124. Fourthly and subsidiarily, the Tribunal in SGS v Pakistan found support for its conclusion in the fact that Article 11 is located at the end of the BIT, after the basic jurisdictional clauses, whereas if it had been intended to impose substantive international obligations it would more naturally have appeared earlier. This factor is entitled to some weight, and it is the case that where it appears (as it does in only a minority of BITs) the 'umbrella' clause is usually located earlier in the text. But the Tribunal does not regard the location of the provision as decisive, having regard to the other considerations recited above. In particular, it is difficult to accept that the same language in other Philippines BITs is legally operative, but that it is legally inoperative in the Swiss-Philippines BIT merely because of its location.

"125. Not only are the reasons given by the Tribunal in SGS v Pakistan unconvincing: the Tribunal failed to give any clear meaning to the 'umbrella clause'. It treated Article 11 as signalling…

> *'an implied affirmative commitment to enact implementing rules and regulations necessary or appropriate to give effect to a contractual or statutory undertaking in favor of investors of another Contracting Party that would otherwise be a dead letter. Secondly, we do not preclude the possibility that under exceptional circumstances, a violation of certain provisions of a State contract with an investor of another State might constitute violation of a treaty provision… enjoining a Contracting Party constantly to guarantee the observance of contracts with investors of another Contracting Party.'*

But Article 11, if it has any effect at all, confers jurisdiction on an international tribunal, and needs to do so with adequate certainty. Jurisdiction is not conferred by way of 'an implied affirmative commitment' or through the characterisation of circumstances as 'exceptional'.

"126. Moreover the SGS v Pakistan Tribunal appears to have thought that the broad interpretation which it rejected would involve a full-scale internationalisation of domestic contracts – in effect, that it would convert investment contracts into treaties by way of what the Tribunal termed 'instant transubstantiation'. But this is not what Article X (2) of the Swiss-Philippines Treaty says. It does not convert non-binding domestic blandishments into binding international obligations. It does not convert questions of contract law into questions of treaty law. In particular it does not change the proper law of the CISS Agreement from the law of the Philippines to international law. Article X (2) addresses not the scope of the commitments entered into with regard to specific investments but the performance of these obligations, once they are ascertained. It is a conceivable function of a provision such as Article X (2) of the Swiss-Philippines BIT to

provide assurances to foreign investors with regard to the performance of obligations assumed by the host State under its own law with regard to specific investments – in effect, to help secure the rule of law in relation to investment protection. In the Tribunal's view, this is the proper interpretation of Article X (2).

"127. To summarize, for present purposes Article X (2) includes commitments or obligations arising under contracts entered into by the host State. The basic obligation on the State in this case is the obligation to pay what is due under the contract, which is an obligation assumed with regard to the specific investment (the performance of services under the CISS Agreement). But this obligation does not mean that the determination of how much money the Philippines is obliged to pay becomes a treaty matter. The extent of the obligation is still governed by the contract, and it can only be determined by reference to the terms of the contract.

"128. To summarize the Tribunal's conclusions on this point, Article X (2) makes it a breach of the BIT for the host State to fail to observe binding commitments, including contractual commitments, which it has assumed with regard to specific investments. But it does not convert the issue of the extent or content of such obligations into an issue of international law. That issue (in the present case, the issue of how much is payable for services provided under the CISS Agreement) is still governed by the investment agreement. In the absence of other factors it could be decided by a tribunal constituted pursuant to Article VIII (2). The proper law of the CISS Agreement is the law of the Philippines, which in any event this Tribunal is directed to apply by Article 42(1) of the ICSID Convention. On the other hand, if some other court or tribunal has exclusive jurisdiction over the Agreement, the position may be different.

"129. Before turning to that question, however, it is appropriate to ask whether the present Tribunal could exercise jurisdiction over contractual disputes concerning an investment by virtue of Article VIII (2) of the BIT, irrespective of any breach of the substantive provisions of the BIT. This issue was debated before the Tribunal and is potentially relevant, for example, in the context of the application of the BIT to claims arising before its entry into force."

'Fork in the road'

In paragraphs 130-135 the Tribunal then went on to deal with another problem highlighted in this chapter, namely 'fork in the road' provisions. The relevant provisions of the BIT are set out in Article VIII (2). The Tribunal stated:

"130. Article VIII of the BIT provides for settlement of 'disputes with respect to investments between a Contracting Party and an investor of the other Contracting Party'. If a dispute is not resolved by consultations between the parties pursuant to Article VIII (1), the investor may submit the dispute 'either to the national jurisdiction of the Contracting Party in whose territory the investment has been made or to international arbitration', and in the latter case, at the investor's option, to ICSID or UNCITRAL arbitration.

"131. Prima facie, Article VIII is an entirely general provision, allowing for submission of all investment disputes by the investor against the host State. The term 'disputes with respect to investments' ('différents relatifs à des divertissements'

in the French text) is not limited by reference to the legal classification of the claim that is made. A dispute about an alleged expropriation contrary to Article VI of the BIT would be a 'dispute with respect to investments' so too would a dispute arising from an investment contract such as the CISS Agreement.

"132. This prima facie conclusion is supported by a number of further considerations, both within the BIT itself and extrinsic to it:

(a) Each of the forums contemplated by Article VIII (2) (the national courts of the host State, ICSID panels and ad hoc tribunals established under the UNCITRAL Rules) has the competence to apply the law of the host State, including its law of contract. Indeed, if the BIT has not been implemented internally, the national courts may only be competent to apply their own law.

(b) The general term 'disputes with respect to investments' may be contrasted with the more specific term '[d]isputes... regarding the interpretation or application of the provisions of this Agreement' in Article IX. If the States Parties to the BIT had wanted to limit investor-State arbitration to claims concerning breaches of the substantive standards contained in the BIT, they would have said so expressly, using this or similar language.

(c) As noted already, the purpose of the BIT is to promote and protect foreign investments. Allowing investors a choice of forum for resolution of investment disputes of whatever character is consistent with this aim. By contrast drawing technical distinctions between causes of action arising under the BIT and those arising under the investment agreement is capable of giving rise to overlapping proceedings and jurisdictional uncertainty. It may be necessary to draw such distinctions in some cases, but it should be avoided to the extent possible, in the interests of the efficient resolution of investment disputes by the single chosen forum.

(d) By definition, investments are characteristically entered into by means of contracts or other agreements with the host State and the local investment partner (or if these are different entities, with both of them). The specific link between investments and contracts is acknowledged by the line of cases dealing with pre-contractual claims. ICSID tribunals have been very reluctant to acknowledge that an investment has actually been made until the contract has been signed or at least approved and acted on. Thus the phrase 'disputes with respect to investments' naturally includes contractual disputes; the same is true of the phrase 'legal dispute arising directly out of an investment' in Article 25(1) of the ICSID Convention.

(e) In other investment protection agreements, when investor-State arbitration is intended to be limited to claims brought for breach of international standards (as distinct from contractual or other claims under national law), this is stated expressly. A well-known example is Chapter 11 of the North American Free Trade Agreement (NAFTA), under which investors may only bring claims for breaches of specified provisions of Chapter 11 itself.

"133. However, a different view of the matter was apparently taken by the ICSID Tribunal in SGS v Pakistan, and it is necessary to consider the reasons given for their conclusion. The equivalent provision of the BIT in that case, Article 9, used the phrase 'disputes with respect to investments': this is the same as

Article VIII of the Swiss-Philippines BIT. The relevant passage of the decision reads as follows:

'161. We recognize that disputes arising from claims grounded on alleged violation of the BIT, and disputes arising from claims based wholly on supposed violations of the PSI [pre-shipment inspection] Agreement, can both be described as "disputes with respect to investments," the phrase used in Article 9 of the BIT. That phrase, however, while descriptive of the factual subject matter of the disputes, does not relate to the legal basis of the claims, or the cause of action asserted in the claims. In other words, from that description alone, without more, we believe that no implication necessarily arises that both BIT and purely contract claims are intended to be covered by the Contracting Parties in Article 9. Neither, accordingly, does an implication arise that the Article 9 dispute settlement mechanism would supersede and set at naught all otherwise valid non-ICSID forum selection clauses in all earlier agreements between Swiss investors and the Respondent. Thus, we do not see anything in Article 9 or in any other provision of the BIT that can be read as vesting this Tribunal with jurisdiction over claims resting ex hypothesi exclusively on contract. Both Claimant and Respondent have already submitted their respective claims sounding solely on the PSI Agreement to the PSI Agreement arbitrator. We recognize that the Claimant did so in a qualified manner and questioned the jurisdiction of the PSI Agreement arbitrator, albeit on grounds which do not appear to relate to the issue we here address. We believe that Article 11.1 of the PSI Agreement is a valid forum selection clause so far as concerns the Claimant's contract claims which do not also amount to BIT claims, and it is a clause that this Tribunal should respect. We are not suggesting that the parties cannot, by special agreement, lodge in this Tribunal jurisdiction to pass upon and decide claims sounding solely in the contract. Obviously the parties can. But we do not believe that they have done so in this case. And should the parties opt to do that, our jurisdiction over such contract claims will rest on the special agreement, not on the BIT.

'162. We conclude that the Tribunal has no jurisdiction with respect to claims submitted by SGS and based on alleged breaches of the PSI Agreement which do not also constitute or amount to breaches of the substantive standards of the BIT.'

"134. The present Tribunal agrees with the concern that the general provisions of BITs should not, unless clearly expressed to do so, override specific and exclusive dispute settlement arrangements made in the investment contract itself. On the view put forward by SGS it will have become impossible for investors validly to agree to an exclusive jurisdiction clause in their contracts; they will always have the hidden capacity to bring contractual claims to BIT arbitration, even in breach of the contract, and it is hard to believe that this result was contemplated by States in concluding generic investment protection agreements. But there are two different questions here: the interpretation of the general phrase 'disputes with respect to investments' in BITs, and the impact on the jurisdiction of BIT tribunals over contract claims (or, more precisely, the admissibility of those claims) when there is an exclusive jurisdiction clause in the contract. It is not plausible to suggest that general language in BITs dealing with all investment

disputes should be limited because in some investment contracts the parties stipulate exclusively for different dispute settlement arrangements. As will be seen, it is possible for BIT tribunals to give effect to the parties' contracts while respecting the general language of BIT dispute settlement provisions.

"135. Interpreting the text of Article VIII in its context and in the light of its object and purpose, the Tribunal accordingly concludes that in principle (and apart from the exclusive jurisdiction clause in the CISS Agreement) it was open to SGS to refer the present dispute, as a contractual dispute, to ICSID arbitration under Article VIII (2) of the BIT." [44]

The two *SGS* cases illustrate the issues concerning 'umbrella' clauses and 'fork in the road' provisions. The apparently conflicting decisions in the two cases also raise the question whether an appellate system is now required for investor-State arbitrations.[45] A less radical solution may the use of mechanisms to ensure that similar facts / similar issues cases are dealt with in such a way that conflicting decisions are less likely to arise: the use of joinder / consolidation (the Rules of the ICJ permit joinder of two or more cases), for example, or the listing of such cases before the same tribunal.

The ICSID Convention – and the Washington Centre created by the Convention – are of considerable importance in the field of investor-State disputes. The ICSID Arbitration Rules and the ICSID Additional Facility Rules are considered in the chapter dealing with the Centre in Part III of the Manual.

6) NAFTA – Chapter 11

The North American Free Trade Agreement (NAFTA) is a trilateral agreement between Canada, Mexico and the United States that is concerned with trade generally. Much of the NAFTA deals with State-to-State dispute settlement, but Chapter 11 is concerned with investment and investor-State arbitration and its provisions are similar to those that may be found in a BIT. Dispute procedures are administered by the NAFTA Secretariat, established under Article 2002 of the Agreement.

Dealing with Chapter 11, the Secretariat says that it *"... establishes a mechanism for the settlement of investment disputes that assures both equal treatment among investors of the Parties to the Agreement in accordance with the principle of international reciprocity and due process before an impartial tribunal. A NAFTA investor who alleges that a host government has breached its investment obligations under Chapter 11 may, at its option, have recourse to one of the following arbitral mechanisms...."*

Reference is then made to ICSID and UNCITRAL. The relevant provisions are set out in Article 1120:

"1. Except as provided in Annex 1120.1, and provided that six months have elapsed since the events giving rise to a claim, a disputing investor may submit the claim to arbitration under:

44 A report of the *SGS v Philippines* case may be found on the World Bank website.

45 See Chapter 14. The ICSID Secretariat has issued a Discussion Paper that raises the possibility of the establishment of an appeal process.

(a) the ICSID Convention, provided that both the disputing Party and the Party of the investor are parties to the Convention;

(b) the Additional Facility Rules of ICSID, provided that either the disputing Party or the Party of the investor, but not both, is a party to the ICSID Convention; or

(c) the UNCITRAL Arbitration Rules.

2. The applicable arbitration rules shall govern the arbitration except to the extent modified by this Section."

7) Energy Charter Treaty – Article 26

Whereas the NAFTA is concerned with trade generally, the Energy Charter Treaty (ECT) is concerned specifically with energy. In his Foreword to a publication on the ECT in September 2004,[46] the Secretary General of the Energy Charter Secretariat, Dr Ria Kemper, said that:

"The Energy Charter Treaty is a unique instrument for the promotion of international cooperation in the energy sector. Following its entry into force on 16 April 1998, the Treaty, together with the related documents contained in this booklet, provides an important legal basis for the creation of an open international energy market.

"The Charter process includes the countries of the enlarged European Union, Central and Eastern Europe, the Russian Federation, Central Asia and the Caucasus, as well as Japan, Australia and Mongolia. The Treaty remains open for accession by all countries committed to observance of its principles. It is very positive in this regard that States such as China, Iran, South Korea and the countries of ASEAN are taking a close interest in the Charter process, thus opening up the prospect of a further extension of its geographical scope."

Dr Kemper continued:

"The primary challenge facing the constituent members of the Energy Charter process in the coming years will be that of ensuring full implementation of the Treaty's commitments. This will entail increased focus on multilateral cooperation over transit, trade, investments, environmental protection and energy efficiency. By continuing to build on its existing work in these areas, the Charter process stands ready to play a key role in translating the aim of a truly open non-discriminatory energy market into reality."

The Secretariat explains that the provisions for resolving investment disputes are contained in Articles 26 and 27 of the ECT, and are *"based on the model of bilateral investment treaties. This is of particular importance for the energy sector, since disputes may often be very complex and involve huge amounts of money."*

Article 26 (2) provides that, if a dispute cannot be resolved amicably within three months, the Investor party to the dispute may choose to submit it for resolution:

"(a) to the courts or administrative tribunals of the Contracting Party party to the dispute; or

(b) in accordance with any applicable, previously agreed dispute settlement procedure; or

46 Energy Charter Secretariat, *The Energy Charter Treaty and Related Documents: A Legal Framework for International Energy Cooperation*, Energy Charter Secretariat, Brussels, 2004.

(c) in accordance with the following paragraphs of this Article."

In the event that an Investor chooses to submit the dispute for resolution under subparagraph (2)(c), Article 26 (4) provides that:

> *"... the Investor shall further provide its consent in writing for the dispute to be submitted to:*
>
> *(a) (i) The International Centre for Settlement of Investment Disputes, established pursuant to the Convention on the Settlement of Investment Disputes between States and Nationals of other States opened for signature at Washington, 18 March 1965 (hereinafter referred to as the 'ICSID Convention'), if the Contracting Party of the Investor and the Contracting Party party to the dispute are both parties to the ICSID Convention; or*
>
> *(ii) The International Centre for Settlement of Investment Disputes, established pursuant to the Convention referred to in subparagraph (a)(i), under the rules governing the Additional Facility for the Administration of Proceedings by the Secretariat of the Centre (hereinafter referred to as the 'Additional Facility Rules'), if the Contracting Party of the Investor or the Contracting Party party to the dispute, but not both, is a party to the ICSID Convention;*
>
> *(b) a sole arbitrator or ad hoc arbitration tribunal established under the Arbitration Rules of the United Nations Commission on International Trade Law (hereinafter* referred to as 'UNCITRAL'); or
>
> *(c) an arbitral proceeding under the Arbitration Institute of the Stockholm Chamber of Commerce."*

It will be noted that, compared with ICSID and the NAFTA, an additional dispute resolution process is brought in – arbitral proceedings under the Stockholm Arbitration Institute (see Chapter 18).

In February 2005 the *Financial Times* carried a report that a claim for some $28 billion had been made by the parent group of Yukos against the Russian Government – perhaps one of the largest arbitration claims ever made. The report stated that: *"Menatep, the original investment vehicle of Mikhail Khodorkovsky, the former Yukos chief executive now defending fraud charges, has brought the action under the 1994 Energy Charter Treaty, the multilateral accord designed to enforce international law in energy investments to which Russia is a signatory."*

The report stated that the Yukos parent had notified the Russian Government in November of its demand for a settlement *"and is now exercising its right under Article 26 of the Energy Charter Treaty to refer the dispute to international arbitration. It says the treaty entitles it to compensation if Russia breaches its obligations."*[47]

Further information on the NAFTA Secretariat and the Energy Charter Secretariat can be found on their websites.[48]

---

47 Neil Buckley, 'Menatep sues over Yukos sale', *Financial Times*, 9 February 2005, www.news.ft.com.

48 www.nafta-sec-alena.org/; www.encharter.org/.

Part III: Supranational Dispute Resolution Bodies

"We may understand the materials upon which Greek philosophers were working if we look at an exhortation addressed by Demosthenes to an Athenian jury. Men ought to obey the law, he said, for four reasons: because laws were prescribed by God, because they were a tradition taught by wise men who knew the good old customs, because they were deductions from an eternal and immutable moral code, and because they were agreements of men with each other binding them because of a moral duty to keep their promises."

Roscoe Pound[49]

49 Roscoe Pound, *An Introduction to the Philosophy of Law*, Yale University Press, 1954, p 5.

10 Introduction

Part III of the Manual deals with the international dispute settlement bodies handling the types of dispute discussed in Part II, namely territorial disputes, maritime delimitation disputes and investor-State disputes.

The inter-State courts and tribunals dealing with these areas of dispute differ in two major ways from the international commercial dispute resolution bodies that will be considered in Part IV. First, they tend to have been created by international conventions or agreements; and second, they are likely to apply international law, rather than national law, in dealing with these types of dispute.

The international dispute settlement organisations considered in this part of the Manual are:

1. the International Court of Justice (ICJ);
2. the Permanent Court of Arbitration (PCA);
3. the International Tribunal for the Law of the Sea (ITLOS);
4. the International Centre for Settlement of Investment Disputes (ICSID).

The ICJ is described in Article 92 of the United Nations Charter as the *"principal judicial organ"* of the United Nations. It was created after the Second World War and superseded the Permanent Court of International Justice, created in 1920 under the Covenant of the League of Nations. The ICJ sits at the Peace Palace in The Hague.

The PCA was established as a consequence of the Hague Peace Conventions of 1899 and 1907. Like the ICJ, the PCA is located in the Peace Palace in The Hague.

ITLOS was created by the 1982 United Nations Convention on the Law of the Sea (UNCLOS III). It is based in Hamburg.

The International Convention on the Settlement of Investment Disputes (ICSID) created the ICSID Centre, located in Washington, DC.

All four supranational courts and tribunals are of major importance in the area of international disputes, where one or more of the parties is likely to be a State.

11 The International Court of Justice

1) Introduction

This chapter considers the International Court of Justice (ICJ), almost certainly the most important Court dealing with inter-State disputes. It looks first at the history of the ICJ and then at the relevant provisions of the Charter of the United Nations. The Charter of the ICJ itself is then considered, followed by the Rules and Practice Directions of the Court, all vital to an understanding of how it operates. The final sections of the chapter look at some of the cases with which the ICJ has been dealing.

2) Historical Overview

The ICJ is the principal judicial organ of the United Nations and is located at the Peace Palace in The Hague. It began its work in 1946 when it replaced the Permanent Court of International Justice, which had functioned in the Peace Palace since 1922. The ICJ operates under a Statute largely similar to that of its predecessor.

The Court has a dual role: first, to settle (in accordance with international law) the legal disputes submitted to it by States; and second, to give advisory opinions on legal questions referred to it by duly authorised international organs and agencies.

The Court is composed of 15 judges elected for nine-year terms of office by the UN General Assembly and Security Council. The Court may not include more than one judge of any nationality. Elections are held every three years for one-third of the seats, and retiring judges may be re-elected. The Members of the Court do not represent their governments but are independent.

Contentious cases

Only States may apply to – and appear before – the ICJ. The Court is competent to entertain a dispute only if the States concerned have accepted its jurisdiction in one or more of the following ways:

i) by the conclusion between them of a special agreement to submit the dispute to the Court;

ii) by virtue of a pre-existing jurisdictional clause – for example, a clause in a treaty providing that, in the event of a disagreement over its interpretation or application, one of the States may refer the dispute to the Court (several hundred treaties or conventions contain a clause to this effect);

iii) through the reciprocal effect of declarations made by States under the Statute whereby each has accepted the jurisdiction of the Court as compulsory in the event of a dispute with another State (the declarations of 64 States are at present in force).

In cases of doubt as to whether the ICJ has jurisdiction, it is the Court itself that decides.

The procedure followed by the Court in contentious cases is defined in its Statute and in the Rules of Court adopted by it under the Statute. The latest version of the Rules was agreed in 1978, particular Rules being from time to time amended.[50] The proceedings include a written phase, in which the parties file and exchange pleadings, and an oral phase consisting of public hearings at which agents and counsel address the Court. As the Court has two official languages (English and French), everything written or said in one language is translated into the other.

After the oral proceedings the Court deliberates in camera and then delivers its judgment at a public sitting. The judgment is final and without appeal. Should one of the States involved fail to comply with it, the other party may have recourse to the UN Security Council.

Since 1946 the ICJ has delivered 79 Judgments on disputes concerning, among other things: land frontiers and maritime boundaries; territorial sovereignty; the non-use of force; non-interference in the internal affairs of States; diplomatic relations; hostage-taking; the right of asylum; nationality; guardianship; rights of passage; and economic rights. There has been a problem of compliance in only about five of these.

As noted in Chapter 6, the Court decides in accordance with international treaties and conventions in force, international custom, the general principles of law and, as subsidiary means, judicial decisions and the teachings of the most highly qualified publicists.

Advisory opinions

The advisory procedure of the ICJ is open solely to international organisations. The only bodies at present authorised to request advisory opinions of the Court are five organs of the UN and 16 specialised agencies of the UN.

On receiving a request, the Court decides which States and organisations might provide useful information and gives them an opportunity of presenting written or oral statements. The Court's advisory procedure is otherwise modelled on that for contentious proceedings, and the sources of applicable law are the same. In principle the ICJ's advisory opinions are consultative in character and are therefore not binding on the requesting bodies. Certain instruments or regulations can, however, provide in advance that the advisory opinion shall be binding.

Since 1946 the Court has given 24 Advisory Opinions concerning, among other things: admission to UN membership; reparation for injuries suffered in the service of the UN; territorial status of South-West Africa (Namibia) and Western Sahara; judgments rendered by international administrative tribunals; expenses of certain UN operations; applicability of the UN Headquarters Agreement; the status of human rights rapporteurs; the legality of the threat or use of nuclear weapons; and issues relating to the Palestine Wall.

---

50 The Rules were updated in September 2005, when an amendment was made to Rule 43 in relation to notifications.

3) The Charter of the United Nations

Article 1 of the UN Charter provides that the purposes of the UN are to:

> *"maintain international peace and security, and to that end: to take effective collective measures for the prevention and removal of threats to the peace, and for the suppression of acts of aggression or other breaches of the peace, and to bring about by peaceful means, and in conformity with the principles of justice and international law, adjustment or settlement of international disputes or situations which might lead to a breach of the peace…."*

Articles 33 to 38 of the Charter deal with the pacific settlement of disputes. Article 33 states that the parties to any dispute, the continuance of which is likely to endanger the maintenance of international peace and security, shall first seek a solution by, among other means, negotiation, inquiry, mediation, conciliation, arbitration or judicial settlement. Article 36 provides that the Security Council may, at any stage of a dispute of the nature referred to in Article 33, recommend appropriate procedures. In making recommendations, the Security Council *"should also take into consideration that legal disputes should as a general rule be referred by the parties to the International Court of Justice in accordance with the provisions of the Statute of the Court"*.

Articles 92 to 96 of the Charter deal with the ICJ. Article 92 states that the Court shall be the principal judicial organ of the UN and shall *"function in accordance with the annexed Statute, which is based on the Statute of the Permanent Court of International Justice and forms an integral part of the present Charter"*. Article 94 requires each Member of the UN to comply with the decisions of the ICJ in any case to which it was a party. However, Article 95 states that nothing in the Charter is to prevent Members of the UN from entrusting the resolution of differences to *"other tribunals by virtue of agreements already in existence, or which may be concluded in the future"*.

4) The Charter of the International Court of Justice

Article 34 of the Charter of the ICJ provides that only States may be parties to cases before the Court.

Article 36 deals with the jurisdiction of the Court and provides that it may deal with all cases that the parties have referred to it and all matters specially provided for in the UN Charter, or in treaties and conventions in force. The Article goes on to provide that:

> *"The states parties to the present Statute may at any time declare that they recognize as compulsory ipso facto and without special agreement, in relation to any other state accepting the same obligation, the jurisdiction of the Court in all legal disputes concerning:*
>
> a. *the interpretation of a treaty;*
> b. *any question of international law;*
> c. *the existence of any fact which, if established, would constitute a breach of an international obligation;*
> d. *the nature or extent of the reparation to be made for the breach of an international obligation."*

As noted earlier, the Court has the power to decide whether it has jurisdiction.

Article 38 states that it is the function of the ICJ to decide disputes submitted to it in accordance with international law and is to apply:

"a. international conventions, whether general or particular, establishing rules expressly recognized by the contesting states;

b. international custom, as evidence of a general practice accepted as law;

c. the general principles of law recognized by civilized nations;

d. subject to the provisions of Article 59, judicial decisions and the teachings of the most highly qualified publicists of the various nations, as subsidiary means for the determination of rules of law."

As discussed in Chapter 6, this Article is of great significance, not simply to the Court itself but to international law generally, as it is widely accepted as setting out the sources of international law.

Articles 39 to 64 contain provisions dealing with procedure. The Court may make provisional orders preserving the respective rights of the parties. For these there is an abbreviated procedure. The normal procedure of the Court is to consist of two parts, written and oral. The written proceedings are to include memorials, counter-memorials and, if necessary, replies and rejoinders, together with documents in support. Hearings are to be in public, and the Court is to make orders for the conduct of case, deciding the form and time in which each party must conclude its arguments. The Court is to make all arrangements connected with the taking of evidence, and may call for the production of documents. It may seek expert opinion. During the course of the hearing *"... any relevant questions are to be put to the witnesses and experts under the conditions laid down by the Court..."*.

Article 53 deals with default by one of the parties:

"1. Whenever one of the parties does not appear before the Court, or fails to defend its case, the other party may call upon the Court to decide in favour of its claim.

2. The Court must, before doing so, satisfy itself, not only that it has jurisdiction in accordance with Articles 36 and 37, but also that the claim is well founded in fact and law."

When presentation of the parties' case is completed, the President of the Court declares the hearing closed and the Court withdraws to consider the judgment. Questions are decided by a majority of the judges. In the event of the equality of votes, the President has the casting vote. Any judge may deliver a separate opinion in the event that the judgment is not unanimous. The judgment is to state the reasons on which it is based and is final and without appeal. If there is a dispute as to the meaning or scope of the judgment, the Court may construe its judgment at the request of any party. An application for revision of the judgment may be made, but *"only when it is based upon the discovery of some fact of such a nature as to be a decisive factor, which fact was, when the judgment was given, unknown to the Court and also to the party claiming revision, always provided that such ignorance was not due to negligence."*

An application for revision must be made at the latest within six months of the discovery of a new fact, and in any event before the lapse of 10 years from the date of the judgment.

Provision is made for possible intervention by other States in circumstances where they may be affected by the decision in a particular case (including circumstances involving the construction of a convention).

Articles 65 to 68 make provision for advisory opinions. The Court may give such opinions *"on any legal question at the request of whatever body may be authorized by or in accordance with the Charter of the United Nations to make such a request"*. Such questions are to be laid before the Court by means of a written request containing an exact statement of the questions on which opinion is required. The request is to be accompanied by all documents *"likely to throw a light upon the question"*.

5) ICJ Rules of Court

The Preamble to the Rules of the Court refers to the UN Charter and to the Statute of the Court.

Parts 1 and II

Section A of Part I deals with judges and assessors of the Court, Section B with the Presidency, Section C with the Chamber of Summary Procedure and Section D with the internal functioning of the Court.

Part II is concerned with the Registry.

Part III

Part III deals with proceedings in contentious cases.

Institution of proceedings

Article 38 states that, when proceedings are instituted by means of an application to the Court, that application is to indicate the party making the application, the State against which the claim is brought and the subject of the dispute. The application is to specify the legal grounds on which the jurisdiction of the Court is said to be based and is also to specify the precise nature of the claim, together with *"a succinct statement of the facts and grounds upon which the claim is based"*.

Proceedings may be brought by a 'special agreement'. Copies of the application or notification of a special agreement are to be transmitted to the UN Secretary-General, Members of the UN and other States entitled to appear before the Court.

Written proceedings

Articles 44 to 53 deal with the written proceedings. The Court is to determine the number and order of filing of pleadings and the time limits within which they are to be filed. The pleadings in a case begun by means of an application are to consist of a Memorial and a

Counter-Memorial and, if the Court directs, a Reply and a Rejoinder. In the case of a special agreement, the pleadings are to comprise a Memorial and Counter-Memorial, unless otherwise agreed.

The Court may order joinder of two or more cases and may also direct that the written or oral proceedings, including the calling of witnesses, be in common. Time limits for completion of the steps in the proceedings are to be fixed and shall be *"as short as the character of the case permits"*.

The Memorial is to contain a statement of the relevant facts, the law and the submissions. The Counter-Memorial is to contain an admission or denial of the facts stated in the Memorial and, if necessary, observations concerning the statement of law in the Memorial, with a statement of law in answer, together with that party's submissions. The Reply and Rejoinder, if authorised, shall *"not merely repeat the parties' contentions, but shall be directed to bringing out the issues that still divide them."* Relevant documents are to be annexed to the pleadings.

Oral proceedings, documents, witnesses and experts

Articles 54 to 72 are concerned with the oral proceedings. On the closure of the written proceedings the case is ready for hearing. The Court is to fix the date of the opening of the oral proceedings, and, if it considers it desirable, may decide that the proceedings be held at a place other than the seat of the Court.

The Rules contain detailed provisions dealing with production of documents, evidence, details of witnesses and experts intended to be called *"with indications in general terms of the point or points to which their evidence will be directed"*. The Court is to determine whether the parties shall present their arguments before or after the production of the evidence. The parties are nevertheless entitled to retain the right to comment on the evidence given. The order in which the parties are to be heard, the method of handling the evidence and the examination of witnesses and experts, and indeed the number of counsel and advocates to be heard on behalf of each party, is to be settled by the Court.

The hearing is to be in public and the oral statements made on behalf of each party *"shall be as succinct as possible within the limits of what is requisite for the adequate presentation of that party's contentions at the hearing. Accordingly, they shall be directed to the issues that still divide the parties, and shall not go over the whole ground covered by the pleadings, or merely repeat the facts and arguments these contain."*

This telling direction to advocates is followed by a further warning to the loquacious lawyer: *"... at the conclusion of the last statement made by a party at the hearing, its agent, without recapitulation of the arguments, shall read that party's final submissions"*.

During the hearing the Court may indicate any points or issues to which it would like the parties to address themselves, and may put questions to the agents, counsel and advocates. These are to be answered either immediately or within a time limit fixed by the President. The Court may call on the parties to produce evidence.

Article 64 sets out the form of words to be used by every witness by way of a declaration, and the form of declaration to be made by every expert. The examination of witnesses and experts is by the advocates for the parties, but under the control of the President. Before testifying, witnesses are to remain out of the courtroom.

The Court may make arrangements for inquiries to be carried out or for expert opinion to be obtained. It may also request a public international organisation to furnish information.

Interim measures, etc

Articles 73 to 89 contain provisions dealing with interim protection, preliminary objections, counter-claims and interventions. These have proved substantial elements in the Court's calendar.

Chambers

Articles 90 to 93 deal with proceedings before Chambers. These are the proceedings mentioned in Articles 26 and 29 of the Court's Statute. Article 26 is concerned with Chambers composing three or more judges formed to determine particular categories of case, such as labour cases and cases relating to transit and communications. In practice, Chambers have largely dealt with territorial issues in a particular region.

Article 29 deals with a Chamber formed annually with a view to the speedy dispatch of business. This latter Chamber is composed of five judges and can hear cases by summary procedure.

Judgments

Articles 94 to 97 deal with the judgments of the Court. A judgment, which is to state whether it is given by the Court or by a Chamber, is to contain:

- the date on which it is read;
- the names of the judges participating in it;
- the names of the parties;
- the names of the agents, counsel and advocates of the parties;
- a summary of the proceedings;
- the submissions of the parties;
- a statement of the facts;
- the reasons in point of law;
- the operative provisions of the judgment;
- the decision, if any, in regard to costs;
- the number and names of the judges constituting the majority;
- a statement as to the text of the judgment that is authoritative.

Articles 98 to 100 deal with requests for the interpretation or revision of a judgement. Such request must satisfy the conditions set out in Article 61 of the Statute dealing with the discovery of new and decisive facts.

Part IV

Part IV of the Rules of Court is concerned with advisory proceedings under Article 65 of the Statute. The advisory opinion is to contain similar information as is required in the case of a judgement.

6) Practice Directions of the ICJ

The ICJ has in recent years begun to issue Practice Directions dealing with various aspects of the conduct of litigation before the Court that had not been covered in the Rules. For example, Practice Direction II lays emphasis on the need for clarity: The parties are to bear in mind that pleadings are intended not only to reply to the submissions and arguments of the other party, but also – and above all – are to *"present clearly the submissions and arguments of the party which is filing the proceedings. In the light of this, at the conclusion of the written pleadings of each party, there is to appear a short summary of its reasoning."*

Warning is given against the excessive use of annexes to written pleadings: *"the Court has noticed an excessive tendency towards the proliferation and protraction of annexes to written pleadings. It strongly urges parties to append to their pleadings only strictly selected documents."*

Reference was made earlier to the requirements of Article 60 of the Rules, which provides that all statements made on behalf of each party are to be *"as succinct as possible"*. Practice Direction VI states that the Court requires *"the full compliance with these provisions and observation of the requisite degree of brevity"*. Again, a telling direction to advocates.

As at early 2006, the International Court had issued 12 Practice Directions.

7) The ICJ Caseload

As mentioned earlier, since 1946 the Court has delivered 79 Judgments on disputes dealing with a variety of issues and given 24 Advisory Opinions concerning a range of topics.

In the years 2004-2006, pending cases included a maritime delimitation dispute between Nicaragua and Honduras; a frontier dispute involving Benin and Niger; a territorial and maritime dispute between Nicaragua and Colombia; certain criminal proceedings in France (*Republic of the Congo v France*); armed activities in the Congo (*Democratic Republic of the Congo v Uganda*); maritime delimitation in the Black Sea (*Romania v Ukraine);* a case concerning the application of the Convention on the Prohibition and Punishment of the Crime of Genocide (*Croatia v Serbia and Montenegro*); and claims of genocide (*Bosnia and Herzegovina v Serbia and Montenegro*).[51]

References are made in various parts of the Manual to decisions of the ICJ.

51 The public hearings on the merits in the case concerning the 'Application of the Convention on the Prevention and Punishment of the Crime of Genocide' *(Bosnia and Herzegovina v Serbia and Montenegro)* opened at the ICJ on 27 February 2006. The hearings were expected to last until early May 2006: www.icj-cij.org/icjwww/ipresscom/ipress2006/ipresscom_2006-09_bhy_20060227.htm.

8) Conclusions

It is clear that the ICJ, as the primary judicial organ of the UN, is an institution of considerable importance in the field of dispute resolution between States. The Court's importance in the field of international law is likewise of great significance: Its decisions may well have an impact beyond the Court itself.

The nature of the cases dealt with by the ICJ demonstrates its unique role in the field of inter-State dispute resolution. The number of disputes coming before the ICJ has increased in the last 15 years, and the Court is now resorted to by States from all corners of the world, including many Commonwealth countries: Australia, Botswana, Cameroon, Canada, India, Namibia, Nauru, New Zealand, Nigeria, Pakistan, Singapore, South Africa, Uganda and the United Kingdom.

Judges from the Commonwealth sitting at the ICJ include Judge Rosalyn Higgins of the United Kingdom and Judge Abdul G Koroma of Sierra Leone.

12 The Permanent Court of Arbitration

1) Introduction

The Permanent Court of Arbitration (PCA) is one of the major supranational bodies concerned with international disputes, and its work is complementary to that of the International Court of Justice (ICJ) (see Box 6). Both institutions are housed in the Peace Palace in The Hague.

Box 6: The UN Secretary-General on the Importance of the PCA

The importance of the PCA is shown by UN Secretary-General Kofi Annan's Foreword to the *Basic Documents* of the PCA, in which he said that:

"... the Permanent Court of Arbitration and the International Court of Justice are not merely neighbours in the Hague Peace Palace; they are complementary institutions offering the international community a comprehensive range of options for the peaceful resolution of disputes.

"Settling international disputes by peaceful means, in conformity with the principles of justice and international law, is one of the central purposes of the United Nations set out in Article 1 of the United Nations Charter. Arbitration is among the methods of peaceful settlement cited in Article 33 of the Charter, and the Permanent Court has a long and distinguished history in this regard. In 1993, the General Assembly granted the Court the status of permanent observer, enabling it to participate actively in the discussions of the Assembly's Legal Committee.

"I encourage States, international organizations and private parties to make greater use of the Court's services, which also include fact-finding and conciliation; such recourse would help ease the workload of the International Court of Justice and fill gaps concerning arbitrations involving private parties and international organizations. I also urge States which have not ratified the Hague Conventions to do so. Developing countries, in particular, could well find the flexible instruments of dispute resolution to be invaluable."

An historical overview of the PCA is given in the next section, followed by a consideration of the Hague Peace Convention of 1899. That Convention, and the 1907 Hague Convention, set out the thinking behind the concept of an international body whose function would be to secure the peaceful resolution of disputes. This led to the creation of the PCA.

The chapter then goes on to consider some of the present-day procedures operated by the PCA. Two in particular are considered in some detail: first, the PCA's Optional Rules for Arbitrating Disputes between Two States, which are taken as an example of one of the various sets of Arbitration Rules available from the Court; and second, the PCA's Optional Rules for Conciliation.

The UN has a role to play in the PCA in that many of the Court's dispute resolution procedures – both arbitration and conciliation – are based on United Nations Commission on International Trade Law (UNCITRAL) Rules. Further, the 1976 UNCITRAL Arbitration Rules entrust the Secretary-General of the PCA with the task of designating, on request, an 'appointing authority' for the purpose of appointing the members of an arbitral tribunal. The relationship between the PCA and UNCITRAL is considered in one of the later sections.

The final sections of the chapter look at the work of the PCA and at the type of cases it currently handles.

2) Historical Overview

The PCA was established by the Convention for the Pacific Settlement of International Disputes. That Convention was concluded at The Hague in 1899 during the first Hague Peace Conference, convened on the initiative of Czar Nicolas II of Russia. The aim was to seek *"the most objective means of ensuring to all peoples the benefits of a real and lasting peace, and above all, of limiting the progressive development of existing armaments"*. The most significant achievement of the Conference was the establishment of the PCA, which was the first global mechanism for the settlement of inter-State disputes. The 1899 Convention, which provided the legal basis for the PCA, was revised at the second Hague Peace Conference in 1907.

In recent years there has been a sharp increase in accessions to the Conventions of 1899 and 1907. There are currently 103 States that are parties to one or both of the Conventions.

The Peace Palace in The Hague, completed in 1913, was specifically built to accommodate the Court. The Carnegie Foundation, the Hague Academy of International Law, the Peace Palace International Law Library and, as mentioned earlier, the ICJ are also based at the Peace Palace.

3) Convention for the Pacific Settlement of International Disputes, 1899

Article 1 of the 1899 Convention states that the Signatory Powers have agreed to use their best efforts to ensure the pacific settlement of international differences. Two of the methods of resolving disputes are good offices and mediation. The functions of the mediator are said to consist of *"reconciling the opposing claims and appeasing the feelings of resentment which may have arisen between the States at variance"*.

Two further methods of resolving differences specified in the Convention are international commissions of inquiry and international arbitration. Article 15 states that the latter has for its object *"the settlement of differences between States by judges of their own choice, and on the basis of respect for law"*.

Article 16 states that in questions of a legal nature, and especially in the interpretation or application of international conventions, *"... arbitration is recognized by the Signatory Powers as the most effective, and at the same time the most equitable, means of settling disputes which diplomacy has failed to settle"*.

Article 20 of the Convention makes provision for the setting up of the PCA: *"With the object of facilitating an immediate recourse to arbitration for international differences, which it has not been possible to settle by diplomacy, the Signatory Powers undertake to organize a Permanent Court of Arbitration, accessible at all times and operating, unless otherwise stipulated by the parties, in accordance with the Rules of Procedure inserted in the present Convention."*

Article 23 provides that each Signatory Power is to select four arbitrators (known as 'Members of the Court'). They are to be persons *"... of known competency in questions of international law, of the highest moral reputation, and disposed to accept the duties of Arbitrators"*.

Article 28 makes provision for the setting up of a Permanent Administrative Council. Composed of *"the Diplomatic Representatives of the Signatory Powers accredited to The Hague and of the Netherlands Minister for Foreign Affairs, who will act as President,* [it] *shall be instituted in this town as soon as possible after the ratification of the present Act by at least nine Powers"*. That Council would be charged with the establishment and organisation of an International Bureau that would, among other things, settle Rules of Procedure and all other necessary Regulations.

The Rules of Procedure referred to in Article 20 are contained in Chapter III of the Convention. Article 30 states that, with a view to encouraging the development of arbitration, the Signatory Powers have agreed on the Rules that are to be applicable to arbitral procedure.

The Powers who wish to have recourse to arbitration are to sign a special Act or *'Compromis'* in which the subject of the difference is to be defined. The *Compromis* *"implies the undertaking of the parties to submit loyally to the Award"* (Article 31).

The Convention then goes on to set out detailed rules for the conduct of an arbitration:

- the appointment of the arbitrators;
- the place of arbitration (the Tribunal is to sit at The Hague, unless the parties decide otherwise);
- the Tribunal is to decide on the choice of language to be used;
- the arbitral procedure is to comprise two distinct phases, namely preliminary examination (which involves the communication of documents containing argument) and discussion (which consists of the parties' oral argument to the Tribunal);
- the Tribunal may require the production of documents, and may demand explanations;
- the Tribunal is entitled to decide its competence by interpreting the *Compromis* and by interpreting any relevant Treaties, and also by applying *"the principles of international law"*;

- the Tribunal may issue Rules of Procedure for the conduct of the arbitration and can decide the forms and periods within which each party is to conclude its arguments;
- when all explanations and evidence have been presented, the hearing is closed.

The Tribunal then deliberates in private. The Award is to be by a majority of votes and accompanied by a *"statement of reasons. It is drawn up in writing and signed by each member of the Tribunal."* Any members in the minority may record their dissent when signing. The Award *"puts an end to the dispute definitively and without appeal"*.

The parties are entitled to provide in the *Compromis* for the right to demand a revision of the Award. The demand for revision is to be addressed to the Tribunal that made the Award. The revision can only be made on the ground of *"the discovery of some new fact calculated to exercise a decisive influence on the Award, and which, at the time the discussion was closed, was unknown to the Tribunal and to the party demanding the revision"*.

It is interesting to note that the detailed provisions made over 100 years ago for the conduct of arbitrations between States differ very little from the kind of provisions to be found in present-day arbitrations. Indeed, the concept of international dispute resolution as conceived by the 1899 Convention can be said to be the precursor of present-day international dispute resolution, in the fields of both inter-State dispute resolution and pure commercial arbitration. Further, at a time when mediation is still viewed by some with suspicion, it is worth noting that the Convention included mediation as one of the four methods of resolving international disputes between States.

Revisions were made to the 1899 Convention by the 1907 Convention.

4) Present-Day Rules and Procedures

While the Conventions of 1899 and 1907 established the PCA, a series of comparatively new procedural rules are based on international dispute resolution processes currently in use worldwide. The PCA today makes available a considerable array of procedures for dealing with international disputes.

The PCA Rules are largely based on the UNCITRAL Rules and include Optional Rules for arbitrating disputes between two States; for arbitrating between two parties, of which only one is a State; for arbitrating between international organisations and States; for arbitrating between international organisations and private parties; and for arbitrating disputes relating to natural resources.

There are Guidelines for adapting the PCA Arbitration Rules to disputes arising under multilateral agreements and multiparty contracts.

The PCA also provides Optional Rules for Fact-finding Commissions of Inquiry. In addition, there are Optional Conciliation Rules and specific conciliation rules relating to natural resources and the environment.

Model Clauses are available in relation to these various sets of Rules. For example, the Model Clause in relation to the Rules for arbitrating disputes between two States provides first for a clause dealing with future disputes:

> *"Parties to a bilateral treaty or other agreement who wish to have any dispute referred to arbitration under these Rules may insert in the treaty or agreement an arbitration clause in the following form:*
>
> 1. *If any dispute arises between the parties as to the interpretation, application or performance of this [treaty] [agreement], including its existence, validity or termination, either party may submit the dispute to final and binding arbitration in accordance with the Permanent Court of Arbitration Optional Rules for Arbitrating Disputes between Two States, as in effect on the date of this [treaty] [agreement].*
>
> *Parties may wish to consider adding:*
>
> 2. *The number of arbitrators shall be…*
> 3. *The language(s) to be used in the arbitral proceedings shall be…*
> 4. *The appointing authority shall be…"*

The Model Clause for use in the case of an existing dispute provides:

> *"The parties agree to submit the following dispute to final and binding arbitration in accordance with the Permanent Court of Arbitration Optional Rules for Arbitrating Disputes between Two States, as in effect on the date of this agreement: … [insert brief description of dispute]."*

The PCA suggests that the parties may wish to consider adding to this paragraphs 2-4 of the arbitration clause for future disputes.

5) The PCA Rules for Arbitrating Disputes Between Two States

An example of the PCA's arbitration rules is the Optional Rules for Arbitrating Disputes Between Two States. The introduction to these Rules explains that they *"… have been elaborated for use in arbitrating disputes arising under treaties or other agreements between two States; they can be modified for use in connection with multilateral treaties. The Rules are based on the UNCITRAL Arbitration Rules with changes…."*

The Rules are in the four sections:

Section I: Introductory rules

Section II: The composition of the arbitral tribunal

Section III: The arbitral process

Section IV: The award

Section I: Introductory rules

Article 1 states that *"Where the parties to a treaty or other agreement have agreed in writing that disputes shall be referred to arbitration under the Permanent Court of*

Arbitration Optional Rules for Arbitrating Disputes between Two States, then such disputes shall be settled in accordance with these Rules subject to such modification as the parties may agree in writing".

Article 2 contains provisions dealing with notices and calculations of periods of time. Commencement of the arbitration is by way of service of a notice of arbitration. Article 3 states that the party initiating recourse to arbitration – the claimant – *"shall give to the other party (hereinafter called the 'respondent') a notice of arbitration"*. The arbitral proceedings are deemed to commence on the date on which the notice of arbitration is received by the respondent. The notice of arbitration is to contain the following information:

"(a) A demand that the dispute be referred to arbitration;

(b) The names and addresses of the parties;

(c) A reference to the arbitration clause or the separate arbitration agreement that is invoked;

(d) A reference to the treaty or other agreement out of or in relation to which the dispute arises;

(e) The general nature of the claim and an indication of the amount involved, if any;

(f) The relief or remedy sought;

(g) A proposal as to the number of arbitrators (i.e., one, three or five), if the parties have not previously agreed thereon."

The notice of arbitration may also include the statement of claim referred to in Article 18.

Article 4 deals with representation and assistance.

Section II: The composition of the arbitral tribunal

Articles 5 to 8 of Section II of the Rules contain provisions dealing with the composition of the arbitral tribunal: one, three or five arbitrators (with a presiding arbitrator in the case of a three- or five-member tribunal). If the parties cannot agree on an appointment, that appointment is to be made either by an appointing authority or by the Secretary-General of the PCA.

Articles 9 to 12 deal with the challenge of arbitrators. Article 9 requires a prospective arbitrator to disclose *"... any circumstances likely to give rise to justifiable doubts as to his/her impartiality or independence. An arbitrator, once appointed or chosen, shall disclose such circumstances to the parties unless they have already been informed by him/her of these circumstances."*

An arbitrator may be challenged if circumstances exist that give rise to justifiable doubts as to his or her impartiality or independence. In the case of a party seeking to challenge an arbitrator appointed by another party, the reasons relied on may only be those that came to the notice of a party after the appointment had been made (Article 10).

Where necessary, a substitute arbitrator is appointed. Article 13 makes provision for the appointment of a substitute arbitrator in the event of the death or resignation of an arbitrator during the course of the arbitral proceedings. Where a sole or presiding arbitrator is replaced, any hearings held previously are to be repeated. Whether such hearings are to be repeated in the case of the replacement of any other arbitrator is a matter for the discretion of the tribunal.

Section III: The arbitral process

Section III deals with the conduct of the arbitral proceedings. Article 15 states that, subject to the Rules, the arbitral tribunal *"may conduct the arbitration in such manner as it considers appropriate, provided that the parties are treated with equality and that at any stage of the proceedings each party is given a full opportunity of presenting its case"*.

Either party may request an oral hearing. If no such request is made, the tribunal will decide whether the arbitration proceeds to an oral hearing or is dealt with on a documents-only basis.

Place and language of the arbitration

Articles 16 and 17 deal with the place of arbitration and the language to be used. Unless the parties have agreed otherwise, the place of arbitration is The Hague. The award is to be made at the place of arbitration.

Subject to the agreement of the parties, the tribunal is to determine the language or languages to be used in the proceedings. That determination applies to the pleadings, any further written statements and to any oral hearing.

Pleadings and documents

Articles 18 to 20 deal with the statement of claim and the statement of defence, and with amendment of those pleadings. Article 18 provides that, unless the statement of claim was contained in the notice of arbitration, the claimant is to serve a written statement of claim on the respondent and the tribunal. A copy of the treaty or other agreement (and of the arbitration agreement, if not contained in the treaty or agreement) is to be annexed. The statement of claim is to include a precise statement of the following matters:

- *(a) The names and addresses of the parties;*
- *(b) A statement of the facts supporting the claim;*
- *(c) The points at issue;*
- *(d) The relief or remedy sought.*

The claimant may *"annex to its statement of claim all documents it deems relevant or may add a reference to the documents or other evidence it will submit"*.

Article 19 deals with the service of the statement of defence, which is to reply to the particulars contained in (b), (c) and (d) of the statement of claim. The respondent may annex documents relied on or may add a reference to documents or other evidence that will be submitted. The respondent may include in its statement of defence a counterclaim or set-off *"arising out of the same treaty or other agreement or rely on a claim arising out of the same treaty or other agreement for the purpose of a set-off"*.

Article 20 states that either party may amend or supplement its claim or defence *"unless the arbitral tribunal considers it inappropriate to allow such amendment having regard to the delay in making it or prejudice to the other party or any other circumstances. However, a claim may not be amended in such a manner that the amended claim falls outside the scope of the arbitration clause or separate arbitration agreement."*

Time limits are to be fixed by the tribunal for the service of the pleadings.

Jurisdiction of the tribunal

Article 21 contains provisions dealing with 'competence / competence': the power of the tribunal to rule on objections that *"it has no jurisdiction, including any objections with respect to the existence or validity of the arbitration clause or of the separate arbitration agreement"*.

The tribunal has power *"to determine the existence or the validity of the treaty or other agreement of which an arbitration clause forms a part. For the purposes of article 21, an arbitration clause which forms part of the treaty or agreement and which provides for arbitration under these Rules shall be treated as an agreement independent of the other terms of the treaty or agreement. A decision by the arbitral tribunal that the treaty or agreement is null and void shall not entail ipso jure the invalidity of the arbitration clause."*

A plea that the tribunal does not have jurisdiction must be raised no later than in the statement of defence or, in relation to a counter-claim, in the reply to such counter-claim. The arbitral tribunal should generally rule on a plea concerning its jurisdiction as a preliminary question. However, it is entitled to proceed with the arbitration and rule on the matter of its jurisdiction in the final award.

Further written submissions

Articles 22 and 23 deal with further written submissions and periods of time. The tribunal is to decide which further written statements, in addition to the statements of claim and defence, are to be required from the parties, and shall fix the periods of time for communicating such statements. Article 23 lays down that the periods of time fixed by the tribunal for service of pleadings.

Evidence and hearings

Provisions relating to evidence and hearings are set out in Articles 24 and 25. Article 24 states that each party has the burden of proving the facts on which it relies to support its claim or defence. The tribunal may require a party *"to deliver to the tribunal and to the other party, within such a period of time as the arbitral tribunal shall decide, a summary of the documents and other evidence which that party intends to present in support of the facts in issue set out in its statement of claim or statement of defence"*. Furthermore, the tribunal may at any time during the proceedings call on the parties to produce documents, exhibits or other evidence. It is to take note of any refusal to do so, as well as any reasons given for such refusal.

Important provisions relating to the conduct of oral hearings are contained in Article 25. The tribunal is to give the parties adequate advance notice of the date, time and place of the oral hearing. If witnesses are to be heard, at least 30 days prior to the hearing each party is to communicate to the tribunal and the other party the names and addresses of the witnesses it intends to call, the subject matter of the testimony of those witnesses and the language in which such testimony will be given. Where appropriate, arrangements will be made for the translation of oral statements made. Hearings are held in camera unless the parties agree otherwise. The tribunal is entitled to require the retirement of any witnesses during the testimony of other witnesses and to determine the manner in which witnesses are to be examined. The evidence of witnesses may be in the form of written statements. The tribunal determines the admissibility, relevance, materiality and weight of the evidence.

Interim measures

Article 26 gives power to the tribunal to make interim orders of protection aimed at preserving the respective rights of the parties. Such interim measures may be dealt with by way of an interim award, and the tribunal is entitled to require security for the costs of such measures. A request for interim measures to a judicial authority *"shall not be deemed incompatible with the agreement to arbitrate, or as a waiver of that agreement"*.

Experts

Provisions relating to the appointment of experts are contained in Article 27. The tribunal is entitled to appoint one or more experts to report to it on specific issues. The parties are to give such experts any relevant information and produce to them for inspection any relevant documents or goods. The tribunal is to provide the parties with a copy of the experts' reports. The parties can comment on the reports, and may request that the tribunal-appointed experts attend the hearing for interrogation. The parties are entitled to present their own expert witnesses to testify on the points at issue.

Default

Article 28 contains default provisions:

> *"If, within the period of time fixed by the arbitral tribunal, the claimant has failed to communicate its claim without showing sufficient cause for such failure, the arbitral tribunal shall issue an order for the termination of the arbitral proceedings. If, within the period of time fixed by the arbitral tribunal, the respondent has failed to communicate its statement of defence without showing sufficient cause for such failure, the arbitral tribunal shall order that the proceedings continue."*

In the event that one of the parties fails to appear at the hearing *"without showing sufficient cause for such failure"*, the tribunal may proceed with the arbitration. Where a party invited to produce documentary evidence fails to do so without good cause, the tribunal may make the award on the evidence before it.

Close of pleadings and waiver

The tribunal declares the hearings closed, having first inquired of the parties whether they have any further proof to offer, witnesses to be heard or submissions to make. However, if it considers it necessary owing to exceptional circumstances, the tribunal may reopen the hearings at any time before the award is made (Article 29).

The final Article in Section III deals with waiver: Any party who knows that any provision or requirement of the Rules has not been complied with is deemed to have waived its right to object, unless it has promptly stated its objection to such non-compliance.

Section IV: The award

The final Section of the Rules deals with the award, applicable law, settlement and other grounds of termination of the arbitration, interpretation and correction of the awards, additional awards and costs.

Awards: interim, interlocutory, partial and final

Article 31 provides that where there are three or five arbitrators, any award or other decision of the tribunal is to be made by a majority of the arbitrators. Where there is no majority, or when the tribunal authorises, the presiding arbitrator may decide questions of procedure (subject to any revision by the tribunal).

Article 32 states that, in addition to making a final award, the tribunal is entitled to make interim, interlocutory or partial awards. It will be recalled that Article 26 stated that interim measures of protection may be made in the form of an interim award.

The award is to be in writing and is to state the reasons on which it is based, unless the parties have agreed otherwise. It is to be signed by the arbitrators and is to contain the date on which and the place where it was made. If there are three or five arbitrators and any one of them fails to sign, the award is to state the reason for the absence of signatures. The award is final and binding on the parties, who *"undertake to carry out the award without delay"*. The award cannot be made public without the consent of the parties.

Applicable law, international law and *ex aequo et bono*

Article 33 deals with applicable law. The arbitral tribunal is to apply the law chosen by the parties or, in the absence of agreement, is to decide in accordance with international law by applying:

"(a) International conventions, whether general or particular, establishing rules expressly recognized by the contesting States;

(b) International custom, as evidence of a general practice accepted as law;

(c) The general principles of law recognized by civilized nations;

(d) Judicial and arbitral decisions and the teachings of the most highly qualified publicists of the various nations, as subsidiary means for the determination of rules of law."

These provisions "*shall not prejudice the power of the arbitral tribunal to decide a case* ex aequo et bono, *if the parties agree thereto*".

It will be recalled that Article 38 of the Charter of the ICJ contains similar provisions.

Termination: settlement, etc

Article 34 deals with termination of the arbitral process by settlement or otherwise. If, before the award is made, the parties agree on a settlement of the dispute: *"the arbitral tribunal shall either issue an order for the termination of the arbitral proceedings or, if requested by both parties and accepted by the tribunal, record the settlement in the form of an arbitral award on agreed terms. The arbitral tribunal is not obliged to give reasons for such an award."*

In addition, if the continuation of the proceedings *"becomes unnecessary or impossible"* before the award is made, the tribunal is to inform the parties of its intention to issue an order for the termination of the proceedings.

Interpretation and correction of the award

Within 60 days after the receipt of the award either party, on serving notice on the other party, may request the tribunal to give an interpretation of the award. This is to be given in writing within 45 days of the receipt of that request and is to form part of the award (Article 35). Article 36 contains provisions for the tribunal to correct the award in relation to errors in computation, clerical or typographical errors or errors of a similar nature. A request for correction is to be made within 60 days of receipt of the award. Alternatively, the tribunal on its own initiative may make such corrections within 30 days after the communication of the award.

Additional awards

Article 37 provides that, within 60 days of the receipt of the award, either party may request the tribunal to make an additional award *"as to claims presented in the arbitral proceedings but omitted from the award"*. If the tribunal considers that the request is justified and that the omission can be rectified without any further hearings or evidence, it may complete its award within 60 days of the receipt of the request.

Costs

The remaining Articles 38 to 41 deal with costs.

6) The PCA Optional Conciliation Rules

i) Introduction

Having considered one example of the various sets of PCA Arbitration Rules, it may now be useful to look at the PCA Conciliation Rules. The PCA Introduction to the Rules, which outlines their purpose, is well worth reading as it explains the nature of conciliation in a practical way and also seeks to allay fears that many still have concerning the conciliation process.

"Parties who have disputes that they are unable to settle through consultation and negotiation with each other may wish to consider conciliation as a method for resolving their differences without the need to resort to arbitration or judicial means.

"Although the benefits of conciliation are widely recognized, some parties may hesitate to enter into conciliation because they may be unfamiliar with the process or may have different views concerning how a conciliation should be conducted. In order to facilitate greater use of conciliation, the Permanent Court of Arbitration has, with the approval of the Administrative Council, established these Optional Conciliation Rules ('the PCA Optional Conciliation Rules'). These Rules are based on the UNCITRAL Conciliation Rules, with changes to indicate, inter alia, the availability of the Secretary-General of the Permanent Court of Arbitration to assist in appointing conciliators and of the International Bureau to furnish administrative support (art. 4, para. 3 and art. 8).

"The purpose of these Rules is to provide a convenient basis for mutual agreement of parties on practical procedures that are useful in the conciliation process. Thus, for example, the Rules describe how to start a conciliation, how to appoint conciliators, what functions conciliators are expected to perform, and how to encourage parties to speak freely and candidly with conciliators while at the same time preserving necessary confidentiality. These Rules also describe how, if the conciliation is unsuccessful, it may be easily terminated so as not to delay or prejudice recourse to arbitration, judicial procedures or other means for ultimately resolving the dispute."

The Introduction deals with the scope of the Rules, which are meant to assist in resolving disputes where the parties seek an amicable settlement.

"[The Rules] *are intended for use in conciliating disputes in which one or more of the parties is a State, a State entity or enterprise, or an international organization. Thus, for example, the same Rules may be used in disputes between two States and also in disputes between two parties only one of which is a State.*

"The PCA recognizes the importance and complexity of disputes that involve more than two parties. These Rules are also appropriate for use in connection with multiparty disputes, provided that changes are made to reflect participation by more than two parties. The Secretary-General of the Permanent Court of Arbitration is available to consult with interested parties concerning modifications that may be considered in adapting these Rules for use in multiparty disputes.

"These Rules, and the services of the Secretary-General and the International Bureau, are available for use by all States and their entities and enterprises, and are not restricted to disputes in which the State is a party to either the Hague Convention on the Pacific Settlement of International Disputes of 1899, or that of 1907, nor is the choice of conciliators limited to persons who are listed as Members of the Permanent Court of Arbitration."

The Introduction makes the point that there may be little real practical difference between what is described as mediation and what is described as conciliation: *"In modern international practice, the word ' mediation' is sometimes used to designate a process that is very similar to the procedures for 'conciliation' described in these Rules. In such cases, these Rules can also be used for mediation, it being necessary only to change the words 'conciliation' to 'mediation' and 'conciliator' to ' mediator'."*

The Introduction then goes on to deal with the main characteristics of the conciliation process: it is voluntary, the procedure is flexible and the Conciliation Rules are part of an integrated PCA dispute resolution, with the result that procedures for conciliation may be linked to arbitration under the various PCA Optional Arbitration Rules.

That particular characteristic is useful

> *"because if a dispute is not resolved by conciliation, parties may wish to move promptly to final and binding arbitration. Therefore, these Rules provide several important safeguards that apply in the event that arbitration, or recourse to judicial means, follows an unsuccessful conciliation.*
>
> *"The ultimate safeguard against using conciliation to delay commencement of arbitration is the key provision of these Rules that... permits one party to terminate conciliation if it reaches the conclusion that the conciliation is no longer desirable. Moreover, by agreeing to conciliation under these Rules, the parties undertake that if the conciliation does not result in a settlement they will not introduce in any subsequent arbitration, or judicial proceedings, certain specified evidence that might be harmful. The evidence thus barred by these Rules consists of: (i) any views expressed by either party concerning possible settlement of the dispute; (ii) any admissions made by either party in the conciliation; (iii) any proposals made by the conciliator(s); or (iv) the fact that a party indicated willingness to accept a proposal for settlement made by the conciliator (art. 20). These provisions effectively protect parties and thereby encourage candor and a free exchange of views during the conciliation. Additional safeguards in these Rules include that the parties and conciliator undertake that, unless the parties vary the Rules, a conciliator will not act as an arbitrator or representative of a party in any arbitration or judicial proceeding in respect of a dispute that is subject to the conciliation, and that no party will present a conciliator as a witness in any such proceeding (art. 19)."*

Model Clauses are available.

ii) The Conciliation Rules

There are 20 Rules dealing with general matters, commencement of proceedings, the number and appointment of conciliators, submissions, the role of the conciliator, the conciliation process, settlement, confidentiality, termination of the process and, where necessary, resort to judicial or arbitral proceedings.

Scope of the conciliation process

Article 1 sets out the application of the Rules and provides that they apply to conciliation of disputes:

> *"1 ...arising out of or relating to a contractual legal relationship or other circumstances where the parties seeking an amicable settlement of their disputes have agreed that the Permanent Court of Arbitration Optional Conciliation Rules apply.*
>
> *2. The parties may agree to exclude or vary any of these Rules at any time.*
>
> *3. Where any of these Rules is in conflict with a provision of law from which the parties cannot derogate, that provision prevails."*

Commencement of the conciliation process

The conciliation process is initiated by one party sending to the other a written invitation to conciliation under the Rules, briefly identifying the subject matter of the dispute. If the invitation is rejected, the conciliation cannot take place (Article 2).

Appointment of conciliators

Where the parties agree to conciliation, Articles 3 and 4 deal with the appointment of conciliators. There shall be one, two or three conciliators. In cases of difficulty in appointment, assistance can be sought from, among others, the Secretary-General of the PCA.

Conduct of the conciliation

The conciliator will request from each party a brief written statement setting out the general nature of the dispute and the points at issue (copied to the other party). The conciliator may also request each party to submit further written statements of its position, and the facts and grounds in support, supplemented by such documents or other evidence considered necessary (Article 5).

Article 6 states that the parties may be represented or assisted by persons of their choice.

Role of the conciliator

Important provisions are contained in Article 7 relating to the role of the conciliator. These explain the nature of conciliation and are at the very heart of any mediation / conciliation process.

Article 7 (1) states that the conciliator assists the parties:

> *"... in an independent and impartial manner in their attempt to reach an amicable settlement of their dispute.*
>
> *2. The conciliator will be guided by principles of objectivity, fairness and justice, giving consideration to, among other things, the rights and obligations of the parties and the circumstances surrounding the dispute, including any previous practices between the parties.*

3. *The conciliator may conduct the conciliation proceedings in such a manner as he considers appropriate, taking into account the circumstances of the case, the wishes the parties may express, including any request by a party that the conciliator hear oral statements, and any special need for a speedy settlement of the dispute.*
4. *The conciliator may, at any stage of the conciliation proceedings, make proposals for a settlement of the dispute. Such proposals need not be in writing and need not be accompanied by a statement of the reasons therefore."*

Administrative assistance may be sought to aid the conciliation process, including from the PCA (Article 8).

'Caucus' sessions – and confidentiality

Article 9 deals with communications between the conciliator and the parties, and contains provisions relating to what is arguably one of the most valuable processes in a conciliation (or mediation): what is often referred to as the 'caucus' sessions. The conciliator may invite the parties to meet with him or her (or may communicate with them orally or in writing) and *"may meet or communicate with the parties together or with each of them separately"*.

Article 10 contains provisions that are perhaps linked to the caucus concept. Where the conciliator receives factual information from one party, he or she discloses the substance of the information to the other party, who then has the opportunity to present any explanation. However, *"when a party gives any information to the conciliator subject to a specific condition that it be kept confidential, the conciliator does not disclose that information to the other party"*.

Good faith and co-operation

The success of any conciliation / mediation process requires the good faith of the parties. Article 11 states that the parties *"will in good faith co-operate with the conciliator and, in particular, will endeavor to comply with requests by the conciliator to submit written materials, provide evidence and attend meetings"*.

Settlement / termination

Article 12 contains provisions that again may be linked to the caucus concept: Each party, either on its own initiative or at the invitation of the conciliator, may submit to the conciliator suggestions for the settlement of the dispute.

Article 13 deals with settlement, and shows that the conciliator may take the lead in proposing possible terms of settlement. Article 13 (1) states that:

> *"When it appears to the conciliator that there exist elements of a settlement which would be acceptable to the parties, he formulates the terms of a possible settlement and submits them to the parties for their observations. After receiving the observations of the parties, the conciliator may reformulate the terms of a possible settlement in the light of such observations.*

2. *If the parties reach agreement on a settlement of the dispute, they draw up and sign a written settlement agreement. If requested by the parties, the conciliator draws up, or assists the parties in drawing up, the settlement agreement.*
3. *The parties by signing the settlement agreement put an end to the dispute and are bound by the agreement."*

Article 14 provides for the confidentiality of the conciliation process and states that, unless the parties agree otherwise *"or the disclosure is required in connection with judicial proceedings pursuant to article 16 hereof, the conciliator and the parties shall keep confidential all matters relating to the conciliation proceedings. Confidentiality extends also to the settlement agreement, except where its disclosure is necessary for purposes of implementation and enforcement."*

The conciliation proceedings are terminated in any of the following ways:

"(a) By the signing of the settlement agreement by the parties, on the date of the agreement; or

(b) By a written declaration of the conciliator, after consultation with the parties, to the effect that further efforts at conciliation are no longer justified, on the date of the declaration; or

(c) By a written declaration of the parties addressed to the conciliator to the effect that the conciliation proceedings are terminated, on the date of the declaration; or

(d) By a written declaration of a party to the other party and the conciliator, if appointed, to the effect that the conciliation proceedings are terminated, on the date of the declaration" (Article 15).

Commencement of other proceedings during the conciliation process

Article 16 states that the parties undertake not to initiate any arbitral or judicial proceedings during the course of the conciliation process *"except that a party may initiate arbitral or judicial proceedings where, in its opinion, such proceedings are necessary for preserving its rights".*

Costs

Articles 17 and 18 deals with costs and deposits. Costs of the conciliation are fixed by the conciliator and are to be borne equally by the parties (unless the settlement agreement provides otherwise). The parties bear their own costs.

The conciliator may request a deposit as an advance on the costs that he or she expects will be incurred, and may request supplementary deposits during the conciliation. Failure to pay the deposits may result in the conciliator suspending the process.

Use of conciliation material, etc, in other proceedings

The conciliation process may fail and it is therefore necessary to make provision for (i) the role of the conciliator in some other process that may follow on from the conciliation, and (ii) the admissibility of evidence in such other process.

Article 19 states that the parties and the conciliator undertake that, unless the parties have agreed otherwise, the conciliator *"will not act as an arbitrator or as a representative or counsel of a party in any arbitral or judicial proceedings in respect of a dispute that is the subject of the conciliation proceedings. The parties also undertake that they will not present the conciliator as a witness in any such proceedings."*

Article 20, dealing with the admissibility of evidence in other proceedings, states that the parties undertake:

> *"not to rely on or introduce as evidence in arbitral or judicial proceedings, whether or not such proceedings relate to the dispute that is the subject of the conciliation proceedings:*
>
> *(a) Views expressed or suggestions made by the other party in respect of a possible settlement of the dispute;*
>
> *(b) Admissions made by the other party in the course of the conciliation proceedings;*
>
> *(c) Proposals made by the conciliator;*
>
> *(d) The fact that the other party had indicated its willingness to accept a proposal for settlement made by the conciliator."*

7) The PCA and UNCITRAL

The 1976 United Nations Commission on International Trade Law (UNCITRAL) Arbitration Rules entrust the Secretary-General of the PCA with the task of designating, on request of a party to arbitration proceedings, an 'appointing authority' for the purpose of appointing the members of an arbitral tribunal and ruling on challenges to arbitrators. The parties may also designate the Secretary-General himself as appointing authority under the UNCITRAL Rules or other instruments.

The PCA provides procedural guidelines for requesting designation of an appointing authority by the Secretary-General of the PCA under the UNCITRAL Arbitration Rules, together with model clauses for PCA services under the UNCITRAL Rules.

Mention has been made earlier of the fact that many of the PCA Rules – both Arbitration and Conciliation – are based on the UNCITRAL Rules.

8) The PCA Caseload – Pending and Recent Cases

In 2004 Mr Tjaco T van den Hout, the Secretary-General of the PCA, stated that the Court's current caseload was then at an all-time high (see Box 7).

Box 7: Comments on the PCA by the Secretary-General of the Court

Speaking at an International Oil and Gas Conference in the City of London in April 2004, Mr Tjaco T van den Hout, the Secretary-General of the PCA, considered aspects of the PCA's cases of relevance to the oil and gas industry, in particular in relation to arbitral tribunals convened under Annex VII of the 1982 United Nations Convention on the Law of the Sea (UNCLOS III). He stated that the PCA was currently serving as registry for three tribunals hearing inter-State disputes arising under the 1982 Convention, and that there had been a sharp increase in the number of Annex VII arbitrations initiated over the past year by States in the Caribbean, Latin America and Asia. These cases dealt with a broad range of issues regarding natural resources, the environment and marine delimitation, he said, and "no doubt a number of them are prompted by attempts of governments to secure clear and unambiguous title to an area, presumed rich in natural resources, that lies in a contest zone".

One of the Annex VII cases currently pending before a PCA tribunal was the *MOX Plant Case* between Ireland and the United Kingdom. Mr van den Hout stated that Ireland had instituted proceedings against the United Kingdom pursuant to Article 287 and Article 1 of Annex I of UNCLOS III and a five-member tribunal had been constituted. He said that the case concerned discharges into the Irish Sea from a mixed oxide (MOX) fuel plant located at the Sellafield nuclear facility in the United Kingdom, and related movements of radioactive material through the Irish Sea.

A further PCA-administered arbitration in which oil and gas were relevant was the Eritrea-Yemen case. The arbitration was divided into two phases: the first dealing with territorial sovereignty and the second covering maritime delimitation. Evidence of petroleum agreements and concessions was introduced into both phases. In the first phase, the Tribunal concluded that, while the offshore petroleum contracts entered into by the two Governments failed to *"establish or significantly strengthen the claims of either party to sovereignty over the disputed islands"*, they did *"lend a measure of support to a median line between the opposite coasts of Eritrea and Yemen, drawn without regard to the islands, dividing the respective jurisdiction of the Parties"*.

The following were some of the pending and recent PCA cases (some proceedings under the PCA auspices may be excluded from listing for reasons of confidentiality).

Pending cases

Malaysia / Singapore

In this dispute the PCA is acting as Registry. The case concerns land reclamation by Singapore in and around the Straits of Johor and was instituted by Malaysia on 4 July 2003 pursuant to Article 287 of UNCLOS III and Article 1 of the Convention's Annex VII.

Guyana / Suriname

This case commenced in February 2004 when Guyana gave written notification and a statement of claim to Suriname, submitting a dispute concerning the delimitation of its maritime boundary with Suriname. The arbitral tribunal will be constituted under Annex VII of UNCLOS III.

Barbados / Trinidad

The PCA is acting as Registry in an arbitration between Barbados and the Republic of Trinidad and Tobago relating to the delimitation of the exclusive economic zone and continental shelf between the two parties. The arbitration was submitted under UNCLOS III.

Telekom Malaysia Berhad / Government of Ghana

The PCA is serving as registry for an arbitration under the UNCITRAL Arbitration Rules concerning an investment dispute between Telekom Malaysia Berhad, a Malaysian company, and the Government of the Republic of Ghana.

Belgium / Netherlands

The Kingdom of Belgium and the Kingdom of the Netherlands have submitted a dispute to an arbitral tribunal established under the auspices of the PCA. The dispute concerns the so-called 'Iron Rhine Railway' case.

MOX Plant case

The Permanent Court is serving as Registry in arbitration proceedings between Ireland and the United Kingdom. Those proceedings were initiated pursuant to Annex VII of UNCLOS III.

Saluka Investments B.V. v Czech Republic

The International Bureau of the PCA is serving as Registry in an arbitration that is being conducted under the UNCITRAL Arbitration Rules.

Eritrea-Ethiopia Boundary Commission

The International Bureau serves as Registry for a Commission established pursuant to an Agreement made in December 2000 between the Government of the State of Eritrea and the Government of the Federal Democratic Republic of Ethiopia. The Commission has a mandate *"to delimit and demarcate the colonial treaty border based on pertinent colonial treaties (1900, 1902 and 1908) and applicable international law"*.

Eritrea-Ethiopia Claims Commission

This Commission was established and operates pursuant to Article 5 of the Agreement signed in Algiers on 12 December 2000 between Eritrea and Ethiopia. The Commission is directed to: *"decide through binding arbitration all claims for loss, damage or injury by one Government against the other, and by nationals (including both natural and juridical persons) of one party against the Government of the other party or entities owned or controlled by the other party that are (a) related to the conflict that was the subject of the Framework Agreement, the Modalities for its Implementation and the Cessation of Hostilities Agreement, and (b) result from violations of international humanitarian law, including the 1949 Geneva Conventions, or other violations of international law."*

Recent cases

Decisions of the PCA are referred to in various parts of the Manual. Some recent arbitrations include the following.

Netherlands / France

The International Bureau served as Registry for an arbitration relating to the Convention of 3 December 1976 on the Protection of the Rhine against Pollution by Chlorides and the Additional Protocol of 25 September 1991. A Final Award was rendered on 12 March 2004.

Bank for International Settlements

The Tribunal concerning the Bank for International Settlements rendered a Final Award in September 2003. That Award determined the compensation to be paid for shares that had been withdrawn by the Bank.

Ireland v United Kingdom

The International Bureau served as Registry in these arbitration proceedings initiated pursuant to the 1992 Convention for the Protection of the Marine Environment of the North-East Atlantic (OSPAR Convention). A week of hearings began in October 2002 at the Peace Palace. By agreement of the parties, the hearings were open to the public, and the written pleadings are available on the PCA website.[52] The Tribunal issued its final award on 2 July 2003.

Larsen / Hawaiian Kingdom

By the terms of an agreement to arbitrate made between the parties, it was agreed that a dispute alleged in the Complaint for Injunctive Relief filed on 4 August 1999 be referred to final and binding arbitration in accordance with the PCA's *Optional Rules for Arbitrating Disputes between Two Parties of which Only One Is a State*. One allegation by Lance Paul Larsen, a Hawaiian subject, was that the Government of the Hawaiian Kingdom was in continual violation of its 1849 Treaty of Friendship, Commerce and Navigation with the United States of America, and in violation of the principles of international law laid down in the 1969 Vienna Convention on the Law of Treaties. Mr Larsen relied on the alleged unlawful imposition of American municipal laws over the claimant's person within the territorial jurisdiction of the Hawaiian Kingdom.

9) Conclusions

The PCA is the world's oldest inter-governmental arbitration institution. Although the Court was conceived for the purpose of dealing with disputes between States, its mandate is flexible and allows it to respond to the ever-changing dispute resolution needs of the international community.

For example, in relation to disputes between a State and a non-State party, the PCA's *Optional Rules for Arbitrating Disputes Between Two Parties of Which Only One Is a State* can provide a means for resolving a wide variety of cases involving international trade, investment and intellectual property.

The range of dispute resolution processes provided by the PCA makes the Court suitable for the resolution of disputes by way of both arbitration and conciliation.

52 www.pca-cpa.org.

13 The International Tribunal for the Law of the Sea and Dispute Settlement under UNCLOS III

1) Introduction

The International Tribunal for the Law of the Sea (ITLOS) is the third international dispute settlement body to be considered in this part of the Manual. It was created by the 1982 United Nations Convention on the Law of the Sea (UNCLOS III). The Convention provides for dispute resolution by way of both arbitration and conciliation, permits disputes to be decided *ex aequo et bono* (provided the parties agree) and makes provisions for the establishment of a fact-finding Tribunal.

Part XV of UNCLOS III contains the provisions relating to the settlement of disputes. Article 284 in Part XV contains provisions dealing with Conciliation (the detail is set out in Annex V). Article 287 contains the choice of four means for the settlement of disputes relating to the interpretation and application of the Convention: through the Tribunal itself (the ITLOS Statute is set out in Annex VI); through the International Court of Justice (ICJ); through Arbitration (the relevant provisions are contained in Annex VII); or through Special Arbitration (the provisions are set out in Annex VIII).

This chapter will look at the Law of the Sea Convention, the Statute of ITLOS, cases decided by the Tribunal, the Conciliation provisions, the Arbitration provisions and the Special Arbitration provisions.

2) Historical Overview

UNCLOS III came into force on 16 November 1994. In October 1996, the Tribunal began to function at its seat in Hamburg.

The other supranational dispute resolution bodies considered in the Manual – the ICJ, the Permanent Court of Arbitration (PCA) and the International Centre for Settlement of Investment Disputes (ICSID) – were all made the primary court or tribunal by the instruments that created them: the United Nations Charter, the 1899 Hague Peace Conference and the ICSID Convention.

UNCLOS III, on the other hand, gave jurisdiction to resolve disputes not only to ITLOS but also to other tribunals. In all, as noted above, there are four procedures for dispute resolution under the 1982 Convention. The UNCLOS dispute settlement procedures are complex. This is hardly surprising given the complexity of the subject matter: two-thirds of the Earth's surface is covered by water, and the Convention contains a universal legal regime dealing with, among other things, the territorial sea, exclusive economic zones, the continental shelf and delimitation.

3) The Dispute Resolution Provisions of Part XV of UNCLOS III

Parts of UNCLOS III have been considered earlier in the Manual. For example, Part II of the Convention deals with the territorial sea and contiguous zone; Part V with the exclusive economic zone; and Part VI with the continental shelf. The Part to be considered now is Part XV, which is concerned with dispute resolution.

Part XV is divided into three Sections: Section 1 (Articles 279-285) contains general provisions dealing with peaceful settlement by non-binding means such as negotiation and conciliation; Section 2 (Articles 286-296) deals with compulsory procedures entailing binding decisions; and Section 3 (Articles 297-299) deals with limitations and exceptions.

Section 1: General provisions

Section 1 sets out the requirement that disputes be settled by peaceful means (Articles 279-281). Article 282 deals with the situation where other agreements, such as bilateral agreements, apply:

> *"If the States Parties which are parties to a dispute concerning the interpretation or application of this Convention have agreed, through a general, regional or bilateral agreement or otherwise, that such dispute shall, at the request of any party to the dispute, be submitted to a procedure that entails a binding decision, that procedure shall apply in lieu of the procedures provided for in this Part, unless the parties to the dispute otherwise agree."*

Article 283 provides that the States Parties are under an obligation to exchange views regarding the settlement of the dispute by negotiation or other peaceful means. They can agree to submit their dispute to conciliation in accordance with the procedures under Annex V or another conciliation procedure (Article 284).

Article 285 deals with disputes under Part XI, which is concerned with the Seabed Disputes Chamber.

Section 2: Compulsory procedures

Article 286 deals with compulsory dispute settlement procedures. It states that where no settlement has been reached by recourse to the provisions contained in Section 1, the dispute is to be submitted to the court or tribunal having jurisdiction under Section 2. The provisions are important, and deal with the four settlement procedures referred to earlier. Article 287 (1) provides for a choice, by means of a written declaration, of one or more of the following means for the settlement of disputes:

> *"(a) the International Tribunal for the Law of the Sea established in accordance with Annex VI;*
>
> *(b) the International Court of Justice;*
>
> *(c) an arbitral tribunal constituted in accordance with Annex VII;*
>
> *(d) a special arbitral tribunal constituted in accordance with Annex VIII for one or more of the categories of disputes specified therein."*

Article 287 (3) provides that a State party that is a party to a dispute not covered by a declaration in force *"shall be deemed to have accepted arbitration in accordance with Annex VII"*.

If the parties have accepted the same dispute settlement procedure, the dispute may be submitted only to that procedure (unless the parties otherwise agree). However, Article 287 (5) states that if the parties to the dispute have not accepted the same procedure, the dispute *"may be submitted only to arbitration in accordance with Annex VII, unless the parties otherwise agree"*.

Declarations may be made when signing, ratifying or acceding to the Convention or at any time thereafter and are to be lodged with the UN Secretary-General.

Article 288 deals with the jurisdiction of the various courts or tribunals referred to in Article 287:

> *"1. A court or tribunal referred to in article 287 shall have jurisdiction over any dispute concerning the interpretation or application of this Convention which is submitted to it in accordance with this Part.*
>
> *2. A court or tribunal referred to in article 287 shall also have jurisdiction over any dispute concerning the interpretation or application of an international agreement related to the purposes of this Convention, which is submitted to it in accordance with the agreement.*
>
> *3. The Seabed Disputes Chamber of the International Tribunal for the Law of the Sea established in accordance with Annex VI, and any other chamber or arbitral tribunal referred to in Part XI, section 5, shall have jurisdiction in any matter which is submitted to it in accordance therewith.*
>
> *4. In the event of a dispute as to whether a court or tribunal has jurisdiction, the matter shall be settled by decision of that court or tribunal."*

The court or tribunal exercising jurisdiction in a dispute involving scientific or technical matters may select no fewer than two scientific or technical experts to sit with the court or tribunal. The experts do not have the right to vote (Article 289).

Article 290 deals with provisional measures. Article 290 (1) provides that the relevant court or tribunal has the power to order provisional measures that *"it considers appropriate under the circumstances to preserve the respective rights of the parties to the dispute or to prevent serious harm to the marine environment, pending the final decision"*.

Under Article 290 (5), ITLOS is competent to prescribe provisional measures on a mandatory basis pending the constitution of an arbitral tribunal. When arbitral proceedings are instituted (e.g., in the event that the parties did not make a declaration under Article 287 of the Convention), the constitution of the arbitral tribunal may take some months before it becomes effective. In the meantime, since the rights of the parties need to be preserved, it may be necessary to prevent serious harm being caused to the environment. The Tribunal is therefore competent to prescribe provisional measures *"within two weeks from the date of the request for provisional measures"*. To date, four cases have been dealt with by the Tribunal under this paragraph.

Access to the dispute settlement procedures is only open to States Parties. Entities other than States Parties may use the procedures only as specifically provided for in the Convention (Article 291).

The prompt release of vessels and crews is dealt with in Article 292. The *M/V "Saiga" Case* and various other cases referred to later in this chapter were concerned with this Article.

Article 293 specifies that the court or tribunal having jurisdiction under the compulsory procedures of Section 2 is to apply *"this Convention and other rules of international law not incompatible with this Convention"* (Article 293 (1)). However, it may decide a case *ex aequo et bono*, if the parties agree (Article 293 (2)).

The relevant court or tribunal has power under Article 294 to decide whether a claim made under Article 297 (concerning the exercise by a coastal state of its sovereign rights or jurisdiction) constitutes an abuse of legal process.

Article 295 deals with the exhaustion of local remedies: *"Any dispute between States Parties concerning the interpretation or application of this Convention may be submitted to the procedures provided for in this section only after local remedies have been exhausted where this is required by international law."*

A decision rendered by the court or tribunal having jurisdiction under Section 2 is final *"and shall be complied with by all the parties to the dispute"*.

Section 3: Limitations and exceptions

The final Section of Part XV sets out limitations on the applicability of Section 2. Article 297 provides that disputes relating to the exercise by a coastal State of its sovereign rights or jurisdiction are subject to the Section 2 procedures in the various cases that are listed: for example, when the coastal State has acted in contravention of the provisions of the Convention in relation to the freedoms and rights of navigation, overflight or the laying of pipelines.

Article 298 deals with optional exceptions to the applicability of Section 2. When signing, ratifying or acceding to the Convention, or at any time thereafter, a State may declare in writing that it does not accept any one or more of the procedures provided for in Section 2 in relation to the various categories of disputes set out in Article 298.

Notwithstanding the provisions of Articles 297 and 298, the parties may nevertheless be able to make use of the dispute review processes contained in Section 2. Article 299 (1) states that a dispute *"excluded under article 297 or excepted by a declaration made under article 298 from the dispute settlement procedures provided for in section 2 may be submitted to such procedures only by agreement of the parties to the dispute"*.

Article 299 (2) states that nothing in Section 2 impairs the right of the parties to the dispute *"to agree to some other procedure for the settlement of such dispute or to reach an amicable settlement"*.

4) The Statute of ITLOS – the Tribunal: Annex VI

It was seen earlier that Article 287 in Part XV stated that one of the four means of settling disputes under UNCLOS III was by way of the international Tribunal *"established in accordance with Annex VI"*.

Annex VI of the Convention contains the Statute of the ITLOS, commencing with the provision creating the Tribunal in Article 1:

> *"1. The International Tribunal for the Law of the Sea is constituted and shall function in accordance with the provisions of this Convention and this Statute.*
>
> *"2. The seat of the Tribunal shall be in the Free and Hanseatic City of Hamburg in the Federal Republic of Germany...."*

Article 1 is followed by five sections.

Section 1: Organisation of the Tribunal

Section 1 (Articles 2-19) deals with the organisation and composition of the Tribunal, which comprises 21 members of recognised competence in the law of the sea. The representation of the principal legal systems of the world and equitable geographical distribution is assured – Article 3 provides that there shall be no fewer than three members from each geographical group as established by the UN General Assembly. At present, the Tribunal is composed of five judges from Africa, five from Asia, four from Latin America and the Caribbean, four from Western Europe and others, and three from Eastern Europe. There is to be a President, Vice-President and Registrar. Eleven members constitute a quorum.

The establishment of a Seabed Disputes Chamber is provided for in Article 14, and the Tribunal may form special chambers to deal with particular categories of disputes (Article 15). The Tribunal is to frame rules, in particular rules of procedure.

Section 2: Competence / jurisdiction of the Tribunal and applicable law

Section 2 (Articles 20-22) deals with the competence of the Tribunal. The Tribunal is open to States Parties, and also to entities other than States Parties *"in any case expressly provided for in Part XI or in any case submitted pursuant to any other agreement conferring jurisdiction on the Tribunal which is accepted by all the parties to that case"*. Further, the parties to a treaty or convention already in force and that concerns the subject matter covered by the Convention may agree that *"any disputes concerning the interpretation or application of such treaty or convention may, in accordance with such agreement, be submitted to the Tribunal"* (Article 22).

Article 23 deals with the applicable law. The Tribunal is to decide all disputes and applications in accordance with Article 293, which provides that the relevant court or tribunal is to apply the Convention and other rules of international law not incompatible with the Convention and may also, if the parties agree, decide a case *ex aequo et bono*.

Section 3: Procedure of the Tribunal

Section 3 (Articles 24-34) of Annex VI is concerned with procedure. Article 24 contains provisions dealing with the institution of proceedings before the Tribunal:

"1. Disputes are submitted to the Tribunal, as the case may be, either by notification of a special agreement or by written application, addressed to the Registrar. In either case, the subject of the dispute and the parties shall be indicated.

2. The Registrar shall forthwith notify the special agreement or the application to all concerned.

3. The Registrar shall also notify all States Parties."

Article 25 provides that the Tribunal (and its Seabed Disputes Chamber) has power to prescribe provisional measures in accordance with Article 290 of the Convention. That Article in Part XV states that the relevant court or tribunal has jurisdiction to prescribe provisional measures aimed at preserving the respective rights of the parties and preventing serious harm to the maritime environment, pending a final decision. Hearings shall be in public, unless the Tribunal decides otherwise or the parties demand that the public should not be admitted (Article 26).

The Tribunal makes orders for the conduct of the case, and decides *"the form and time in which each party must conclude its arguments, and make all arrangements connected with the taking of evidence"*.

Article 28 makes provision for proceedings in default in the event that one of the parties does not appear or fails to defend its case: *"the other party may request the Tribunal to continue the proceedings and make its decision. Absence of a party or failure of a party to defend its case shall not constitute a bar to the proceedings. Before making its decision, the Tribunal must satisfy itself not only that it has jurisdiction over the dispute, but also that the claim is well founded in fact and law."*

Decisions are by a majority of the members of the Tribunal. In the event of an equal vote, the President (or the member acting in this place) has the casting vote (Article 29). The judgement of the Tribunal is to state reasons and contain the names of the members who have taken part in the decision. If the judgement is not unanimous, any member is entitled to deliver a separate opinion (Article 30).

Articles 31 and 32 make provisions for intervention. A State Party that considers that it has an interest *"of a legal nature which may be affected by the decision in any dispute"* may submit a request to the Tribunal to be permitted to intervene. If the Tribunal grants such a request, its decision in respect of the dispute is binding on the intervening State Party. Furthermore, whenever the interpretation or application of the Convention is in question, the Registrar is to notify all States Parties, who are entitled to intervene. Similarly, where the interpretation or application of an international agreement is in question (Article 21 and 22) the parties to the agreement may intervene. Intervening parties are bound by the judgement of the Tribunal.

The decision of the Tribunal is final and binding (although the Tribunal can construe the meaning and scope of its decision) (Article 33).

Article 34 deals with costs. Unless otherwise decided, each party bears its own costs.

Section 4: Seabed Disputes Chamber

Section 4 (Articles 35-40) deals with the Seabed Disputes Chamber. Article 35 sets out provisions relating to the composition of the Chamber: 11 members, selected by a majority of the elected members of the Tribunal. The Chamber elects a President, and a quorum comprises seven members. The Chamber may create an ad hoc chamber for dealing with specific disputes (Article 36).

Articles 37 and 38 deal with access to the Chamber and with applicable law. The Chamber is open to the States Parties, the International Seabed Authority and the other entities referred to in Section 5 of Part XI. It is to apply the rules, regulations and procedures of the Authority and the terms of contracts concerning activities in the Area in matters relating to those contracts. Additionally, the Chamber is to apply the provisions of Article 293, namely the Convention and other rules of international law not incompatible with the Convention. The Chamber may also decide the case *ex aequo et bono*, if the parties agree.

Decisions of the Chamber are enforceable in the territories of the States Parties *"in the same manner as judgments or orders of the highest court of the State Party in whose territory the enforcement is sought"* (Article 39).

Other sections of Annex VI that are not incompatible with Section 4 apply to the Chamber.

Section 5

Section 5 of the Statute deals with amendments to Annex VI. The Tribunal has framed detailed Rules of Procedure in accordance with Article 16 of Annex VI. The Rules concern the organisation of the Tribunal and the procedure to be followed in proceedings before ITLOS and the Seabed Disputes Chamber. In addition, to assist parties appearing in proceedings before it, the Tribunal has also established Guidelines concerning the preparation and presentation of cases. The text of the Rules of the Tribunal and the Guidelines can be found on the ITLOS website.[53]

5) The ITLOS Caseload and Some Decisions

When he addressed the UN General Assembly in 2004 (see Box 8), the President of ITLOS, Dolliver Nelson, noted that the Tribunal had to that point dealt with 12 cases involving 17 State parties. Subsequently, Case No. 13, the *Juno Trader (Saint Vincent and the Grenadines v Guinea-Bissau), Prompt Release,* was submitted to the Tribunal on 18 November 2004 and judgment was delivered on 18 December 2004.

53 www.itlos.org.

Box 8: Comments by the President of ITLOS on the Tribunal

Addressing the 59th session of the UN General Assembly in November 2004, the President of ITLOS, Dolliver Nelson, looked back over the eight-year existence of the Tribunal and noted that 17 State parties had been involved in the 12 cases dealt with by the Tribunal at that time. In those cases, six judgements and 26 orders had been delivered: *"This bears favourable comparison with the record of other international courts and tribunals in the initial stages of their existence. It is gratifying to note that 17 States Parties from different regions of the world have been engaged in proceedings before the Tribunal. It should also be remarked, and this is generally agreed, that the Tribunal has rendered its decisions within remarkably short periods."*

The President stated that, although the Tribunal had often been used successfully to assist States to settle their maritime disputes without resorting to litigation, it had not been put to full use by prospective litigants – and had therefore been unable to develop its potential as the specialised judicial organ under the Convention for the settlement of maritime disputes.

In this context, President Nelson stressed the ready availability of the Tribunal to States Parties, and he drew the attention of the General Assembly to the possibility of submitting disputes to special chambers of the Tribunal as a viable alternative to arbitration. He said that the Tribunal *"has already made some contribution to the development of international law with regard to issues such as the nationality of claims, reparation, use of force in law enforcement activities, hot pursuit and the question of the genuine link between the vessel and the flag State. It can be fairly said that the Tribunal has also developed a coherent jurisprudence in prompt release proceedings under article 292 of the Convention."*

The cases are as follows:

- *The M/V "Saiga" Case (Saint Vincent and the Grenadines v Guinea), Prompt Release;*
- *The M/V "Saiga" (No. 2) Case (Saint Vincent and the Grenadines v Guinea), Merits;*
- *Southern Bluefin Tuna Cases (New Zealand v Japan; Australia v Japan), Provisional Measures;*[54]
- *The "Camouco" Case (Panama v France), Prompt Release;*
- *The "Monte Confurco" Case (Seychelles v France), Prompt Release;*
- *Case concerning the Conservation and Sustainable Exploitation of Swordfish Stocks in the South-Eastern Pacific Ocean (Chile / European Community);*
- *The "Grand Prince" Case (Belize v France), Prompt Release;*
- *The "Chaisiri Reefer 2" Case (Panama v Yemen), Prompt Release;*
- *The MOX Plant Case (Ireland v United Kingdom), Provisional Measures;*

54 Cases nos. 3 and 4.

- *The "Volga" Case (Russian Federation v Australia), Prompt Release;*
- *Case concerning Land Reclamation by Singapore in and around the Straits of Johor (Malaysia v Singapore), Provisional Measures;*
- *The "Juno Trader" Case (Saint Vincent and the Grenadines v Guinea-Bissau), Prompt Release.*

A selection of ITLOS cases will now be considered.

i) The M/V "Saiga" Case

The International Tribunal received its first case – the *M/V "Saiga" Case (Saint Vincent and the Grenadines v Guinea), Prompt Release* – in November 1997. The case related to an application for the prompt release of a vessel and its crew.

The application on behalf of Saint Vincent and the Grenadines instituted proceedings against the Government of Guinea with regard to the alleged arrest of the M/V Saiga off the coast of West Africa. It requested the Tribunal to order the prompt release of the vessel and its cargo and crew detained in Conakry, Guinea. The vessel was allegedly *"attacked by representatives of the Guinean Government who shot at the ship and crew and injured four of them before taking control of the vessel. The vessel was brought into Conakry, Guinea at around 21:00 on 28 October 1997. Two seriously injured crew have since been allowed to leave. The vessel and remaining crew continue to be held hostage at Conakry."*

The application was based on Article 292 of UNCLOS III, which provides that:

"- *where the authorities of a government of a State that is a party to the Convention have detained a vessel flying the flag of another State which is also party to the Convention, and*

- *it is alleged that the detaining State has not complied with the requirements of the Convention for the prompt release of the vessel or its crew upon the posting of a reasonable bond or other financial security, then*
- *the question of release from detention may be submitted to the Tribunal if the parties have not agreed (within 10 days from the time of detention) to submit the case to another court or tribunal."*

The application of Saint Vincent and the Grenadines stated that:

> *"Guinea has not to date sought any bond or other financial security in respect of the detention of the 'Saiga', nor has it advised any interested party of the reasons for its action, nor has it allowed their representatives access to the crew remaining on board."*

The Registry transmitted a copy of the application with all its attachments to the Government of Guinea. Guinea had until 24 hours before the date of the opening of the hearing to provide its response to the application.

There were 21 members of the Tribunal that heard and determined the case. The hearing opened on 21 November 1997 and, at the request of Guinea, was postponed until

27 November 1997. The Tribunal concluded its hearing on 28 November 1997 and six days later delivered its judgement. It:

> *"... ordered the prompt release of the oil tanker M/V 'Saiga' and its crew from detention in Conakry, Guinea. In addition to the cargo of gas oil, Saint Vincent and the Grenadines is to deposit 400,000 United States Dollars as a security for the release.*
>
> *"... Guinea claimed that the M/V 'Saiga' was engaged in smuggling activities off its coast when arrested. The arrest, at a point outside Guinean waters, allegedly following a chase, was claimed to be in the exercise of the right of hot pursuit. Guinea also maintained that the Tribunal had no jurisdiction in the matter and that the claim was inadmissible. Saint Vincent and the Grenadines accused Guinea of piracy.*
>
> *"The arrest took place on 28 October 1997.*
>
> *"In view of the urgency attached to these proceedings and the humanitarian considerations for the crew, the Tribunal was obliged by the United Nations Convention on the Law of the Sea, to which both Countries are parties, and the Rules of the Tribunal to act rapidly.*
>
> *Within ten days of the arrest there had been no agreement between the parties to go before any other court. The application for release was then filed with the Tribunal by Saint Vincent and the Grenadines on 13 November.*
>
> *Within ten days of the filing of the application, the Judges convened to hear the case.*
>
> *Within ten days of the Tribunal convening, written statements were filed by the parties and two days of oral proceedings were held.*
>
> *Within ten days of the end of the oral proceedings the Judgment was delivered.*
>
> *"The whole procedure before the Tribunal has taken exactly three weeks.*
>
> *"The Judges of the Tribunal heard oral argument on 27 and 28 November. It also heard oral testimony from two witnesses called by Saint Vincent and the Grenadines: Mr. Sergiy Klyuyev, Second Officer of the 'Saiga', and Mr. Mark Vervaet, representative in Senegal of the charterers of the 'Saiga'. Mr. Klyuyev told the Tribunal under oath how he received fragments of a bullet in his arm when the Guinean authorities arrested the ship.*
>
> *"The Judges heard evidence on the activities and the route of the M/V 'Saiga', which was bunkering fishing boats in the coastal waters of Guinea, supplying them with gas oil. They were also told that the captain of the vessel was still kept imprisoned in Guinea. Extracts from the logbook of the M/V 'Saiga' were also submitted to the Tribunal.*
>
> *"Agents and Counsel of both Saint Vincent and the Grenadines and Guinea participated at the hearings.*
>
> *"The Judges, having completed their deliberations on the case, set up a drafting committee in accordance with the Internal Judicial Practice of the Tribunal. The Committee is composed of five Judges holding the majority opinion. The draft Judgment produced by this Committee went through two readings after which a final vote was taken to adopt the Judgment. The Judgement was delivered, six days after the end of the oral proceedings.*

> *"The Judgment was unanimous as to the Tribunal having jurisdiction, but divided 12 to 9 on the question of the release. The dissenting Judges filed two collective dissenting opinions and two dissenting opinions by individual Judges."*[55]

The decision of the Tribunal dealing with the merits of the *M/V "Saiga" Case* – in an award released in July 1999 – is considered later.

The Tribunal has dealt with seven other applications for the prompt release of a vessel and its crew.

ii) The Southern Bluefin Tuna Cases

In 1999 the role of the Tribunal in the *Southern Bluefin Tuna Cases (New Zealand v Japan; Australia v Japan), Provisional Measures* was restricted to the prescription of provisional measures. Following that, the dispute was dealt with by an arbitral tribunal constituted under the provisions of Annex VII of the 1982 Convention.

The Registry reported that:

> *"Australia and New Zealand filed with the Registrar of the Tribunal requests for the prescription of provisional measures (interim injunction) in a case against Japan. The dispute between Australia and New Zealand on one side and Japan on the other concerned the conservation of the population of Southern Bluefin Tuna. The species is, according to the applicants, significantly overfished and is below commonly accepted thresholds for biologically safe parental biomass.*
>
> *"In the absence of agreement between the parties for the settlement of the merits (substance) of the dispute between them, the Governments of Australia and New Zealand decided to submit their dispute with Japan to an arbitration procedure under Annex VII of the United Nations Convention on the Law of the Sea. Pending the constitution of such an arbitral tribunal, the Governments of Australia and New Zealand have requested the International Tribunal for the Law of the Sea to prescribe provisional measures, pursuant to paragraph 5 of Article 290 of the Convention."*[56]

iii) The Mox Plant Case

The *Mox Plant Case (Ireland v United Kingdom), Provisional Measures* in 2001 again involved a dispute in which the parties came before the Tribunal in relation to a request for provisional measures, with the merits of the dispute later being heard and determined by an arbitral tribunal constituted under Annex VII to the Convention.

The *MOX Plant Case* concerned objections by Ireland to the United Kingdom's construction of a mixed oxide (MOX) plant. These included the possibility that the plant or shipments of radioactive material associated with the plant might release radioactive material into the Irish Sea.

---

55 See *M/V "SAIGA" (Saint Vincent and the Grenadines v Guinea), Prompt release, Judgment, ITLOS Reports 1997*, p 16. The judgment and dissenting opinions can also be found on the ITLOS website at www.itlos.org.

56 See *Southern Bluefin Tuna (New Zealand v Japan; Australia v Japan), Provisional Measures, Order of 27 August 1999, ITLOS Reports 1999*, p 280. The order concerning the Southern Bluefin Tuna Cases can also be found on the ITLOS website.

In the Notification and Statement of Claim of 25 October 2001, Ireland requested the Annex VII arbitral tribunal to adjudge and declare:

"1) That the United Kingdom has breached its obligations under Articles 192 and 193 and/or Article 194 and/or Article 207 and/or Articles 211 and 213 of UNCLOS in relation to the authorisation of the MOX plant, including by failing to take the necessary measures to prevent, reduce and control pollution of the marine environment of the Irish Sea from (1) intended discharges of radioactive materials and/or wastes from the MOX plant, and/or (2) accidental releases of radioactive materials and/or wastes from the MOX plant and/or international movements associated [with] the MOX plant, and/or (3) releases of radioactive materials and/or wastes from the MOX plant and/or international movements associated the MOX plant ....

"2) That the United Kingdom has breached its obligations under Articles 192 and 193 and/or Article 194 and/or Article 207 and/or Articles 211 and 213 of UNCLOS in relation to the authorisation of the MOX plant by failing (1) properly or at all to assess the risk of terrorist attack on the MOX plant and international movements of radioactive material associated with the plant, and/or (2) properly or at all to prepare a comprehensive response strategy or plan to prevent, contain and respond to terrorist attack on the MOX plant and international movements of radioactive waste associated with the plant;

"3) That the United Kingdom has breached its obligations under Articles 123 and 197 of UNCLOS in relation to the authorisation of the MOX plant, and has failed to cooperate with Ireland in the protection of the marine environment of the Irish Sea inter alia by refusing to share information with Ireland and/or refusing to carry out a proper environmental assessment of the impacts on the marine environment of the MOX plant and associated activities and/or proceeding to authorise the operation of the MOX plant whilst proceedings relating to the settlement of a dispute on access to information were still pending...."

On 3 December 2001 the International Tribunal prescribed a provisional measure. The Tribunal:

"1. Unanimously,

Prescribes, pending a decision by the Annex VII arbitral tribunal, the following provisional measure under article 290, paragraph 5, of the Convention:

Ireland and the United Kingdom shall cooperate and shall, for this purpose, enter into consultations forthwith in order to:

(a) exchange further information with regard to possible consequences for the Irish Sea arising out of the commissioning of the MOX plant;

(b) monitor risks or the effects of the operation of the MOX plant for the Irish Sea;

(c) devise, as appropriate, measures to prevent pollution of the marine environment which might result from the operation of the MOX plant.

"2. Unanimously,

Decides that Ireland and the United Kingdom shall each submit the initial report referred to in article 95, paragraph 1, of the Rules not later than 17 December 2001, and authorizes the President of the Tribunal to request such further reports and information as he may consider appropriate after that date.

> *"3. Unanimously,*
>
> *Decides that each party shall bear its own costs."*[57]

iv) The M/V "Saiga" (No 2) Case: decision on the merits

The decision of the Tribunal in the *M/V "Saiga" Case* prompt release case was considered earlier. Now the decision of the Tribunal in the later case on the merits will be considered.

On 1 July 1999, by eighteen votes to two, ITLOS declared that Guinea had violated the rights of Saint Vincent and the Grenadines in arresting the M/V Saiga and awarded US$2,123,357 with interest as compensation. This included compensation for the detention of the Captain and the crew, for the gunshot injuries to the Second Officer and another, for the confiscated cargo and for the damage to the vessel. The Tribunal also decided that Guinea had used excessive force when arresting the vessel.

The Tribunal rejected the claim by Saint Vincent and the Grenadines that Guinea violated its rights by naming it as civilly responsible in the schedule of summons against the Master of the Saiga. The Tribunal also rejected Saint Vincent's claim that Guinea violated its rights by failing to promptly release the Saiga and its crew. In previous proceedings, the Tribunal ordered its release on the deposit of a security.

The Tribunal in its award first set out the factual background to the case:

> *"The Saiga is an oil tanker. At the time of its arrest on 28 October 1997, it was owned by Tabona Shipping Company Ltd. of Nicosia, Cyprus, and managed by Seascot Shipmanagement Ltd. of Glasgow, Scotland. The ship was chartered to Lemania Shipping Group Ltd. of Geneva, Switzerland. The Saiga was provisionally registered in Saint Vincent and the Grenadines on 12 March 1997. The Master and crew of the ship were all of Ukrainian nationality. There were also three Senegalese nationals who were employed as painters. The Saiga was engaged in selling gas oil as bunker and occasionally water to fishing and other vessels off the coast of West Africa. The owner of the cargo of gas oil on board was Addax BV of Geneva, Switzerland.*
>
> *"Under the command of Captain Orlov, the Saiga left Dakar, Senegal, on 24 October 1997 fully laden with approximately 5,400 metric tons of gas oil. On 27 October 1997, between 0400 and 1400 hours and at a point 10°25'03"N and 15°42'06"W, the Saiga supplied gas oil to three fishing vessels, the Giuseppe Primo and the Kriti, both flying the flag of Senegal, and the Eleni S, flying the flag of Greece. This point was approximately 22 nautical miles from Guinea's island of Alcatraz. All three fishing vessels were licensed by Guinea to fish in its exclusive economic zone. The Saiga then sailed in a southerly direction to supply gas oil to other fishing vessels at a pre-arranged place. Upon instructions from the owner of the cargo in Geneva, it later changed course and sailed towards another location beyond the southern border of the exclusive economic zone of Guinea.*
>
> *"At 0800 hours on 28 October 1997, the Saiga, according to its log book, was at a point 09°00'01"N and 14°58'58"W. It had been drifting since 0420 hours while*

57 See *Mox Plant, (Ireland v United Kingdom), Provisional Measures, Order of 3 December 2001, ITLOS. Reports 2001*, p 89. The order may also be found on the ITLOS website.

awaiting the arrival of fishing vessels to which it was to supply gas oil. This point was south of the southern limit of the exclusive economic zone of Guinea. At about 0900 hours the Saiga was attacked by a Guinean patrol boat (P35). Officers from that boat and another Guinean patrol boat (P328) subsequently boarded the ship and arrested it. On the same day, the ship and its crew were brought to Conakry, Guinea, where its Master was detained. The travel documents of the members of the crew were taken from them by the authorities of Guinea and armed guards were placed on board the ship. On 1 November 1997, two injured persons from the Saiga, Mr. Sergey Klyuyev and Mr. Djibril Niasse, were permitted to leave Conakry for Dakar for medical treatment. Between 10 and 12 November 1997, the cargo of gas oil on board the ship, amounting to 4,941.322 metric tons, was discharged on the orders of the Guinean authorities. Seven members of the crew and two painters left Conakry on 17 November 1997, one crew member left on 14 December 1997 and six on 12 January 1998. The Master and six crew members remained in Conakry until the ship was released on 28 February 1998.

"An account of the circumstances of the arrest of the Saiga was drawn up by Guinean Customs authorities in a 'Procès-Verbal' bearing the designation 'PV29'... PV29 contains a statement of the Master obtained by interrogation by the Guinean authorities. A document, 'Conclusions présentées au nom de l'Administration des Douanes par le Chef de la Brigade Mobile Nationale des Douanes' (Conclusions presented in the name of the Customs administration by the Head of the National Mobile Customs Brigade), issued on 14 November 1997 under the signature of the Chief of the National Mobile Customs Brigade, set out the basis of the action against the Master. The criminal charges against the Master were specified in a schedule of summons (cédule de citation), issued on 10 December 1997 under the authority of the Public Prosecutor (Procureur de la République), which additionally named the State of Saint Vincent and the Grenadines as civilly responsible to be summoned (civilement responsable à citer). Criminal proceedings were subsequently instituted by the Guinean authorities against the Master before the Tribunal of First Instance (tribunal de première instance) in Conakry.

"On 13 November 1997, Saint Vincent and the Grenadines submitted to this Tribunal a Request for the prompt release of the Saiga and its crew under article 292 of the Convention. On 4 December 1997, the Tribunal delivered Judgment on the Request. The Judgment ordered that Guinea promptly release the Saiga and its crew upon the posting of a reasonable bond or security by Saint Vincent and the Grenadines. The security consisted of the gas oil discharged from the Saiga by the authorities of Guinea plus an amount of US$400,000 to be posted in the form of a letter of credit or bank guarantee or, if agreed by the parties, in any other form.

"On 17 December 1997, judgment was rendered by the Tribunal of First Instance in Conakry against the Master."

Various articles of Codes and Laws had been cited in support of the charge brought against the Master of the vessel, namely that he had *"imported, without declaring it, merchandise that is taxable on entering national Guinean territory, in this case diesel oil, and that he refused to comply with injunctions by Agents of the Guinean Navy, thus committing the crimes of contraband, fraud and tax evasion"*. The International Tribunal continued:

"The Tribunal of First Instance in Conakry found the Master guilty as charged and imposed on him a fine of 15,354,024,040 Guinean francs. It also ordered the confiscation of the vessel and its cargo as a guarantee for payment of the penalty.

"The Master appealed to the Court of Appeal (cour d'appel) in Conakry against his conviction by the Tribunal of First Instance. On 3 February 1998, judgment was rendered by the Court of Appeal. The Court of Appeal found the Master guilty of the offence of 'illegal import, buying and selling of fuel in the Republic of Guinea' which it stated was punishable under Law L/94/007. The Court of Appeal imposed a suspended sentence of six months imprisonment on the Master, a fine of 15,354,040,000 Guinean francs and ordered that all fees and expenses be at his expense. It also ordered the confiscation of the cargo and the seizure of the vessel as a guarantee for payment of the fine.

"On 11 March 1998, the Tribunal delivered the Order prescribing provisional measures, referred to in paragraph 8. Prior to the issue of its Order, the Tribunal was informed, by a letter dated 4 March 1998 sent on behalf of the Agent of Saint Vincent and the Grenadines, that the Saiga had been released from detention and had arrived safely in Dakar, Senegal. According to the Deed of Release signed by the Guinean authorities and the Master, the release was in execution of the Judgment of the Tribunal of 4 December 1997."

The Tribunal then went on to consider jurisdiction, admissibility, exhaustion of local remedies, nationality of claims, the arrest of the " Saiga", hot pursuit and the use of force.

In respect of the use of force, the Tribunal noted that:

"... Saint Vincent and the Grenadines claims that Guinea used excessive and unreasonable force in stopping and arresting the Saiga. It notes that the Saiga was an unarmed tanker almost fully laden with gas oil, with a maximum speed of 10 knots. It also notes that the authorities of Guinea fired at the ship with live ammunition, using solid shots from large-calibre automatic guns.

"Guinea denies that the force used in boarding, stopping and arresting the Saiga was either excessive or unreasonable. It contends that the arresting officers had no alternative but to use gunfire because the Saiga refused to stop after repeated radio messages to it to stop and in spite of visual and auditory signals from the patrol boat P35. Guinea maintains that gunfire was used as a last resort, and denies that large-calibre ammunition was used. Guinea places the responsibility for any damage resulting from the use of force on the Master and crew of the ship."

The Tribunal them went on to say that, in considering the use of force by Guinea in the arrest of the " Saiga":

"... the Tribunal must take into account the circumstances of the arrest in the context of the applicable rules of international law. Although the Convention does not contain express provisions on the use of force in the arrest of ships, international law, which is applicable by virtue of article 293 of the Convention, requires that the use of force must be avoided as far as possible and, where force is unavoidable, it must not go beyond what is reasonable and necessary in the circumstances. Considerations of humanity must apply in the law of the sea, as they do in other areas of international law.

"These principles have been followed over the years in law enforcement operations at sea. The normal practice used to stop a ship at sea is first to give an auditory or visual signal to stop, using internationally recognized signals. Where this does not succeed, a variety of actions may be taken, including the firing of shots across the bows of the ship. It is only after the appropriate actions fail that the pursuing vessel may, as a last resort, use force. Even then, appropriate warning must be issued to the ship and all efforts should be made to ensure that life is not endangered (S.S. "I'm Alone" case (Canada / United States, 1935), U.N.R.I.A.A., Vol. III, p. 1609; The Red Crusader case (Commission of Enquiry, Denmark – United Kingdom, 1962), I.L.R., Vol. 35, p. 485). The basic principle concerning the use of force in the arrest of a ship at sea has been reaffirmed by the Agreement for the Implementation of the Provisions of the United Nations Convention on the Law of the Sea of 10 December 1982 Relating to the Conservation and Management of Straddling Fish Stocks and Highly Migratory Fish Stocks…."

The Tribunal noted that in the present case, the "Saiga"

"… was almost fully laden and was low in the water at the time it was approached by the patrol vessel. Its maximum speed was 10 knots. Therefore it could be boarded without much difficulty by the Guinean officers. At one stage in the proceedings Guinea sought to justify the use of gunfire with the claim that the Saiga had attempted to sink the patrol boat. During the hearing, the allegation was modified to the effect that the danger of sinking to the patrol boat was from the wake of the Saiga and not the result of a deliberate attempt by the ship. But whatever the circumstances, there is no excuse for the fact that the officers fired at the ship itself with live ammunition from a fast-moving patrol boat without issuing any of the signals and warnings required by international law and practice

" The Guinean officers also used excessive force on board the Saiga. Having boarded the ship without resistance, and although there is no evidence of the use or threat of force from the crew, they fired indiscriminately while on the deck and used gunfire to stop the engine of the ship. In using firearms in this way, the Guinean officers appeared to have attached little or no importance to the safety of the ship and the persons on board. In the process, considerable damage was done to the ship and to vital equipment in the engine and radio rooms. And, more seriously, the indiscriminate use of gunfire caused severe injuries to two of the persons on board.

"For these reasons, the Tribunal finds that Guinea used excessive force and endangered human life before and after boarding the Saiga, and thereby violated the rights of Saint Vincent and the Grenadines under international law."[58]

6) Conciliation: Annex V

It will be recalled that Article 284 in Section 1 of Part XV provides that disputes may be submitted to conciliation in accordance with the procedure under Annex V of UNCLOS III (or indeed in accordance with any other conciliation procedure). The conciliation process is non-binding.

58 A full report of the decision can be found on the ITLOS website.

Section 1 of Annex V is concerned with the voluntary dispute settlement procedures of Section 1 of Part XV. The process is commenced by one party serving written notice on the other party or parties. The UN Secretary-General is to maintain a list of conciliators. Every State Party shall be entitled to nominate four conciliators *"each of whom shall be a person enjoying the highest reputation for fairness, competence and integrity"*. Provisions are made for the constitution of the conciliation commission (Articles 1-3). Unless the parties have agreed otherwise, the commission determines its own procedure with the consent of the parties. It may invite any State Party to submit its views orally or in writing. Its decisions relating to procedural matters, the report and recommendations are to be by a majority vote (Article 4).

The provisions at the heart of the conciliation process are contained in Articles 5 and 6 and are succinct. Article 5 states that: *"The commission may draw the attention of the parties to any measures which might facilitate an amicable settlement of the dispute."* Article 6 states that the functions of the commission are to hear the parties, examine their claims and objections, and make proposals to them with a view to reaching an amicable settlement.

Article 7 contains provisions relating to the commission's report, which is non-binding:

"1. *The commission shall report within 12 months of its constitution. Its report shall record any agreements reached and, failing agreement, its conclusions on all questions of fact or law relevant to the matter in dispute and such recommendations as the commission may deem appropriate for an amicable settlement. The report shall be deposited with the Secretary-General of the United Nations and shall immediately be transmitted by him to the parties to the dispute.*

2. *The report of the commission, including its conclusions or recommendations, shall not be binding upon the parties."*

The conciliation proceedings are terminated when settlement has been reached, when the parties have accepted the recommendations of the report, when one party has rejected those recommendations, or when a period of three months has expired from the date of transmission of the report to the parties (Article 8).

Article 9 deals with fees and expenses of the commission, which must be borne by the parties. The parties may modify the provisions of the Annex (Article 10).

Section 2 contains provisions relating to compulsory submission to conciliation, pursuant to Section 3 of Part XV. Proceedings are instituted by written notice by one party to the other party or parties: *"Any party to the dispute, notified under paragraph 1, shall be obliged to submit to such proceedings"* (Article 11). Article 12 states that failure to reply to notification of institution of proceedings, or to submit to those proceedings, shall not constitute a bar to the conciliation process.

The conciliation commission shall decide a disagreement as to whether it has competence (Article 13). Article 14 applies Articles 2 to 10 of Section 1 of the Annex (namely the provisions as to procedure, amicable settlement, functions of the commission, etc).

7) Arbitration: Annex VII

Annex VII of UNCLOS III contains 13 Articles covering the institution of proceedings, the constitution and functions of the tribunal, procedure and the arbitral award.

Arbitration is instituted by one party giving written notification to the other party to the dispute. The notification is to be accompanied by a statement of claim and the grounds on which the claim is based (Article 1).

The UN Secretary-General is to draw up and maintain a list of arbitrators. Each State Party is entitled to nominate four arbitrators. An arbitrator shall be *"a person experienced in maritime affairs and enjoying the highest reputation for fairness, competence and integrity"* (Article 2). Unless the parties agree otherwise, the arbitral tribunal is to consist of five members.

Article 3 contains detailed provisions dealing with the constitution of the tribunal, which is to function in accordance with Annex VII and the other provisions of the Convention. The tribunal determines its own procedure *"assuring to each party a full opportunity to be heard and to present its case"* (Articles 4 and 5). The parties are to facilitate the work of the tribunal, in particular *"in accordance with their law and using all means at their disposal"*. The parties are to provide the tribunal with all relevant documents, facilities and information, and are to enable it (when necessary) to call witnesses or experts and to visit the localities to which the case relates (Article 6).

Article 7 provides that the expenses of the tribunal are to be borne equally by the parties, unless it decides otherwise because of the particular circumstances of the case.

Decisions of the tribunal are taken by a majority vote: *"The absence or abstention of less than half of the members shall not constitute a bar to the tribunal reaching a decision. In the event of an equality of votes, the President shall have a casting vote"* (Article 8).

Article 9 deals with default of appearance. If one of the parties does not appear before the tribunal or fails to defend its case, the other party may request the tribunal to *"continue the proceedings and to make its award. Absence of a party or failure of a party to defend its case shall not constitute a bar to the proceedings. Before making its award, the arbitral tribunal must satisfy itself not only that it has jurisdiction over the dispute but also that the claim is well founded in fact and law."*

Articles 10 to 12 deal with the award. This is to be confined to the subject matter of the dispute and is to give the reasons on which it is based. It is to contain the names of the members and the date of the award. Any member may attach a separate or dissenting opinion. The award is final and without an appeal, unless the parties have agreed in advance to an appellate procedure. The parties are to comply with the award. Any controversy regarding the interpretation or manner of implementation of the award may be submitted to the tribunal: or, by agreement of all the parties, to another court or tribunal under Article 287.

Article 13 states that the provisions of the Annex apply, *mutatis mutandis*,[59] to any dispute involving entities other than States Parties.

8) Special Arbitration: Annex VIII

Annex VIII contains special arbitration provisions dealing with disputes relating to *"(1) fisheries, (2) protection and preservation of the marine environment, (3) marine scientific research, or (4) navigation, including pollution from vessels and by dumping"*.

The submission to arbitration is by way of written notification to the other party accompanied by a statement of claim and the grounds on which the claim is based (Article 1).

Lists of experts are to be established and maintained in respect of the four fields mentioned above. Article 2 lists the various organisations of the United Nations and the International Maritime Organisation that are to draw up the lists of experts. Each State Party is entitled to nominate two experts in each field whose competence *"in the legal, scientific or technical aspects of such field is established and generally recognized and who enjoy the highest reputation for fairness and integrity"*.

Article 3 concerns the constitution of the special arbitral tribunal. Article 4 provides that the arbitration provisions of Articles 4 to 13 of Annex VII are to apply to the special arbitration proceedings in Annex VIII.

Provision is made in Article 5 for a fact-finding procedure covering the four categories listed in Article 1. The parties can agree to request the special arbitral tribunal to carry out an inquiry and establish the facts giving rise to the dispute. Unless the parties agree otherwise, the findings of fact are to be considered as conclusive between the parties. Further, provided all the parties agree, the special arbitral tribunal *"may formulate recommendations which, without having the force of a decision, shall only constitute the basis for a review by the parties of the questions giving rise to the dispute"*.

9) Conclusions

ITLOS is an international tribunal that performs a function of considerable global importance. Its significance is demonstrated by the powers bestowed on it by the United Nations under the 1982 Convention, and its importance is in no way reduced because of the relatively small number of cases it has handled to date. In part, the number of cases dealt with by the Tribunal may be a result of the various choices of settlement procedures that are provided in UNCLOS III.

The nature of the disputes coming before the Tribunal provides clear evidence that it ranks high among the world's leading dispute settlement bodies.

59 With the necessary changes.

14 The International Centre for Settlement of Investment Disputes

1) Introduction

The International Centre for Settlement of Investment Disputes (the ICSID Centre) was created by the International Convention on the Settlement of Investment Disputes (also known as the Washington Convention). The Centre was briefly mentioned in Chapter 9 of the Manual, which dealt with investor-State disputes and which considered, among other things, the ICSID Convention.

This chapter now looks at the Centre in more detail, and also considers the ICSID Arbitration Rules, Conciliation Rules, Additional Facility Rules and fact-finding procedure, and the ICSID caseload.

Brief mention will be made again of some of the problems arising in investor-State disputes, referred to earlier in Chapter 9.

2) Historical Overview

The Centre states that on a number of occasions in the past, the World Bank as an institution and the President of the Bank in his personal capacity have participated in the mediation or conciliation of investment disputes between governments and private foreign investors. The creation of ICSID in 1966 was thus *"in part intended to relieve the President and the staff of the burden of becoming involved in such disputes. But the Bank's overriding consideration in creating ICSID was the belief that an institution specially designed to facilitate the settlement of investment disputes between governments and foreign investors could help to promote increased flows of international investment."*

The Centre goes on to say that ICSID was established

> *"... under the Convention on the Settlement of Investment Disputes between States and Nationals of Other States (the Convention) which came into force on October 14, 1966. ICSID has an Administrative Council and a Secretariat. The Administrative Council is chaired by the World Bank's President and consists of one representative of each State which has ratified the Convention. Annual meetings of the Council are held in conjunction with the joint Bank / Fund annual meetings.*
>
> *"ICSID is an autonomous international organization. However, it has close links with the World Bank. All of ICSID's members are also members of the Bank. Unless a government makes a contrary designation, its Governor for the Bank sits ex officio on ICSID's Administrative Council. The expenses of the ICSID Secretariat are financed out of the Bank's budget, although the costs of individual proceedings are borne by the parties involved.*
>
> *"Pursuant to the Convention, ICSID provides facilities for the conciliation and arbitration of disputes between member countries and investors who qualify as nationals of other member countries. Recourse to ICSID conciliation and arbitration is*

entirely voluntary. However, once the parties have consented to arbitration under the ICSID Convention, neither can unilaterally withdraw its consent. Moreover, all ICSID Contracting States, whether or not parties to the dispute, are required by the Convention to recognize and enforce ICSID arbitral awards."

Besides providing facilities for conciliation and arbitration under the ICSID Convention, since 1978 the Centre has had a set of Additional Facility Rules authorising the ICSID Secretariat to administer certain types of proceedings between States and foreign nationals that fall outside the scope of the Convention.

"These include conciliation and arbitration proceedings where either the State party or the home State of the foreign national is not a member of ICSID. Additional Facility conciliation and arbitration are also available for cases where the dispute is not an investment dispute, provided it relates to a transaction which has 'features that distinguishes it from an ordinary commercial transaction.' The Additional Facility Rules further allow ICSID to administer a type of proceedings not provided for in the Convention, namely fact-finding proceedings to which any State and foreign national may have recourse if they wish to institute an inquiry ' to examine and report on facts.'"

The Centre goes on to say that the third activity of ICSID in the field of dispute settlement *"has consisted in the Secretary-General of ICSID accepting to act as the appointing authority of arbitrators for ad hoc (i.e., non-institutional) arbitration proceedings. This is most commonly done in the context of arrangements for arbitration under the Arbitration Rules of the United Nations Commission on International Trade Law (UNCITRAL), which are specially designed for ad hoc proceedings."*

Provisions on ICSID arbitration are a common feature of investment contracts between governments of member countries and investors from other member countries, and the Centre notes that advance consents by governments to submit investment disputes to ICSID arbitration can be found in about 20 investment laws and in over 900 bilateral investment treaties (BITS). In addition, *"Arbitration under the auspices of ICSID is similarly one of the main mechanisms for the settlement of investment disputes under four recent multilateral trade and investment treaties (the North American Free Trade Agreement, the Energy Charter Treaty, the Cartagena Free Trade Agreement and the Colonia Investment Protocol of Mercosur)."*

Under the ICSID Convention, proceedings need not be held at the Centre's headquarters in Washington, DC, as the parties to an ICSID proceeding are free to agree to conduct their proceeding at any other place. The Convention's provisions *"facilitate advance stipulations for such other venues when the place chosen is the seat of an institution with which the Centre has an arrangement for this purpose. ICSID has to date entered in such arrangements with the Permanent Court of Arbitration at The Hague, the Regional Arbitration Centres of the Asian-African Legal Consultative Committee at Cairo and Kuala Lumpur, the Australian Centre for International Commercial Arbitration at Melbourne, the Australian Commercial Disputes Centre at Sydney, the Singapore International Arbitration Centre and the GCC Commercial Arbitration Centre at Bahrain. These arrangements have proved their usefulness in many ICSID cases and have helped to promote cooperation between ICSID and these institutions in several other respects."*

As at January 2006, 155 States had signed the ICSID Convention. The Centre states that the number of cases submitted to it – under the ICSID Convention and under the ICSID Additional Facility Rules – has increased significantly in recent years. The full text of ICSID's statement is available on its website.[60]

3) The ICSID Institution of Arbitration and Conciliation Proceedings

The Institution Rules of ICSID set out the process to be used for the commencement of an ICSID arbitration or conciliation. These Rules relate to the time from the filing of a request for arbitration or conciliation to the time of the dispatch of a notice of registration. Transactions after that stage are regulated in accordance with the Arbitration Rules or the Conciliation Rules, as the case may be (these Rules are considered in sections 4 and 5 of this chapter).

Rule 1 of the Institution Rules provides that any Contracting State or any national of a Contracting State wishing to institute arbitration or conciliation proceedings under the ICSID Convention is to do so by means of a written request to the Secretary-General at the Centre. The request may be made jointly by the parties to the dispute.

Rule 2 sets out the detailed information that is to be included in the request. The request is to:

"(a) designate precisely each party to the dispute and state the address of each;

(b) state, if one of the parties is a constituent subdivision or agency of a Contracting State, that it has been designated to the Centre by that State pursuant to Article 25(1) of the Convention;

(c) indicate the date of consent and the instruments in which it is recorded, including, if one party is a constituent subdivision or agency of a Contracting State, similar data on the approval of such consent by that State unless it had notified the Centre that no such approval is required;

(d) indicate with respect to the party that is a national of a Contracting State:

(i) its nationality on the date of consent; and

(ii) if the party is a natural person:

(A) his nationality on the date of the request; and

(B) that he did not have the nationality of the Contracting State party to the dispute either on the date of consent or on the date of the request; or

(iii) if the party is a juridical person which on the date of consent had the nationality of the Contracting State party to the dispute, the agreement of the parties that it should be treated as a national of another Contracting State for the purposes of the Convention;

(e) contain information concerning the issues in dispute indicating that there is, between the parties, a legal dispute arising directly out of an investment; and

(f) state, if the requesting party is a juridical person, that it has taken all necessary internal actions to authorize the request."

60 www.worldbank.org/icsid/.

The information required by subparagraphs (1) (c), (1) (d) (iii) and (1) (f) is to be supported by documentation.

The request may additionally set out any provisions agreed by the parties concerning the number of arbitrators or conciliators and the method of the appointment, as well as any other provisions agreed by them (Rule 3).

Any documentation submitted with the request is to conform with the requirements of Administrative and Financial Regulation 30. On receiving the request, the Secretary-General is to send an acknowledgement to the requesting party, but is to take no further action until he or she has received payment of the prescribed fee. When the fee has been received, the Secretary-General transmits a copy of the request and the documentation to the other party (Rules 4 and 5).

The request is to be registered unless the Secretary-General finds *"on the basis of the information contained in the request, that the dispute is manifestly outside the jurisdiction of the Centre"*. In that event, he or she is to notify the parties that their request has been refused and give the reasons for that refusal (Rule 6).

Rule 7 sets out the detail that is to be entered into the notice of registration of the request, including an invitation to the parties to proceed to the next stage of the process – namely the constitution of a Conciliation or Arbitration Commission. The notice is to:

"(a) record that the request is registered and indicate the date of the registration and of the dispatch of that notice;

(b) notify each party that all communications and notices in connection with the proceeding will be sent to the address stated in the request, unless another address is indicated to the Centre;

(c) unless such information has already been provided, invite the parties to communicate to the Secretary-General any provisions agreed by them regarding the number and the method of appointment of the conciliators or arbitrators;

(d) invite the parties to proceed, as soon as possible, to constitute a Conciliation Commission in accordance with Articles 29 to 31 of the Convention, or an Arbitral Tribunal in accordance with Articles 37 to 40;

(e) remind the parties that the registration of the request is without prejudice to the powers and functions of the Conciliation Commission or Arbitral Tribunal in regard to jurisdiction, competence and the merits; and

(f) be accompanied by a list of the members of the Panel of Conciliators or of Arbitrators of the Centre."

Rule 8 provides that the request may be withdrawn by service of written notice on the Secretary-General prior to registration.

4) The ICSID Rules of Procedure for Arbitration Proceedings

Introduction

Before looking at the detail of the ICSID Arbitration Rules, it may be useful to mention that these Rules broadly follow the same pattern as the Arbitration Rules of the Permanent Court of Arbitration (PCA), which were considered in an earlier chapter of the Manual.

Chapter 1 of the ICSID Arbitration Rules deals with the appointment and replacement of arbitrators. Chapter II contains provisions relating to the procedure of the Tribunal and Chapter III contains general procedural provisions dealing with matters such as time limits. Written and oral procedures are set out in Chapter IV, covering matters such as witnesses and experts. Chapter V deals with matters described as 'Particular Procedures', and contains provisions relating to matters such as objections to jurisdiction. Provisions concerning the award are set out in Chapter VI, and Chapter VII deals with the interpretation, revision and annulment of the award.

Chapter 1: Establishment of the Tribunal

Chapter I is comprised of 12 Rules dealing with the establishment of the Tribunal.

On notification of the registration of the request for arbitration, Rule 1 states that the parties are to proceed with all possible dispatch to constitute a Tribunal. The majority of the arbitrators are to be nationals of States other than the State that is party to the dispute and the State whose national is a party to the dispute *"unless the sole arbitrator or each individual member of the Tribunal is appointed by agreement of the parties. Where the Tribunal is to consist of three members, a national of either of these States may not be appointed as an arbitrator by a party without the agreement of the other party to the dispute. Where the Tribunal is to consist of five or more members, nationals of either of these States may not be appointed as arbitrators by a party if appointment by the other party of the same number of arbitrators of either of these nationalities would result in a majority of arbitrators of these nationalities."*

Where the parties have not agreed on the number and method of appointment of arbitrators, the procedure to be followed is set out in Rule 2:

> *"(1)...(a) the requesting party shall, within 10 days after the registration of the request, propose to the other party the appointment of a sole arbitrator or of a specified uneven number of arbitrators and specify the method proposed for their appointment;*
>
> *(b) within 20 days after receipt of the proposals made by the requesting party, the other party shall:*
>
> *(i) accept such proposals; or*
>
> *(ii) make other proposals regarding the number of arbitrators and the method of their appointment;*
>
> *(c) within 20 days after receipt of the reply containing any such other proposals, the requesting party shall notify the other party whether it accepts or rejects such proposals."*

The communications provided for in paragraph 1 are to be transmitted to the Secretary-General. If no agreement is reached on the appointment of the Tribunal within 60 days after the registration of the request, either party may inform the Secretary-General that it chooses the formula provided for in Article 37 (2) (b) of the Convention.

Rule 3 goes on to deal with the appointment of arbitrators in accordance with provisions of the Convention:

> "*(a) either party shall in a communication to the other party:*
>
> > *(i) name two persons, identifying one of them, who shall not have the same nationality as nor be a national of either party, as the arbitrator appointed by it, and the other as the arbitrator proposed to be the President of the Tribunal; and*
> >
> > *(ii) invite the other party to concur in the appointment of the arbitrator proposed to be the President of the Tribunal and to appoint another arbitrator;*
>
> *(b) promptly upon receipt of this communication the other party shall, in its reply:*
>
> > *(i) name a person as the arbitrator appointed by it, who shall not have the same nationality as nor be a national of either party; and*
> >
> > *(ii) concur in the appointment of the arbitrator proposed to be the President of the Tribunal or name another person as the arbitrator proposed to be President;*
>
> *(c) promptly upon receipt of the reply containing such a proposal, the initiating party shall notify the other party whether it concurs in the appointment of the arbitrator proposed by that party to be the President of the Tribunal.*"

The communications provided for in that Rule are to be transmitted to the Secretary-General.

Where a Tribunal has not been constituted within 90 days following the dispatch by the Secretary-General of the notice of registration, either party may request the Chairman of the Administrative Council to appoint the arbitrator or arbitrators not yet appointed and to designate one arbitrator to be the President of the Tribunal.

Rule 5 contains provisions relating to the acceptance of appointments by arbitrators.

Rule 6 states that the Tribunal is deemed to be constituted, and the proceedings to have begun, when the Secretary-General notifies the parties that all arbitrators have accepted their appointment. Each arbitrator is to sign a declaration in the following form:

> "*To the best of my knowledge there is no reason why I should not serve on the Arbitral Tribunal constituted by the International Centre for Settlement of Investment Disputes with respect to a dispute between ______________________________ and ______________________________.*
>
> "*I shall keep confidential all information coming to my knowledge as a result of my participation in this proceeding, as well as the contents of any award made by the Tribunal.*
>
> "*I shall judge fairly as between the parties, according to the applicable law, and shall not accept any instruction or compensation with regard to the proceeding from any*

> *source except as provided in the Convention on the Settlement of Investment Disputes between States and Nationals of Other States and in the Regulations and Rules made pursuant thereto.*
>
> *"A statement of my past and present professional, business and other relationships (if any) with the parties is attached hereto."*

Any arbitrator failing to sign that declaration by the end of the first session of the Tribunal is deemed to have resigned.

Rules 7 to 9 deal with the replacement, incapacity, resignation and disqualification of arbitrators. At any time prior to the constitution of the Tribunal, any party may replace an arbitrator appointed by that party. Where an arbitrator becomes incapacitated or unable to perform his/her duties, the disqualification procedure set out in Rule 9 is applied. An arbitrator may resign by submitting his/her resignation to the other members of the Tribunal and to the Secretary-General. However, where that arbitrator was appointed by one of the parties, the Tribunal is to consider the reasons for the resignation and decide whether it consents to that resignation. The Rule 9 procedure relating to the disqualification of arbitrators requires a party proposing disqualification, pursuant to Article 57 of the Convention, to file a proposal with the Secretary-General stating the reasons on which it is based. The filing of the disqualification proposal is to be made before the proceeding is declared closed. The Secretary-General is then to:

> *"(a) transmit the proposal to the members of the Tribunal and, if it relates to a sole arbitrator or to a majority of the members of the Tribunal, to the Chairman of the Administrative Council; and*
>
> *(b) notify the other party of the proposal."*

The arbitrator whose disqualification is proposed may *"furnish explanations to the Tribunal or the Chairman, as the case may be"*. Unless the proposal relates to a majority of the members of the Tribunal, the other members *"... shall promptly consider and vote on the proposal in the absence of the arbitrator concerned. If those members are equally divided, they shall, through the Secretary-General, promptly notify the Chairman of the proposal, of any explanation furnished by the arbitrator concerned and of their failure to reach a decision."* The arbitration is suspended until a decision has been taken on the disqualification proposal.

Rules 10 and 11 deal with vacancies on the Tribunal. The Secretary-General is to notify the parties of the disqualification, death, incapacity or resignation of an arbitrator and of the consent, if any, of the Tribunal to a resignation. The proceeding is suspended until the vacancy is filled, which is to be achieved by the same method by which the appointment was originally made. Rule 12 provides that as soon as a vacancy has been filled, the proceeding is to continue *"from the point it had reached at the time the vacancy occurred. The newly appointed arbitrator may, however, require that the oral procedure be recommenced, if this had already been started."*

Chapter II: Procedure of the Tribunal

Chapter II, Rules 13 to 18, contains provisions largely dealing with the Tribunal's own procedures.

Rule 14 provides that the Tribunal is to hold its first session within 60 days of its constitution. The Tribunal will determine the dates of subsequent sessions, after consultation with the Secretary-General and the parties. The Tribunal is to meet at the seat of the Centre, or such other place as has been agreed under the provisions of Article 63 of the Convention.

The President of the Tribunal is to conduct the hearings and, unless the parties agree otherwise, the presence of a majority of the members of the Tribunal is required at the sittings. The deliberations of the Tribunal take place in private and remain secret. Only members of the Tribunal may take part in its deliberations: *"No other person shall be admitted unless the Tribunal decides otherwise."* Decisions of the Tribunal are by a majority of votes, and the Tribunal may take any decision by correspondence among its members.

Should the President of the Tribunal be unable to act, his/her functions are to be performed by another member of the Tribunal, acting in the order in which notice of acceptance of appointment was received by the Secretary-General.

The final Rule of Chapter 2 states that each party may be represented or assisted by agents, counsel or advocates *"... whose names and authority shall be notified by that party to the Secretary-General, who shall promptly inform the Tribunal and the other party"*.

Chapter III: General procedural provisions – pre-hearing conferences, documents, etc

Rules 19 to 28 of Chapter III contain general procedural provisions.

The Tribunal shall make the orders necessary for the conduct of the arbitration proceedings, and as early as possible after the constitution of the Tribunal, the President is to *"... endeavor to ascertain the views of the parties regarding questions of procedure. For this purpose he may request the parties to meet him. He shall, in particular, seek their views on the following matters:*

- *(a) the number of members of the Tribunal required to constitute a quorum at its sittings;*
- *(b) the language or languages to be used in the proceeding;*
- *(c) the number and sequence of the pleadings and the time limits within which they are to be filed;*
- *(d) the number of copies desired by each party of instruments filed by the other;*
- *(e) dispensing with the written or the oral procedure;*
- *(f) the manner in which the cost of the proceeding is to be apportioned; and*
- *(g) the manner in which the record of the hearings shall be kept."*

In the conduct of the proceeding, the Tribunal is to apply any agreement between the parties on procedural matters, except as otherwise provided in the Convention or the Administrative and Financial Regulations (Rule 20).

Rule 21 deals with pre-hearing conferences between the Tribunal and the parties aimed at an exchange of information and the *"stipulation of uncontested facts in order to expedite the proceeding"*. In addition, the parties may request a pre-hearing conference *"to consider the issues in dispute with a view to reaching an amicable settlement"*.

Rule 22 provides that the parties may agree on the use of one or two languages. The Tribunal must approve any language that is not one of the official languages of the Centre (namely, English, French and Spanish).

Rules 23 and 24 deal with copies of instruments and supporting documentation. Except as otherwise provided, every request, pleading, application, written observation, supporting documentation (if any) or other instrument is to be filed in the form of a signed original accompanied by a specified number of copies. Supporting documentation should ordinarily be filed together with the instrument to which it relates. 'Accidental errors' in any instrument or supporting document may, with the consent of the other party or by leave of the Tribunal, be corrected at any time before the award is rendered (Rule 25).

Time limits are dealt with in Rule 26. They shall be fixed by the Tribunal, which shall assign dates for the completion of the various steps in the proceeding. The Tribunal may extend any time limit. Any steps taken after the expiration of the relevant time limit is to be disregarded *"unless the Tribunal, in special circumstances and after giving the other party an opportunity of stating its views, decides otherwise"*.

Waiver is covered in Rule 27: *"A party which knows or should have known that a provision of the Administrative and Financial Regulations, of these Rules, of any other rules or agreement applicable to the proceeding, or of an order of the Tribunal has not been complied with and which fails to state promptly its objections thereto, shall be deemed – subject to Article 45 of the Convention – to have waived its right to object."*

The final Rule of Chapter 3 deals with the costs of the proceeding.

Chapter IV: Written and oral procedures

Chapter IV contains provisions in Rules 29 to 38 dealing with written and oral procedures. Rule 29 states that, unless the parties agree otherwise, the arbitral proceeding is to comprise two distinct phases: a written procedure followed by an oral procedure.

The written procedure

In addition to the request for arbitration, Rule 31 provides that the written procedure is to consist of the following pleadings, which are to be filed within the time limits set by the Tribunal:

"(a) a memorial by the requesting party;

(b) a counter-memorial by the other party; and, if the parties so agree or the Tribunal deems it necessary:

(c) a reply by the requesting party; and

(d) a rejoinder by the other party."

Where the request for arbitration was made jointly by the parties *"each party shall, within the same time limit determined by the Tribunal, file its memorial and, if the parties so agree or the Tribunal deems it necessary, its reply; however, the parties may instead agree that one of them shall, for the purposes of paragraph (1), be considered as the requesting party"*.

The Rules provide succinctly what is to be set out in the pleadings. A memorial is to contain: *"a statement of the relevant facts; a statement of law; and the submissions. A counter-memorial, reply or rejoinder shall contain an admission or denial of the facts stated in the last previous pleading; any additional facts, if necessary; observations concerning the statement of law in the last previous pleading; a statement of law in answer thereto; and the submissions."*

The oral procedure

Rule 32 deals with the oral procedure, which is to consist of the hearing by the Tribunal of the parties, their agents, counsel and advocates, and of witnesses and experts. The Tribunal shall decide, with the consent of the parties, what other persons may attend hearings. Members of the Tribunal may put questions to the parties, their agents, counsel and advocates, and may ask them for explanations.

Rules 33 and 34 deal with evidence. Without prejudice to the rules concerning the production of documents, each party is to communicate to the Secretary-General, for onward transmission to the Tribunal and the other party, *"precise information regarding the evidence which it intends to produce and that which it intends to request the Tribunal to call for, together with an indication of the points to which such evidence will be directed"*.

The Tribunal is to be the judge of the admissibility of any evidence and of the probative value of that evidence. If it considers it necessary, the Tribunal may call on the parties to produce documents, witnesses and experts and may visit any place connected with the dispute or may conduct inquiries there. The parties are to cooperate with the Tribunal in these matters, and it is to take formal note of the failure of a party to comply with its obligations.

Rules 35 and 36 deal with witnesses and experts. They are to be examined before the Tribunal by the parties. Such examination is under the control of the President. Members of the Tribunal may also put questions. Before giving evidence, each witness is to make the following declaration:

> *"I solemnly declare upon my honour and conscience that I shall speak the truth, the whole truth and nothing but the truth."*

Each expert is to make the following declaration before making his/her statement:

> *"I solemnly declare upon my honour and conscience that my statement will be in accordance with my sincere belief."*

In addition, the Tribunal may admit evidence given by a witness or expert in the form of a written deposition. Further, with the consent of the parties, the Tribunal may arrange for the examination of a witness or an expert *"otherwise than before the Tribunal itself. The Tribunal shall define the subject of the examination, the time limit, the procedure to be followed and other particulars. The parties may participate in the examination."*

Article 37 provides that, if the Tribunal considers it necessary, it may visit any place connected with the dispute or may conduct an inquiry at such place. The parties are entitled to participate in any such visit or inquiry.

When the parties have completed their presentation of the case, the Tribunal is to declare the proceeding closed. In exceptional circumstances the Tribunal may, before the award has been rendered, reopen the proceeding on the ground that *"... new evidence is forthcoming of such a nature as to constitute a decisive factor, or that there is a vital need for clarification on certain specific points"*.

Chapter V: 'Particular procedures'

Chapter V in Rules 39 to 45 contains provisions for 'Particular Procedures'. These include provisional measures, ancillary claims, jurisdiction, default, settlement and discontinuance.

Provisional measures

The first particular procedure relates to the important matter of provisional measures in Rule 39:

> *"(1) At any time during the proceeding a party may request that provisional measures for the preservation of its rights be recommended by the Tribunal. The request shall specify the rights to be preserved, the measures the recommendation of which is requested, and the circumstances that require such measures.*
>
> *(2) The Tribunal shall give priority to the consideration of a request made pursuant to paragraph (1).*
>
> *(3) The Tribunal may also recommend provisional measures on its own initiative or recommend measures other than those specified in a request. It may at any time modify or revoke its recommendations.*
>
> *(4) The Tribunal shall only recommend provisional measures, or modify or revoke its recommendations, after giving each party an opportunity of presenting its observations."*

Nothing in the Rule shall prevent the parties, *"provided that they have so stipulated in the agreement recording their consent, from requesting any judicial or other authority to order provisional measures, prior to the institution of the proceeding, or during the proceeding, for the preservation of their respective rights and interests"*.

Ancillary claims

Rule 40 states that, unless the parties have agreed otherwise, a party may present an *"incidental or additional claim or counter-claim arising directly out of the subject-matter of the dispute, provided that such ancillary claim is within the scope of the consent of the parties and is otherwise within the jurisdiction of the Centre".*

An incidental or additional claim is to be presented *"not later than in the reply and a counter-claim no later than in the counter-memorial, unless the Tribunal, upon justification by the party presenting the ancillary claim and upon considering any objection of the other party, authorizes the presentation of the claim at a later stage in the proceeding".*

The Tribunal is to fix a time limit within which the party against which an ancillary claim is presented may file its observations on that claim.

Jurisdiction

Rule 41 relates to the potentially significant matter of objections to jurisdiction. An award made by a tribunal that lacks jurisdiction is subject to annulment.

Any objection that the dispute itself or any ancillary claim is not within the jurisdiction of the Centre, or within the competence of the Tribunal, is to be made as early as possible. The party mounting the challenge *"... shall file the objection with the Secretary-General no later than the expiration of the time limit fixed for the filing of the counter-memorial, or, if the objection relates to an ancillary claim, for the filing of the rejoinder – unless the facts on which the objection is based are unknown to the party at that time".* Additionally, the Tribunal itself may at any stage of the proceeding consider whether the dispute or any ancillary claim before it is within the jurisdiction of the Centre or within its own competence.

Where a formal objection relating to the dispute is raised, the proceeding on the merits is to be suspended. The President of the Tribunal, after consultation with its other members, is to fix a time limit within which the parties may file observations on the objection. The Tribunal decides whether or not the further procedures relating to the objection are to be oral. As is common in arbitral practice generally, the Tribunal may deal with the objection either as a preliminary question or may join it to the merits of the dispute. If the Tribunal overrules the objection or joins it to the merits, it is to fix time limits for the further procedures. However, if it decides that the dispute is not within the jurisdiction of the Centre or not within its own competence *"it shall render an award to that effect".*

Default

Rule 42 provides that if a party, referred to as the 'defaulting party', fails to appear or to present its case, the other party may request the Tribunal to deal with the questions submitted to it and to render an award. The Tribunal is to notify the defaulting party of such a request and, unless it is satisfied that the party in question does not intend to appear or to present its case, is to grant a period of grace on the following basis:

"(a) if that party had failed to file a pleading or any other instrument within the time limit fixed therefor, fix a new time limit for its filing; or

(b) if that party had failed to appear or present its case at a hearing, fix a new date for the hearing."

Without the consent of the other party, the period of grace is not to exceed 60 days. The Tribunal subsequently resumes consideration of the dispute. Any failure on the part of the defaulting party to appear or present its case is not deemed an admission of assertions made by the other party. The Tribunal is then to *"examine the jurisdiction of the Centre and its own competence in the dispute and, if it is satisfied, decide whether the submissions made are well-founded in fact and in law. To this end, it may, at any stage of the proceeding, call on the party appearing to file observations, produce evidence or submit oral explanations."*

Settlement and discontinuance

Under Rule 43, if the parties agree on a settlement of the dispute or otherwise agree to discontinue the proceeding, the Tribunal (or the Secretary-General in a case where the Tribunal has not yet been constituted) is to take note of the discontinuance of the proceeding. If the parties file with the Secretary-General the full and signed text of their settlement, and if they submit a written request for the Tribunal to embody that settlement in an award, the Tribunal *"may record the settlement in the form of its award"*.

Rule 44 states that if a party requests the discontinuance of the proceeding, the Tribunal (or the Secretary-General, if the Tribunal has not yet been constituted) is to fix a time limit within which the other party may state whether it opposes the discontinuance. If no objection is made, that party is deemed to have acquiesced in the discontinuance. If an objection is made, the proceeding is to continue. Rule 45 provides that if the parties fail to take any steps in the proceeding during six consecutive months (or such other period as may be agreed), the Tribunal (or the Secretary General) shall in an order *"take note of the discontinuance"*.

Chapter VI: The award

Rules 46 to 49 deal with the award.

Rule 46 provides that the award (including any individual or dissenting opinion) is to be drawn up and signed within 120 days of the closure of the proceeding. The Tribunal has power to extend that period by a further 60 days. Rule 47 states that the award is to be in writing and is to contain the following:

"(a) a precise designation of each party;

(b) a statement that the Tribunal was established under the Convention, and a description *of the method of its constitution;*

(c) the name of each member of the Tribunal, and an identification of the appointing authority of each;

(d) the names of the agents, counsel and advocates of the parties;

(e) the dates and place of the sittings of the Tribunal;

(f) a summary of the proceeding;

(g) a statement of the facts as found by the Tribunal;

(h) the submissions of the parties;

(i) the decision of the Tribunal on every question submitted to it, together with the reasons upon which the decision is based; and

(j) any decision of the Tribunal regarding the cost of the proceeding."

The award is to be signed by the members of the Tribunal who voted for it, and the date of each signature is to be indicated. Any member of the Tribunal may attach his/her individual opinion to the award, whether dissenting from the majority or not. Any member may attach a statement of dissent.

Rule 48 deals with the rendering of the award. Following signature of the award by all members of the Tribunal, the Secretary-General is to (a) authenticate the original text of the award and deposit it in the archives of the Centre, together with any individual opinions and statements of dissent; and (b) dispatch a certified copy of the award (including individual opinions and statements of dissent) to each party, indicating the date of dispatch on the original text and on all copies.

The award is deemed to have been rendered on the date on which the certified copies were dispatched. The Centre is not to publish the award without the consent of the parties. However, the Centre may *"include in its publications excerpts of the legal rules applied by the Tribunal"*.

Provisions for supplementary decisions and rectification of the award are set out in Rule 49. Within 45 days of the date on which the award was rendered, either party may request (pursuant to Article 49 (2) of the Convention) either a supplementary decision on the award or a rectification of the award. The request is to be addressed in writing to the Secretary-General and is to:

"(a) identify the award to which it relates;

(b) indicate the date of the request;

(c) state in detail:

(i) any question which, in the opinion of the requesting party, the Tribunal omitted to decide in the award; and

(ii) any error in the award which the requesting party seeks to have rectified; and

(d) be accompanied by a fee for lodging the request."

The Secretary-General is to register the request, notify the parties accordingly, and transmit a copy of that request and any accompanying documentation to the other party and to the Tribunal.

The President of the Tribunal is to consult the members as to whether it is necessary to meet in order to consider the request. The Tribunal is to fix a time for the parties to file observations on the request and determine the procedure to be followed for a consideration of the request.

The Secretary-General must refuse to register any request received more than 45 days after the award was rendered.

Chapter VII: Interpretation, revision and annulment of the award

Chapter VII of the Arbitration Rules contains provisions for the interpretation and revision of an ICSID award, together with the significant provisions relating to an application for the annulment of an award pursuant to Article 52 (1) of the ICSID Convention (and provisions for a stay of enforcement where application has been made for annulment or revision of an award).

Rule 50 provides that an application for the interpretation, revision or annulment of an award is to be made in writing to the Secretary-General and is to:

"(a) identify the award to which it relates;

(b) indicate the date of the application;

(c) state in detail:

(i) in an application for interpretation, the precise points in dispute;

(ii) in an application for revision, pursuant to Article 51(1) of the Convention, the change sought in the award, the discovery of some fact of such a nature as decisively to affect the award, and evidence that when the award was rendered that fact was unknown to the Tribunal and to the applicant, and that the applicant's ignorance of that fact was not due to negligence;

(iii) in an application for annulment, pursuant to Article 52(1) of the Convention, the grounds on which it is based. These grounds are limited to the following:

- *that the Tribunal was not properly constituted;*
- *that the Tribunal has manifestly exceeded its powers;*
- *that there was corruption on the part of a member of the Tribunal;*
- *that there has been a serious departure from a fundamental rule of procedure;*
- *that the award has failed to state the reasons on which it is based."*

On receiving the application the Secretary-General is to register it, notify the parties accordingly and transmit to the other party a copy of the application and any documentation. The Secretary-General is to refuse to register applications not made within the time limits specified in the Rules, and is to notify the requesting party accordingly.

The provisions relating to annulment contained in Rule 50 and in Article 52 of the ICSID Convention are in some respects similar to provisions contained in Article V of the New York Convention (relating to the recognition and enforcement of foreign arbitral awards) and to provisions in Articles 34 and 36 of the UNCITRAL Model Law (relating to the setting aside and recognition and enforcement of arbitral awards).

Rules 51 and 52 contain 'further procedures' relating to interpretation and revision and to annulment. If all members of the Tribunal express their willingness to take part in the consideration of the application, the Secretary-General shall so notify the members of the Tribunal and the parties. The Tribunal is deemed to be reconstituted on the dispatch of the relevant notices. However, if it cannot be reconstituted, the Secretary-General is to notify the parties and invite them to proceed to constitute a new Tribunal, which is to comprise the same number of arbitrators (and is to be appointed by the same method) as the original Tribunal (Rule 51). In the case of an annulment, the Secretary-General is to request the Chairman of the Administrative Council to appoint an ad hoc Committee in accordance with Article 52 of the ICSID Convention (Rule 52).

Rule 53 states that the provisions of the rules apply *mutatis mutandis* to the procedures relating to interpretation, revision or annulment. The party that has applied for revision or annulment of an award may well require a stay of enforcement pending the outcome of the application, particularly so in the case of an application for annulment. The relevant provisions are contained in Rule 54. On making the application for revision or annulment the party applying may at the same time (or at any time before the final disposition of the application) request a stay of enforcement in relation to all or part of the award. The other party may make a similar application. Priority is to be given to such a request.

Where an application for revision or annulment contains a request for a stay, the Secretary-General is to inform both parties that a provisional stay has been put into effect. As soon as the Tribunal (or Committee) is constituted it shall, on the request of either party, rule within 30 days on whether the provisional stay should be continued. Unless the stay is continued, it is treated as being automatically terminated.

Rule 54 (3) provides that *"If a stay of enforcement has been granted pursuant to paragraph (1) or continued pursuant to paragraph (2), the Tribunal or Committee may at any time modify or terminate the stay at the request of either party. All stays shall automatically terminate on the date on which a final decision is rendered on the application, except that a Committee granting the partial annulment of an award may order the temporary stay of enforcement of the unannulled portion in order to give either party an opportunity to request any new Tribunal constituted pursuant to Article 52(6) of the Convention to grant a stay pursuant to Rule 55(3)."*

Requests for a stay are to specify the circumstances that require the stay or its modification or termination. Each party is to have an opportunity of presenting its observations on the stay application. The Secretary-General is to notify the parties of the outcome.

Rule 55 deals with the resubmission of a dispute following annulment. A request is to be made in writing to the Secretary-General and is to:

"(a) identify the award to which it relates;

(b) indicate the date of the request;

(c) explain in detail what aspect of the dispute is to be submitted to the Tribunal."

The Secretary-General invites the parties to proceed to the constitution of a new Tribunal. This is to include the same number of arbitrators, appointed by the same method, as the original Tribunal.

Where the original award is only annulled in part, the new Tribunal is not to reconsider the unannulled part. However, it may apply the stay provisions to the annulled portion.

The Rules apply to a resubmitted dispute in the same manner as if such dispute had been submitted under the Institution Rules.

Chapter VIII

Rule 56 states that the text of the Rules is equally authentic in each of the official languages (English, French and Spanish).

5) The ICSID Rules of Procedure for Conciliation

Introduction

The ICSID Conciliation Rules follow a similar pattern to the Arbitration Rules. The bulk of them can therefore simply be outlined.

Chapter I deals with the establishment of the Commission of Conciliators: general obligations; method of constituting the commission; appointment, resignation, disqualification and replacement of Conciliators; and resumption of proceedings. Chapter II sets out provisions mainly concerned with the Commission's own procedure: sessions, sittings, deliberations and decisions of the Commission and incapacity of the President. It also deals with the representation of the parties. Chapter III is concerned with general procedural provisions: procedural orders; preliminary procedural consultation; and languages.

The crucial section of the Rules dealing with the conciliation process is contained in Chapter IV, and this will be considered in more detail. It is important to bear in mind that the result of the conciliation process, unlike the arbitration process, is non-binding.

Chapter IV

The Conciliation Procedures are set out in Chapter IV. Rules 22 and 23 are of particular importance.

Rule 22

Rule 22 is at the heart of the conciliation process, since it sets out the functions of the Commission of Conciliators. Rule 22 (1) provides that, in order to clarify the issues in dispute between the parties, the Commission:

"(1) *shall hear the parties and shall endeavor to obtain any information that might serve this end. The parties shall be associated with its work as closely as possible.*

"(2) *In order to bring about agreement between the parties, the Commission may, from time to time at any stage of the proceeding, make – orally or in writing – recommendations to the parties. It may recommend that the parties accept specific terms of settlement or that they refrain, while it seeks to bring about agreement between them, from specific acts that might aggravate the dispute; it shall point out to the parties the arguments in favor of its recommendations. It may fix time limits within which each party shall inform the Commission of its decision concerning the recommendations made.*

"(3) The Commission, in order to obtain information that might enable it to discharge its functions, may at any stage of the proceeding:

(a) request from either party oral explanations, documents and other information;

(b) request evidence from other persons; and

(c) with the consent of the party concerned, visit any place connected with the dispute or conduct inquiries there, provided that the parties may participate in any such visits and inquiries."

Rule 23

Rule 23 (1) makes the important point that the good faith of the parties is a vital requirement of the conciliation process. It states that:

> *"The parties shall cooperate in good faith with the Commission and, in particular, at its request furnish all relevant documents, information and explanations as well as use the means at their disposal to enable the Commission to hear witnesses and experts whom it desires to call. The parties shall also facilitate visits to and inquiries at any place connected with the dispute that the Commission desires to undertake."*

Rule 23 (2) requires the parties to comply with any time limits.

Rules 24 to 28

As soon as the Commission is constituted, the Secretary-General is to transmit to each member of the Commission a copy of the request, supporting documentation, the notice of registration and any communications from the parties (Rule 24).

Provisions relating to written statements are contained in Rule 25. The President of the Commission is to invite each party to file a *"written statement of its position"*. The time limit is 30 days. Every written statement or other instrument may be accompanied by supporting documentation, which should ordinarily be filed together with the instrument to which it relates (Rule 26).

Rule 27 makes provisions for hearings. These are to take place in private, and unless the parties agree otherwise, are to remain secret. The Commission is to decide, with the consent of the parties, which other persons – besides the parties and their agents, counsel, advocates, witnesses and experts – may attend the hearings.

The parties may request the Commission to hear witnesses and experts, who shall be examined before the Commission. Such examination is by the parties, but under the control of the President. Questions may also be put by any member of the Commission. If a witness or expert cannot attend the hearing, the Commission (with the agreement of the parties) may make arrangements for the relevant evidence to be given in a written deposition or to be taken by examination at another place (Rule 28).

Chapters V and VI

Chapter V contains the provisions dealing with termination of the proceeding: objections to jurisdiction; closure of the proceeding; preparation of the conciliation Report; provisions relating to the Report; and communication of that Report.

Rule 32 states that the Report is to contain:

"(a) a precise designation of each party;

(b) a statement that the Commission was established under the Convention, and a description of the method of its constitution;

(c) the names of the members of the Commission, and an identification of the appointing authority of each;

(d) the names of the agents, counsel and advocates of the parties;

(e) the dates and place of the sittings of the Commission; and

(f) a summary of the proceeding."

The Report is also to record *"any agreement of the parties, pursuant to Article 35 of the Convention, concerning the use in other proceedings of the views expressed or statements or admissions or offers of settlement made in the proceeding before the Commission or of the report or any recommendation made by the Commission"*.

Chapter VI contains the Final Provisions.

6) The ICSID Additional Facility Rules and the Fact-finding Provisions

Introduction

The Administrative Council of the Centre adopted Additional Facility Rules that authorise the Secretariat of ICSID to administer certain categories of proceedings between States and nationals of other States that fall outside the scope of that provision in the ICSID Convention.

Given that proceedings under the Additional Facility Rules are not governed by the Convention, it is important to appreciate that arbitrations conducted under these Rules are not protected from national laws. Therefore recognition and enforcement of awards will be governed by the law of the place of enforcement – the 'self-enforcing' machinery of the ICSID Convention does not apply.

ICSID's Introduction to the Additional Facility Rules explains the extent of the Centre's jurisdiction by analogy with Article 25 (1) of the ICSID Convention. That Article provides that the jurisdiction of the Centre *"shall extend to any legal dispute arising directly out of an investment, between a Contracting State (or any constituent subdivision or agency of a Contracting State designated to the Centre by that State) and a national of another Contracting State, which the parties to the dispute consent in writing to submit to the Centre"*. The Introduction explains that the additional categories of proceedings are:

"(i) fact-finding proceedings; (ii) conciliation or arbitration proceedings for the settlement of investment disputes between parties one of which is not a

Contracting State or a national of a Contracting State; and (iii) conciliation and arbitration proceedings between parties at least one of which is a Contracting State or a national of a Contracting State for the settlement of disputes that do not arise directly out of an investment, provided that the underlying transaction is not an ordinary commercial transaction."

The Introduction states that the Additional Facility Rules *"comprise a principal set of Rules Governing the Additional Facility and their three schedules: Fact-Finding Rules (Schedule A), Conciliation Rules (Schedule B) and Arbitration Rules (Schedule C). On September 29, 2002, the Administrative Council approved amendments of the Additional Facility Rules. These amendments came into effect on January 1, 2003."*

The Additional Facility Rules

Article 1 of the Rules contains definitions. Article 2 states that the Secretariat of the Centre is authorised to administer proceedings between a State and a national of another State that fall within the following categories:

"(a) conciliation and arbitration proceedings for the settlement of legal disputes arising directly out of an investment which are not within the jurisdiction of the Centre because either the State party to the dispute or the State whose national is a party to the dispute is not a Contracting State;

(b) conciliation and arbitration proceedings for the settlement of legal disputes which are not within the jurisdiction of the Centre because they do not arise directly out of an investment, provided that either the State party to the dispute or the State whose national is a party to the dispute is a Contracting State; and

(c) fact-finding proceedings."

Article 3 makes clear that, because the proceedings envisaged by Article 2 are outside the jurisdiction of the Centre, none of the provisions of the Convention are applicable to those proceedings or to recommendations, awards or reports.

Article 4 (1) states that any agreement providing for conciliation or arbitration proceedings under the Additional Facility in respect of existing or future disputes requires the approval of the Secretary-General. The rest of Article 4 sets out the conditions to be satisfied for such approval to be granted:

"(2) In the case of an application based on Article 2(a), the Secretary-General shall give his approval only if (a) he is satisfied that the requirements of that provision are fulfilled at the time, and (b) both parties give their consent to the jurisdiction of the Centre under Article 25 of the Convention (in lieu of the Additional Facility) in the event that the jurisdictional requirements ratione personae of that Article shall have been met at the time when proceedings are instituted.

(3) In the case of an application based on Article 2(b), the Secretary-General shall give his approval only if he is satisfied (a) that the requirements of that provision are fulfilled, and (b) that the underlying transaction has features which distinguish it from an ordinary commercial transaction.

(4) If in the case of an application based on Article 2(b) the jurisdictional requirements ratione personae of Article 25 of the Convention shall have been met and the Secretary-General is of the opinion that it is likely that a Conciliation Commission or Arbitral Tribunal, as the case may be, will hold that the dispute arises directly out of an investment, he may make his approval of the application conditional upon consent by both parties to submit any dispute in the first instance to the jurisdiction of the Centre."

Proceedings for fact-finding, conciliation and arbitration under the Additional Facility are to be conducted in accordance with the respective Rules set out in Schedules A, B and C. Schedules B and C contain detailed provisions dealing with conciliation and arbitration that are similar to the ICSID Conciliation and Arbitration rules already considered.

The fact-finding provisions

Schedule A contains the fact-finding provisions. There are four Chapters: Chapter I deals with the institution of proceedings; Chapter II with the Committee and its workings; Chapter III with the termination of the proceedings; and Chapter IV includes a requirement of good faith.

Chapter I: Commencement of the process and appointment of the Committee

Article 1 of Chapter I sets out the nature of a 'fact-finding proceeding':

> *"Any State or national of a State wishing to institute an inquiry under the Additional Facility to examine and report on facts (hereinafter called a 'fact-finding proceeding') shall send a request to that effect in writing to the Secretariat at the seat of the Centre...."*

The request may be made jointly by the parties. Article 2 states that the request is to:

"(a) designate precisely each party to the fact-finding proceeding and state the address of each;

(b) set forth the agreement between the parties providing for recourse to the fact-finding proceeding; and

(c) state the circumstances to be examined and reported on."

The request is also to set out any provisions agreed by the parties regarding *"the number of commissioners, their qualifications, appointment, replacement, resignation and disqualification, the extent of the powers of the Committee, the appointment of its President, and the place of its sessions, as well as the procedure to be followed in the fact-finding proceeding (hereinafter called the 'Procedural Arrangement')".*

Provisions relating to the registration of the request by the Secretary-General are set out in Article 3. The other party may object to the request (Article 4). Such objection is to be made in writing to the Secretary-General and is to indicate which of the following grounds are relied on. Namely, that:

"(a) the other party is under no obligation to have recourse to fact-finding;

(b) the circumstances indicated in the request as the circumstances to be examined and reported on are wholly or partly outside the scope of the agreement between the parties for recourse to fact-finding."

The Secretary-General is to send a copy of the notice of objections to the other party and is to invite the parties *"to meet with him in order to seek to resolve the objections by agreement"*. If no agreement is reached, the parties are to be invited to designate a 'Special Commissioner' to rule on the objections. If the parties do not designate a Special Commissioner within the period allowed (and are not willing to allow the designation to be made by the Chairman of the Administrative Council or some other authority), the Secretary-General is to inform the parties that *"the fact-finding proceeding cannot be held, recording the failure of the parties or one of them to cooperate"*.

If the Special Commissioner is appointed, he or she is to rule on the objections after hearing both parties and decide whether or not the fact-finding proceeding is to continue. If it is to continue, the Special Commissioner is to determine the scope of the proceeding (Article 5).

To the extent that the parties have not agreed the fact-finding procedure to be followed, Article 6 provides that the Procedural Arrangement is to be drawn up by the Chairman, in consultation with the parties. Unless the parties agree otherwise, that Arrangement is to provide for the appointment of three commissioners, and:

"(a) qualifications, appointment, replacement, resignation, and disqualification of the commissioners, filling up of the vacancies and consequential resumption of proceeding; and (b) incapacity of the President of the Committee and procedural matters, including procedural languages, shall, to the extent practicable, be similar to those applicable to conciliators and conciliation proceedings under the Conciliation (Additional Facility) Rules."

Chapter II: Procedure of the Committee

Unless the parties agree otherwise, the Committee is to consist of a sole Commissioner or any uneven number of Commissioners. If it consists of three or more, one is to be appointed President (Article 7). Following their appointment, Article 8 requires each member of the Committee to sign a declaration similar to that required under the Arbitration Rules.

Each investigation, and each examination of a locality, is to be in the presence of agents and counsel of the parties (Article 10). Decisions of the Committee are to be taken by a majority of votes of the members (Article 11). Article 12 provides that the Secretary-General shall make the necessary arrangements for the serving of notices by the Committee. The constitution of that Committee and its procedures are to be governed by the Procedural Arrangement. Any matters not provided for in that Arrangement, or in any of the Rules, are to be determined by the agreement of the parties or, failing that, by the Committee (Article 13).

Chapter III: Termination of the proceedings and the Report of the Committee

After the parties have presented their explanations and evidence, and any witnesses have been heard, the President of the Committee is to declare the fact-finding proceedings closed. The Committee then adjourns to deliberate and to draw up its Report.

If one of the parties has failed to appear, to participate in the proceeding or to cooperate with the Committee, and the Committee determines that as a result it is unable to carry out its task, it is to give notice to the parties, *"close the proceeding and draw up its Report, noting the reference to fact-finding under the Additional Facility and recording the failure of that party to appear, participate or cooperate"* (Article 14).

Article 15 states that the Report of the Committee is to be adopted by a majority of the Commissioners and signed by them. The refusal of a Commissioner to sign shall not invalidate the Report. A Commissioner who dissents may attach to the Report a statement explaining his/her reasons.

Article 15 (4) contains the significant provision that *"The Report shall be limited to findings of fact. The Report shall not contain any recommendations to the parties nor shall it have the character of an award"*. Article 16 contains the equally significant provision that the parties shall be *"entirely free as to the effect to be given to the Report"*.

Chapter IV: Good faith

Article 17 contains what is in effect a 'good faith' requirement that the parties cooperate with the Committee. The parties are to:

> *"undertake to facilitate the work of the Committee and to supply it with all means and facilities necessary to enable it to become fully acquainted with, and to accurately understand, the facts in question. Without prejudice to the generality of the foregoing, the parties in particular undertake to supply the Committee to the greatest possible extent with all relevant documents and information, as well as to use the means at their disposal to allow the Committee to visit the localities in question and to summon and hear witnesses or experts."*

7) The ICSID Centre's Caseload

The increasing use of – and reliance on – bilateral and multilateral investment treaties has led in recent years to a considerable increase in the Centre's caseload. This fact was stressed by the Senior Counsel at ICSID, Mr Ucheroa Onwuamaegbu, when he spoke at the 2004 International Oil and Gas Conference in London (see Box 9). Although cases traditionally brought to the Centre were mostly commenced on the basis of the agreement of the parties in their investment contracts, or on the basis of consents of governments contained in national investment laws, Mr Onwuamaegbu said that in the past decade more cases had been commenced on the authority of the consents provided by governments in various bilateral and multilateral treaties that provide for ICSID arbitration for the resolution of their investment disputes. Indeed, about 80 per cent of the cases then pending at the Centre were commenced on the basis of consents contained in BITs.

Box 9: Comments on ICSID by the Centre's Senior Counsel

Speaking at the 2004 International Oil and Gas Conference at the Guildhall in the City of London, ICSID's Senior Counsel Mr Ucheroa Onwuamaegbu stated that the Centre provided facilities for the arbitration and conciliation under the ICSID Convention of legal disputes arising directly out of an investment between member States and nationals of other member States. By way of example, he said that the Centre had recently registered a request for arbitration by a Dutch company against the Government of Tunisia concerning alleged breaches of rights and obligations under the Tunisian foreign investment law.

He added that in addition to the Convention cases, ICSID also administered cases under the Additional Facility Rules, where one of the parties was not a member country or a national of a member country, or where the dispute did not directly arise out of an investment. Therefore a country like Canada (or its national) could be a party to proceedings at the Centre under those Rules. He pointed out that such proceedings were not covered by the provisions of the Convention and could therefore be subject to the control of national courts.

Of cases pending at ICSID, 14 related to oil and gas and of those all but three involved the Government of Argentina as a respondent. All of the cases involving Argentina concerned complaints of similar measures of the Government, which claimants alleged had breached their rights guaranteed under BITs. This fact raised challenging issues for ICSID in relation to administering multiple cases involving the same respondent and similar legal and factual issues. One approach taken by the Centre, with the cooperation of the parties, had been to appoint the same arbitrators wherever possible to deal with different claims that involved similar issues. Some of the pending cases raised common issues – for example, jurisdictional matters raised when a claimant alleged a breach of a contract and a breach of a treaty in the same dispute.

To date, ICSID had dealt with four conciliation cases, and was taking steps to encourage increased use of the Conciliation Rules.

In concluding, Mr Onwuaemaegbu stressed that an award made by a Tribunal under the ICSID Convention could be enforced in 140 countries as if it were a *"final judgement of a court"* in each of those countries. Such an award was also free from interference by the local courts.

In the year 2004 there were more than 70 pending cases. By early 2006, the number of pending cases exceeded 100. These cases included disputes dealing with the following:

- Debt instruments
- Cobalt and copper mining concessions
- Natural gas transportation

- Hydrocarbon concession and electricity generation project
- Water and sewer services concession agreement
- Concession agreement regarding a port
- Electric power generating station project
- Energy enterprise
- Oil and gas development contract
- Waterway construction project
- Dam construction project
- Diamond mining concessions
- Airport project / construction of an airport terminal
- Electricity generation and distribution enterprise
- Oil refinery
- Cotton processing and trading enterprise
- Sunflower oil joint venture
- Cement production enterprise
- Railway concession agreement
- Dredging project
- Thermal energy station project

States involved in the cases included Argentina, Bolivia, Burundi, Democratic Republic of the Congo, Ecuador, Egypt, Jordan, Kazakhstan, Kenya, Mexico, Pakistan, Peru, Philippines, Romania, Seychelles, Slovak Republic, Trinidad and Tobago, Turkey and the United States of America.

8) Problems Arising in Investor-State Disputes

Some of the difficulties that may arise in investment treaty arbitration were considered in Chapter 9 of the Manual, which dealt with investor-State disputes.

The problems looked at were 'umbrella' / *pacta sunt servanda* clauses, 'fork in the road' provisions, and the difficulties caused by different tribunals arriving at different decisions in cases involving similar facts / similar issues. The decisions *in SGS v Pakistan* and *SGS v the Philippines* were taken as an example of the problems. The chapter also considered possible solutions to those problems that might be provided by listing similar facts / similar issues cases before the same tribunals, or by using mechanisms such as joinder or consolidation.

A more radical proposal, which was being considered by ICSID in 2004, was the setting up of an appellate process – a single optional mechanism for the appeal of awards in investor-State disputes as an alternative to individual appeal mechanisms that could be created under different treaties by member countries.

9) Proposed Changes to the ICSID Rules

The possibility of setting up an appellate process was raised in a 'Discussion Paper on Possible Improvements of the Legal Framework for ICSID Arbitration', released by the Secretariat of the ICSID Centre in October 2004.[61] The Secretariat sought comments on the Discussion Paper from, among others, business groups, civil society groups and arbitration experts and institutions around the world.

In May 2005 ICSID issued a Working Paper that outlined the results of that extensive consultation and set out a number of proposed changes to the Rules. According to the Working Paper, the Discussion Paper had

> *"... suggested some changes to the ICSID Arbitration Rules and the Additional Facility Arbitration Rules. The suggested changes concerned preliminary procedures; publication of awards; access of third parties to the proceedings; and disclosure requirements of arbitrators. The Discussion Paper also suggested that ICSID might strengthen its conciliation services and expand its training activities. A further possibility considered in the Discussion Paper was the establishment by ICSID of a mechanism for the appeal of awards in investment arbitrations. The Discussion Paper explained that this was a possibility that ICSID might pursue as an alternative to the creation of individual appeal mechanisms under different investment treaties of member countries."*

For example, the proposed changes to ICSID Arbitration Rule 39 dealing with preliminary procedures are set out in an Annex to the Working Paper. The Note explaining the reasons for the proposed amendments stated:

> *"As noted in the Secretariat's Discussion Paper of October 22, 2004, under the ICSID Arbitration Rules, provisional measures may only be sought from national courts if provided for in the consent to arbitration of the parties. Even where such measures are urgently needed, the parties must await the review and registration of the request for arbitration, and the constitution of the arbitral tribunal, before filing a request. Thereafter, the tribunal would have to allow the parties enough time to file observations before it could recommend provisional measures.*
>
> *"The suggested changes introduce a procedure for the expedited filing of requests for provisional measures, and of all the observations of the parties on such a request, prior to the constitution of a tribunal. Such a procedure would reduce delay and ensure that the tribunal is able to consider the request once it is constituted, especially where the measures are urgently required."*

However, the Working Paper did not make any proposals in relation to the difficult question of an appellate system. Paragraph 4 of the Working Paper explained why:

> *"The members of the Administrative Council and others who provided comments on the Discussion Paper expressed appreciation for the initiative to review the framework for ICSID arbitration and identify possible improvements. There was general agreement that, if international appellate procedures were to be introduced*

61 Further information on the Discussion Paper can be found on the World Bank website.

for investment treaty arbitrations, then this might best be done through a single ICSID mechanism rather than by different mechanisms established under each treaty concerned. Most, however, considered that it would be premature to attempt to establish such an ICSID mechanism at this stage, particularly in view of the difficult technical and policy issues raised in the Discussion Paper. The Secretariat will continue to study such issues to assist member countries when and if it is decided to proceed towards the establishment of an ICSID appeal mechanism."

10) Conclusions

The ICSID system is a supranational system created specifically for the purpose of handling investment disputes. The Centre, through the ICSID Convention and the various sets of ICSID Rules, provides a wide range of investment dispute resolution processes to both States and nationals of States. One of the system's many benefits is the fact that, in relation to arbitration, it provides a self-contained enforcement mechanism.

The increased use of and reliance on bilateral and multilateral investment treaties has resulted in an increase in the volume of the Centre's caseload, a situation that seems likely to continue into the future.

Part IV: International Commercial Dispute Resolution

"Given the prodigious expansion of international commercial arbitration over the past half-century (the increase of trade being its fundamental cause, and the 1958 New York Convention on the Recognition and Enforcement of Foreign Arbitral Awards its primary instrument) modern practitioners may be excused for believing that we are living in an unprecedented golden age of international arbitration. They would be surprised to learn how vast international arbitral jurisprudence was in the 19th Century. In the period between 1814 and 1898, for example, one study enumerated no less than 158 different international tribunals, including the celebrated commissions created in 1853 between Britain and the US; in 1868 between Mexico and the US; and in 1880 between France and the US....

"The list did not include the commissions created under the famous Jay Treaty, UK/US, 8 Stat. 116, which was concluded in 1794 for the purposes, inter alia, of adjudicating claims of British creditors who were unsatisfied by their treatment at the hands of US courts, and vice versa. All of these bodies were created by treaty, some to resolve only one dispute, but others to deal with many cases over a period of years."

Jan Paulsson[62]

62 Jan Paulsson, "International Arbitration and the Generation of Legal Norms: Treaty Arbitration and International Law", paper delivered at the 18th Congress of the International Council for Commercial Arbitration in Montreal, June 2006.

15 Introduction

Parts II and III of the Manual dealt with supranational dispute resolution and supranational dispute resolution bodies. The types of disputes were those where one or more of the parties is likely to be a State. The dispute resolution bodies dealt exclusively either with disputes between States or with disputes where one or more of the parties is likely to be a State.

This part of the Manual will deal with international commercial disputes. It may be helpful to approach the topic by looking first at the kind of dispute resolution provisions that are likely to be found in a commercial contract. These are of vital importance, and contractual provision will normally be made at a minimum for the following:

i) *Forum:* in what country should the dispute resolution process take place?

ii) *Choice of law:* which country's law is to govern the contract? It is, of course, always open to the parties to provide for a choice of laws rather than a choice of law and to provide that disputes will be resolved by way of reference to general principles of international law or *lex mercatoria.*[63] However, the choice of a national law is likely to be the norm.

iii) *Dispute resolution process:* broadly speaking, as discussed earlier, there are four dispute resolution processes in common use: litigation, arbitration, alternative dispute resolution (ADR) and expert determination. The questions that then arise are:

- If litigation, which country's courts are to have jurisdiction?
- If arbitration, is this to be institutional or ad hoc? If institutional, which institution? London Court of International Arbitration (LCIA), International Chamber of Commerce (ICC), American Arbitration Association (AAA), etc.?
- If ADR, should some form of ADR filter mechanism be inserted into the contract, arbitration then only being triggered off in the event that the ADR process fails?
- Or is expert determination the appropriate way to resolve disputes?

The following chapters look at those four dispute resolution processes, and at some of the institutions and other bodies providing facilities for the resolution of disputes in the pure commercial field.

63 Law merchant, originally a body of rules and principles relating to merchants and mercantile transactions.

16 Litigation

1) Introduction

Litigation between States in the International Court of Justice (ICJ) was considered earlier in the Manual. This chapter will look at litigation in the national courts. National courts may be used in the context of international commercial disputes for a variety of purposes, for example:

- as a forum for resolving disputes in cases where one or more of the parties is an 'overseas' or foreign party;
- as support machinery for the arbitral process;
- as a forum for challenging or enforcing foreign commercial arbitral awards.

2) National Courts as a Dispute Resolution Forum

Despite the increasing use of international commercial arbitration backed up by the New York Convention, litigation in the national courts is probably still the major international dispute resolution process in use.

In the context of international contracts, the major problem in relation to litigation is the prospect for one of the parties of that litigation taking place in the courts of a foreign country, conducted in a foreign language and under a foreign system of law. However, litigation may be the dispute resolution process used for a variety of reasons:

- No contractual provision is made for dispute resolution;
- The bargaining power of one party is such that it is able to insist that litigation takes place in the courts of a country of its choosing;
- It is a deliberate, consensual choice of the parties. For example, parties may choose the English courts as the forum for resolution of any disputes that may arise under the contract, and additionally may choose English law as the law to govern that contract. More than 80 per cent of the cases heard in the Commercial Court in London have no connection with England in the sense that either the subject matter of the contract has no connection with the country or one or more of the parties is not English.[64]

An example of overseas parties litigating in the English courts is given in Box 10.

64 England and Wales have a separate court system from Scotland and Northern Ireland and, broadly speaking, a separate system of law. For the sake of brevity, reference is made in this Manual to the English courts and English law.

Box 10: National Courts as a Dispute Resolution Forum: *BHP v Dalmine*

In the case of *BHP Billiton Petroleum and others v Dalmine SpA*, the Defendant, Dalmine, appealed to the Court of Appeal against a judgment of Mr Justice Cresswell. The Claimant, BHP, was the operator of an oil and gas field in the Irish Sea. Dalmine, an Italian steel maker, manufactured steel pipes used in the construction of a sub-sea gas pipeline. The pipeline suffered sulphide stress corrosion cracking. The cracks started in the weld root between the sections of pipe and then propagated through the weld metal on the adjacent pipe. BHP found that the pipes adjacent to the leak sites were out of specification because the carbon equivalent value exceeded 0.40 per cent, making the steel less resistant to crack propagation.

In proceedings against Dalmine, BHP discovered that the steel maker had fraudulently misrepresented the carbon value of the pipes during the manufacturing and supply process. Dalmine accepted responsibility for that fraud and accepted that BHP had relied on the false documents.

Mr Justice Cresswell found that on the balance of probability the incorporation of non-compliant pipe did cause the pipeline to fail and that the pipeline would not otherwise have failed. The Judge found in favour of BHP and ordered damages to be assessed. The Court of Appeal dismissed the appeal.

A full report of the case can be found at [2003] EWCA Civ 170.

3) National Courts as Support Machinery for the Arbitral Process: The English Arbitration Act

i) Introduction

Most states support the arbitral process while at the same time exercising a degree of control over that process. For example, the English Arbitration Act of 1996 supports arbitration in a number of ways, both by filling gaps where the parties have failed to make some necessary provision for the operation of the arbitral process and by giving powers to the court to assist the arbitral process. (The UNCITRAL Model Law on International Commercial Arbitration, on which the English Act is structured, is considered in Chapter 17.)

The 'gap-filling' aspect of the English Act may be of less importance to an international commercial arbitration held in England in circumstances where the parties have provided in their contract for arbitration under the Rules of one of the major international commercial arbitral institutions, such as the London Court of International Arbitration (LCIA) or the International Chamber of Commerce (ICC). Such Rules contain detailed provisions for the conduct of an arbitration, running from the commencement of the arbitration through to the making of the final award.

However, where the arbitration provisions made in the relevant contract are sketchy *("arbitration London")*, the English Act gives full supporting machinery for the conduct of an arbitration whose 'seat' is England. The framework provided by the Act operates from the commencement of the arbitration and the appointment of the tribunal right through to the making of and enforcement of the award.

The Departmental Advisory Committee on Arbitration Law (DAC), under the chairmanship of Lord Justice Mustill (now Lord Mustill), advised the British Government on the proposed Act. In its Report in June 1989, the DAC advised against England, Wales and Northern Ireland adopting the UNCITRAL Model Law and recommended instead that there should be a new and improved Arbitration Act that should comprise a statement in statutory form of the more important principles of the English law of arbitration. However, consideration should be given *"to ensuring that any such new statute should, as far as possible, have the same structure and language as the Model Law, so as to enhance its accessibility to those who are familiar with the Model Law"*.

The DAC also recommended that the new Act should apply both to domestic and international arbitrations and should not be limited to the subject matter of the Model Law.

ii) An overview of the Act

Part I of the 1996 English Arbitration Act deals with introductory matters; the arbitration agreement; stay of legal proceedings; commencement of arbitral proceedings; the arbitral tribunal (appointment, resignation, death and the filling of vacancies); jurisdiction of the arbitral tribunal; the arbitral proceedings; powers of the court in relation to arbitral proceedings; the award; costs; powers of the court in relation to the award; and miscellaneous and supplementary provisions.

Part II is largely concerned with domestic arbitration. Part III deals with the recognition and enforcement of foreign arbitral awards, namely Geneva Convention awards and New York Convention awards. Part IV contains general provisions.

The English Act leaves the arbitral process largely in the hands of the parties. For example, the parties may make provisions in their arbitration agreement relating to the appointment of a tribunal. But to the extent that the parties have failed to make those provisions, the Act contains the necessary framework for the appointment and replacement of arbitrators. However, there are certain 'mandatory provisions' that apply regardless of the will of the parties. These include the provisions in Section 9 relating to the stay of litigation where parties have agreed to arbitrate, and the provisions in Section 66 relating to the enforcement of the award.

iii) 'Gap- filling' and supportive provisions in the Act

Stay of litigation

Section 9 of the Act contains a major support mechanism for the arbitral process. It operates to prohibit one of the parties from using litigation in circumstances where an agreement has been made between the parties to utilise arbitration as the dispute resolution process: *"a party to an arbitration agreement against whom legal proceedings are brought… in respect of a matter which under the agreement is to be referred to arbitration may... apply to the court in which the proceedings have been brought to stay the proceedings so far as they concern that matter".*

The court shall grant the application unless satisfied that the arbitration agreement is *"null and void, inoperative, or incapable of being performed"* – the wording of the provision contained in Article II.3 of the New York Convention.

Composition of the tribunal

Sections 15-27 of the Act contain provisions dealing with the appointment of the arbitral tribunal in circumstances where the parties themselves have not agreed such provisions. The Sections deal also with the resignation and death of arbitrators and the filling of vacancies. In addition, Section 24 gives power to the court to remove an arbitrator: Any party to arbitral proceedings may apply to the court to remove an arbitrator on various grounds, including the existence of circumstances that *"give rise to justifiable doubts as to his impartiality".*

Jurisdiction of the tribunal

Section 30 contains another important 'gap-filling' provision dealing with *competence / competence:*

> *"Unless otherwise agreed by the parties, the arbitral tribunal may rule on its own substantive jurisdiction, that is, as to –*
>
> *(a) whether there is a valid arbitration agreement,*
>
> *(b) whether the tribunal is properly constituted, and*
>
> *(c) what matters have been submitted to arbitration in accordance with the arbitration agreement."*

Duty of the tribunal

Section 33 lays down the general duty of an arbitral tribunal, which shall

> *"(a) act fairly and impartially as between the parties, giving each party a reasonable opportunity of putting his case and dealing with that of his opponent, and*
>
> *(b) adopt procedures suitable to the circumstances of the particular case, avoiding unnecessary delay or expense, so as to provide a fair means for the resolution of the matters falling to be determined."*

The general duty imposed by the Act in Section 33 is linked to one of the few opportunities given to a party to challenge an arbitral award. Section 68 provides that a party to an arbitral award may apply to the court to challenge the award on the grounds of 'serious irregularity', one such irregularity being the failure by the tribunal to comply with the general duty set out in Section 33.

Powers of the tribunal

Section 38 stresses the freedom of the parties to agree on the powers exercisable by the tribunal. However, unless the parties have agreed otherwise, the Act gives to the tribunal various powers including:

- the power to order a claimant to provide security costs;
- the power to give directions relating to the preservation of property;
- the power to direct that a party or witness be examined on oath or affirmation;
- the power to give directions to a party for the preservation of evidence.

Section 39 states that the parties are free to agree that the tribunal shall have the power to make provisional awards.

Section 41 sets out the powers of a tribunal in case of a party's default (save where the parties have agreed otherwise):

- the power to make an award dismissing a claim where one party has been guilty of inordinate and inexcusable delay;
- the power to continue with proceedings in the absence of a party who has failed to attend or has failed to submit evidence or make submissions;
- the power to deal with a party who fails to comply with any order or direction of the tribunal.

Section 43 deals with the securing of the attendance of witnesses at an arbitration hearing. It provides that a party to arbitral proceedings may *"use the same court procedures as are available in relation to legal proceedings to secure the attendance before the tribunal of a witness in order to give oral testimony or to produce documents or other material evidence"*.

Powers of the court

Section 44 gives extensive powers to the court to support arbitral proceedings. Unless the parties have agreed otherwise, the court has power to make orders relating to:

- the taking of evidence of witnesses;
- the preservation of evidence;
- the inspection, preservation or detention of property;
- the taking of samples;
- the sale of goods;
- the granting of interim injunctions or the appointment of receivers.

Section 45 contains potentially useful provisions dealing with the determination of a preliminary point of law. Unless the parties have agreed otherwise, the court may *"on the application of a party to arbitral proceedings... determine any question of law arising in the course of the proceedings which the court is satisfied substantially affects the rights of one or more of the parties"*.

Governing law, conflict of laws, *ex aequo et bono* and *amiable compositeur*[65]

Section 46 deals with the vitally important matters of governing law in Section 46 (1) and (2) and conflict of laws in Section 46 (3).

First, the Act states that a tribunal is to decide a dispute *"... in accordance with the law chosen by the parties as applicable to the substance of the dispute, or if the parties so agree, in accordance with such other considerations as are agreed by them or determined by the tribunal"*. It therefore makes it clear that, in accordance with the generally accepted international view, the parties are free to choose the governing law: for example, Italian law. Alternatively, the parties are entitled to specify that the tribunal may decide a dispute on the basis of "other considerations". This can be read as meaning that it may decide on the basis of general equitable principles, i.e., *ex aequo et bono* or acting as *amiable compositeur.*

This is because the Act is based on the UNCITRAL Model Law, which in Article 28 states that the tribunal *"shall decide* ex aequo et bono *or as* amiable compositeur *only if the parties have expressly authorized it to do so"*.

Those who drafted the English Act, however, deliberately avoided using those two terms, instead referring to "other considerations". The DAC Report of February 1996 explained the position: *"... [T]he parties may agree that their dispute is not to be decided in accordance with a recognised system of law but under what in this country are often called 'equity clauses' or arbitration* 'ex aequo et bono' *or* 'amiable composition' *i.e. general considerations of justice and fairness etc. It will be noted that we avoided using this description in the Bill, just as we have avoided using the Latin and French expressions found in the Model Law.'*[66]

Section 46 (2) makes it clear that the requirement that an arbitral tribunal is to decide the dispute in accordance with the law chosen by the parties is a reference to the substantive laws of a country (e.g., the laws of Italy) and not to that country's conflict of laws rules.

To the extent that the parties have failed to make a choice *"... the tribunal shall apply the law determined by the conflict of law rules which it considers applicable"* (Section 46 (3)). Most developed systems of law contain rules to be used to discover the law to be applied where the parties to a contract have failed to specify what that law should be. These 'conflict of law' rules, which differ from country to country, may be based on 'connecting factors'. Take the example of a case involving a dispute between French and German companies that comes before an arbitral tribunal sitting in England. The parties failed to specify which country's law should govern their contract, but the contract was signed in Germany, written in German and was to be performed in Germany. The application of the English conflict of law rules might determine that the substantive law to be applied by the tribunal was the law of Germany.

---

65 *Amiable compositeur* means the arbitrator has the power to abate the strictness of law in favour of general principles of equity.

67 Departmental Advisory Committee on Arbitration Law, *Report on the Arbitration Bill,* February 1996, p 49.

Awards on different issues, etc

Section 47 gives to the tribunal (unless the parties have otherwise agreed) the practical and useful power to make awards on different issues: "... *the tribunal may make more than one award at different times on different aspects of the matters to be determined*".

Settlement and agreed awards

Section 51 deals with settlement. It provides that, if the parties settle the dispute during the arbitral proceedings, the tribunal is to terminate the substantive proceedings and, if requested by the parties and not objected to by the tribunal, it "... *shall record the settlement in the form of an agreed award*". This is an important provision in relation to the New York Convention.

Finality of awards

Section 58 contains one of the vitally significant provisions relating to arbitration, namely the finality of awards. It states that, unless the parties have agreed otherwise, an award is "... *final and binding both on the parties and on any persons claiming through or under them*". The proviso to Section 58 states that the finality of the award does not affect the rights of a person to challenge the award by any *"available arbitral process of appeal or review"*, or in accordance with the provisions of the Act. The latter is a reference to the provisions of Sections 67, 68 and 69 (see below).

Challenging awards and appeals on points of law

Section 67 contains provisions enabling a party to challenge an award in relation to the substantive jurisdiction of the tribunal.

Section 68 contains provisions enabling an award to be challenged on the grounds of a *"serious irregularity"* that the court considers has caused or will cause *"substantial injustice"*. The types of irregularity are listed in Section 68 (2):

"(a) failure by the tribunal to comply with section 33 (general duty of tribunal);

(b) the tribunal exceeding its powers (otherwise than by exceeding its substantive jurisdiction: see section 67);

(c) failure by the tribunal to conduct the proceedings in accordance with the procedure agreed by the parties;

(d) failure by the tribunal to deal with all the issues that were put to it;

(e) any arbitral or other institution or person vested by the parties with powers in relation to the proceedings or the award exceeding its powers;

(f) uncertainty or ambiguity as to the effect of the award;

(g) the award being obtained by fraud or the award or the way in which it was procured being contrary to public policy;

(h) failure to comply with the requirements as to the form of the award; or

(i) any irregularity in the conduct of the proceedings or in the award which is admitted by the tribunal or by any arbitral or other institution or person vested by the parties with powers in relation to the proceedings or the award."

Section 69 deals with appeals on points of law. Unless the parties have agreed otherwise, a party may appeal to the court on a question of law arising out of an award. The right to appeal on a point of law is limited and such an appeal cannot be brought except:

"(a) with the agreement of all the other parties to the proceedings, or

(b) with the leave of the court."

The right to appeal is also subject to the restrictions in Section 70(2) and (3). Leave to appeal will only be given if the court is satisfied,

"(a) that the determination of the question will substantially affect the rights of one or more of the parties,

(b) that the question is one which the tribunal was asked to determine,

(c) that, on the basis of the findings of fact in the award –

(i) the decision of the tribunal on the question is obviously wrong, or

(ii) the question is one of general public importance and the decision of the tribunal is at least open to serious doubt, and

(d) that, despite the agreement of the parties to resolve the matter by arbitration, it is just and proper in all the circumstances for the court to determine the question."

Section 70 (2) provides that an application or appeal may not be brought if the applicant or appellant has not first exhausted

"(a) any available arbitral process of appeal or review, and

(b) any available recourse under section 57 (correction of award or additional award)."

Section 70 (3) states that any application or appeal *"must be brought within 28 days of the date of the award or, if there has been any arbitral process of appeal or review, of the date when the applicant or appellant was notified of the result of that process"*.

Recognition and enforcement of awards

Section 66 of the Act deals with enforcement of the award. It states that an award may, by leave of the court, be enforced *"... in the same manner as a judgement or award of court to the same effect"*. This Section relates to the enforcement of domestic awards and of international awards made in England. An international arbitral award made in England is not, for purposes of recognition and enforcement, a New York Convention award (Article 1.1 of the New York Convention and Section 100 of the Act). The provisions relating to the recognition and enforcement of awards made *outside* England (i.e., mainly New York Convention awards) are dealt with in Sections 99 to 104.

Section 66 (4) states that:

"Nothing in this section affects the recognition or enforcement of an award under any other enactment or rule of law, in particular under Part II of the Arbitration Act 1950 (enforcement of awards under Geneva Convention) or the provisions of Part III of this Act relating to the recognition and enforcement of awards under the New York Convention or by an action on the award."

Section 99 deals with the enforcement of Geneva Convention awards by simply continuing the provisions of the Arbitration Act 1950. Since this Convention is not longer in effect between contracting States that are parties to the New York Convention, there are now obviously very few such awards.

Section 100 deals with New York Convention awards. It defines such an award as one *"made, in pursuance of an arbitration agreement, in the territory of a state (other than the United Kingdom) which is a party to the New York Convention".*

Section 101 contains the provisions dealing with the recognition and enforcement of New York Convention awards, stating that such an award *"... shall be recognised as binding on the persons as between whom it was made, and may accordingly be relied on by those persons by way of defence, set-off or otherwise in any legal proceedings in England and Wales or Northern Ireland".* The award is enforced by leave of the court *"in the same manner as a judgment or order of the court to the same effect".*

Section 102 is concerned with the evidence that is to be produced by the party seeking recognition or enforcement of a New York Convention award, which is:

"(a) the duly authenticated original award or a duly certified copy of it, and

(b) the original arbitration agreement or a duly certified copy of it".

Section 103 sets out the grounds for the refusal of recognition or enforcement of a New York Convention award. These provisions are based on the Convention itself (which is considered in the next chapter). The Section provides that recognition or enforcement of a Convention award is not to be refused except in the cases listed in Section 103 (2). Recognition or enforcement may be refused if the person against whom the award is invoked proves:

"(a) that a party to the arbitration agreement was (under the law applicable to him) under some incapacity;

(b) that the arbitration agreement was not valid under the law to which the parties subjected it or, failing any indication thereon, under the law of the country where the award was made;

(c) that he was not given proper notice of the appointment of the arbitrator or of the arbitration proceedings or was otherwise unable to present his case;

(d) that the award deals with a difference not contemplated by or not falling within the terms of the submission to arbitration or contains decisions on matters beyond the scope of the submission to arbitration (but see subsection (4));

(e) that the composition of the arbitral tribunal or the arbitral procedure was not in accordance with the agreement of the parties or, failing such agreement, with the law of the country in which the arbitration took place;

(f) that the award has not yet become binding on the parties, or has been set aside or suspended by a competent authority of the country in which, or under the law of which, it was made."

Recognition or enforcement of an award may also be refused if the award *"is in respect of a matter which is not capable of settlement by arbitration, or if it would be contrary to public policy to recognise or enforce the award"* (Section 103 (3)).

Section 103 (4) states that: *"An award which contains decisions on matters not submitted to arbitration may be recognised or enforced to the extent that it contains decisions on matters submitted to arbitration which can be separated from those on matters not so submitted."* The court has the power to adjourn its decision on the recognition or enforcement of an award: *"Where an application for the setting aside or suspension of the award has been made to such a competent authority as is mentioned in subsection (2)(f)"* (Section 103 (5)).

Section 104 makes provision for the retention of the right to enforce a New York Convention award under common law or under Section 66. An example of the enforcement of a foreign arbitral award by the English courts is given in the next section of this chapter.

For the purposes of this Manual, arguably the most important provisions in the English Arbitration Act are Section 9, dealing with the stay of litigation where parties have agreed to arbitrate disputes; Section 66, dealing with the enforcement of international awards made in England; and Sections 100 to 103, dealing with the recognition and enforcement of New York Convention awards made outside England.

4) National Courts as a Forum for Enforcing and Challenging International Arbitral Awards

National courts may also be used both to challenge foreign arbitral awards and to enforce such awards. This aspect of the national courts' jurisdiction seems to be increasing and is likely to increase further for two reasons: first, because of the growth of world trade; and second, because of the increasing use of arbitration as a means of resolving international commercial disputes. Examples are given below of cases that have come before courts in England, the United States and China.

i) England: Commercial Court in London

An example of a case concerning the enforcement of a foreign arbitral award in the English national courts is that of *Minmetals Germany GMBH v Ferco Steel Ltd (1999)*.

The case was heard by Mr Justice Colman in the Commercial Court and concerned a New York Convention award. An application was made by the defendant to set aside leave granted under Section 101 of the English Arbitration Act 1996 to enforce two arbitration awards – one in an initial arbitration and one in a resumed arbitration – made by the China International Economic Trade Arbitration Commission (CIETAC), Beijing.

The issue concerned a contractual dispute in which the contract in question contained a Chinese arbitration clause. The awards, subject only to intervention by the Beijing court, were final and enforceable under Chinese law. Applications to the Beijing court to have the awards revoked were rejected.

The applicant made the following contentions: (i) the awards contained decisions on matters beyond the scope of the submission to arbitration within Section 103 (2) (d) of the 1996 Act, in that the arbitrators relied on evidence derived from their own investigations and not previously provided to the applicant; (ii) the applicant had been prevented from presenting its case; (iii) the decision had been reached by an arbitral procedure that was not in accordance with the agreement between the parties and therefore fell within Section 103 (2) (e) of the 1996 Act; and (iv) the decision was contrary to the requirements of substantial justice as expounded in *Adams v Cape Industries* [1990] 2 WLR 657.

Mr Justice Colman held that:

1. The *"scope of the submission to arbitration"* fell to be defined by reference to the issues to be resolved by the arbitrators and not by reference to the procedure to be adopted. The evidence relied on by the tribunal went to a central issue within the overall dispute referred to arbitration. This head of objection to arbitration therefore failed.
2. Article V of the New York Convention provided that an award might be avoided if the enforcee had not been given any reasonable opportunity to present its case in relation to the arbitration tribunal's investigation. In the instant case the defendant had not availed itself of the opportunity to present its case and therefore had not brought itself within that exception to enforcement under the Convention.
3. By the arbitration clause, article 53 of the CIETAC Rules was clearly and expressly applicable to the conduct of the arbitrators in making their award. There had been two hearings and a resumed hearing under the auspices of the CIETAC, and following the Beijing court's order for a resumed hearing the evidence relied on by the arbitrators at the first hearing was open to challenge. However, no such challenge had been made so the defendant had under article 45 of the Rules waived its right to object.
4. Where an enforcee alleged that a New York Convention award should not be enforced because this would lead to substantial injustice and be contrary to English public policy, the considerations that would be relevant were: (i) the nature of the procedural injustice; (ii) whether the enforcee had invoked the supervisory jurisdiction of the seat of the arbitration; (iii) whether a remedy was available under that jurisdiction; (iv) whether the courts of that jurisdiction had conclusively determined the enforcee's complaint in favour of upholding the award; and (v) if the enforcee had failed to invoke that remedial jurisdiction, his reason for such failure, and whether he had acted unreasonably in failing to do so.
5. In the instant case the enforcement of the award would not have led to substantial injustice. The unreasonable conduct of the applicant in the manner of its subsequent conduct of the arbitration had, in effect, deprived it of its local remedies and had left it in exactly the same position in substance as if it had wholly ignored the availability of such remedies. Even taking account of a continuing feature of injustice in the failure to disclose the sub-sale award prior to the second award and of the possibility that the arbitrators would have arrived at a more favourable conclusion if disclosure had been made, the countervailing policy considerations in favour of enforcement of the awards were so strong that they displaced the policy consideration of non-enforcement in the face of procedural defects going to a breach of natural justice.

The application was dismissed.[67]

67 A report of the case appeared in *The Times* on 1 March 1999.

ii) United States: US Court of Appeals for the Fifth Circuit

An example of a challenge to a foreign arbitral award in the courts of the United States of America is the case of *Bridas Corporation and Others v Government of Turkmenistan and Others, and State Concern Turkmenneft.*

Plans for an oil/gas pipeline from Turkmenistan through Afghanistan to Pakistan form part of the background to this case. The case initially involved an International Chamber of Commerce (ICC) arbitration award and an application to a US District Court. Bridas applied to a District Court for the Southern District of Texas to confirm an ICC award made in its favour in the sum of US$495 million. The District Court confirmed the award made against the Government of Turkmenistan and others, and State Concern Turkmenneft. The Turkmenistan parties then appealed to the US Court of Appeals for the Fifth Circuit.

The Court of Appeals judgement

The Court judgment, delivered in September 2003, dealt with complex areas of law. It recounted that Bridas had entered into a Joint Venture Agreement in February 1993 with Turkmenneft, the second Defendant. The Government of Turkmenistan, the first Defendant, was not a signatory. The agreement related to hydrocarbon operations in Keimir, western Turkmenistan. It provided for disputes to be settled by arbitration under the Rules of the ICC, the law governing that agreement being the law of England. Bridas claimed that in 1995 the Government of Turkmenistan had ordered it to suspend work in Keimir and had prohibited it from importing or exporting into or out of Turkmenistan.

In 1996 Bridas had initiated the ICC arbitration proceedings. Although the agreement contemplated that the arbitration would be held in Stockholm, the parties agreed that it would take place in Houston, Texas. The arbitration hearing lasted 19 days. The ICC Tribunal had found for Bridas and awarded damages of US$495 million. Following motions by both parties to the District Court of the Southern District of Texas, that Court confirmed the ICC award.

The Turkmenistan parties then launched the appeal to the US Court of Appeals, which considered two issues. The first issue related to jurisdiction: whether the Government, which had not signed the agreement, was bound by that agreement. Had the ICC Tribunal properly exercised jurisdiction over the Government? The Court considered a number of arguments – agency, alter ego, estoppel, third-party beneficiary – before vacating and remanding the District Court's decision on this issue.

The second issue involved a challenge to the quantum of damages. The Court of Appeals rejected arguments based on the discount rate applied by the Tribunal and on the contention that the Tribunal had impliedly awarded punitive damages, and held that the District Court had not erred on this issue. It affirmed the District Court's decision in refusing to vacate or modify the Tribunal's award of US$495 million.[68]

68 *Bridas S.A.P.I.C. v Government of Turkmenistan*, 345 F.3d 347 (5th Cir. 2003).

A further consideration of the case

The Court of Appeals considered the case yet again in a decision rendered on 21 April 2006:

> *"This court, in Bridas S.A.P.I.C. v Government of Turkmenistan ("Bridas I"), 345 F.3d 347 (5th Cir. 2003), considered several theories that could bind a non signatory to an arbitration agreement: agency, alter ego, estoppel, and third-party beneficiary. Rejecting all but one of those theories, Bridas I remanded for further consideration of the alter ego doctrine, as it found the district court's analysis of this 'highly fact-based' issue incomplete and insufficient. The district court was instructed to 'take into account all of the aspects of the relationship between the Government and Turkmenneft.' Because this court resolved other issues concerning the award in Bridas's favor, the sole issue on remand was reconsideration of the alter ego theory. The district court on remand reviewed many of the factors identified by this court as pertinent and held that there was 'an insufficient showing of complete domination or extensive control so as to warrant a finding that Turkmenneft was the alter ego of the Government of Turkmenistan.' Bridas has appealed from the district court's resulting decision to vacate the award against the Government."*

On the alter ego issue the Court of Appeals for the Fifth Circuit concluded that:

> *"Despite some indicia of separateness, the reality was that when the Government's export ban forced Bridas out of the joint venture, the Government then exercised its power as a parent entity to deprive Bridas of a contractual remedy. Intentionally bleeding a subsidiary to thwart creditors is a classic ground for piercing the corporate veil. It is true that the standard for this equitable remedy should be more stringent in breach of contract cases, because the creditor has willingly transacted business with a subsidiary and, as here, forewent the opportunity to obtain a guarantee of Turkmenneft's debts by the Government. The standard is met in this case, however, because Turkmenneft assumed full responsibility for its obligations under the joint venture. The Government, as Turkmenneft's owner, made it impossible for the objectives of the joint venture to be carried out. In this rare case, we are compelled to reverse the district court's finding and conclude that the Government acted as the alter ego of Turkmenneft in regard to this Joint Venture Agreement with Bridas. Accordingly, the judgment of the district court is reversed, and judgment rendered for Bridas authorizing enforcement of the arbitration award."*[69]

iii) China: Beijing No. 1 Intermediate People's Court

An example of a case concerning the enforcement in the People's Republic of China of a foreign arbitral award is *Food Industries Planning and Servicing Ltd (Switzerland)* ("Food Industries") v *China Hua Yang Technology and Trade Corporation* ("Hua Yang"). The case was heard by the Beijing No 1 Intermediate People's Court.

The dispute arose between the parties when Hua Yang failed to make certain payments to Food Industries under a turnkey contract for a fruit juice processing plant. Food Industries commenced an arbitration against Hua Yang before the Arbitration Institute of the

69 *Bridas S.A.P.I.C. v Gov't of Turkmenistan*, No. 04-20842, 2006 WL 1046963 at *1 (5th Cir. Apr. 21, 2006); www.ca5.uscourts.gov/opinions/pub/04/04-20842-CV0.wpd.pdf

Stockholm Chamber of Commerce, which ordered the Respondent, Hua Yang, to pay the Claimant, Food Industries, more than US$2 million, together with interest. The Respondent failed to comply with the award and the Claimant therefore brought proceedings in China for the recognition and enforcement of the award.

The Beijing Court held that the arbitral award complied with the provisions of the New York Convention and should therefore be recognised and enforced. The Court ruled that Hua Yang should perform its obligations under the arbitral award within 15 days.[70]

70 The case is referred to in Jingzhou Tao, *Arbitration Law and Practice in China,* Kluwer Law International, 2003.

17 International Commercial Arbitration

1) Introduction

This chapter looks at international commercial arbitration. The subject is vast. As with other topics considered in the Manual, the hope is that what is set out here will give an overview of the subject, highlighting certain areas and pointing in the direction where more detailed information can be found.[71] With that in mind, the chapter considers the agreement to arbitrate; the course of an international arbitration; arbitration and national laws; the UNCITRAL Model Arbitration Law; and the New York Convention. First, however, it looks at the advantages and disadvantages of arbitration over litigation.

While the International Court of Justice (ICJ) deals with disputes between States, there is no international court to deal with pure international commercial disputes. Therefore if no provision is made in a contract for dispute resolution, any disputes arising out of that contract that cannot be resolved by negotiation between the parties are likely to have to be dealt with by litigation in the national courts.

As mentioned in Chapter 16, resort to litigation in these circumstances will probably mean that one of the parties will have to fight a case in a foreign court, in a foreign language and under a foreign legal system.

The way to avoid that problem is to make provision for some other method of resolving disputes. One obvious dispute resolution process to include in an international commercial contract is arbitration. The parties can agree that, instead of their disputes being dealt with in the national courts, any disputes will be heard by an arbitral tribunal.

Advantages of arbitration

The advantages of arbitration over litigation are clear.

Control of the parties over the procedure, etc

Because arbitration is a consensual process, the parties have far more control over it than would be the case with litigation in a national court. For example, the parties can decide which language shall be used for the purposes of the arbitration and which law shall govern their contractual relationship – a matter of considerable significance. It is generally accepted worldwide, in both the common law and civil law countries, that – subject to certain constraints – the parties are to be allowed to choose the law that will govern the contract between them.

---

71 See in particular Alan Redfern and Martin Hunter, *Law and Practice of International Arbitration*, Sweet and Maxwell, 2004 (4th edition); and Gary Born, *International Commercial Arbitration: Commentary and Materials*, Transnational Publishers Inc, 2001 (2nd edition).

Selection of the tribunal

Because of the degree of control that they exercise over the process, the parties can select the tribunal that is to decide the dispute. In an ad hoc arbitration the parties may have complete control and can name the arbitrator or arbitrators. In an institutional arbitration the parties will generally be able to name arbitrators, although in those circumstances the choice may be limited to arbitrators listed in the panel of the particular arbitral institution. The obvious benefit is that the parties have the opportunity to choose arbitrators who are known and respected in the field of international commercial arbitration and/or who are experts in the area of the dispute in question.

Neutral venue

Again, because of the degree of control that the parties exercise over the arbitration process, it is open to them to specify the country in which the arbitration will take place. Parties from State A and State B may agree that the arbitration be held in neutral State C.

Flexibility

Arbitration is a far more flexible process than litigation in the national courts. The parties can choose an arbitral procedure that suits them – for example, arbitration under the rules of one of the international arbitral institutions such as the London Court of International Arbitration (LCIA), the International Chamber of Commerce (ICC) or the American Arbitration Association (AAA). Or they can choose ad hoc arbitration, where they agree to adopt the United Nations Commission on International Trade Law (UNCITRAL) Arbitration Rules.

Finality

While many judgements handed down by national courts are subject to appeal, arbitral awards are final and subject only to challenge in very limited circumstances.

Enforceability

The New York Convention has provided a very successful means of enforcing arbitral awards. Generally speaking, the international enforcement of arbitral awards is a far more effective process than is available for the enforcement internationally of judgements made in national courts.

Confidentiality

Because arbitration is a private dispute resolution process, the parties will know that, subject to certain exceptions, the proceedings will be confidential.

Cost and speed

Arbitration may – indeed in many cases should – prove to be a cheaper and quicker means of resolving disputes than litigation in the national courts.

Disadvantages of arbitration

However, arbitration does have its disadvantages. Because it is a consensual process, the powers of the arbitrators are limited to those that are given to them either by the parties or by national legislation. Arbitrators therefore do not have the range of powers that are vested in judges sitting in national courts. One particular example is the general inability of arbitrators to order joinder of parties or consolidation of issues. These are powers that can be exercised by judges and that are aimed at ensuring that different courts do not reach different decisions on the same issues – a problem referred to in the earlier chapters dealing with investor-State disputes.

Similarly, arbitrators do not possess the same coercive powers as judges. To take a simple and obvious example, arbitrators cannot order committal to prison on failure of a party to comply with a direction made by the tribunal.

2) The Agreement to Arbitrate

Given that arbitration may be used as a dispute resolution process only as a consequence of the agreement between the parties, the wording of that agreement is of considerable importance. It can either relate to future disputes (a *'clause compromissoire')* or to an existing dispute (a *'compromis')*. The agreement in relation to future disputes is likely to be contained within the trading or commercial contract. An agreement in relation to an existing dispute will probably be a one-off contract drawn up following the emergence of the dispute.

Most international arbitral institutions provide model forms of arbitration clauses. For example, the LCIA model clause relating to future disputes provides:

> *"Any dispute arising out of or in connection with this contract, including any question regarding its existence, validity or termination, shall be referred to and finally resolved by arbitration under the LCIA Rules, which Rules are deemed to be incorporated by reference to this clause.*
>
> *The number of arbitrators shall be [one / three].*
>
> *The seat, or legal place, of arbitration shall be [City and/or Country].*
>
> *The language to be used in the arbitral proceedings shall be [ ].*
>
> *The governing law of the contract shall be the substantive law of [ ]."*

The model clause for a dispute that has already arisen provides:

> *"A dispute having arisen between the parties concerning [ ], the parties hereby agree that the dispute shall be referred to and finally resolved by arbitration under the LCIA Rules.*
>
> *The number of arbitrators shall be [one / three].*
>
> *The seat, or legal place, of arbitration shall be [City and/or Country].*
>
> *The language to be used in the arbitral proceedings shall be [ ].*
>
> *The governing law of the contract [is / shall be] the substantive law of [ ]."*

3) The Course of an International Arbitration

A general idea of the course that an international commercial arbitration is likely to follow can be gathered from the outline of the English Arbitration Act given earlier, from the UNCITRAL Model Law referred to later and from the Notes provided by UNCITRAL for the organisation of arbitral proceedings.

UNCITRAL Notes on Organising Arbitral Proceedings

The matters listed in the UNCITRAL Notes for possible consideration indicate the potential complexity of an international commercial arbitration. UNCITRAL states that the purpose of the Notes *"... is to assist arbitration practitioners by listing and briefly describing questions on which appropriately timed decisions on organizing arbitral proceedings may be useful. The text, prepared with a particular view to international arbitrations, may be used whether or not the arbitration is administered by an arbitral institution."*[72]

The Notes list the following questions:

1 Set of arbitration rules: if the parties have not agreed on a set of arbitration rules, would they wish to do so

2 Language of proceedings

- (a) Possible need for translation of documents, in full or in part
- (b) Possible need for interpretation of oral presentations
- (c) Cost of translation and interpretation

3 Place of arbitration

- (a) Determination of the place of arbitration, if not already agreed on by the parties
- (b) Possibility of meetings outside the place of arbitration

4 Administrative services that may be needed for the arbitral tribunal to carry out its functions

5 Deposits in respect of costs

- (a) Amount to be deposited
- (b) Management of deposits
- (c) Supplementary deposits

6 Confidentiality of information relating to the arbitration

7 Routing of written communications among the parties and the arbitrators

8 Telefax and other electronic means of sending documents

- (a) Telefax
- (b) Other electronic means (e.g. electronic mail and magnetic or optical disk)

9 Arrangements for the exchange of written submissions

- (a) Scheduling of written submissions
- (b) Consecutive or simultaneous submissions

72 The full text of the UNCITRAL Notes can be viewed on the UNCITRAL website: www.uncitral.org/.

10 Practical details concerning written submissions and evidence (e.g. method of submission, copies, numbering, references)

11 Defining points at issue; order of deciding issues; defining relief or remedy sought

(a) Should a list of points at issue be prepared

(b) In which order should the points at issue be decided

(c) Is there a need to define more precisely the relief or remedy sought

12 Possible settlement negotiations and their effect on scheduling proceedings

13 Documentary evidence

(a) Time-limits for submission of documentary evidence intended to be submitted by the parties; consequences of late submission

(b) Whether the arbitral tribunal intends to require a party to produce documentary evidence

(c) Should assertions about the origin and receipt of documents and about the correctness of photocopies be assumed as accurate

(d) Are the parties willing to submit jointly a single set of documentary evidence

(e) Should voluminous and complicated documentary evidence be presented through summaries, tabulations, charts, extracts or samples

14 Physical evidence other than documents

(a) What arrangements should be made if physical evidence will be submitted

(b) What arrangements should be made if an on-site inspection is necessary

15 Witnesses

(a) Advance notice about a witness whom a party intends to present; written witnesses' statements

(b) Manner of taking oral evidence of witnesses

(i) Order in which questions will be asked and the manner in which the hearing of witnesses will be conducted

(ii) Whether oral testimony will be given under oath or affirmation and, if so, in what form an oath or affirmation should be made

(iii) May witnesses be in the hearing room when they are not testifying

(c) The order in which the witnesses will be called

(d) Interviewing witnesses prior to their appearance at a hearing

(e) Hearing representatives of a party

16 Experts and expert witnesses

(a) Expert appointed by the arbitral tribunal

(i) The expert's terms of reference

(ii) The opportunity of the parties to comment on the expert's report, including by presenting expert testimony

(b) Expert opinion presented by a party (expert witness)

17 Hearings
  - (a) Decision whether to hold hearings
  - (b) Whether one period of hearings should be held or separate periods of hearings
  - (c) Setting dates for hearings
  - (d) Whether there should be a limit on the aggregate amount of time each party will have for oral arguments and questioning witnesses
  - (e) The order in which the parties will present their arguments and evidence
  - (f) Length of hearings
  - (g) Arrangements for a record of the hearings
  - (h) Whether and when the parties are permitted to submit notes summarising their oral arguments

18 Multi-party arbitration

19 Possible requirements concerning filing or delivering the award

International arbitral bodies

Many commercial contracts in which the parties have agreed to have their disputes resolved by arbitration will specify one of the well-known international arbitral bodies considered later. The Rules of these institutions will similarly indicate the course that an international arbitration is likely to follow:

- commencement of the arbitration;
- appointment of the arbitral tribunal, challenge and replacement of arbitrators;
- powers of the tribunal (including *competence / competence,* interim measures, and the power to make different types of award at different stages of the arbitral process);
- language and place of the arbitration;
- governing law, conflict of laws, any right of the tribunal to decide *ex aequo et bono* or to act as *amiable compositeur;*
- conduct of the arbitration: pleadings, evidence (including documents), factual witnesses and experts, oral and written submissions, conduct of the hearing;
- the award: revision of the award, additional awards and the finality of the award.

4) Arbitration and National Laws

International commercial arbitrations conducted under the Rules of international arbitral bodies must be conducted in accordance with the relevant national laws – and with an eye to the New York Convention.

As to national laws, it is clear that arbitration – as a private dispute resolution system separate from the litigation systems of the national courts – can only operate with the consent of national governments. Broadly speaking, national governments support arbitration as a 'private' dispute resolution system principally in two ways: first, by staying litigation in the national courts in circumstances where the parties have agreed to arbitrate; and second, by enforcing in the national courts the awards made by arbitral tribunals.

In addition, the national courts may aid the arbitral process by, say, granting injunctions. But in return the State expects to exercise a degree of control over the arbitral process by, for example, allowing appeals / challenges in certain circumstances to the national courts against arbitration awards. The position under the English Arbitration Act was considered earlier.

The situation obviously varies from country to country. It was with a view to standardising the arbitral process internationally that UNCITRAL adopted the Model Arbitration Law. The English Arbitration Act was structured on the Model Law. Other countries – one example is Scotland – have adopted the Model Law.

5) The UNCITRAL Model Arbitration Law

i) Introduction

The United Nations Commission on International Trade Law (UNCITRAL) is the core legal body of the United Nations in the field of international trade law. It has specialised in commercial law reform on a worldwide basis for over 30 years. Its Secretariat, the International Trade Law Branch of the UN Office of Legal Affairs, is located in Vienna.

UNCITRAL was established by the UN General Assembly in 1966. The General Assembly recognised that differences in national laws dealing with international trade law were creating *"obstacles to the flow of trade, and it regarded the Commission as the vehicle by which the United Nations could play a more active role in reducing or removing these obstacles"*. It gave to the Commission a mandate to *"further the progressive harmonization and unification of the law of international trade"*. The Commission is currently composed of 36 member States elected by the General Assembly, but will be expanded to a total of 60 States. Membership is structured so as to be representative of the world's various geographic regions and its principal economic and legal systems.

UNCITRAL has adopted various measures in the field of international commercial arbitration. These include the UNCITRAL Notes on Organising Arbitral Proceedings, adopted in 1996 (outlined above) and the Arbitration Rules, adopted in 1976, which are discussed in the next chapter. The vitally important New York Convention was prepared by the UN prior to the creation of UNCITRAL, but promotion of the Convention is a major part of the Commission's work. The New York Convention is considered later in this chapter.

The Model Law on International Commercial Arbitration was adopted in 1985. This was designed to assist States in *"reforming and modernizing their laws on arbitral procedure so as to take into account the particular features and needs of international commercial arbitration"*. As at April 2004, over 40 countries had enacted legislation based on the Model Law.

The Law consists of eight Chapters and thirty-six Articles. Chapter 1 contains general provisions; Chapter II deals with the arbitration agreement and Chapter III with the composition of the arbitral tribunal; Chapter IV contains provisions dealing with the jurisdiction of the tribunal and Chapter V deals with the conduct of the arbitral proceedings; Chapter VI deals with the award and the termination of the arbitral proceedings; Chapter VII contains provisions dealing with recourse against the award; and the provisions of Chapter VIII are concerned with recognition and enforcement of awards.

ii) The Model Law

Chapter I: General provisions

Article 1 states that the Model Law applies to *"international commercial arbitration, subject to any agreement in force between this State and any other State or States"*. With certain exceptions, the Law applies only if the place of arbitration is in the territory of *"this State"*. Arbitration is *"international"* only if:

> *"(a) the parties to an arbitration agreement have, at the time of the conclusion of that agreement, their places of business in different States; or*
>
> *(b) one of the following places is situated outside the State in which the parties have their places of business:*
>
> *(i) the place of arbitration if determined in, or pursuant to, the arbitration agreement;*
>
> *(ii) any place where a substantial part of the obligations of the commercial relationship is to be performed or the place with which the subject-matter of the dispute is most closely connected; or*
>
> *(c) the parties have expressly agreed that the subject-matter of the arbitration agreement relates to more than one country."*

Article 1(5) states that the Law *"shall not affect any other law of this State by virtue of which certain disputes may not be submitted to arbitration or may be submitted to arbitration only according to provisions other than those of this Law"*.

Article 2 contains various definitions and Articles 3 and 4 deal with written communications and waiver of the right to object. Article 5 provides that in matters governed by the Law *"no court shall intervene except where so provided in this Law"*.

Article 6 makes provision for each State in enacting the Law to specify the court or courts or other competent authority to perform functions referred to in Articles 11 (3), 11 (4), 13 (3), 14, 16 (3) and 34 (2). Those articles deal with the appointment of arbitrators and recourse against the award.

Chapter II: Arbitration agreement, stay of litigation and interim measures

Article 7 states that the arbitration agreement is *"an agreement by the parties to submit to arbitration all or certain disputes which have arisen or which may arise between them in respect of a defined legal relationship, whether contractual or not. An arbitration agreement may be in the form of an arbitration clause in a contract or in the form of a separate agreement."* The agreement is to be in writing and may be contained in an exchange of documents.

Provisions relating to the stay of litigation are contained in Article 8. A court before which action is brought in a matter that is the subject of an arbitration agreement is to refer the parties to arbitration *"unless it finds that the agreement is null and void, inoperative or incapable of being performed"* (the wording in the New York Convention). However, the request to a court for interim measures of protection is not incompatible with an arbitration agreement (Article 9).

Chapter III: Composition of arbitral tribunal

Articles 10 and 11 deal with the number of arbitrators (three, unless the parties determine otherwise) and their appointment. Articles 12 and 13 contain the provisions relating to the grounds of challenge to arbitrators and the challenge procedure. An arbitrator may be challenged only if *"circumstances exist that give rise to justifiable doubts as to his impartiality or independence, or if he does not possess qualifications agreed to by the parties"*.

Article 14 contains provisions dealing with the situation where an arbitrator is unable to perform his/her functions or fails to act without undue delay. Article 15 deals with the appointment of substitute arbitrators.

Chapter IV: Jurisdiction of arbitral tribunal

The *'competence / competence'* provisions are contained in Article 16: *"The arbitral tribunal may rule on its own jurisdiction, including any objections with respect to the existence or validity of the arbitration agreement. For that purpose, an arbitration clause which forms part of a contract shall be treated as an agreement independent of the other terms of the contract. A decision by the arbitral tribunal that the contract is null and void shall not entail ipso jure the invalidity of the arbitration clause."*

A plea that the tribunal does not have jurisdiction is to be raised not later than the submission of the statement of the defence. The tribunal may rule on such a plea either as a preliminary question or in the award on the merits. Unless the parties have agreed otherwise, the arbitral tribunal has power to order interim measures (Article 17).

Chapter V: Conduct of arbitral proceedings

The parties are to be treated with equality and each party *"shall be given a full opportunity of presenting his case"* (Article 18).

Subject to the provisions of the Law, the parties are free to agree on the procedure to be followed. Failing such agreement, the tribunal may conduct the arbitration in such a manner as it considers appropriate: *"The power conferred upon the arbitral tribunal includes the power to determine the admissibility, relevance, materiality and weight of any evidence"* (Article 19).

The parties are free to agree on the place of arbitration, but failing such agreement the place is to be determined by the tribunal *"having regard to the circumstances of the case, including the convenience of the parties"*. However, the tribunal (unless the parties have agreed otherwise) may meet at any place it considers appropriate for consultation among its members, for hearing witnesses / experts / the parties, or for inspections (Article 20).

Unless agreed otherwise, the arbitral proceedings commence on the date on which a request for the dispute to be referred to arbitration is received by the respondent (Article 21). Article 22 provides that (unless the parties agree otherwise) the language or languages to be used in the arbitration are to be determined by the tribunal.

Pleadings and relevant documents are dealt with an Article 23. The claimant is to *"state the facts supporting his claim, the points at issue and the relief or remedy sought"*, and the respondent is to *"state his defence in respect of these particulars, unless the parties have otherwise agreed as to the required elements of such statements"*. The parties may submit with their statements all documents they consider to be relevant or *"may add a reference to the documents or other evidence they will submit"*. The parties may amend or supplement the claim and defence, unless they have agreed otherwise, or unless the arbitral tribunal considers it inappropriate having regard to the delay.

Whether the arbitration should proceed by way of an oral hearing or whether it should be conducted on a documents-only basis is a matter of decision for the tribunal (unless, again, the parties have decided otherwise). In relation to evidence *"All statements, documents or other information supplied to the arbitral tribunal by one party shall be communicated to the other party. Also any expert report or evidentiary document on which the arbitral tribunal may rely in making its decision shall be communicated to the parties"* (Article 24).

Article 25 makes provision for party default in the event that the parties have not agreed otherwise. If, without showing sufficient cause:

"(a) the claimant fails to communicate his statement of claim in accordance with article 23(1), the arbitral tribunal shall terminate the proceedings;

(b) the respondent fails to communicate his statement of defence in accordance with article 23(1), the arbitral tribunal shall continue the proceedings without treating such failure in itself as an admission of the claimant's allegations;

(c) any party fails to appear at a hearing or to produce documentary evidence, the arbitral tribunal may continue the proceedings and make the award on the evidence before it."

Article 26 deals with experts appointed by the tribunal. Unless the parties have agreed otherwise, the tribunal:

"(a) may appoint one or more experts to report to it on specific issues to be determined by the arbitral tribunal;

(b) may require a party to give the expert any relevant information or to produce, or to provide access to, any relevant documents, goods or other property for his inspection."

Article 26 (2) states that *"Unless otherwise agreed by the parties, if a party so requests or if the arbitral tribunal considers it necessary, the expert shall, after delivery of his written or oral report, participate in a hearing where the parties have the opportunity to put questions to him and to present expert witnesses in order to testify on the points at issue."*

The final Article of Chapter V deals with court assistance in relation to the taking of evidence. Both the tribunal and the parties – with the approval of the tribunal – may request *"from a competent court of this State assistance in taking evidence. The court may execute the request within its competence and according to its rules on taking evidence"* (Article 27).

Chapter VI: Governing law; the award; settlement and termination of proceedings

The first Article of Chapter VI deals with the rules applicable to the substance of the dispute. The tribunal is to decide the dispute *"in accordance with such rules of law as are chosen by the parties as applicable to the substance of the dispute. Any designation of the law or legal system of a given State shall be construed, unless otherwise expressed, as directly referring to the substantive law of that State and not to its conflict of laws rules."*

Failing a designation of the parties, the tribunal is to apply the law *"determined by the conflict of laws rules which it considers applicable"*. Article 28 then states expressly that the tribunal *"shall decide* ex aequo et bono *or as* amiable compositeur *only if the parties have expressly authorized it to do so"*.

Article 28 (4) states that in all cases *"the arbitral tribunal shall decide in accordance with the terms of the contract and shall take into account the usages of the trade applicable to the transaction"*. That provision, like the express reference to *ex aequo et bono* and *amiable compositeur*, does not appear in the English Arbitration Act.

Article 29 deals with decisions made by the panel: *"In arbitral proceedings with more than one arbitrator, any decision of the arbitral tribunal shall be made, unless otherwise agreed by the parties, by a majority of all its members. However, questions of procedure may be decided by a presiding arbitrator, if so authorized by the parties or all members of the arbitral tribunal."*

If the dispute has been settled during the course of the proceedings, the tribunal is to *"terminate the proceedings and, if requested by the parties and not objected to by the arbitral tribunal, record the settlement in the form of an arbitral award on agreed terms.... An award on agreed terms shall be made in accordance with the provisions of article 31 and shall state that it is an award. Such an award has the same status and effect as any other award on the merits of the case"* (Article 30). This provision is important in the context of the New York Convention as only an 'arbitral award' is enforceable under the Convention.

Article 31 contains provisions dealing with the form and contents of the award, which is to be in writing and signed by the tribunal. Where there is more than one arbitrator, the signatures of the majority of the tribunal suffice *"provided that the reason for any omitted signature is stated"*. Unless the parties have agreed otherwise (or unless it is an award on agreed terms under Article 30), the award is to state the reasons on which it is based. It is to state its date and the place of arbitration, and a copy signed by the arbitrators is to be delivered to each party.

Article 32 states that the arbitral proceedings are terminated by the final award or by an order of termination issued by the tribunal when:

"(a) the claimant withdraws his claim, unless the respondent objects thereto and the arbitral tribunal recognizes a legitimate interest on his part in obtaining a final settlement of the dispute;

(b) the parties agree on the termination of the proceedings;

(c) the arbitral tribunal finds that the continuation of the proceedings has for any other reason become unnecessary or impossible."

The tribunal's mandate ends with the termination of the arbitral proceedings, subject to the provisions of Article 33 and Article 34 (4) (re-correction, etc of and recourse against the award – see below).

Article 33 contains provisions for the correction and interpretation of the award and for the making of an additional award. Within 30 days of receipt of the award (unless some other period of time has been agreed by the parties):

"(a) a party, with notice to the other party, may request the arbitral tribunal to correct in the award any errors in computation, any clerical or typographical errors or any errors of similar nature;

(b) if so agreed by the parties, a party, with notice to the other party, may request the arbitral tribunal to give an interpretation of a specific point or part of the award."

If the tribunal considers that the request is justified, it is to make the correction or give the interpretation, which forms part of the award. In addition, the tribunal may correct errors on its own initiative. Unless the parties have agreed otherwise, a party may also request the tribunal to make an additional award *"as to claims presented in the arbitral proceedings but omitted from the award. If the arbitral tribunal considers the request to be justified, it shall make the additional award within sixty days."* The correction and interpretation provisions apply also to any additional award.

Chapter VII: Recourse against the award

Article 34 contains provisions for recourse to a court against the award. Article 36 (in Chapter VIII) contains the grounds for refusing recognition and enforcement of the award. Both are based on Article V of the New York Convention, save that Article 34 does not contain the Article V (1) (e) provision of the Convention relating to a situation where the award has not yet become binding on the parties, or has been set aside or suspended. They will both nevertheless be set out in full since they are important in the field of international trade and international commercial arbitration.

Under Article 34, recourse to a court against an arbitral award may only be made by an application for setting aside. Such setting aside may only be made by the court specified by the particular State in Article 6, and may only be done if:

"(a) the party making the application furnishes proof that:

(i) a party to the arbitration agreement referred to in article 7 was under some incapacity; or the said agreement is not valid under the law to which the

parties have subjected it or, failing any indication thereon, under the law of this State; or

(ii) *the party making the application was not given proper notice of the* appointment of an arbitrator or of the arbitral proceedings or was otherwise unable to present his case; or

(iii) *the award deals with a dispute not contemplated by or not falling within the terms of the submission to arbitration, or contains decisions on matters beyond the scope of the submission to arbitration, provided that, if the decisions on matters submitted to arbitration can be separated from those not so submitted, only that part of the award which contains decisions on matters not submitted to arbitration may be set aside; or*

(iv) *the composition of the arbitral tribunal or the arbitral procedure was not in accordance with the agreement of the parties, unless such agreement was in conflict with a provision of this Law from which the parties cannot derogate, or, failing such agreement, was not in accordance with this Law;* or

(b) *the court finds that:*

(i) *the subject-matter of the dispute is not capable of settlement by arbitration under the law of this State; or*

(ii) *the award is in conflict with the public policy of this State."*

Article 34 (3) states that an application for setting aside *"may not be made after three months have elapsed from the date on which the party making that application had received the award or, if a request had been made under article 33, from the date on which that request had been disposed of by the arbitral tribunal".*

Article 34 (4) states that the court, when asked to set aside an award *"may, where appropriate and so requested by a party, suspend the setting aside proceedings for a period of time determined by it in order to give the arbitral tribunal an opportunity to resume the arbitral proceedings or to take such other action as in the arbitral tribunal's opinion will eliminate the grounds for setting aside".*

Chapter VIII: Recognition and enforcement of awards

Articles 35 and 36 deal with recognition and enforcement of awards. Article 35 states that an award *"irrespective of the country in which it was made, shall be recognized as binding and, upon application in writing to the competent court, shall be enforced subject to the provisions of this article and of article 36".*

The party relying on the award or applying for its enforcement is to supply *"the duly authenticated original award or a duly certified copy thereof, and the original arbitration agreement referred to in article 7 or a duly certified copy thereof. If the award or agreement is not made in an official language of this State, the party shall supply a duly certified translation thereof into such language."*

These provisions are similar to those contained in Article IV of the New York Convention.

The grounds for refusing recognition or enforcement are set out in Article 36. These are very similar to the Article 34 recourse against the award provisions, but with the additional *"not yet binding, etc"* ground contained in Article V (1) (e) of the New York Convention. Recognition or enforcement of an arbitral award, irrespective of the country in which the award was made, may be refused only:

"(a) at the request of the party against whom it is invoked, if that party furnishes to the competent court where recognition or enforcement is sought proof that:

(i) a party to the arbitration agreement referred to in article 7 was under some incapacity; or the said agreement is not valid under the law to which the parties have subjected it or, failing any indication thereon, under the law of the country where the award was made; or

(ii) the party against whom the award is invoked was not given proper notice of the appointment of an arbitrator or of the arbitral proceedings or was otherwise unable to present his case; or

(iii) the award deals with a dispute not contemplated by or not falling within the terms of the submission to arbitration, or it contains decisions on matters beyond the scope of the submission to arbitration, provided that, if the decisions on matters submitted to arbitration can be separated from those not so submitted, that part of the award which contains decisions on matters submitted to arbitration may be recognized and enforced; or

(iv) the composition of the arbitral tribunal or the arbitral procedure was not in accordance with the agreement of the parties or, failing such agreement, was not in accordance with the law of the country where the arbitration took place; or

(v) the award has not yet become binding on the parties or has been set aside or suspended by a court of the country in which, or under the law of which, that award was made; or

(b) if the court finds that:

(i) the subject-matter of the dispute is not capable of settlement by arbitration under the law of this State; or

(ii) the recognition or enforcement of the award would be contrary to the public policy of this State."

Article 36 (2) provides that: *"If an application for setting aside or suspension of an award has been made to a court referred to in paragraph (1)(a)(v) of this article, the court where recognition or enforcement is sought may, if it considers it proper, adjourn its decision and may also, on the application of the party claiming recognition or enforcement of the award, order the other party to provide appropriate security."*

An Explanatory Note by the UNCITRAL Secretariat states that *"By modelling the recognition and enforcement rules on the relevant provisions of the 1958 New York Convention, the Model Law supplements, without conflicting with, the regime of recognition and enforcement created by that successful Convention."*

iii) Case law relating to the Model Law

Two cases decided on the provisions of the UNCITRAL Model Law are set out below. These and other case reports can be found on the UNCITRAL website as part of the Case Law on UNCITRAL Texts (CLOUT) system.[73]

Europcar v Alba Tours

Canada has enacted legislation based on the Model Law. The case of *Europcar Italia S.p.A v Alba Tours International Inc* was heard in the Ontario Court of Justice by Mr Justice Paul Dilks in January 1997. The case concerned Articles 35 and 36 of the Model Law (referred to in the report as MAL).

The CLOUT report of the case states that:

"Europcar Italia S.p.A ('Europcar'), a major European motor vehicle rental agency, and Alba Tours International Inc. ('Alba'), a tour operator based in Toronto, entered into an agreement in Rome for car rental services. A dispute brought the parties to arbitration resulting in an award in favour of Europcar. Alba Tours asked the Italian courts to set aside the award on the ground that the arbitrator had made a serious error of fact which resulted in a loss of his jurisdiction. In the interim, Europcar sought enforcement of the arbitral award against Alba in Ontario.

"The Court began by noting that, in accordance with article 35 of the MAL, it was obliged to recognize an arbitral award unless one of the grounds for refusal, listed in article 36, was available. Even then, it noted that a discretion remained to recognize the award under that provision on the basis that the word 'may' is used in the preamble to article 36(2). The Court found that it is 'therefore clear that even should one of the circumstances [set out in article 36(1)] exist, enforcement could still be ordered in the exercise of judicial discretion'.

"Alba objected to recognition on the basis of article 36(1)(a)(iii) and (v). Under the first provision, Alba argued that by misinterpreting the agreement, the arbitrator lost jurisdiction, and that accordingly his award contained decisions on matters beyond the scope of the submission to arbitration. The Court rejected this argument on two grounds: first, that this issue was already before the Italian courts and should therefore not be considered by the Ontario Court, and second, that in any event, the evidence did not indicate that any errors committed by the arbitrator substantially affected his conclusions. The Court also rejected the submission based on subparagraph (v), holding that the conditions for its application had not been met.

"The Court considered that the conditions for the application of article 36(2) had been met by Alba's appeal in Italy. The only issue was the exercise of the Court's discretion under article 36(2). In exercising its discretion, the Court considered the balance of convenience to the parties. It found that Alba Tours would suffer extreme prejudice if the award were enforced in Ontario only to be set aside later in Italy. The Court thus ordered an adjournment of the enforcement proceedings in Ontario, conditional upon Alba furnishing security pending a determination of the appeal in Italy."[74]

---

73 www.uncitral.org/uncitral/en/case_law.html.

74 CLOUT Case 366.

Skandia International Insurance Company v Al Amana Insurance

Bermuda is another example of a Model Law jurisdiction. In January 1994 the Supreme Court of Bermuda dealt with a case concerning Article 16 of the Model Law. Mr Justice Vincent Meerabux gave judgement in *Skandia International Insurance Company and Mercantile & General Reinsurance Company, and others v Al Amana Insurance.*

A report of the case in CLOUT states that proceedings were initiated in the Supreme Court by Skandia and other insurance companies seeking an injunction to restrain Al Amana Insurance and other insurance companies from continuing legal proceedings against Skandia and others in Kuwait:

> *"Skandia and others were reinsurers of Al Amana, a company incorporated under the laws of Bermuda, in respect of real and personal property located in Kuwait and belonging to Alghanim Industries ('Alghanim') and its associated companies. Alghanim sustained extensive property damage in Kuwait during and consequential to the invasion of Kuwait by Iraq in August 1990. Disputes arose as to whether the losses sustained by Alghanim were excluded by virtue of a War Risks Exclusion Clause contained in the reinsurance agreements between Al Amana and Skandia and others.*
>
> *"Al Amana was sued by Alghanim in Kuwait and joined Skandia and others as third parties. Skandia and others argued that the Kuwaiti court had no jurisdiction over them as there were arbitration provisions in the reinsurance agreements with Al Amana. In the meantime, Skandia and others served notices of arbitration on Al Amana and initiated the proceedings in the Supreme Court of Bermuda for an injunction to restrain Al Amana from continuing legal proceedings against them in Kuwait on the ground that there existed an agreement to have their disputes determined by arbitration 'at the seat of the defendant party' (i.e., Bermuda).*
>
> *"Al Amana challenged, inter alia, the existence of an arbitration clause in one of the reinsurance agreements. Al Amana argued that article 7(2) MAL requires that, for incorporating an arbitration clause by reference into another document, the reference has to be 'such as to make that clause part of the contract.' Al Amana submitted that a reference to insurance coverage 'as per wording attached' simply incorporated the description of the risks in respect of which reinsurance was effected, but could not incorporate the entirety of the policy and was inadequate to incorporate the arbitration clause contained in another document.*
>
> *"The Supreme Court held that there was prima facie evidence that the arbitration agreement existed and satisfied the requirements of article 7(1) MAL and Article II(2) of the Convention on the Recognition and Enforcement of Foreign Arbitral Awards (New York, 1958). The Supreme Court held, under reference to the travaux préparatoires of the MAL, that the contractual documents do not need to make an explicit reference to the arbitration clause and that general words of incorporation suffice under article 7 MAL. The Supreme Court pointed out, however, that, in any event, a challenge to the existence, validity and scope of the arbitration agreement was a matter to be first determined by the arbitral tribunal under article 16(3) MAL. Accordingly, the Supreme Court granted the injunction restraining Al Amana from continuing with the proceedings brought by it against Skandia and others in Kuwait."*[75]

75 CLOUT Case 127.

6) The New York Convention

i) Introduction

The United Nations Convention on the Recognition and Enforcement of Foreign Arbitral Awards, commonly referred to as the New York Convention, is the third of the three international conventions mentioned at the beginning of the Manual as being of particular significance to international trade and investment. The other two Conventions have been referred to in earlier chapters: the 1982 United Nations Law of the Sea Convention (UNCLOS III) and the World Bank's International Convention on the Settlement of Investment Disputes (ICSID).

The 1958 New York Convention is widely accepted as being the cornerstone of international commercial arbitration. Enforcement of the award made by the tribunal is the ultimate object of international commercial arbitration. The purpose of the Convention is to provide for the mutual recognition and enforcement of arbitral awards made in countries that are parties to it.

Over 130 states have ratified, acceded to or succeeded to the Convention. These include the world's major trading nations.[76] Thus, for example, in the case of a dispute between Canadian and Nigerian companies, an award made in Switzerland against the Canadian company could be enforced by the Nigerian company in Canada through the Canadian courts. And if the Canadian company had assets in, say, France and Italy, the Nigerian company could likewise enforce the award through the French and Italian courts, since both France and Italy have ratified the Convention.

The late Sir Michael Kerr, a former English Court of Appeal Judge and distinguished international arbitrator, described the New York Convention as *"the foundation on which the whole of the edifice of international arbitration rests. Without the Convention the process could have no effective existence."*[77] The Convention was also described by Alan Redfern and Martin Hunter in the first edition of their work *Law and Practice of International Commercial Arbitration* as *"...easily the most important international treaty relating to international commercial arbitration. Indeed, its general level of success may be regarded as one of the factors responsible for the rapid development of arbitration as a means of resolving international trade disputes in recent decades."*[78]

The Convention is the successor to the Geneva Protocol and the Geneva Convention. As noted above, it was prepared by the United Nations prior to the creation of the UN Commission on International Trade Law (UNCITRAL), but the promotion of the Convention is an important aspect of UNCITRAL's work.

Put shortly, the New York Convention:

- requires Contracting States to recognise relevant arbitration agreements;

---

76 See the list of States on the UNCITRAL website: www.uncitral.org/uncitral/en/uncitral_texts/arbitration/NYConvention_status.html.

77 [1997] 13 Arbitration International, 121-143 at p 127.

78 Sweet and Maxwell, 1986, p 46.

- requires the courts of Contracting States to refer disputes to arbitration where a relevant agreement to arbitrate has been made, unless the Court finds that the agreement is null and void, inoperative or incapable of being performed;
- requires a Convention State to recognise and enforce a foreign arbitral award made in another Convention State, only refusing recognition and enforcement on the limited specified grounds set out in Article V of the Convention. These comprise five procedural defects that must be proved (e.g., failure to give proper notice of the appointment of the arbitrator) and two additional defences that a court can find on its own motion: first, the subject matter of the difference is not capable of settlement by arbitration; and second, that recognition or enforcement would be contrary to public policy.

ii) The Convention

The New York Convention is, by the standard of international conventions, relatively short. It comprises 16 articles.

Article I (1) sets out the scope of the Convention. It applies to *"the recognition and enforcement of arbitral awards made in the territory of a State other than the State where the recognition and enforcement of such awards are sought, and arising out of differences between persons, whether physical or legal. It shall also apply to arbitral awards not considered as domestic awards in the State where their recognition and enforcement are sought."*

Article I (2) defines 'arbitral awards'. They include *"not only awards made by arbitrators appointed for each case but also those made by permanent arbitral bodies to which the parties have submitted"*.

When signing, ratifying or acceding to this Convention (or notifying extension under Article X), any State *"may on the basis of reciprocity declare that it will apply the Convention to the recognition and enforcement of awards made only in the territory of another Contracting State. It may also declare that it will apply the Convention only to differences arising out of legal relationships, whether contractual or not, which are considered as commercial under the national law of the State making such Declaration"* (Article I (3)).

Article II (1) deals with the recognition of arbitration agreements. Each Contracting State *"shall recognize an agreement in writing under which the parties undertake to submit to arbitration all or any differences which have arisen or which may arise between them in respect of a defined legal relationship, whether contractua1 or not, concerning a subject matter capable of settlement by arbitration"*.

Article II (2) defines 'agreement in writing'. It shall include *"an arbitral clause in a contract or an arbitration agreement, signed by the parties or contained in an exchange of letters or telegrams"*.

Article II (3) contains the requirement that a court of a Contracting State must stay litigation where there is a relevant agreement to arbitrate.

The combined powers of a national court to 'stay' litigation and to enforce arbitral awards are arguably the most vital support mechanisms in the field of arbitration, both domestic and international.

The Article states that a court of a Contracting State *"when seized of an action in a matter in respect of which the parties have made an agreement within the meaning of this article, shall, at the request of one of the parties, refer the parties to arbitration, unless it finds that the said agreement is null and void, inoperative or incapable of being performed."* The reference to agreements being *"null and void, inoperative or incapable of being performed"* appears in the UNCITRAL Model Law and in the English Arbitration Act.

Article III contains the recognition and enforcement provisions: each Contracting State *"shall recognize arbitral awards as binding and enforce them in accordance with the rules of procedure of the territory where the award is relied upon, under the conditions laid down in the following articles. There shall not be imposed substantially more onerous conditions or higher fees or charges on the recognition or enforcement of arbitral awards to which this Convention applies than are imposed on the recognition or enforcement of domestic arbitral awards."*

The requirements for obtaining recognition and enforcement are set out in Article IV. The party applying *"shall, at the time of the application, supply:*

(a) The duly authenticated original award or a duly certified copy thereof;

(b) The original agreement referred to in article II or a duly certified copy thereof."

If either the award or the agreement is not made in an official language of the country concerned, the party applying for recognition and enforcement of the award *"shall produce a translation of these documents into such language. The translation shall be certified by an official or sworn translator or by a diplomatic or consular agent."*

Article V contains the grounds on which recognition and enforcement of an award may be refused (referred to in the earlier section on the UNCITRAL Model Law).

Article V (1) sets out the five procedural defects grounds:

"Recognition and enforcement of the award may be refused, at the request of the party against whom it is invoked, only if that party furnishes to the competent authority where the recognition and enforcement is sought, proof that:

(a) The parties to the agreement referred to in article II were, under the law applicable to them, under some incapacity, or the said agreement is not valid under the law to which the parties have subjected it or, failing any indication thereon, under the law of the country where the award was made; or

(b) The party against whom the award is invoked was not given proper notice of the appointment of the arbitrator or of the arbitration proceedings or was otherwise unable to present his case; or

(c) The award deals with a difference not contemplated by or not falling within the terms of the submission to arbitration, or it contains decisions on matters beyond the scope of the submission to arbitration, provided that, if the decisions on

matters submitted to arbitration can be separated from those not so submitted, that part of the award which contains decisions on matters submitted to arbitration may be recognized and enforced; or

(d) The composition of the arbitral authority or the arbitral procedure was not in accordance with the agreement of the parties, or, failing such agreement, was not in accordance with the law of the country where the arbitration took place; or

(e) The award has not yet become binding on the parties, or has been set aside or suspended by a competent authority of the country in which, or under the law of which, that award was made."

Article V (2) deals with the two additional grounds on which recognition and enforcement may be refused by the court on its own motion:

"Recognition and enforcement of an arbitral award may also be refused if the competent authority in the country where recognition and enforcement is sought finds that:

(a) The subject matter of the difference is not capable of settlement by arbitration under the law of that country; or

(b) The recognition or enforcement of the award would be contrary to the public policy of that country."

Article VI states that if an application for the setting aside or suspension of the award has been made to a competent authority referred to in Article V (1) (e) *"the authority before which the award is sought to be relied upon may, if it considers it proper, adjourn the decision on the enforcement of the award and may also, on the application of the party claiming enforcement of the award, order the other party to give suitable security".*

Article VII (1) deals with recognition and enforcement of arbitral awards under multilateral or bilateral investment treaties or other processes: *"The provisions of the present Convention shall not affect the validity of multilateral or bilateral agreements concerning the recognition and enforcement of arbitral awards entered into by the Contracting States nor deprive any interested party of any right he may have to avail himself of an arbitral award in the manner and to the extent allowed by the law or the treaties of the country where such award is sought to be relied upon."*

For example, the World Bank's ICSID Convention contains its own enforcement mechanism, and the Framework Agreement between the United Kingdom and Norway concerning the laying of inter-connecting submarine pipes under the North Sea between the two countries (discussed in Chapter 8) provides that a decision of the relevant arbitral tribunal shall be treated as if it was an agreement between the two Governments.

Article VII (2) provides that the predecessors of the New York Convention, the Geneva Protocol of 1923 and the Geneva Convention of 1927, shall cease to have any effect between Contracting States on their becoming bound by the New York Convention.

Article XIV provides that a Contracting State *"shall not be entitled to avail itself of the present Convention against other Contracting States except to the extent that it is itself bound to apply the Convention".*

The remaining Articles VIII to XVI are concerned with signature, accession, the extension of the Convention to territories for which a State has responsibility for international relations, federal or non-unitary States, the date of coming into force of the Convention, denunciation of the Convention, notification by the UN Secretary-General of Article VIII matters, and the authentic texts of the Convention (Chinese, English, French, Russian and Spanish).

iii) Case law relating to the New York Convention

Set out below are brief notes on two New York Convention cases decided in the English courts.

Westacre v Jugoimport

The English Court of Appeal considered the public policy ground in Article V (2) (b) in relation to refusing recognition and enforcement of a New York Convention award.

The case of *Westacre Investments Inc v (1) Jugoimport-SDRP Holding Co Ltd (2) Beogradska Banka DD* came before the Court of Appeal on 12 May 1999, on appeal from a decision of Mr Justice Colman. The appeal was against the refusal by Mr Justice Colman to set aside a Swiss arbitration award on the ground of illegality, and for leave to re-amend the defence by relying on fresh evidence showing that the claimant's evidence at the arbitration was perjured.

The respondent to the appeal accepted that if the appellants were entitled to establish the facts now alleged, and if it was assumed those facts were correct, enforcement of the award should be refused as contrary to public policy. Two of the issues before the Court of Appeal were:

- Whether the court should allow the facts as found by the arbitrators to be re-opened;
- Whether, on the authority of *Lemenda Trading Co Ltd v African Middle East Petroleum Co* [1998] 1 QB 448 and *Soleimany v Soleimany* [1998] 3 WLR 811, the English courts should not enforce an English law contract that fell to be performed abroad as a matter of public policy.

The Court of Appeal held (with Lord Justice Waller dissenting) that the attempt to re-open the facts should be refused. Swiss law was both the proper law of the contract and the curial law of the arbitration and Switzerland, like the United Kingdom, was a party to the New York Convention. The allegation of bribery in the arbitration had been made and been rejected. Had it not been rejected the claim would have failed, Swiss and English public policy being indistinguishable in this respect. In those circumstances and without fresh evidence, there could be no justification for refusing to enforce the award.

The seriousness of the alleged illegality was not a factor to be considered at the stage of deciding whether or not to mount a full-scale inquiry. It was something to be taken into account as part of the balancing exercise between the competing public policy considerations of finality and illegality, which could only be performed in response to the question, if it arose, of whether the award should be enforced.

In addition, although the award was not isolated from the underlying contract, it was relevant that the English court was considering the enforcement of the former and not the latter. It was legitimate to conclude that there was nothing that offended English public policy if an arbitral tribunal enforced a contract that did not offend the domestic public policy under either the proper law of the contract or its curial law, even if English domestic public policy might have taken a different view. Mr Justice Colman was right on the *Lemenda* point and, unless the appellants were entitled to go behind the facts as found by the arbitrators, there was no public policy answer to the enforcement of the award.

The Court of Appeal dismissed the appeal.[79] In October 1999 the House of Lords refused an application for leave to appeal the decision of the Court of Appeal.

Omnium v Hilmarton

Omnium de Traitement et de Valorisation SA v Hilmarton Ltd involved an arbitration award made in Geneva under Swiss law. Omnium applied:

- to set aside an ex parte order giving effect in England to an ICC award in favour of Hilmarton, and
- for an order that the award be refused enforcement in England under Section 103 of the English Arbitration Act 1996 (which contains the grounds for refusing recognition and enforcement of New York Convention awards – including the public policy ground).

Omnium had appointed Hilmarton to be its legal and tax consultant and to carry out certain work relating to the design and completion of a drainage project in Algiers. The fees payable were conditional on a public contract being awarded to Omnium by the City of Algiers. The contract was awarded, but Omnium only paid Hilmarton half the agreed fees. The claim arising as a result led to the commencement of an ICC arbitration and an award.

The relevant arbitration clause in the agreement between the parties established Swiss law as the proper law. The agreement provided for ICC arbitration and specified Geneva as the seat of the arbitration. Omnium argued that the award should not be enforced in England because such enforcement would be contrary to public policy. Omnium relied on the fact that the law of Algeria prohibited the intervention of a middleman in connection with any public contract or agreement within the ambit of foreign trade. The principal issue was the manner in which the term 'public policy' was to be assessed in such an international context.

Mr Justice Timothy Walker held that the enforcement of a New York Convention award was to be refused only in certain limited circumstances. One ground was that it would be contrary to public policy to enforce the award. It had to be established that enforcement would be contrary to public policy in English law: *Soleimany v Soleimany* [1998] WLR 811. Omnium must also establish not merely that the agreement was unlawful in its place of performance but also that the unlawfulness infected the award itself.

79 A full report of the case can be found in [1999] 2 Lloyd's Reports 65.

Following *Westacre Investments Inc v Jugoimport*, Mr Justice Walker held that, despite the fact that performance was contrary to domestic public policy in its place of performance (Algeria), because it was not contrary to the domestic public policy of the country of the proper law (Switzerland) or the curial law (Swiss law), enforcement should be allowed. There were therefore no public policy grounds on which enforcement of the award could be refused.

The application was refused.[80]

---

80 (a) A full report of the case can be found in [1999] 2 Lloyd's Reports 222.

(b) The case of *Hilmarton (UK), Appellant v Omnium (France), Appellee* is reported in the *ICCA Yearbook Commercial Arbitration*, Volume XIX, 1994, p. 665: a decision of the Cour d'Appel, Paris in December 1991.

18 International Commercial Arbitral Institutions and Other International Bodies

A. *International Commercial Arbitral Institutions and Their Arbitration Rules*

1) Introduction

The last chapter looked briefly at international commercial arbitration, including the United Nations Commission on International Trade Law (UNCITRAL) Model Arbitration Law and the New York Convention. Part A of this chapter looks at a number of the international commercial arbitral institutions and their arbitration rules, Part B considers the Arbitration Rules of UNCITRAL and Part C looks at arbitration under the Rules of the Chartered Institute of Arbitrators.

It is obviously not possible in this Manual to consider all of the international arbitral institutions: there are many, and only a small selection can be looked at in the space available.[81] Moreover, because their rules tend to follow a similar pattern, it is unnecessary to look in detail at each and every one of them. Instead, only the rules of the first institution considered – the London Court of International Arbitration (LCIA) – will be looked at in any detail.

The structure of the arbitration rules of the institutions considered includes:

- commencement of the arbitration;
- constitution of the arbitral tribunal: number of arbitrators, appointment, challenge and replacement of arbitrators;
- duties of arbitrators;
- powers of the tribunal, including *competence / competence* and interim and conservatory measures;
- place and language of the arbitration;
- governing law, and whether the tribunal may decide *ex aequo et bono* or act as *amiable compositeur;*
- pleadings: statement of case, statement of reply, etc;
- documentary evidence and factual and expert evidence;
- provisions as to hearings, which may include provisions relating to the examination of witnesses;
- provisions as to the award, including correction and interpretation and finality of the award.

81 For example, four Regional International Commercial Arbitration Centres in Cairo, Kuala Lumpur, Lagos and Tehran have been set up under the auspices of the Asian-African Legal Consultative Organisation (AALCO). A fifth Regional Centre is due to open in Nairobi. AALCO has 47 member countries and has UN Observer Status.

However, the rules of different institutions have their particular features. For example:

- The LCIA Rules contain a provision for the expedited constitution of the tribunal in cases of exceptional urgency. The Rules also lay emphasis on the general duty of the tribunal, a reflection of provisions in the English Arbitration Act, and include the warning that arbitrators shall not *"act in the arbitration as advocates for any party"*. The Rules are unusual in that, in the provisions relating to pleadings, there is an express requirement that a Reply be served.
- The International Chamber of Commerce (ICC) Rules provide for Terms of Reference and for the scrutiny of the draft award by the ICC Court.
- The International Rules of the American Arbitration Association's (AAA) international division, the International Centre for Dispute Resolution, contain a very useful provision for a preparatory conference with the parties *"for the purpose of organizing, scheduling and agreeing to procedures to expedite the subsequent proceedings"*. The Rules also contain a provision excluding the award of punitive damages, as well as a unique provision that permits a party to seek emergency relief through the appointment of an emergency arbitrator (who will be appointed within one day of a request for such relief).
- One of the significant features of the China International Economic and Trade Arbitration Commission (CIETAC) Rules is the emphasis on the *"combination of arbitration with conciliation"*.

The next section will consider in some detail the LCIA Arbitration Rules, thus enabling the other institutional rules to be dealt with more briefly.

2) London Court of International Arbitration

i) Introduction

The LCIA is one of the longest established of the major international commercial arbitral institutions and is a truly international organisation. Although it is based in London, there is no more reason for an LCIA arbitration to be held in that city than there is for an ICC arbitration to be held in Paris.

The LCIA operates under a three-tier structure, comprising the Company, the Arbitration Court and the Secretariat. The formation of the Arbitration Court in 1985 is regarded by the LCIA as a major step towards its internationalisation:

> *"The LCIA Court is made up of up to thirty-five members, selected to provide and maintain a balance of leading practitioners in commercial arbitration, from the major trading areas of the world. UK membership of the LCIA Court is restricted to 25 per cent. Other members are drawn from as far afield as Hungary and Australia, Nigeria and the United States, Tunisia and China.*
>
> *"The LCIA Court is the final authority for the proper application of the LCIA Rules. Its principal functions are the appointment of tribunals, the determination of challenges to arbitrators, and the control of costs. The functions of the LCIA Court are performed, in the name of the LCIA Court, by the President, by a Vice President or by a Division*

of the LCIA Court of three or five members, of whom one will be the President or a Vice President, or, in the case of administrative functions, by the Registrar.

"It is the LCIA's view that a carefully selected and, therefore, specifically suitable tribunal will issue a reasoned, well-drafted award in which the parties may have confidence, without the need for external scrutiny. There is, therefore, no LCIA Court scrutiny of LCIA awards, so parties receive their award promptly, and subject only to the payment of the costs of the arbitration."

The Secretariat of the LCIA is based at the International Dispute Resolution Centre in Fleet Street, London. The Secretariat, headed by the Registrar, is responsible for the administration of arbitrations referred to the LCIA. It *"aims to assist the parties and their counsel promptly and with the minimum of bureaucracy, as and when required, and to ensure that proceedings are not allowed to flounder for want of proper supervision."*

"The Secretariat also organises all necessary back-up for hearings and meetings, including video and teleconferences, court reporting and simultaneous translation. The Secretariat receives many requests for information each day. Many of these enquiries do not relate to LCIA cases, either projected or pending. The LCIA provides a free information service in the interest of promoting private dispute resolution generally. The aim of the LCIA is first and foremost to provide a service to its users."

The LCIA has established Users' Councils around the world that are aimed at keeping the LCIA *"informed about developments in other jurisdictions and provide local support and advice for the London Secretariat"*. The Users' Councils are

- the European Council, covering Europe and the Middle East;
- the North American Council, covering North America and adjacent countries;
- the Asia-Pacific Council, covering South East Asia and the Pacific Rim;
- the Pan-African Council, covering the whole of Africa; and
- the Latin American Council, covering Central and South America and the Caribbean.

The LCIA says that the nature and value of its arbitration casework is

"very substantial, with major international users entrusting the administration of their arbitrations to the LCIA. Many of the cases are technically and legally complex and sums in issue can run into billions of US dollars. Parties come from a very large number of jurisdictions, of both civil law and common law traditions.

"The subject matter of contracts in dispute is wide and varied, and includes all aspects of international commerce, including, in particular, telecommunications, insurance, oil and gas exploration, construction, shipping, aviation, pharmaceuticals, IT, finance and banking."

Full information concerning the LCIA can be found on its website.[82]

82 www.lcia-arbitration.com.

ii) The LCIA Arbitration Rules

The current LCIA Arbitration Rules came into effect on 1 January 1998. The revision of the Rules was to some extent made in the light of the new English Arbitration Act of 1996.

Request for Arbitration

The commencement of an LCIA arbitration is made by a Request for Arbitration. The Request seeks a considerable amount of detailed information. Article 1 of the Rules provides that a written request is to be sent to the Registrar and is to contain or be accompanied by:

> *"(a) the names, addresses, telephone, facsimile, telex and e-mail numbers (if known) of the parties to the arbitration and of their legal representatives;*
>
> *(b) a copy of the written arbitration clause or separate written arbitration agreement invoked by the Claimant ('the Arbitration Agreement'), together with a copy of the contractual documentation in which the arbitration clause is contained or in respect of which the arbitration arises;*
>
> *(c) a brief statement describing the nature and circumstances of the dispute, and specifying the claims advanced by the Claimant against another party to the arbitration ('the Respondent');*
>
> *(d) a statement of any matters (such as the seat or language(s) of the arbitration, or the number of arbitrators, or their qualifications or identities) on which the parties have already agreed in writing for the arbitration or in respect of which the Claimant wishes to make a proposal;*
>
> *(e) if the Arbitration Agreement calls for party nomination of arbitrators, the name, address, telephone, facsimile, telex and e-mail numbers (if known) of the Claimant's nominee;*
>
> *(f) the fee prescribed in the Schedule of Costs (without which the Request shall be treated as not having been received by the Registrar and the arbitration as not having been commenced);*
>
> *(g) confirmation to the Registrar that copies of the Request (including all accompanying documents) have been or are being served simultaneously on all other parties to the arbitration by one or more means of service to be identified in such confirmation."*

The date on which the Registrar receives the Request is treated as the commencement date of the arbitration. However, this is subject to the Article 1.1 (f) provision that the Request shall be treated as not having been received, and the arbitration as not having been commenced, if the prescribed registration fee has not been paid.

Response

Article 2 provides for service of a Response by the Respondent that is to contain or be accompanied by:

> *"(a) confirmation or denial of all or part of the claims advanced by the Claimant in the Request;*

(b) a brief statement describing the nature and circumstances of any counterclaims advanced by the Respondent against the Claimant;

(c) comment in response to any statements contained in the Request, as called for under Article 1.1(d), on matters relating to the conduct of the arbitration;

(d) if the Arbitration Agreement calls for party nomination of arbitrators, the name, address, telephone, facsimile, telex and e-mail numbers (if known) of the Respondent's nominee; and

(e) confirmation to the Registrar that copies of the Response (including all accompanying documents) have been or are being served simultaneously on all other parties to the arbitration by one or more means of service to be identified in such confirmation."

Failure by the Respondent to send a Response *"shall not preclude the Respondent from denying any claim or from advancing a counterclaim in the arbitration. However, if the Arbitration Agreement calls for party nomination of arbitrators, failure to send a Response or to nominate an arbitrator within time or at all shall constitute an irrevocable waiver of that party's opportunity to nominate an arbitrator."*

LCIA Court and Registrar

Article 3 deals with the functions of the LCIA Court and the Registrar.

Notices and periods of time

Provisions as to notices and periods of time are contained in Article 4. The Arbitral Tribunal may extend time (even where the period has expired) or abridge any period of time, both under the Rules and under the Arbitration Agreement (Article 4.7).

Formation of the Arbitral Tribunal

Article 5 sets out the provisions relating to the formation of the Arbitral Tribunal, which Article 5.1 defines as including *"a sole arbitrator or all the arbitrators where more than one"*. Article 5.2 deals with impartiality and independence. All arbitrators conducting an arbitration under the LCIA rules *"shall be and remain at all times impartial and independent of the parties; and none shall act in the arbitration as advocates for any party. No arbitrator, whether before or after appointment, shall advise any party on the merits or outcome of the dispute."*

In that respect, Article 5.3 states that before appointment by the LCIA Court *"each arbitrator shall furnish to the Registrar a written résumé of his past and present professional positions; he shall agree in writing upon fee rates conforming to the Schedule of Costs; and he shall sign a declaration to the effect that there are no circumstances known to him likely to give rise to any justified doubts as to his impartiality or independence, other than any circumstances disclosed by him in the declaration. Each arbitrator shall thereby also assume a continuing duty forthwith to disclose any such circumstances to the LCIA Court, to any other members of the Arbitral Tribunal and to all the parties if such circumstances should arise after the date of such declaration and before the arbitration is concluded."*

Article 5.4 deals with the timescale within which the LCIA Court is to appoint the Arbitral Tribunal, which is as soon as practicable after the receipt by the Registrar of the Response, or 30 days after the service of the Request if no response is received.

Only the LCIA Court is empowered to appoint arbitrators. The Court *"will appoint arbitrators with due regard for any particular method or criteria of selection agreed in writing by the parties. In selecting arbitrators consideration will be given to the nature of the transaction, the nature and circumstances of the dispute, the nationality, location and languages of the parties and (if more than two) the number of parties"* (Article 5.5).

In the case of a three-member Tribunal, the chairman – who will not be a party-nominated arbitrator – will be appointed by the LCIA Court (Article 5.6). This provision is sometimes misunderstood as meaning that the parties may not jointly select the Chairman, or that the party nominees may not do so. That is not the case. The provision is intended to say that, where there is party nomination, neither of the party-nominated arbitrators may preside. In all cases, all arbitrators must be *appointed* by the LCIA Court, irrespective of who nominates them.

Tribunal and the nationality of arbitrators

Article 6 contains detailed provisions dealing with the nationality of arbitrators. Where parties are of different nationalities *"a sole arbitrator or chairman of the Arbitral Tribunal shall not have the same nationality as any party unless the parties who are not of the same nationality as the proposed appointee all agree in writing otherwise"*. The nationality of parties includes that of controlling shareholders or interests. A person who is a citizen of two or more States *"shall be treated as a national of each State; and citizens of the European Union shall be treated as nationals of its different Member States and shall not be treated as having the same nationality"*.

Tribunal – party and other nominations

Article 7 demonstrates the strict control that the LCIA maintains over the appointment of arbitrators. Article 7.1 states that

> *" If the parties have agreed that any arbitrator is to be appointed by one or more of them or by any third person, that agreement shall be treated as an agreement to nominate an arbitrator for all purposes. Such nominee may only be appointed by the LCIA Court as arbitrator subject to his prior compliance with Article 5.3. The LCIA Court may refuse to appoint any such nominee if it determines that he is not suitable or independent or impartial."*

Article 7.2 contains default provisions in relation to the nomination and appointment of arbitrators:

> *"Where the parties have howsoever agreed that the Respondent or any third person is to nominate an arbitrator and such nomination is not made within time or at all, the LCIA Court may appoint an arbitrator notwithstanding the absence of the nomination and without regard to any late nomination. Likewise, if the Request for Arbitration does not contain a nomination by the Claimant where the parties have howsoever agreed that the Claimant or a third person is to nominate an arbitrator, the LCIA Court*

may appoint an arbitrator notwithstanding the absence of the nomination and without regard to any late nomination."

Tribunal – three or more parties

Article 8 contains default provisions for the appointment of the Tribunal in an arbitration where there are three or more parties:

> *"Where the Arbitration Agreement entitles each party howsoever to nominate an arbitrator, the parties to the dispute number more than two and such parties have not all agreed in writing that the disputant parties represent two separate sides for the formation of the Arbitral Tribunal as Claimant and Respondent respectively, the LCIA Court shall appoint the Arbitral Tribunal without regard to any party's nomination."*

In those circumstances, the Arbitration Agreement is to be treated as a written agreement by the parties for the appointment of the Tribunal by the LCIA Court.

Expedited formation of Tribunal

Article 9 makes provision for the expedited formation of an Arbitral Tribunal. Article 9.1 states that in cases of exceptional urgency, on or after the commencement of the arbitration *"any party may apply to the LCIA Court for the expedited formation of the Arbitral Tribunal, including the appointment of any replacement arbitrator under Articles 10 and 11 of these Rules"*.

The application is to be made in writing to the LCIA Court (copied to all the parties) and is to set out the grounds relied on for the exceptional urgency in the formation of the Tribunal. The Court has a discretion whether to abridge or curtail any time limit under the Rules for formation of the Tribunal, including *"service of the Response and of any matters or documents adjudged to be missing from the Request. The LCIA Court shall not be entitled to abridge or curtail any other time-limit."*

Revocation of arbitrator's appointment

Provisions relating to the revocation, challenge and replacement of arbitrators are contained in Articles 10 and 11. Article 10.1 states that

> *"If either (a) any arbitrator gives written notice of his desire to resign as arbitrator to the LCIA Court, to be copied to the parties and the other arbitrators (if any) or (b) any arbitrator dies, falls seriously ill, refuses, or becomes unable or unfit to act, either upon challenge by a party or at the request of the remaining arbitrators, the LCIA Court may revoke that arbitrator's appointment and appoint another arbitrator. The LCIA Court shall decide upon the amount of fees and expenses to be paid for the former arbitrator's services (if any) as it may consider appropriate in all the circumstances."*

Article 10.2 provides that

> *"If any arbitrator acts in deliberate violation of the Arbitration Agreement (including these Rules) or does not act fairly and impartially as between the parties or does not conduct or participate in the arbitration proceedings with reasonable diligence,*

> *avoiding unnecessary delay or expense, that arbitrator may be considered unfit in the opinion of the LCIA Court."*

An arbitrator may also be challenged *"by any party if circumstances exist that give rise to justifiable doubts as to his impartiality or independence. A party may challenge an arbitrator it has nominated, or in whose appointment it has participated, only for reasons of which it becomes aware after the appointment has been made"* (Article 10.3).

Article 10.4 states that a party who intends to challenge an arbitrator *"shall, within 15 days of the formation of the Arbitral Tribunal or (if later) after becoming aware of any circumstances referred to in Article 10.1, 10.2 or 10.3, send a written statement of the reasons for its challenge to the LCIA Court, the Arbitral Tribunal and all other parties. Unless the challenged arbitrator withdraws or all other parties agree to the challenge within 15 days of receipt of the written statement, the LCIA Court shall decide on the challenge."*

Nomination and replacement of arbitrators

The nomination and replacement provisions are contained in Article 11: *"In the event that the LCIA Court determines that any nominee is not suitable or independent or impartial or if an appointed arbitrator is to be replaced for any reason, the LCIA Court shall have a complete discretion to decide whether or not to follow the original nominating process".* If the Court does so decide, *"any opportunity given to a party to make a re-nomination shall be waived if not exercised within 15 days (or such lesser time as the LCIA Court may fix), after which the LCIA Court shall appoint the replacement arbitrator".*

Majority power to continue proceedings

Provisions to deal with the situation where an arbitrator on a three-member Tribunal persistently fails to participate in the process are set out in Article 12:

> *"If any arbitrator on a three-member Arbitral Tribunal refuses or persistently fails to participate in its deliberations, the two other arbitrators shall have the power, upon their written notice of such refusal or failure to the LCIA Court, the parties and the third arbitrator, to continue the arbitration (including the making of any decision, ruling or award), notwithstanding the absence of the third arbitrator."*

In deciding whether to continue with the arbitration, the other two arbitrators are to take into account *"the stage of the arbitration, any explanation made by the third arbitrator for his non-participation and such other matters as they consider appropriate in the circumstances of the case. The reasons for such determination shall be stated in any award, order or other decision made by the two arbitrators without the participation of the third arbitrator."*

Where those two arbitrators decide not to continue without the participation of the third arbitrator *"the two arbitrators shall notify in writing the parties and the LCIA Court of such determination; and in that event, the two arbitrators or any party may refer the matter to the LCIA Court for the revocation of that third arbitrator's appointment and his replacement under Article 10."*

Communications between parties and the Arbitral Tribunal

Provisions dealing with communications between the parties and the Tribunal are set out in Article 13. Until the Tribunal is formed, all communications are through the Registrar. Communications continue through the Registrar after formation, unless the Tribunal decides otherwise.

Conduct of the proceedings

The Rules now move to the conduct of the arbitral proceedings. Article 14.1 states that the parties may agree on the conduct of their arbitral proceedings and are encouraged to do so

> *"consistent with the Arbitral Tribunal's general duties at all times:*
>
> *(i) to act fairly and impartially as between all parties, giving each a reasonable opportunity of putting its case and dealing with that of its opponent; and*
>
> *(ii) to adopt procedures suitable to the circumstances of the arbitration, avoiding unnecessary delay or expense, so as to provide a fair and efficient means for the final resolution of the parties' dispute."*

That reference to the Tribunal's general duties mirrors the provisions of Article 33 of the English Arbitration Act.

Any agreement made by the parties is to be recorded in writing. Unless the parties agree otherwise, Article 14.2 provides that the Tribunal *"shall have the widest discretion to discharge its duties allowed under such law(s) or rules of law as the Arbitral Tribunal may determine to be applicable; and at all times the parties shall do everything necessary for the fair, efficient and expeditious conduct of the arbitration"*.

Where there is a three-member Tribunal, the Chairman, with the consent of the other two arbitrators, may make procedural rulings alone.

Submission of written statements and documents

Save to the extent that the parties have agreed otherwise under Article 14.1 (or the Tribunal determines differently), the provisions for the written stage of the arbitral process are set out in Article 15. Article 15.2 provides that:

> *"Within 30 days of receipt of written notification from the Registrar of the formation of the Arbitral Tribunal, the Claimant shall send to the Registrar a Statement of Case setting out in sufficient detail the facts and any contentions of law on which it relies, together with the relief claimed against all other parties, save and insofar as such matters have not been set out in its Request."*

Within 30 days of the receipt of that Statement of Case (or a written notice from the Claimant that it elects to treat the Request as its Statement of Case) Article 15.3 requires the Respondent to *"send to the Registrar a Statement of Defence setting out in sufficient detail which of the facts and contentions of law in the Statement of Case or Request (as the case may be) it admits or denies, on what grounds and on what other facts and contentions of law it relies. Any counterclaims shall be submitted with the Statement of Defence in the same manner as claims are to be set out in the Statement of Case."*

The LCIA Rules are unusual in that they expressly require the service of a Statement of Reply. Article 15.4 states that within 30 days of the receipt of the Statement of Defence *"the Claimant shall send to the Registrar a Statement of Reply which, where there are any counterclaims, shall include a Defence to Counterclaim in the same manner as a defence is to be set out in the Statement of Defence."* Where the Statement of Reply contains a Defence to Counterclaim, the Respondent is to serve a Statement of Reply to Counterclaim within 30 days (Article 15.5).

The pleadings are to be accompanied by copies of documents or lists: *"All Statements referred to in this Article shall be accompanied by copies (or, if they are especially voluminous, lists) of all essential documents on which the party concerned relies and which have not previously been submitted by any party, and (where appropriate) by any relevant samples and exhibits."* Following the receipt of the pleadings, the Tribunal is to proceed with the arbitration *"in such manner as has been agreed in writing by the parties or pursuant to its authority under these Rules"*.

Default provisions are contained in Article 15.8: *"If the Respondent fails to submit a Statement of Defence or the Claimant a Statement of Defence to Counterclaim, or if at any point any party fails to avail itself of the opportunity to present its case in the manner determined by Article 15.2 to 15.6 or directed by the Arbitral Tribunal, the Arbitral Tribunal may nevertheless proceed with the arbitration and make an award."*

Seat of arbitration, place of hearings and law applicable to the arbitration

The provisions relating to the seat of the arbitration and the place of the hearings are contained in Article 16. Article 16.1 provides that the parties may agree in writing *"the seat (or legal place) of their arbitration. Failing such a choice, the seat of arbitration shall be London, unless and until the LCIA Court determines in view of all the circumstances, and after having given the parties an opportunity to make written comment, that another seat is more appropriate."*

While the seat of the arbitration is fixed, hearings, meetings and deliberations may be held *"at any convenient geographical place in its discretion; and if elsewhere than the seat of the arbitration, the arbitration shall be treated as an arbitration conducted at the seat of the arbitration and any award as an award made at the seat of the arbitration for all purposes"*.

The law applicable to the arbitration (if any) *"shall be the arbitration law of the seat of arbitration, unless and to the extent that the parties have expressly agreed in writing on the application of another arbitration law and such agreement is not prohibited by the law of the arbitral seat"*.

The law applicable to the conduct of the arbitral proceedings is to be distinguished from the law governing the contract, which is dealt with in Article 22.3 of the LCIA Rules.

Language of arbitration

Article 17 deals with the language of the arbitration. Article 17.1 states that the initial language of the arbitration *"shall be the language of the Arbitration Agreement, unless the parties have agreed in writing otherwise and providing always that a non-participating or defaulting party shall have no cause for complaint if communications to and from the Registrar and the arbitration proceedings are conducted in English".*

Where the Arbitration Agreement is written in more than one language *"the LCIA Court may, unless the Arbitration Agreement provides that the arbitration proceedings shall be conducted in more than one language, decide which of those languages shall be the initial language of the arbitration".*

Once the Tribunal has been formed (and unless the parties have agreed otherwise) *"the Arbitration Tribunal shall decide upon the language(s) of the arbitration, after giving the parties an opportunity to make written comment and taking into account the initial language of the arbitration and any other matter it may consider appropriate in all the circumstances of the case".*

As to documents: *"If any document is expressed in a language other than the language(s) of the arbitration and no translation of such document is submitted by the party relying upon the document, the Arbitral Tribunal or (if the Arbitral Tribunal has not been formed) the LCIA Court may order that party to submit a translation in a form to be determined by the Arbitral Tribunal or the LCIA Court, as the case may be."*

Party representation

The parties may be represented by legal practitioners or other representatives (Article 18). The Tribunal *"may require from any party proof of authority granted to its representative(s) in such form as the Arbitral Tribunal may determine".*

Hearings

Unless the parties have agreed in writing on a documents-only arbitration, *"Any party which expresses a desire to that effect has the right to be heard orally before the Arbitral Tribunal on the merits of the dispute."* The Tribunal is to fix the date, time and place of any meetings and hearings in the arbitration, giving reasonable notice to the parties.

In advance of any hearing, the Tribunal may *"submit to the parties a list of questions which it wishes them to answer with special attention".*

Unless the parties agree otherwise, or unless the Tribunal directs otherwise, meetings and hearings are to be in private. The Tribunal has authority to establish time limits for such meetings and hearings (Article 19).

Witnesses and experts

Article 20 and 21 deal with witnesses and with experts to the Tribunal.

Article 20 states that: *"Before any hearing, the Arbitral Tribunal may require any party to give notice of the identity of each witness that party wishes to call (including rebuttal witnesses), as well as the subject matter of that witness's testimony, its content and its relevance to the issues in the arbitration."* The Tribunal may determine *"the time, manner and form in which such materials should be exchanged between the parties and presented to the Arbitral Tribunal; and it has a discretion to allow, refuse, or limit the appearance of witnesses (whether witness of fact or expert witness)".*

Unless the Tribunal orders otherwise, the testimony of a witness may be in written form, either as a signed statement or as a sworn affidavit. However, any party may request that a witness attend the hearing for oral questioning. If the witness fails to attend without good cause *"the Arbitral Tribunal may place such weight on the written testimony (or exclude the same altogether) as it considers appropriate in the circumstances of the case".* A witness giving oral evidence may be questioned by the parties – but under the control of the Tribunal – and the Tribunal itself may put questions. Article 20.6 states that, subject to the mandatory provisions of any applicable law *"it shall not be improper for any party or its legal representatives to interview any witness or potential witness for the purpose of presenting his testimony in written form or producing him as an oral witness".*

Article 20.7 provides that any individual intending to testify to the Tribunal, either on any issue of fact or of expertise *"shall be treated as a witness under these Rules notwithstanding that the individual is a party to the arbitration or was or is an officer, employee or shareholder of any party".*

Article 21.1 states that, unless otherwise agreed by the parties in writing, the Tribunal

> *"(a) may appoint one or more experts to report to the Arbitral Tribunal on specific issues, who shall be and remain impartial and independent of the parties throughout the arbitration proceedings; and*
>
> *(b) may require a party to give any such expert any relevant information or to provide access to any relevant documents, goods, samples, property or site for inspection by the expert".*

The Tribunal-appointed experts may be required to attend the hearing: *"Unless otherwise agreed by the parties in writing, if a party so requests or if the Arbitral Tribunal considers it necessary, the expert shall, after delivery of his written or oral report to the Arbitral Tribunal and the parties, participate in one or more hearings at which the parties shall have the opportunity to question the expert on his report and to present expert witnesses in order to testify on the points at issue"* (Article 21.2).

Under Article 24 the fees and expenses of any such expert are to be paid out of the deposits payable by the parties and form part of the costs of the arbitration.

Additional powers of the Arbitral Tribunal

Article 22 contains a series of important provisions relating to the additional powers of the Tribunal – including production of documents, rectification, joinder of parties and governing law. Article 22.1 sets out a list of procedural powers. Unless the parties have agreed otherwise in writing:

> *"the Arbitral Tribunal shall have the power, on the application of any party or of its own motion, but in either case only after giving the parties a reasonable opportunity to state their views:*

(a) to allow any party, upon such terms (as to costs and otherwise) as it shall determine, to amend any claim, counterclaim, defence and reply

(b) to extend or abbreviate any time-limit provided by the Arbitration Agreement or these Rules for the conduct of the arbitration or by the Arbitral Tribunal's own orders;

(c) to conduct such enquiries as may appear to the Arbitral Tribunal to be necessary or expedient, including whether and to what extent the Arbitral Tribunal should itself take the initiative in identifying the issues and ascertaining the relevant facts and the law(s) or rules of law applicable to the arbitration, the merits of the parties' dispute and the Arbitration Agreement;

(d) to order any party to make any property, site or thing under its control and relating to the subject matter of the arbitration available for inspection by the Arbitral Tribunal, any other party, its expert or any expert to the Arbitral Tribunal;

(e) to order any party to produce to the Arbitral Tribunal, and to the other parties for inspection, and to supply copies of, any documents or classes of documents in their possession, custody or power which the Arbitral Tribunal determines to be relevant;

(f) to decide whether or not to apply any strict rules of evidence (or any other rules) as to the admissibility, relevance or weight of any material tendered by a party on any matter of fact or expert opinion; and to determine the time, manner and form in which such material should be exchanged between the parties and presented to the Arbitral Tribunal;

(g) to order the correction of any contract between the parties or the Arbitration Agreement, but only to the extent required to rectify any mistake which the Arbitral Tribunal determines to be common to the parties and then only if and to the extent to which the law(s) or rules of law applicable to the contract or Arbitration Agreement permit such correction; and

(h) to allow, only upon the application of a party, one or more third persons to be joined in the arbitration as a party provided any such third person and the applicant party have consented thereto in writing, and thereafter to make a single final award, or separate awards, in respect of all parties so implicated in the arbitration...."

The joinder power contained in Article 22.1 (h) is a significant power – and may well be without parallel in any other major set of Arbitration Rules. The provision permits a willing third party (or parties), which is a party neither to the arbitration agreement nor to the contract in dispute, to be joined to the arbitration on the application of *one* of the parties to the arbitration. This is so notwithstanding the objection of another party to the arbitration, although all parties will have their say on the joinder application.

By agreeing to LCIA arbitration *"the parties shall be treated as having agreed not to apply to any state court or other judicial authority for any order available from the Arbitral Tribunal under Article 22.1, except with the agreement in writing of all parties".*

Article 22.3 deals with the vitally important matter of governing law and rules of law:

"The Arbitral Tribunal shall decide the parties' dispute in accordance with the law(s) or rules of law chosen by the parties as applicable to the merits of their dispute. If and to the extent that the Arbitral Tribunal determines that the parties have made no such

choice, the Arbitral Tribunal shall apply the law(s) or rules of law which it considers appropriate."

Article 22.4 states that the Tribunal shall only apply to the merits of the dispute principles deriving from *"ex aequo et bono"*, *"amiable composition"* or *"honourable engagement"* where the parties have so agreed expressly in writing. The LCIA is happy to use the Latin and French terms avoided in Section 46 of the English Arbitration Act.

Jurisdiction of the Arbitral Tribunal

The jurisdiction of a Tribunal is a matter of considerable significance in international commercial arbitration. The question of *competence / competence* is dealt with in Article 23. The Tribunal:

> *"shall have the power to rule on its own jurisdiction, including any objection to the initial or continuing existence, validity or effectiveness of the Arbitration Agreement. For that purpose, an arbitration clause which forms or was intended to form part of another agreement shall be treated as an arbitration agreement independent of that other agreement. A decision by the Arbitral Tribunal that such other agreement is non-existent, invalid or ineffective shall not entail ipso jure the non-existence, invalidity or ineffectiveness of the arbitration clause."*

Article 23.2 states that:

> *"A plea by a Respondent that the Arbitral Tribunal does not have jurisdiction shall be treated as having been irrevocably waived unless it is raised not later than the Statement of Defence; and a like plea by a Respondent to Counterclaim shall be similarly treated unless it is raised no later than the Statement of Defence to Counterclaim. A plea that the Arbitral Tribunal is exceeding the scope of its authority shall be raised promptly after the Arbitral Tribunal has indicated its intention to decide on the matter alleged by any party to be beyond the scope of its authority, failing which such plea shall also be treated as having been waived irrevocably. In any case, the Arbitral Tribunal may nevertheless admit an untimely plea if it considers the delay justified in the particular circumstances."*

The Tribunal may determine the matter of its jurisdiction or authority either in an interim award or in the award on the merits (Article 23.3). Article 23.4 states that by agreeing to LCIA arbitration *"the parties shall be treated as having agreed not to apply to any state court or other judicial authority for any relief regarding the Arbitral Tribunal's jurisdiction or authority, except with the agreement in writing of all parties to the arbitration or the prior authorisation of the Arbitral Tribunal or following the latter's award ruling on the objection to its jurisdiction or authority"*.

Deposits

Article 24 deals with deposits. The LCIA Court may direct the parties to make interim or final payments on account costs. In the event that a party fails or refuses to provide a deposit, the Court *"may direct the other party or parties to effect a substitute payment to allow the arbitration to proceed (subject to any award on costs). In such circumstances, the party paying the substitute payment shall be entitled to recover that amount as a debt immediately due from the defaulting party."* Failure by a claimant or counterclaiming party to provide a deposit *"may be treated by the LCIA Court and the Arbitral Tribunal as a withdrawal of the claim or counterclaim respectively".*

Interim and conservatory measures

Article 25 contains provisions relating to interim and conservatory measures. Article 25.1 states that, unless the parties have agreed otherwise in writing, the Tribunal has the power on the application of any party

> *"(a) to order any respondent party to a claim or counterclaim to provide security for all or part of the amount in dispute, by way of deposit or bank guarantee or in any other manner and upon such terms as the Arbitral Tribunal considers appropriate. Such terms may include the provision by the claiming or counterclaiming party of a cross-indemnity, itself secured in such manner as the Arbitral Tribunal considers appropriate, for any costs or losses incurred by such respondent in providing security. The amount of any costs and losses payable under such cross-indemnity may be determined by the Arbitral Tribunal in one or more awards;*
>
> *(b) to order the preservation, storage, sale or other disposal of any property or thing under the control of any party and relating to the subject matter of the arbitration; and*
>
> *(c) to order on a provisional basis, subject to final determination in an award, any relief which the Arbitral Tribunal would have power to grant in an award, including a provisional order for the payment of money or the disposition of property as between any parties."*

Article 25.2 gives power to the Tribunal to order the provision of security for its legal or other costs.

Article 25.3 deals with the right of parties to apply to state courts for interim or conservatory measures prior to the formation of the Tribunal, and, in exceptional circumstances, even after the formation of a Tribunal: *"Any application and any order for such measures after the formation of the Arbitral Tribunal shall be promptly communicated by the applicant to the Arbitral Tribunal and all other parties. However, by agreeing to arbitration under these Rules, the parties shall be taken to have agreed not to apply to any state court or other judicial authority for any order for security for its legal or other costs available from the Arbitral Tribunal...."*

Awards – separate awards, consent awards and finality of awards

Articles 26 and 27 deal with awards. The award is to be in writing and, unless the parties have agreed otherwise, is to state the reasons on which is based. The award is to state the date it was made and the seat of the arbitration. It is to be signed by the Tribunal.

Article 26.2 states that if any arbitrator *"fails to comply with the mandatory provisions of any applicable law relating to the making of the award, having been given a reasonable opportunity to do so, the remaining arbitrators may proceed in his absence and state in their award the circumstances of the other arbitrator's failure to participate in the making of the award".*

Decision is by a majority. Failing a majority decision on any issue, the chairman decides that issue. If any arbitrator refuses or fails to sign the award, *"the signatures of the majority or (failing a majority) of the chairman shall be sufficient, provided that the reason for the omitted signature is stated in the award by the majority or chairman".*

The sole arbitrator or chairman delivers the award to the LCIA Court, which transmits certified copies to the parties (provided that the costs have been paid). The award may be expressed in any currency and simple compound interest may be awarded *"at such rates as the Arbitral Tribunal determines to be appropriate, without being bound by legal rates of interest imposed by any state court, in respect of any period which the Arbitral Tribunal determines to be appropriate ending not later than the date upon which the award is complied with".*

The Tribunal has power to make separate awards on different issues at different times.

Article 26.8 makes provision for a Consent Award in the event of a settlement of the dispute during the arbitral process:

> *"In the event of a settlement of the parties' dispute, the Arbitral Tribunal may render an award recording the settlement if the parties so request in writing (a 'Consent Award'), provided always that such award contains an express statement that it is an award made by the parties' consent. A Consent Award need not contain reasons. If the parties do not require a Consent Award, then on written confirmation by the parties to the LCIA Court that a settlement has been reached, the Arbitral Tribunal shall be discharged and the arbitration proceedings concluded, subject to payment by the parties of any outstanding costs of the arbitration under Article 28."*

Article 26.9 contains the important provisions on finality of the arbitral award. All awards shall be final and binding on the parties: *"By agreeing to arbitration under these Rules, the parties undertake to carry out any award immediately and without any delay (subject only to Article 27); and the parties also waive irrevocably their right to any form of appeal, review or recourse to any state court or other judicial authority, insofar as such waiver may be validly made."*

Correction of awards and additional awards

The above reference to Article 27 is to the provisions relating to correction of awards and to additional awards. On the request of a party, or on its own initiative, the Tribunal has the power *"to correct in the award any errors in computation, clerical or typographical errors or any errors of a similar nature. If the Arbitral Tribunal considers the request to be justified, it shall make the corrections within 30 days of receipt of the request. Any correction shall take the form of separate memorandum dated and signed by the Arbitral Tribunal or (if three arbitrators) those of its members assenting to it; and such memorandum shall become part of the award for all purposes."*

The Tribunal also has power on the written application of a party *"to make an additional award as to claims or counterclaims presented in the arbitration but not determined in any award. If the Arbitral Tribunal considers the request to be justified, it shall make the additional award within 60 days of receipt of the request. The provisions of Article 26 shall apply to any additional award."*

Arbitration and legal costs

Article 28 contains detailed provisions dealing with arbitration and legal costs. The allocation of costs in the award is dealt with in Article 28.2:

> *"The Arbitral Tribunal shall specify in the award the total amount of the costs of the arbitration as determined by the LCIA Court. Unless the parties agree otherwise in writing, the Arbitral Tribunal shall determine the proportions in which the parties shall bear all or part of such arbitration costs. If the Arbitral Tribunal has determined that all or any part of the arbitration costs shall be borne by a party other than a party which has already paid them to the LCIA, the latter party shall have the right to recover the appropriate amount from the former party."*

The parties' legal and other costs may be determined by the Tribunal: *"The Arbitral Tribunal shall also have the power to order in its award that all or part of the legal or other costs incurred by a party be paid by another party, unless the parties agree otherwise in writing. The Arbitral Tribunal shall determine and fix the amount of each item comprising such costs on such reasonable basis as it thinks fit"* (Article 28.3).

The 'costs follow the event' principle is reflected in Article 28.4: *"Unless the parties otherwise agree in writing, the Arbitral Tribunal shall make its orders on both arbitration and legal costs on the general principle that costs should reflect the parties' relative success and failure in the award or arbitration, except where it appears to the Arbitral Tribunal that in the particular circumstances this general approach is inappropriate. Any order for costs shall be made with reasons in the award containing such order."*

Article 28.5 makes provision for costs where the arbitration is abandoned, suspended or concluded before a final award is made.

Decisions by the LCIA Court

Article 29 deals with decisions by the LCIA Court. Such decisions are conclusive and binding on the parties and the Tribunal, and are to be treated as *"administrative in nature and the LCIA Court shall not be required to give any reasons"*. Further, to the extent permitted by the law of the seat of the arbitration *"the parties shall be taken to have waived any right of appeal or review in respect of any such decisions of the LCIA Court to any state court or other judicial authority. If such appeals or review remain possible due to mandatory provisions of any applicable law, the LCIA Court shall, subject to the provisions of that applicable law, decide whether the arbitral proceedings are to continue, notwithstanding an appeal or review."*

However, although under the Rules the LCIA is not required to give reasons for its decisions, its publicly stated policy is nevertheless to give reasons where it is required to decide on a challenge to an arbitrator. That is because the LCIA believes that it is important that the parties and the challenged arbitrator understand why the decision has been made.

Confidentiality

Article 30 states that the arbitral proceedings are confidential:

> *"Unless the parties expressly agree in writing to the contrary, the parties undertake as a general principle to keep confidential all awards in their arbitration, together with all materials in the proceedings created for the purpose of the arbitration and all other documents produced by another party in the proceedings not otherwise in the public domain – save and to the extent that disclosure may be required of a party by legal duty, to protect or pursue a legal right or to enforce or challenge an award in bona fide legal proceedings before a state court or other judicial authority" (Article 30.1).*

Similarly, the deliberations of the Tribunal are confidential to its members *"save and to the extent that disclosure of an arbitrator's refusal to participate in the arbitration is required of the other members of the Arbitral Tribunal under Articles 10, 12 and 26".*

Article 30.3 states that the LCIA Court does not publish any award or part of an award without the prior written consent of the parties and the Tribunal.

The English Arbitration Act (see Chapter 16) does not contain provisions dealing with confidentiality. The Report of the Departmental Advisory Committee (DAC) of December 1996 stated that a small number of key areas had not been included in the draft Arbitration Bill: *"one such example concerns privacy and confidentiality in arbitration.... Privacy and confidentiality have long been assumed as general principles in English commercial arbitration, subject to important exceptions. It is only recently that the English courts have been required to examine both the legal basis of such principles and the breadth of certain of these exceptions, without seriously questioning the existence of the general principles themselves."*

The Report considered various decisions of the English and Australian courts and noted that the decision of the High Court of Australia in *Esso/BHP v Plowman* had *"troubled users of commercial arbitration far outside Australia. The first response has been for arbitral institutions to amend their arbitration rules to provide expressly for confidentiality and privacy. The new WIPO Rules have sought to achieve this and we understand that both the ICC and the LCIA are currently amending their respective rules to similar effect."*

The DAC concluded that no attempt should be made to codify English law on the privacy and confidentiality of English arbitration in the Bill, but stated that *"none doubt at English law the existence of the general principles of confidentiality and privacy.... Where desirable, institutional rules can stipulate for these general principles, even where the arbitration agreement is not governed by English law."*

Exclusion of liability

Provisions dealing with the exclusion of liability in relation to the LCIA, the LCIA Court, the Registrar, arbitrators and tribunal experts are set out in Article 31.1, save to the extent that *"the act or omission is shown by that party to constitute conscious and deliberate wrongdoing committed by the body or person alleged to be liable to that party".*

Article 31.2 states that after the award has been made *"and the possibilities of correction and additional awards referred to in Article 27 have lapsed or been exhausted, neither the LCIA, the LCIA Court (including its President, Vice Presidents and individual members), the Registrar, any deputy Registrar, any arbitrator or expert to the Arbitral Tribunal shall be under any legal obligation to make any statement to any person about any matter concerning the arbitration, nor shall any party seek to make any of these persons a witness in any legal or other proceedings arising out of the arbitration"*.

General rules

The final Article deals with waiver and matters not specifically provided for in the Rules. Article 32.1 states that: *"A party who knows that any provision of the Arbitration Agreement (including these Rules) has not been complied with and yet proceeds with the arbitration without promptly stating its objection to such non-compliance, shall be treated as having irrevocably waived its right to object."*

Article 32.2 states that: *"In all matters not expressly provided for in these Rules, the LCIA Court, the Arbitral Tribunal and the parties shall act in the spirit of these Rules and shall make every reasonable effort to ensure that an award is legally enforceable."*

iii) Other LCIA dispute resolution processes

Like many of the other major international commercial arbitral institutions, the LCIA will not only administer arbitrations under its own Rules. For example, the LCIA will administer ad hoc arbitrations subject to the UNCITRAL Arbitration Rules (considered later in this chapter).

The LCIA also provides other dispute resolution procedures such as mediation. Alternative dispute resolution (ADR) is considered in the next chapter.

3) The International Chamber of Commerce

i) Introduction

The International Chamber of Commerce (ICC) is arguably the most well known of the international arbitral institutions. The ICC's International Court of Arbitration was established in 1923 and, according to its website, *"pioneered international commercial arbitration as it is known today. The Court took the lead in securing the worldwide acceptance of arbitration as the most effective way of resolving international commercial disputes. Since its creation, the Court has administered well over 13,000 international arbitration cases involving parties and arbitrators from more than 100 countries and territories. Demand for its services grows in line with the expansion of international trade and the rapid globalization of the world economy."*

The dispute resolution mechanisms developed by the ICC *"have been conceived specifically for business disputes in an international context. These disputes pose unique difficulties and challenges. Usually, the parties will be of different nationalities, with different linguistic, legal and cultural backgrounds. They may also have very different expectations about how a dispute can be resolved reasonably and fairly. Distrust may be relatively strong, accompanied by uncertainty or a lack of information about the course to follow. These difficulties may be compounded by distance and the disadvantages one party may face in submitting to a procedure on the other's home ground."*

The full background to the ICC and to the International Court of Arbitration can be found on the ICC's website.[83]

ii) The ICC Arbitration Rules

Introductory provisions

The first section of the Rules deals with Introductory Provisions. Article 1, dealing with the ICC Court, states that the Court itself does not settle disputes but ensures the application of the Rules. Article 2 contains definitions and Article 3 deals with written notifications or communications and time limits.

Commencement of the arbitration

Articles 4, 5 and 6 are concerned with the commencement of the arbitration. Article 4 deals with the Request for Arbitration and Article 5 with the Answer to the Request and Counterclaims. The Claimant is to file a Reply to any Counterclaim within a certain time limit. Article 6 deals with the effect of the arbitration agreement: For example, if a plea is raised concerning the existence, validity or scope of the arbitration agreement, the ICC Court may decide that the arbitration shall proceed if it is satisfied *prima facie* that an arbitration agreement under the Rules may exist. The decision as to the jurisdiction of the Tribunal is then to be taken by the Tribunal itself.

The arbitral tribunal

Articles 7 to 12 deal with the arbitral tribunal. Article 7 contains general provisions – for example, the requirement regarding the independence of arbitrators. The number of arbitrators is dealt with in Article 8: either a sole arbitrator or three arbitrators. Article 9 deals with the appointment and confirmation of arbitrators. Provisions dealing with the appointment of arbitrators where there are multiple parties are set out in Article 10. The challenge to arbitrators and replacement of arbitrators are dealt with in Articles 11 and 12.

The arbitral proceedings – including the Terms of Reference

The arbitral proceedings provisions are contained in Articles 13 to 23. These include transmission of the file by the Secretariat to the Tribunal (Article 13); the place of arbitration – fixed by the Court, unless agreed on by the parties (Article 14); and Rules governing the proceedings (Article 15). The ICC Rules govern, and the Tribunal is to *"act fairly and impartially and ensure that each party has a reasonable opportunity to present its case"*.

83 www.iccarbitration.org. See also W Laurence Craig, William Park and Jan Paulsson, *International Chamber of Commerce Arbitration*, ICC Publication N° 594.

Unless the parties have agreed on the language of the arbitration, the matter is to be determined by the Tribunal (Article 16).

Article 17 deals with the applicable rules of law. If not decided by the parties, the Tribunal applies the rules of law *"which it determines to be appropriate"*. In all cases the Tribunal is to take account of the provisions of the contract and the relevant trade usages. Only if the parties have agreed may the Tribunal assume the powers of *amiable compositeur* or decide *ex aequo et bono*.

The Terms of Reference and the procedural timetable are dealt with in Article 18. The Tribunal is to draw up, in the presence of the parties and on the basis of the documents and submissions, a document that sets out various particulars. These include a summary of the parties' claims and the relief sought; an indication (if possible) of the amount claimed or counterclaimed; a list of issues to be determined (unless the Tribunal considers it inappropriate); the place of arbitration; and particulars of the applicable procedural rules (and whether there is power conferred on the Tribunal to act as *amiable compositeur* or decide *ex aequo et bono*). The Tribunal and the parties sign the Terms of Reference. A provisional timetable is also to be drawn up.

The Terms of Reference and the procedural timetable are peculiar to ICC arbitration and have been criticised by some. However, the requirement that the Tribunal draw up a Terms of Reference is a great benefit to the forward planning of the course of the arbitration. Indeed, the very process of drawing them up may result in a narrowing of the issues. Unless the Tribunal so authorises, no new claims or counterclaims are to be made that fall outside the limits of the Terms of Reference (Article 19).

The Tribunal is to proceed to establish the facts of the case (Article 20). Provisions as to hearings are set out in Article 21. When the Tribunal is satisfied that the parties have had a reasonable opportunity to present their cases, it is to declare the proceedings closed (Article 22). Unless the parties have agreed otherwise, the Tribunal has power to order interim or conservatory measures.

The award – including scrutiny of the award

Articles 24 to 29 deals with awards. The time limit for rendering the award is six months from the date of the Terms of Reference. The Court can extend the time limit (Article 24). Where there is more than one arbitrator, the award is by majority decision. Failing a majority the award is made by the chairman alone. Reasons must be given for this (Article 25).

If a settlement is reached, such settlement is to be recorded in the form of an award made by consent, if requested by the parties and if the Tribunal agrees (Article 26).

Article 27 contains the scrutiny of award provisions. Again, these provisions are a unique feature of ICC arbitration and, as in the case of the Terms of Reference provisions, they have been criticised by some as being an interference with the role of the Tribunal. However, it is reasonable to argue that the scrutiny provisions are necessary to ensure the high standard of ICC awards in circumstances where many such awards are made by arbitrators from different parts of the world. The ICC's stamp of approval on an international arbitral award is beyond any doubt a matter of importance and value.

Article 27 states that, before the signing of the award, the Tribunal is to submit it in draft form to the Court. The Court *"may lay down modifications as to the form of the Award and, without affecting the Arbitral Tribunal's liberty of decision, may also draw its attention to points of substance. No award shall be rendered by the Arbitral Tribunal until it has been approved by the Court as to its form."*

Provisions concerning the notification, deposit and enforceability of the award are set out in Article 28. The Tribunal may correct clerical, computational and typographical errors, subject to the approval of the Court. A party may apply for interpretation of the award (Article 29).

Costs and miscellaneous provisions

Articles 30 and 31 deals with costs. Miscellaneous provisions relating to modified time limits, waiver, exclusion of liability and the general rule relating to matters not expressly provided for in the Rules are contained in Articles 32 to 35.

iii) Other ICC dispute resolution processes

The ICC provides amicable dispute resolution services that will be considered in Chapter 19 on alternative dispute resolution.

Chapter 23 in Part V of the Manual, which deals with online dispute resolution, will consider the ICC's specialist system for dealing with documentary credit disputes: DOCDEX.

4) The American Arbitration Association at the International Centre for Dispute Resolution

i) Introduction

The American Arbitration Association (AAA) – commonly referred to as the triple A – was founded in 1926. It is the leading arbitral institution in the United States, where it has over 30 regional offices. Its Commercial Arbitration Rules are used in domestic arbitrations.

In the 1990s the AAA promulgated its International Arbitration Rules, which are largely based on an administered version of the UNCITRAL Arbitration Rules, and established its international division: the International Centre for Dispute Resolution (ICDR). The ICDR maintains offices in New York and Dublin, Ireland. In addition, the ICDR established an office in Mexico City through a cooperative agreement with the Commission of the Mexico City National Chamber of Commerce, and announced a joint venture with the Singapore International Arbitration Centre to establish a dispute resolution centre in Singapore.

The AAA says that the international business community *"uses arbitration to resolve commercial disputes arising in the global marketplace. Supportive laws are in place. The New York Convention of 1958 has been widely adopted, providing a favorable legislative climate that enables the enforcement of arbitration clauses. International commercial arbitration awards are recognized by national courts in most parts of the world, even more than foreign court judgments."*

Of the ICDR, the AAA says that its *"experience, international expertise and multilingual staff form an integral part of the dispute resolution process. The ICDR's international system is premised on its ability to move the matter forward, facilitate communications, ensure that qualified arbitrators and mediators are appointed, control costs, understand cultural sensitivities, resolve procedural impasses and properly interpret and apply its International Arbitration and Mediation Rules. Additionally, the ICDR has many cooperative agreements with arbitral institutions around the world for facilitating the administration of its international cases."*

ii) The AAA's International Arbitration Rules

Commencing the arbitration

Article 1 provides that where the parties have agreed in writing to arbitrate disputes *"under these International Arbitration Rules or have provided for arbitration of an international dispute by the International Centre for Dispute Resolution or the American Arbitration Association without designating particular rules, the arbitration shall take place in accordance with these rules, as in effect at the date of commencement of the arbitration, subject to whatever modifications the parties may adopt in writing."*

The Rules govern the arbitration, except that where *"any such rule is in conflict with any provision of the law applicable to the arbitration from which the parties cannot derogate, that provision shall prevail"*.

The Rules specify the duties and responsibilities of the administrator: *"the International Centre for Dispute Resolution, a division of the American Arbitration Association. The administrator may provide services through its Centre, located in New York, or through the facilities of arbitral institutions with which it has agreements of cooperation."*

Article 2 provides for the initiation of the arbitration process by service of a written notice by the claimant on both the respondent and the administrator. The notice of arbitration is to contain details of the claim. The respondent is to serve a defence and any counterclaim (Article 3). The pleadings may be amended (Article 4).

The Tribunal

Articles 5 to 11 deal with the Tribunal: the number of arbitrators; appointment of arbitrators; impartiality and independence of arbitrators; and challenge and replacement of arbitrators.

General Conditions

The General Conditions (Articles 12 to 37) deal with the arbitration process following the appointment of the Tribunal.

Pleas as to jurisdiction

Article 15 contain provisions relating to pleas as to jurisdiction: *"The tribunal shall have the power to rule on its own jurisdiction, including any objections with respect to the existence, scope or validity of the arbitration agreement."*

Conduct of the arbitration

Article 16 states that: *"Subject to these rules, the tribunal may conduct the arbitration in whatever manner it considers appropriate, provided that the parties are treated with equality and that each party has the right to be heard and is given a fair opportunity to present its case."*

Article 16 (2) contains the extremely useful provision, less detailed than the ICC's Terms of Reference, that the Tribunal in its discretion may hold a preparatory conference with the parties *"for the purpose of organizing, scheduling and agreeing to procedures to expedite the subsequent proceedings"*.

A further very practical provision is set out in Article 16 (3): *"The tribunal may in its discretion direct the order of proof, bifurcate proceedings, exclude cumulative or irrelevant testimony or other evidence, and direct the parties to focus their presentations on issues the decision of which could dispose of all or part of the case."*

Further written statements

Article 17 states that the Tribunal has the power to decide whether the parties shall present further pleadings in addition to the statements of claim, counterclaim and defence.

Notices and evidence

Article 18 contains provisions as to notices and Article 19 deals with evidence.

Hearings

Hearings are dealt with in Article 20. The Tribunal is to give the parties at least 30 days advance notice of the date, time and place of the initial oral hearing, and reasonable notice of any subsequent hearings. At least 15 days before the hearings *"each party shall give the tribunal and the other parties the names and addresses of any witnesses it intends to present, the subject of their testimony and the languages in which such witnesses will give their testimony"*. The Tribunal may require witnesses to retire during the testimony of other witnesses. The evidence of witnesses may also be given in the form of written statements. The Tribunal is to determine *"the admissibility, relevance, materiality and weight of the evidence offered by any party. The tribunal shall take into account applicable principles of legal privilege, such as those involving the confidentiality of communications between a lawyer and client."*

Interim and emergency measures of protection

Articles 21 and 37 deal with measures of protection. Article 21 addresses the subject of interim measures of protection and the authority of arbitrators to award such relief during the arbitral proceeding and after the tribunal is appointed. Article 37, however, deals with the procedure for making available emergency measures of protection. This procedure is unique among the rules of international arbitration providers, and permits a party to seek emergency relief prior to the constitution of the tribunal. Pursuant to Article 37 (2), a party in need of emergency relief *"shall notify the administrator and all other parties in writing of the nature of the relief sought and the reasons why such relief is required on an emergency basis*". The ICDR thereafter, within one business day, appoints a single emergency arbitrator to rule on the application after a reasonable opportunity to be heard is provided to the parties. Article 37 (5) gives the emergency arbitrator the "*power to order or award any interim or conservancy measure the arbitrator deems necessary*". In addition, the emergency arbitrator has no further power to act after the tribunal is constituted, and may not serve as a member of the tribunal unless the parties agree otherwise.

Experts

Article 22 contains provisions dealing with experts.

Default

Default of the parties in relation to the filing of statements, appearance at hearings and production of evidence is set out in Article 23.

Closure of hearing

Article 24 deals with the closure of hearings and provides that: *"After asking the parties if they have any further testimony or evidentiary submissions and upon receiving negative replies or if satisfied that the record is complete, the tribunal may declare the hearings closed."* The Tribunal has a discretion, either on its own motion or on an application by a party, to reopen the hearings at any time before the award is made.

Waiver

Waiver provisions are contained in Article 25: *"A party who knows that any provision of the rules or requirement under the rules has not been complied with, but proceeds with the arbitration without promptly stating an objection in writing thereto, shall be deemed to have waived the right to object."*

Awards, decisions and rulings

Articles 26 and 27 deal with awards, decisions and rulings. Awards may be made by a majority of arbitrators. The presiding arbitrator may be authorised to make rulings on questions of procedure. The award is final and binding and the parties undertake to carry it out without delay. The award is to state reasons and may be made public only with the consent of the parties *"or as required by law"*. The Tribunal is authorised to make interim, interlocutory or partial orders and awards.

Provisions are made in Article 34 for correction and interpretation of the award.

Applicable laws and punitive damages

Applicable laws and remedies are dealt with in Article 28. The Tribunal is to apply the substantive law or rules of law designated by the parties, failing which it will apply the law or rules of law that it determines to be appropriate. In arbitrations involving the application of contracts *"the tribunal shall decide in accordance with the terms of the contract and shall take into account usages of the trade applicable to the contract"*. Unless the parties expressly authorise it, the Tribunal *"shall not decide as* amiable compositeur *or* ex aequo et bono*"*.

Article 28 (5) contains provisions specifically dealing with the award of damages:

> *"Unless the parties agree otherwise, the parties expressly waive and forego any right to punitive, exemplary or similar damages unless a statute requires that compensatory damages be increased in a specified manner. This provision shall not apply to any award of arbitration costs to a party to compensate for dilatory or bad faith conduct in the arbitration."*

That provision may be peculiar to US arbitration. The courts in the United States may award punitive damages. In relation to arbitration, however, the New York Court of Appeals in *Garrity v Lyle Stuart*[84] held that the award of such damages is a means of punishment and deterrence and has no place in private arbitration.

Settlement or other reasons for termination

Article 29 deals with settlement or other reasons for termination of the arbitral process.

Costs and compensation

Articles 31 to 33 cover costs and arbitrators' compensation.

Confidentiality

Confidentiality is dealt with in Article 34, which provides that: *"Confidential information disclosed during the proceedings by the parties or by witnesses shall not be divulged by an arbitrator or by the administrator. Except as provided in Article 27, unless otherwise agreed by the parties, or required by applicable law, the members of the tribunal and the administrator shall keep confidential all matters relating to the arbitration or the award."*

Exclusion of liability and interpretation of the rules

Article 35 covers exclusion of liability in relation to the members of the Tribunal and the administrator. Article 36 gives power to the Tribunal to interpret the rules in so far as they relate to the powers and duties of Tribunal. The administrator is to interpret and apply all other rules. As mentioned earlier, Article 37 contains the provisions dealing with emergency measures of protection.

The average time frame from commencement of an arbitration to the issue of an award in an ICDR-administered arbitration in 2005 was 357 days.

iii) ***Other AAA dispute resolution processes at the ICDR***

Among the various dispute resolution processes provided by the AAA is a comprehensive set of international mediation rules.

iv) ***Dublin***

One of the four AAA international centres is based in Dublin. Ireland has adopted the UNCITRAL Model Law and in 1998 enacted the Arbitration (International Commercial) Act. Ireland ratified the New York Convention in 1981.

---

84 [1976] 40 NY2d 354.

Further details of the AAA and of its International Centre for Dispute Resolution in Dublin can be found on the AAA's website.[85]

5) The China International Economic and Trade Arbitration Commission

i) Introduction

The China International Economic and Trade Arbitration Commission (CIETAC) was established in 1954 within the China Council for the Promotion of International Trade (CCPIT). The objective of CIETAC is to settle – by means of arbitration – disputes arising from economic and trade transactions, particularly disputes between foreign companies and Chinese companies.

The headquarters of CIETAC is in Beijing. Because of CIETAC's increasing caseload, Sub-Commissions have been set up in Shenzhen and Shanghai. In fact, on a caseload basis, CIETAC is probably the busiest international arbitral institution in the world. Facilities for holding arbitrations are available at all three premises.

The scope of CIETAC's jurisdiction is extensive and includes international or foreign-related disputes. It has a multi-national panel of arbitrators. CIETAC has entered into co-operation agreements with various institutions in a number of countries including Belgium, France, Germany, Ghana, India, Italy, Korea, Sweden, Switzerland and the United Kingdom.

CIETAC arbitration has its distinctive features, perhaps the most notable being the combination of arbitration with conciliation. The tribunal may conciliate the case before or after the commencement of the arbitration proceedings, provided the parties agree. If the conciliation fails, the tribunal will continue the arbitration proceedings in accordance with the Arbitration Rules.

The CIETAC Arbitration Rules have been revised from time to time, the most recent being the 2005 revision, effective as from 1 May 2005.

ii) Significant changes in the 2005 Rules

The following changes are of particular significance, and bring the CIETAC Rules more into line with other major international commercial arbitral rules.

Choice / nationality of arbitrators

Perhaps one of the most significant changes is that parties can, by agreement, choose arbitrators from outside of the CIETAC Panel. However, any arbitrator chosen outside of the panel must be approved by the Chairman of CIETAC. Additionally, if the parties cannot agree on the choice of the presiding arbitrator, CIETAC will make the appointment from its own panel.

85 www.icdr.org.

This provision is not unusual. The LCIA Rules, for example, permit party *nomination* (Article 7.1), but state that only the LCIA Court may actually *appoint* an arbitrator (Article 5.5). In the case of a three-member Tribunal, the LCIA Court alone may make the appointment of the chairman *"who will not be a party-nominated arbitrator"* (Article 5.6).

Seat of arbitration

The 2005 Rules permit CIETAC arbitrations to be held outside China.

Procedure

Arbitrators are now permitted to conduct 'adversarial' or 'inquisitorial' proceedings, and provision is made for pre-hearing conferences, the issuing of directions and the establishment of terms of reference.

iii) The 2005 CIETAC Arbitration Rules

There are 71 Articles in the new Rules, which are divided into Chapters.

Chapter I

Chapter I contains general provisions, including the Article 3 provisions relating to the jurisdiction of CIETAC: Cases accepted by CIETAC include those involving international or foreign-related disputes. Article 6 contains the *competence / competence* provisions: if CIETAC is satisfied on prima facie evidence that an arbitration agreement exists, then the arbitration may proceed.

Article 8 contains the usual waiver provisions.

Chapter II

This chapter deals with the arbitral proceedings. Section 1 covers the request for arbitration, defence and counterclaim, and amendment of pleadings. Provision is made for applications relating to the preservation of property and the protection of evidence.

Section 2 contains the rules dealing with the arbitral Tribunal. Article 19 states that an arbitrator *"shall not represent either party and shall remain independent of the parties and treat them equally"*.

The panel is to consist of either one or three arbitrators. Article 21 (2) contains the new provision that *"where the parties have agreed to appoint arbitrators from outside of CIETAC's Panel of Arbitrators, the arbitrators so appointed by the parties or nominated according to the agreement of the parties may act as co-arbitrator, presiding arbitrator or sole arbitrator after the appointment has been confirmed by the Chairman of the CIETAC in accordance with the law"*.

In the case of a three-person panel, each party may appoint one arbitrator. Article 22 (3) contains a 'listing provision' whereby the parties may put forward a list of three candidates as presiding arbitrator, such presiding arbitrator to be approved by the

Chairman of CIETAC. Article 24 contains provisions dealing with the appointment of the Tribunal in the case of a multi-party arbitration.

Article 25 deals with the impartiality of arbitrators, and Articles 26 and 27 with the challenge and replacement of arbitrators.

Article 29 contains significant new provisions relating to the conduct of the hearing. The Tribunal shall *"examine the case in any way that it deems appropriate, unless otherwise agreed by the parties"*. Further, *"the arbitral tribunal may adopt an inquisitorial or adversarial approach when examining the case, having regard to the circumstances of the case"*. The tribunal *"may hold deliberation at any place or in any manner that it considers appropriate"* and, if it considers it necessary, may *"issue procedural directions and lists of questions, hold pre-hearing meetings and preliminary hearings, and produce terms of reference, etc, unless otherwise agreed by the parties"*.

Further new and significant provisions are contained in Articles 31 and 32, which deal with place of arbitration and the place of the oral hearing. Where the parties have agreed on the place of arbitration in writing, *"the parties' agreement shall prevail"*. Otherwise, the place of arbitration is the domicile of CIETAC (or its Sub-Commission). The award is deemed to have been made at the place of arbitration. The parties can agree on the place where the oral hearings are to be held; failing such agreement, the place is Beijing (or the location of the relevant Sub-Commission).

Articles 36 and 37 deal with evidence. Each party has the burden of *"proving the facts relied on to support its claim, defense or counterclaim"*. The Tribunal *"may, on its own initiative, undertake investigations and collect evidence, as it considers necessary"*.

Article 40 contains the classic CIETAC provision dealing with the combination of conciliation and arbitration: *"where both parties have the desire for conciliation… the arbitral tribunal may conciliate the case during the course of the arbitration proceedings… where the conciliation fails, the arbitral tribunal shall proceed with the arbitration and render an arbitral award"*.

Chapter III

Chapter III contains provisions dealing with the arbitral award. This is to be made within six months from the date of the formation of the Tribunal. The Tribunal shall *"independently and impartially make its arbitral award on the basis of the facts, in accordance with the law and terms of the contract, with reference to international practices, and in compliance with the principle of fairness and reasonableness"*.

Article 44 authorises the making of interlocutory and partial awards, and Article 45 states that the Tribunal shall submit its draft award to CIETAC *"for scrutiny before signing the award. The CIETAC may remind the arbitral tribunal of issues in the award on condition that the arbitral tribunal's independence in rendering the award is not affected."* This provision is similar to that found in the ICC Rules.

Articles 47 and 48 deal with the correction of the award and the making of additional awards.

Chapter IV

Articles 50-66 contain provisions for summary procedure where the amounts in disputes do not exceed 500,000 yuan. Pleadings are to be served within 20 days, and 15 days' notice is to be given in relation to any oral hearing. The award is to be made within three months from the date on which the Tribunal was formed – half the time limit of the main CIETAC Arbitration Rules.

The remaining provisions of the Rules deal with language, the service of documents, fees and expenses, interpretation and the date of their coming into force: 1 May 2005.

iii) Other CIETAC dispute resolution processes

CIETAC operates a specific arbitration system relating to financial disputes.

As mentioned above, contained within the main arbitration procedure is provision for the arbitral tribunal to act as conciliators: the *"arbitration with conciliation"* process.

Information on CIETAC can be found on its website.[86] The conciliation procedures operated by CCPIT are considered in Chapter 19 of the Manual.

6) The Arbitration Institute of the Stockholm Chamber of Commerce

i) Introduction

The Stockholm Chamber of Commerce (SCC) is a voluntary business organisation with 2,000 member companies, ranging from world giants to small entrepreneurs. An important part of its work is to facilitate international trade and to establish contacts between companies in the Stockholm region and companies all over the world.

The Arbitration Institute, established in 1917, is an independent entity within the SCC. It was recognised in the 1970s by the United States and the former Soviet Union as a neutral centre for the resolution of East-West trade disputes. The Institute has extended its activities to over 40 countries worldwide and is recognised as one of the world's leading international arbitral institutions. Its current Rules entered into force in April 1999.

ii) The Arbitration Rules of the SCC

The SCC Rules contain 42 Articles.

Part I (Articles 1-4) deals with the organisation of the SCC Institute.

Part 2 contains the Arbitration Rules. Articles 5-15 cover the initiation of proceedings, including the Request for Arbitration (to contain a summary of the dispute); the Respondent's Reply; the place of arbitration; and the appointment of the Tribunal.

86 www.cietac.org.cn.

Articles 16-19 set out the provisions relating to the Tribunal: the number of arbitrators and the method of their appointment; impartiality and independence of arbitrators; and challenge and removal of arbitrators.

Proceedings before the Tribunal are dealt with in Articles 20-31: procedures of the Tribunal; statement of claim and defence; amendments of pleadings; language; applicable law; oral hearings; evidence; experts; default of the parties; waiver / failure to object to procedural irregularities; majority vote / vote of the Chairman; and interim measures.

Articles 32-38 set out the provisions relating to the award: place and date of the award; settlement recorded as award; time for rendering award (six months); separate awards; finality of award; correction and interpretation of award; and additional awards.

Costs are dealt with in Articles 39-41: arbitration and party costs; and allocation of costs between the parties.

Finally, Article 42 makes provision for the exclusion of liability of the SCC Institute and arbitrators, save in the case of wilful misconduct or gross negligence.

iii) Other dispute resolution processes of the SCC Arbitration Institute

The SCC Institute also has available Rules for Expedited Arbitration; separate Rules for Insurance Arbitration; Mediation Rules; and procedures for arbitration under the UNCITRAL Rules.

Further information on the SCC and the Arbitration Institute, and the Arbitration Rules, can be found on the SCC website.[87]

7) The Netherlands Arbitration Institute

i) Introduction

The Netherlands Arbitration Institute (NAI) was founded in 1949. One of the founders was Professor Pieter Sanders, the doyen of international commercial arbitration, who participated in the drafting of the New York Convention.

The NAI is an independent, non-profit-making organisation whose objective is to facilitate the resolution of disputes by providing arbitral services, guidelines and information. It has no connection with government and receives no subsidies. Arbitration is administered by the NAI Secretariat, based in Rotterdam.

ii) The NAI Arbitration Rules

The Rules consist of seven Sections comprising 67 Articles.

87 www.sccinstitute.com.

Section One

This Section deals with General Provisions, including definitions, notices and periods of time.

Section Two

Section Two contains the provisions concerning the Commencement of the Arbitration.

Section Three

This Section deals with the Appointment of Arbitrators, and includes provisions relating to the impartiality and independence of arbitrators; the number of arbitrators and methods of appointment; nationality of arbitrators; and the challenge and replacement of arbitrators.

Section Four

Section Four contains provisions dealing with Procedure:

- place of arbitration;
- memorials: statement of claim, statement of defence and – at the discretion of the Tribunal – reply and rejoinder;
- amendment;
- hearing;
- evidence: documents, witnesses and experts (party-appointed and Tribunal-appointed experts);
- default;
- summary arbitral proceedings: including detailed provisions for emergency applications where the place of arbitration is the Netherlands (but a hearing will not necessarily be held, even if the place of arbitration is the Netherlands);
- provisional measures;
- costs and deposits;
- language;
- third parties: a third-party who has an interest in the outcome of the arbitral proceedings may apply to the Tribunal for permission to be joined or to intervene;
- non-compliance by a party.

Section Four A contains 15 Articles dealing with a Summary Arbitral process:

> *"A request can be made for such summary process where an immediate provisional measure is required. The Request for the summary process is to set out the basis of claim and the reasons for the urgency of the matter. The request is made under Section Four A where the arbitrators have not yet been appointed. However, where the arbitrators have already been appointed, an application for an order in summary arbitral proceedings is made under Article 37 in Section 4."*

Section Five

Section Five deals with the Award and Applicable Law:

- period of time for rendering the award: *"all due dispatch"*;
- types of award: partial, interim and final;
- Rules of Law / Applicable Law / trade usages: the Tribunal is to decide the dispute on the basis of Rules of Law, unless the parties have authorised it to decide as *amiable compositeur* – the Rules of Law are those chosen by the parties, and failing such choice, such Rules as the Tribunal considers appropriate; the Tribunal is also to take into account any applicable trade usages (the reverse is the case in a national, as opposed to an international, arbitration, where the Tribunal *must* decide as *amiable compositeur*, unless the parties have otherwise authorised);
- majority vote: a dissenting opinion is to be set out in a separate document and is not considered part of the award (again, this applies only in the case of an international arbitration);
- the award: to be in writing, give reasons and be signed by the Tribunal – a copy of an award rendered in the Netherlands is deposited with the registry of the district court within whose district the place of arbitration is located;
- a copy of the award to be retained by the NAI Secretariat for 10 years;
- *res judicata*: the award is binding and the parties are deemed to have undertaken to carry out the award without delay;
- rectification or correction of the award;
- additional award;
- award on agreed terms: any settlement may be recorded in an award – however, the Tribunal may refuse to make an award on agreed terms and need not give reasons for refusing to do so – any such award must be signed by all the parties.
- publication of the award: unless the parties serve notice objecting, the NAI may publish the award, but without names and deleting any details that might disclose the identity of the parties.

Section Six

This Section deals with various aspects of Costs, including:

- administration costs of the NAI;
- fees and disbursements of arbitrators;
- deposits for costs;
- allocation of costs against the losing party.

Section Seven

Section Seven contains the Final Provisions:

- waiver: *"the violation of the Rules"*;
- powers of the Court where the arbitration takes place within the Netherlands: the President of the District Court of Rotterdam has jurisdiction to deal with certain matters such as the appointment of arbitrators;

- unforeseen matters: any matter not covered by the Rules will be dealt with in accordance with the spirit of the Rules;
- exclusion of liability in relation to the NAI and arbitrators and others;
- amendment of Rules: power is vested in the Governing Body of the NAI to make amendments.

iii) Other dispute resolution processes of the NAI

The Netherlands Arbitration Institute operates a Minitrial process, which is a form of alternative dispute resolution (ADR) (see Chapter 19).

Further information on the NAI can be found on its website.[88]

8) The World Intellectual Property Organization

i) Introduction

Based in Geneva, Switzerland, the World Intellectual Property Organization (WIPO) Arbitration and Mediation Center was established in 1994 to offer ADR options including *"arbitration and mediation services for the resolution of international commercial disputes between private parties"*.

> *"Developed by leading experts in cross-border dispute settlement, the arbitration and mediation procedures offered by the Center are widely recognized as particularly appropriate for technology, entertainment and other disputes involving intellectual property."*

An increasing number of arbitrations and mediations are being filed with the Center under the WIPO Arbitration, Expedited Arbitration and Mediation Rules. The subject matter of these proceedings *"includes both contractual disputes (e.g. patent and software licenses, trademark coexistence agreements, distribution agreements for pharmaceutical products and research and development agreements) and non-contractual disputes (e.g. patent infringement). WIPO disputes have involved parties based in different jurisdictions including Austria, China, France, Germany, Hungary, Ireland, Israel, Italy, Japan, the Netherlands, Panama, Spain, Switzerland, the United Kingdom and the United States of America."*

In addition to appointing arbitrators and mediators in WIPO cases *"the Center is also frequently asked to recommend neutrals or to act as appointing authority, by parties to disputes that are not subject to the WIPO Rules but that require experience in arbitration or mediation and specialized knowledge of the intellectual property rights in dispute"*.

The Center has also focused significant resources *"on establishing an operational and legal framework for the administration of disputes relating to the Internet and electronic commerce. For example, today the Center is recognized as the leading dispute resolution*

88 www.nai-nl.org/english/.

service provider for disputes arising out of the abusive registration and use of Internet domain names. In addition, the Center is frequently consulted on other specialised dispute resolution services. An independent and impartial body, the Center administratively is part of the International Bureau of the World Intellectual Property Organization."

WIPO's online dispute resolution service is considered in Chapter 23 of the Manual.

ii) The WIPO Arbitration Rules

The WIPO Arbitration Rules are divided into eight Sections.

Section I

This Section contains General Provisions – including the documents to be submitted to the Center.

Section II

Section II deals with the Commencement of the Arbitration (Request and Answer).

Section III

Section III covers the Composition and Establishment of the Tribunal:

- Number of Arbitrators (Article 14)
- Appointment Pursuant to Procedure Agreed Upon by the Parties (Article 15)
- Appointment of a Sole Arbitrator (Article 16)
- Appointment of Three Arbitrators (Article 17)
- Appointment of Three Arbitrators in Case of Multiple Claimants or Respondents (Article 18)
- Default Appointment (Article 19)
- Nationality of Arbitrators (Article 20)
- Communication Between Parties and Candidates for Appointment as Arbitrator (Article 21)
- Impartiality and Independence (Article 22)
- Availability, Acceptance and Notification (Article 23)
- Challenge of Arbitrators (Articles 24 to 29)
- Release from Appointment (Articles 30 to 32)
- Replacement of an Arbitrator (Articles 33 and 34)
- Truncated Tribunal (Article 35)
- Pleas as to the Jurisdiction of the Tribunal (Article 36)

Section IV

Articles 37 to 58 contain the provisions dealing with the Conduct of the Arbitration:

- Transmission of the File to the Tribunal (Article 37)
- General Powers of the Tribunal (Article 38)
- Place of Arbitration (Article 39)
- Language of Arbitration (Article 40)
- Statement of Claim (Article 41)
- Statement of Defense (Article 42)
- Further Written Statements (Article 43)
- Amendments to Claims or Defense (Article 44)
- Communication Between Parties and Tribunal (Article 45
- Interim Measures of Protection and Security for Claims and Costs (Article 46)
- Preparatory Conference (Article 47)
- Evidence (Article 48)
- Experiments (Article 49)
- Site Visits (Article 50)
- Agreed Primers and Models (Article 51)
- Disclosure of Trade Secrets and Other Confidential Information (Article 52)
- Hearings (Article 53)
- Witnesses (Article 54)
- Experts Appointed by the Tribunal (Article 55)
- Default (Article 56)
- Closure of Proceedings (Article 57)
- Waiver (Article 58)

Section V

Articles 59 to 66 deal with the Award and Other Decisions:

- Laws Applicable to the Substance of the Dispute, the Arbitration and the Arbitration Agreement (Article 59)
- Currency and Interest (Article 60)
- Decision-Making (Article 61)
- Form and Notification of Awards (Article 62)
- Time Period for Delivery of the Final Award (Article 63)
- Effect of Award (Article 64)
- Settlement or Other Grounds for Termination (Article 65)
- Correction of the Award and Additional Award (Article 66)

Sections VI, VII and VIII

These Sections cover Fees and Costs, Confidentiality and Miscellaneous Matters.

iii) Other WIPO dispute resolution processes

As mentioned earlier, WIPO operates a number of dispute resolution systems including a Domain Name Dispute Resolution system (considered in Chapter 23) and mediation procedures (referred to in Chapter 19).

Information on the WIPO Center's work in conventional arbitration and mediation may be found on its website.[89]

B *The UNCITRAL Arbitration Rules*

i) Introduction

The United Nations Commission on International Trade Law (UNCITRAL) was established by the General Assembly of the United Nations in 1966 and was given a general mandate to *"further the progressive harmonization and unification of the law of international trade"*. UNCITRAL and its Model Arbitration Law were considered in the earlier chapter dealing with international commercial arbitration.

The Model Law was adopted by UNCITRAL in 1985 with the intention of assisting States in *"reforming and modernizing their laws on arbitral procedure so as to take into account the particular features and needs of international commercial arbitration"*.

The UNCITRAL Arbitration Rules predate the Model Law, having been adopted in 1976. Resolution 31/98 adopted by the UN General Assembly in December of that year stated that the General Assembly recognised the value of arbitration as a method of settling disputes arising in the context of international commercial relations and was convinced *"that the establishment of rules for ad hoc arbitration that are acceptable in countries with different legal, social and economic systems would significantly contribute to the development of harmonious international economic relations…"*. The Resolution noted that the Arbitration Rules had been prepared by UNCITRAL *"after extensive consultation with arbitral institutions and centres of international commercial arbitration…"*.

The UNCITRAL Rules were thus intended for use in arbitrations that are not conducted under the Rules of one of the international commercial arbitral bodies such as those considered earlier in this chapter. Arbitrations conducted by, for example, the LCIA or NAI have a framework of rules that will carry the arbitration from its commencement through to the making of the final award. An ad hoc arbitration has no such procedural framework. The object of the UNCITRAL Model Rules was to provide a framework of rules that would be acceptable globally, by civil law and common law countries, by countries in the East and the West, by developed and developing countries and by countries of varying political systems.

The success of the UNCITRAL Arbitration Rules is shown by the fact that they have additionally been used as a model for institutional rules – in much the same way as the UNCITRAL Model Law has been used as a guide for national arbitration legislation (one example considered earlier in the Manual is the English Arbitration Act of 1996).

---

89 http://arbiter.wipo.int/.

Some of the international arbitral institutions, in addition to offering arbitration under their own Rules, also offer to supervise international arbitrations under the UNCITRAL Arbitration Rules. Two examples are the LCIA and the Arbitration Institute of the SCC.

ii) The UNCITRAL Arbitration Rules

The Rules are divided into four Sections.

Section 1: Introductory Rules

Articles 1 to 4 cover:

- The scope of the Rules: agreement in writing to arbitration under the Rules (a model arbitration clause is provided);
- Notices and calculation of periods of time;
- Commencement of the arbitration by service of a Notice of Arbitration;
- Representation and assistance.

Section II: Composition of the Arbitral Tribunal

Articles 5 to 14 deal with:

- Number of arbitrators (one or three);
- Appointment of arbitrators (provision is made for the Secretary-General of the Permanent Court of Arbitration to designate an appointing authority where necessary);
- Challenge and replacement of arbitrators;
- Repetition of the hearings on replacement of an arbitrator.

Section III: Arbitral proceedings

Articles 15 to 30 contain:

- General provisions: *"Subject to these Rules, the arbitral tribunal may conduct the arbitration in such manner as it considers appropriate, provided that the parties are treated with equality and that at any stage of the proceedings each party is given a full opportunity of presenting his case"* (Article 15 (1));
- Place of arbitration;
- Language of arbitration;
- Pleadings: statement of claim; statement of defence; amendment of claim or defence;
- Pleas as to the jurisdiction of the tribunal (*competence / competence*): *"The arbitral tribunal shall have the power to rule on objections that it has no jurisdiction, including any objections with respect to the existence or validity of the arbitration clause or of the separate arbitration agreement."* In general, the tribunal should rule on a plea concerning its jurisdiction as a preliminary question; however, it may deal with such a plea in the final award;

- Further written statements;
- Periods of time (including periods for service of the statement of claim and statement of defence);
- Evidence: *"The arbitral tribunal may, if it considers it appropriate, require a party to deliver to the tribunal and to the other party, within such a period of time as the arbitral tribunal shall decide, a summary of the documents and other evidence which that party intends to present in support of the facts in issue set out in his statement of claim or statement of defence";*
- Hearings: *"Hearings shall be held in camera unless the parties agree otherwise. The arbitral tribunal may require the retirement of any witness or witnesses during the testimony of other witnesses. The arbitral tribunal is free to determine the manner in which witnesses are examined."* Evidence of witnesses may also be presented in the form of written statements;
- Interim measures of protection: including measures for the conservation of goods. The interim measures may be dealt with in the form of an interim award: *"A request for interim measures addressed by any party to a judicial authority shall not be deemed incompatible with the agreement to arbitrate, or as a waiver of that agreement";*
- Tribunal-appointed experts;
- Default by the parties in relation to service of pleadings, appearance at hearings and failure to produce evidence;
- Closure of hearings: *"The arbitral tribunal may inquire of the parties if they have any further proof to offer or witnesses to be heard or submissions to make and, if there are none, it may declare the hearings closed."* The tribunal may reopen the hearings at any time before the award is made;
- Waiver of rules: a party who proceeds with the arbitration, knowing that a provision or requirement of the Rules has not been complied with, is deemed to have waived the right to object.

Section IV: The award

A number of significant provisions are contained in this part of the UNCITRAL Rules (Articles 31-41).

- Decisions: by majority where there are three arbitrators;
- The form and the effect of the award:
  - The tribunal may make interim, interlocutory and partial awards in addition to the final award;
  - The award is to be in writing and is final and binding on the parties;
  - The award is to state reasons (unless the parties agree otherwise);
  - The award is to be signed by the arbitrators, stating the date on which and the place where the award was made: *"where there are three arbitrators and one of them fails to sign, the award shall state the reason for the absence of the signature";*
  - The award may be made public only with the consent of both parties;

- Applicable law and *amiable compositeur:*
  - The tribunal is to apply the law designated by the parties as applicable to the substance of the dispute. Failing such designation, the tribunal is to apply the law determined *"by the conflict of law rules which it considers applicable";*
  - In all cases the tribunal is to decide *"in accordance with the terms of the contract and shall take into account the usages of the trade applicable to the transaction";*
- Settlement or other grounds of termination:
  - if the parties agree on a settlement before the award is made, the tribunal shall issue an order for the termination of the proceedings. Alternatively, if requested by both parties and provided the tribunal agrees, the settlement may be recorded in the form of an arbitral award;
  - if the continuation of the arbitral proceedings *"becomes unnecessary or impossible for any reason not mentioned in paragraph 1 the arbitral tribunal shall inform the parties of its intention to issue an order for the termination of the proceedings. The arbitral tribunal shall have the power to issue such an award unless a party raises justifiable grounds for objection";*
- Interpretation of the award;
- Correction of the award;
- Additional award;
- Costs:
  - The costs of the arbitration *"shall in principle be borne by the unsuccessful party";* the tribunal is free to determine which party shall bear the costs of legal representation or may apportion such costs between the parties;
  - Deposit of costs: on establishment of the tribunal, each party may be requested to pay an equal amount as an advance on costs. During the course of the proceedings the tribunal may request supplementary deposits. If the required deposits are not paid within 30 days *"the arbitral tribunal shall so inform the parties in order that one or another of them may make the required payment. If such payment is not made, the arbitral tribunal may order the suspension or termination of the arbitral proceedings".*

iii) Other UNCITRAL dispute resolution procedures

The UNCITRAL Conciliation Rules are considered in the following chapter on ADR.

C *The Chartered Institute of Arbitrators*

i) Introduction

The Chartered Institute of Arbitrators was founded in 1915. Its purpose was to provide a membership organisation for arbitrators, and it says it is *"now the world's leading centre of excellence for the promotion and facilitation of dispute resolution".*

The Institute goes on to say that it is

> *"a registered charity with 10,500 members from more than 90 countries and an international network of 30 Branches. Recognised as the professional home for all dispute resolvers, the Institute provides the highest educational standards and is an international resource centre for practitioners, policy makers, academics and those in business concerned with the cost effective and early settlement of disputes.*
>
> *"In facilitating the determination of disputes, the Institute operates in a wide variety of business and commercial sectors including: financial services, insurance, shipping, commodities, the media, medicine, sport, travel, telecommunications and technology industries, construction, engineering and the automobile industry. The Institute's sphere of interest is constantly being widened to encompass other sectors. For example, we are developing the use of ADR to resolve personal injury, media, foreign investment and IT disputes.*
>
> *"The Institute offers education and training throughout the world, providing assured global standards – giving confidence to arbitration and ADR users that the very best practitioner is helping to resolve their dispute. Chartered status for Arbitrators was introduced in 1999 as a 'gold standard' for practitioners. A similar programme is in development towards Chartered status for mediators. We are currently working with partners in China, the Middle East and Russia to raise standards.*
>
> *"In addition to its educational activities, the Institute conducts 'Dispute Resolution Services' – administering more than 100 bespoke schemes for consumer and commercial markets, providing cost-effective and timely resolution of disputes. The Institute also offers nominating and appointing services for ad-hoc arbitration, adjudication and mediation."*

ii) The Arbitration Rules of the Chartered Institute of Arbitrators

The Chartered Institute is not an international arbitral institution like those considered in Section A of this Chapter. In contrast to, for example, the NAI, the primary purpose of the Institute is not the administration of international commercial arbitrations. Rather, one of its main roles is as an educational body.

However, the Institute has published Arbitration Rules (and various other dispute resolution procedures). These Rules may be used without reference to the Institute, although the Institute is prepared to administer arbitrations.

The Institute will also act as an Appointing Authority:

> *"The Institute publishes Rules to help parties and arbitrators take maximum advantage of the flexible procedures available in arbitration for the resolution of disputes quickly and economically. The Rules incorporate relevant provisions of the Arbitration Act 1996 and have also taken cognisance of the new Civil Procedure Rules effective from 26 April 1999. The Rules provide that the wishes of parties regarding procedure will be respected so far as possible, but they also seek to ensure that the arbitrator will have sufficient powers to direct the proceedings if the parties cannot*

agree on procedure or will not co-operate. The Rules may be used without reference to the Institute unless the Institute is required to act as Appointing Authority in accordance with Article 3."

Article 1 of the Rules makes it clear that they are intended to cover arbitrations under the English Arbitration Act 1996.

Information concerning the Chartered Institute and its various dispute resolution processes and services can be found on the Institute's website.[90]

90 www.arbitrators.org.

19 Alternative Dispute Resolution

1) Introduction

"God did not decree that the job of a litigator is to lay waste to the adversaries and win all for client.

"Our system of civil litigation was crafted by men, incorporating a Hegelian dialectic of thesis – antithesis – synthesis; both sides beat themselves bloody, and a judge or jury decides what truths have emerged from the process.

"In the economic and cultural milieu in which this system was developed hundreds of years ago, it worked reasonably well. Times change. Today it can be described as functional only by a definition of 'functional' that countenances clients routinely billed more in transactional costs for the litigation process than the amount of the settlement or judgement, and society taxed with the collateral costs and disruption of protracted and proliferating litigation.

"We might want to pause before we drag this time-hallowed system with us – or let it drag us with it – into the new millennium."

This quotation is taken from an article by Antonio C Piazza, a partner in the San Francisco firm of Gregorio, Haldeman and Piazza.[91] His telling and graphic description of what many see as the defects in the litigation system serves as a fitting introduction to this chapter of the Manual on alternative dispute resolution (ADR).[92]

The chapter looks at what ADR is, its development and types; ADR in an international context; ADR as a pre-arbitral dispute mechanism; using a combination of mediation and arbitration; institutions offering ADR systems, including the Netherlands Arbitration Institute's Minitrial Rules; the UN Commission on International Trade Law (UNCITRAL) Model Law on International Commercial Conciliation and the UNCITRAL Conciliation Rules; ADR in action; and the future development of international ADR.

2) ADR: An Overview

What is ADR?

ADR is generally taken to cover all forms of dispute resolution other than litigation and arbitration. The reason for this is clear: both litigation and arbitration operate regardless of the will of the parties and result in a binding and enforceable outcome. The Defendant / Respondent against whom litigation / arbitration proceedings are launched has no

---

91 CPR Institute for Dispute Resolution, *Into the 21st Century: Thought Pieces on Lawyering, Problem Solving and ADR*, CPR Institute for Dispute Resolution, New York, 2001.

92 Some now prefer to refer to it as *amicable dispute resolution*. As noted later in the chapter, the International Chamber of Commerce (ICC) uses this latter description so as to distinguish mediation and other forms of non-binding dispute resolution from binding systems such as arbitration.

choice as to whether to participate and may be faced with a judgment / award that can be enforced in the national courts. In litigation the process is imposed by the State. In arbitration the result follows from the parties' agreement to arbitrate, coupled with the State's support of the arbitral system.

But ADR in its various forms – the most familiar being mediation and conciliation – is a consensual process: The parties do not have to take part in it. And if they do, they do not have to abide by the outcome. Generally speaking, national courts will not enforce ADR agreements and the ADR process – unlike arbitration – is not subject to any statutory code (in England at any rate).

The development of ADR

There is nothing new in the concept of ADR: Mediation and conciliation have been used in the East for centuries. What is new is the kind of techniques that have been developed in the United States, which has led the way in developing new methods of dispute resolution other than by way of litigation and arbitration.

This writer's view on the topic was set out in an article entitled 'The Role of ADR in the Resolution of International Disputes', published in 1996 in *Arbitration International*, the Journal of the London Court of International Arbitration (LCIA):

> *"Alternative Dispute Resolution (ADR) has developed alongside litigation and arbitration as a means of resolving commercial disputes in accordance with procedures aimed at avoiding the inherent costs and delays of the adversarial process. Those costs and delays have been felt most acutely in the United States, where pre trial obligations are the most burdensome. The United States has accordingly led the way in developing innovative ways of keeping parties away from the courts and arbitration.... But the methods used are not always new. The philosophy of the East has always been in favour of a non-contentious approach to dispute resolution.... The pressures resulting from litigation and arbitration are far from unique to the United States and recent years have seen the English courts take active steps to promote the use of ADR alongside the formal court system."*

This writer's conclusions in that article were that ADR

> *"in its various forms is emerging as a genuine complement to arbitration and litigation, both through increasing support in domestic courts for its active consideration and, more significantly, through increasing initial recourse to non-binding dispute resolution techniques in major international contracts. Whilst recourse to ADR in contracts is likely to lead to a multi-stage process which may, in certain circumstances, lead to increased delay, the hope is that the vast majority of disputes will be filtered out at the ADR stage of the process, thereby saving the costs, time and antagonism which usually accompany formal litigation or arbitration."*[93]

Since 1996 when that article was published there has been an increasing interest in ADR in England, particularly by the English courts. Lord Woolf's reform of the Civil Procedure Rules in 1998 laid great emphasis on ADR.

93 [1996] 12 Arbitration International 47-55.

Types of ADR

Mediation and conciliation

The terms 'mediation' and 'conciliation' tend to be used interchangeably, notwithstanding the fact that some commentators have sought to give them different meanings. It will be seen later that the UNCITRAL Model Conciliation Law attributes the same meaning to both terms, as does the CPR Institute for Dispute Resolution. The Permanent Court of Arbitration (PCA) – considered in Part III of the Manual – also takes the view that there is no real difference between the two.

Both expressions refer to a system that involves the use of a third party neutral who seeks to bring the parties to a settlement, but who has no power to impose this. The use of the term 'mediation' would seem to be taking the lead, at any rate in the commercial context in countries like England and the United States.

The process of 'caucusing' is perhaps (at any rate in the experience of this writer) the most significant feature of mediation and is the mechanism that is most likely to produce a successful outcome. The mediator holds a series of separate meetings with the parties in dispute in order to identify any hidden agendas and explore problem-solving proposals. The mediator may only divulge what has been said to him by one party in a caucus session if express permission is given. As the American Arbitration Association (AAA) explains, caucusing enables the mediator to *"selectively use the information derived from each side to:*

- *reduce the hostility between the parties and help them to engage in a meaningful dialogue on the issues at hand;*
- *open discussions into areas not previously considered or inadequately developed;*
- *communicate positions or proposals in understandable or more palatable terms;*
- *probe and uncover additional facts and the real interests of parties;*
- *help each party to better understand the other parties' views and evaluations of a particular issue, without violating confidences;*
- *narrow the issues and each party's positions, and deflate extreme demands;*
- *gauge the receptiveness for a proposal or suggestion;*
- *explore alternatives and search for solutions;*
- *identify what is important and what is expendable;*
- *prevent regression or raising of surprise issues; and*
- *structure a settlement to resolve current problems and future parties' needs."*[94]

Minitrials

The minitrial is often used in disputes between corporations. A 'hearing' takes place before a neutral third party and senior executives of the business organisations involved. Those executives will not have been concerned in the dispute itself. Each side presents its case. It is open to the third party neutral to indicate the consequences in terms of time and

94 www.adr.org/.

money should the minitrial process fail. This system has enjoyed considerable success in the United States.

The CPR Institute and the Netherlands Arbitration Institute both have a set of Minitrial Rules, which are considered later in this chapter.

ADR in an international context

Although ADR in its present form developed in the United States, it is now in use worldwide. ADR in the context of international dispute resolution was considered in the *Arbitration International* article.

Many of the major international arbitration institutions, such as the LCIA, the ICC and the American Arbitration Association (AAA), offer a wide range of dispute resolution processes that include both arbitration and ADR.

ADR as a pre-arbitral dispute mechanism

Construction projects

ADR has been used with great success as a pre-arbitral dispute mechanism in major construction projects around the world since it is of particular use in contracts involving a considerable number of parties. Disputes on such projects need to be settled swiftly in order to avoid disrupting the progress of the works.

The kind of contractual provision that is likely to be found in connection with such projects will require disputes to go through some form of ADR 'filter' before proceeding to arbitration. The obvious hope is that the ADR process will in fact render arbitration unnecessary. The types of ADR mechanisms that are used as 'filters' are likely to comprise such processes as adjudication by a panel of experts or by a Dispute Review Board. It was this kind of procedure that was used in the *Channel Tunnel Group Limited v Balfour Beattie Construction Limited* case.[95]

Similar ADR mechanisms have been used in the Boston Central Artery / Tunnel Project (see Box 1) and in the Hong Kong Airport Core Programme.

These projects and the ADR filter mechanisms were also considered in the *Arbitration International* article mentioned earlier.

An ICC scheme

In late 2004 the ICC produced a set of Dispute Board (DB) Rules, in force as from 1 September 2004. DBs *"are normally set up at the outset of a contract and remain in place and are remunerated throughout its duration"*. The members of the DB – one or three members – are thoroughly acquainted with the contract and assist the parties to resolve disagreements that arise. They make recommendations or decisions regarding disputes referred to the Board.

---

95 [1993] 2 WLR 262 HL.

There are various types of DBs – Dispute Review Board, Dispute Adjudication Board and Combined Dispute Board – and the DB process can be followed by ICC arbitration if required. More information on this new ICC scheme is available from the Dispute Boards Centre's website.[96]

Combining mediation and arbitration

In addition to using ADR as a filter mechanism, it is possible to use a mixture of arbitration and mediation or mediation and arbitration – indeed, whatever combination of mechanisms the parties choose.

The notion of switching from arbitration to mediation may be difficult for Western lawyers and arbitrators to accept, since this must always involve the prospect of a mediator having to revert to the role of arbitrator. But such a course would be regarded as perfectly natural in, say, China. For example, provision is made in the China International Economic and Trade Arbitration Commission (CIETAC) Arbitration Rules for an arbitral tribunal to switch to acting as conciliator.

3) Institutions Offering ADR systems

Introduction

ADR is not the answer to every dispute. There are some circumstances in which an order made by a national court may be the only realistic option. In other circumstances, however, ADR – say in the form of mediation / conciliation – is a sensible and practical option that has much to offer as a dispute resolution process. Examples are where the costs of litigation or arbitration may be out of all proportion to what is at stake or where the parties need to work together in the future.

It is difficult to know the extent to which ADR is being used worldwide. It is still viewed with suspicion by many. However, its use is likely to increase as the nature of ADR begins to be better understood and its benefits thus more appreciated – not least the financial benefits of using it as opposed to litigation or arbitration.

There are many international institutions that offer ADR systems, only a handful of which can be considered in the Manual. Some of these institutions are primarily ADR bodies: for example, the CPR Institute for Dispute Resolution. Others are primarily arbitration bodies that offer ADR systems as part of a broad menu of dispute resolution processes: for example, the LCIA and the AAA. The World Intellectual Property Organization (WIPO) is a specialist body that offers a wide variety of dispute resolution procedures, including online dispute resolution.

Some of the institutions were considered in the earlier chapter on international commercial arbitral institutions. Others, like the CPR, are considered for the first time in this chapter. Fairly extensive references are made to the descriptions by some of the institutions of the mediation / conciliation process, and the views set out should give a clear understanding of the nature of ADR and how it works.

---

96 www-old.iccwbo.org/drs/english/dispute_boards/all_topics.asp.

Since the chapter began with the quote from Antonio Piazza, it is perhaps appropriate to start with the CPR Institute.

i) The CPR Institute for Dispute Resolution

Introduction

The CPR Institute for Dispute Resolution is a non-profit organisation based in New York and made up of 500 major corporations and law firms.[97] Its aim is to *"resolve business and public disputes through innovative forms of alternative dispute resolution. The CPR seeks to develop ADR by involving the best of the profession and academia in its agenda of problem-solving, research, education and ADR advocacy, and in the dispute resolution services it provides through its Distinguished CPR Panels of Neutrals."*

CPR's mission is to *"spearhead innovation and promote excellence in public and private dispute resolution, and to serve as a primary multinational resource for avoidance, management and resolution of business-related and other disputes. To fulfil its mission, CPR is engaged in an integrated agenda of research and development, education, advocacy and dispute resolution. It is the leading proponent of ADR that is managed by the parties and a highly qualified neutral, or self-administered ADR."*

The CPR European Mediation Procedure

The CPR European Mediation Procedure is an informal process in which the mediator *"facilitates negotiation among the parties and their lawyers to help them reach settlement .... [It] is designed to provide a model for the format and procedure of a mediation, although the emphasis is on flexibility and minimising the imposition of rules on the parties."*

The mediator *"can help the parties identify interests, develop settlement options and overcome barriers to settlement."* He or she is *"a third party neutral"* who *"sits down with the disputing parties and actively assists them in reaching a settlement. CPR uses the expression 'mediation' to cover both the concepts of mediation and conciliation. The process is designed to assist parties in reaching a commercially attractive settlement, with minimum time and cost.*

The Procedure is in nine sections:

1 Proposing mediation,
2 Selecting the mediator,
3 Ground rules of proceeding,
4 Exchange of information,
5 Presentation to the mediator,
6 Negotiation of terms,
7 Settlement,
8 Failure to agree and
9 Confidentiality.

97 Detailed information is available on the CPRs website: www.cpradr.org.

Subject to any changes on which the parties and the mediator agree, the Section 3 Ground Rules include the following provisions, which give a clear overview of the mediation process:

> *"3.1The process is voluntary and depends on the co-operation of the parties. The mediator does not issue a binding decision.*
>
> *3.2 Each party may withdraw at any time by written notice to the mediator and the other party or parties.*
>
> *3.3 The mediator is neutral, independent and impartial.*
>
> *3.4 The mediator controls the procedural aspects of the mediation. The parties cooperate fully with the mediator.*
>
> *(a) The mediator is free to meet and communicate separately with each party.*
>
> *(b) The mediator decides when to hold joint meetings with the parties and when to hold separate meetings. The mediator fixes the time and place of each session and its agenda in consultation with the parties. There is no formal written, audio or video record of any meeting. Formal rules of evidence or procedure do not apply.*
>
> *(c) Unless otherwise agreed by the parties, the mediator decides, if necessary, the language in which the mediation is to be conducted and whether any documents should be translated.*
>
> *3.5 Each party is represented at each mediation conference by a business executive authorized to negotiate a resolution of the dispute and to execute a settlement agreement. Each party may be represented by more than one person, e.g. a business executive and a lawyer. The mediator may limit the number of persons representing each party.*
>
> *3.6 The process is to be conducted expeditiously. Each representative undertakes to make every effort to be available for meetings.*
>
> *3.7 The mediator does not transmit information received in confidence from any party to any other party or any third party, unless authorised to do so by the party transmitting the information, or unless ordered to do so by a court of competent jurisdiction.*
>
> *3.8 The mediator and any persons assisting the mediator is disqualified as a witness, consultant or expert in any pending or future investigation, action or proceeding relating to the subject matter of the mediation (including any investigation, action or proceeding which involves persons not party to this mediation).*
>
> *3.9 If the dispute goes into arbitration, the mediator will not serve to as an arbitrator."*

Section 5 dealing with Presentation to the Mediator includes the following provisions concerning the submission of written statements:

> *"At least five business days before the first substantive mediation conference, unless otherwise agreed, each party submits to the mediator a written statement summarising the background and present status of the dispute and such other material and information as it deems helpful to familiarise the mediator with the*

dispute. The parties may agree to submit jointly certain other materials. The mediator may request any party to provide clarification and additional information. The mediator may limit the length of written statements and supporting material. The mediator may direct the parties to exchange concise written statements and other materials they submit to the mediator to further each party's understanding of the other party's viewpoints."

The Negotiation of Terms provisions in Section 6 state that the mediator

> *"may promote settlement in any manner the mediator believes is appropriate. The mediator helps the parties focus on their underlying interests and concerns, explore resolution alternatives and develop settlement options. The mediator decides when to hold joint meetings, and when to confer separately with each party. The mediator expects the parties to make settlement proposals. Finally, if the parties fail to develop mutually acceptable settlement terms, before terminating the procedure, and only with the consent of the parties, (a) the mediator may submit to the parties a final settlement proposal which the mediator considers fair and equitable to all parties; and (b) if the mediator believes he/she is qualified to do so, the mediator may give the parties an evaluation (which if the parties choose will be in writing) of the likely outcome of the case if it were tried to final judgment."*

If a settlement is reached, Section 8 provides that the representatives of the parties are to draft terms of settlement: *"Initially, a preliminary memorandum of understanding may be prepared at the mediation and executed by the parties; the memorandum should make it expressly clear whether it is intended to be binding or not. If litigation is pending, the settlement may provide that the parties will request the court to make an appropriate order disposing of the case promptly upon execution of the settlement agreement. The settlement agreement may also be entered as a consent judgment."*

If the ADR process fails to produce a settlement, the mediator discusses with the parties the possibility of agreeing on arbitration or another form of dispute resolution.

ii) The American Arbitration Association

Introduction

On its website[98] the AAA looks at the difference between mediation and arbitration:

> *"Arbitration is less formal than litigation, and mediation is even less formal than arbitration. Unlike an arbitrator, a mediator does not have the power to render a binding decision. A mediator does not hold evidentiary hearings as would an arbitrator but instead conducts informal joint and separate meetings with the parties to understand the issues, facts, and positions of the parties. The separate meetings are known as caucuses. In contrast, arbitrators hear testimony and receive evidence in a joint hearing, on which they render a final and binding decision known as an award."*

98 www.adr.org/

The AAA describes the process of the mediation as follows:

> *"The parties should come to the mediation conference prepared with all of the evidence and documentation they feel will be necessary to discuss their respective cases. Parties are, of course, entitled to representation by counsel.*
>
> *"At the outset, mediators describe the procedures and ground rules covering each party's opportunity to talk, order of presentation, decorum, discussion of unresolved issues, use of caucuses, and confidentiality of proceedings.*
>
> *"After these preliminaries, each party describes respective views of the dispute. The initiating party discusses his/her understanding of the issues, the facts surrounding the dispute, what he/she wants, and why. The other party then responds and makes similar presentations to the mediator. In this initial session, the mediator gathers as many facts as possible and clarifies discrepancies. The mediator tries to understand the perceptions of each party, their interests, and their positions on the issues.*
>
> *"When joint discussions have reached a stage where no further progress is being made, the mediator often meets with each party in caucuses. While holding separate sessions with each party, the mediator may shuttle back and forth between parties and bring them back to joint sessions at appropriate intervals. During each caucus, the mediator attempts to clarify each party's version of the facts, priorities, and positions, loosen rigid stances, explore alternative solutions, and seek possible tradeoffs. The mediator probes, tests, and challenges the validity of each party's positions. The mediator serves not as an advocate but as an 'agent of reality.' The mediator must make each party think through demands, priorities, and views, and deal with the other party's arguments.*
>
> *"An effective mediator knows that demands and priorities shift as ideas meet opposition, different facts are considered, and underlying circumstances change as parties reappraise and modify positions. In effect, the mediator increases the parties' perceptions of their cases in order to construct a settlement range within which the parties can assess the consequences of continuing or resolving the dispute. By having parties focus on the risks and burdens of litigation, the mediator creates in the minds of the parties the idea that there are alternatives to seek. The parties articulate these possibilities by moving toward tradeoffs and acceptable accommodations.*
>
> *"During the final caucuses and joint sessions, the mediator narrows the differences between the parties and obtains agreement on major and minor issues. The mediator reduces a disagreement into a workable solution. At appropriate times, the mediator makes suggestions about a final settlement, stresses the consequences of failure to reach agreement, emphasizes the progress which has been made, and formalizes offers to gain an agreement.*
>
> *"The mediator acts as a facilitator to keep discussions focused and avoid new outbreaks of disagreement. The mediator will often have the parties negotiate the final terms of a settlement in a joint session. The mediator will then verify the specifics of an agreement and make sure that the terms are comprehensive, specific, and clear in the final session."*

The AAA's International Mediation Rules

The AAA's International Mediation Rules may be used for mediation or conciliation of international disputes under the auspices of their International Centres for Dispute Resolution (ICDR) in New York and Dublin. There are 18 Rules.

Rule M-1 deals with the agreement to mediate. Provisions for the initiation of the mediation process are contained in Rules M-2 and 3, and the request for mediation is to contain a brief statement of the nature of the dispute. Rule M-4 provides for the appointment of the mediator: *"Upon receipt of a request for mediation, the ICDR will appoint a qualified mediator to serve. Normally, a single mediator will be appointed unless the parties agree otherwise or the ICDR determines otherwise. If the agreement of the parties names a mediator or specifies a method of appointing a mediator, that designation or method shall be followed."*

Rules M-5 and 6 deal with qualifications of the mediator and the filling of vacancies, and Rules M-7 and 8 with representation for the parties and the date, time and place of mediation. At least 10 days prior to the mediation session, each party is to provide the mediator with a brief memorandum, setting out their position with regard to the issues to be resolved: *"at the discretion of the mediator, such memoranda may be mutually exchanged by the parties"*. At the first session, the parties are expected to produce all information reasonably required for the mediator to understand the issues.

Rule M-10 contains important provisions setting out the authority of the mediator. These are at the heart of the mediation process:

> *"The mediator does not have the authority to impose a settlement on the parties but will attempt to help them reach a satisfactory resolution of their dispute. The mediator is authorized to conduct joint and separate meetings with the parties and to make oral and written recommendations for settlement. Whenever necessary, the mediator may also obtain expert advice concerning technical aspects of the dispute, provided that the parties agree and assume the expenses of obtaining such advice. Arrangements for obtaining such advice shall be made by the mediator or the parties, as the mediator shall determine.*
>
> *"The mediator is authorized to end the mediation whenever, in the judgment of the mediator, further efforts at mediation would not contribute to a resolution of the dispute between the parties."*

Rules M-11, 12 and 13 deal with privacy and confidentiality.

The process is to be terminated:

> *"(a) by the execution of a settlement agreement by the parties;*
>
> *(b) by a written declaration of the mediator to the effect that further efforts at mediation are no longer worthwhile; or*
>
> *(c) by a written declaration of a party or parties to the effect that the mediation proceedings are terminated."*

The remaining Rules deal with matters such as exclusion of liability, interpretation and expenses.

iii) The International Chamber of Commerce

Introduction

Among the various dispute resolution processes available from the ICC are the ICC ADR Rules.[99] The ICC states that these Rules:

> *"offer a framework for the amicable settlement of commercial disputes with the assistance of a neutral. They were launched in 2001 to replace the 1988 Rules of Conciliation. Under the ICC ADR Rules, parties may freely choose the settlement technique they consider most appropriate to their situation. This may be mediation, whereby a neutral helps the parties to settle their differences through negotiation; a mini-trial, in which a panel comprising a neutral and a manager from each party proposes a solution or gives an opinion; or a neutral evaluation of a point of law or fact. Common to all these techniques is the fact that the decision reached by or in collaboration with the neutral is not binding upon the parties, unless they agree otherwise. The success of the chosen technique will depend largely on the qualities of the neutral. He or she may be designated directly by the parties or appointed by ICC. In the latter case, the parties may specify certain requirements as to the qualifications or attributes the neutral should possess. Lastly, the parties are not limited to a single technique, but may find it useful to apply a combination of settlement techniques."*

The ICC ADR Rules

The first particularity of the ICC ADR Rules is that the acronym ADR stand for 'amicable dispute resolution' rather than the traditional 'alternative dispute resolution'. This was done in order to avoid confusion with arbitration. The intention is to clearly separate arbitration and other binding techniques from techniques such as mediation and neutral evaluation, which do not result in a decision or award that can be enforced at law.

The parties are free to choose any ADR technique that is best adapted to their particular dispute. Thus, the parties may choose mediation, neutral evaluation or minitrial, or may also choose a combination of techniques. For example, mediation could be chosen, but the Neutral could be asked to give his or her evaluation of a particular issue. The ICC Rules are flexible and are party-controlled to the largest extent possible.

Article 1 of the ICC ADR Rules states that all business disputes, whether or not of an international character, may be referred to ADR proceedings under the Rules. Where the parties agree to refer their dispute to the ICC ADR Rules, the process is commenced by written request to the ICC that describes the dispute.

Article 3 deals with the selection of the Neutral. The Neutral discusses with the parties the settlement technique to be used and the specific ADR procedure to be followed: *"in the absence of an agreement of the parties on the settlement technique to be used, mediation shall be used"*. The Neutral is to conduct the procedure *"in such manner as the Neutral sees fit. In all cases the Neutral shall be guided by the principles of fairness and impartiality and by the wishes of parties."* Each party is to cooperate in good faith with the Neutral.

99 See www.iccadr.org.

The circumstances in which the ADR proceedings terminate include the signing by the parties of a settlement agreement and notification by the Neutral to the parties that in his/her opinion the process will not lead to settlement.

Article 7 provides that the ADR process (subject to the applicable law) is private and confidential and any settlement agreement between the parties is likewise confidential, save to the extent that disclosure is required for the purposes of implementation or enforcement. Furthermore *"Unless required to do so by applicable law and in the absence of any agreement of the parties to the contrary, a party shall not in any manner produce as evidence in any judicial, arbitration or similar proceedings:*

- *a) any documents, statements or communications which are submitted by another party or by the Neutral in the ADR proceedings, unless they can be obtained independently by the party seeking to produce them in the judicial, arbitration or similar proceedings;*
- *b) any views expressed or suggestions made by any party within the ADR proceedings with regard to the possible settlement of the dispute;*
- *c) any admissions made by another party within the ADR proceedings;*
- *d) any views or proposals put forward by the Neutral; or*
- *e) the fact that any party had indicated within the ADR proceedings that it was ready to accept a proposal for a settlement."*

Additionally, unless the parties otherwise agree, a Neutral *"shall not act nor shall have acted in any judicial, arbitration or similar proceedings relating to the dispute which is or was the subject of the ADR proceedings, whether as a judge, as an arbitrator, as an expert or as a representative or advisor of a party".*

And, unless required by the applicable law or otherwise agreed by the parties, a Neutral shall not *"give testimony in any judicial, arbitration or similar proceedings concerning any aspect of the ADR proceedings".*

iv) The London Court of International Arbitration

The first two Articles of the LCIA Mediation Rules deal with the commencement of the mediation, both where there is a prior agreement to mediate and where there is no such prior agreement. Article 3 deals with the appointment of the mediator and the impartiality and independence of that mediator.

The parties are free to agree how they will inform the mediator of their respective cases. But unless they have agreed otherwise, each party is to submit to the mediator, no less than seven days before the date of the first mediation session, a brief written statement summarising their case, the background to the dispute and the issues to be resolved. Each written statement is to be accompanied by copies of any documents referred to, and a copy of the statement and supporting documents is to be submitted to the other party or parties (Article 4).

Article 5 contains the provisions dealing with the conduct of the mediation:

> *"The mediator may communicate with the parties orally or in writing, together, or individually, and may convene a meeting or meetings at a venue to be determined by the mediator after consultations with the parties.*
>
> *"Nothing which is communicated to the mediator in private during the course of the mediation shall be repeated to the other party or parties, without the express consent of the party making the communication."*

Article 6 deals with the conclusion of mediation, which will end when either:

"(a) a settlement agreement is signed by the parties; or

(b) the parties advise the mediator that it is their view that a settlement cannot be reached and that it is their wish to terminate the mediation; or

(c) the mediator advises the parties that, in his or her judgement, the mediation process will not resolve the issues in dispute; or

(d) the time limit for mediation provided in a Prior Agreement has expired and the parties have not agreed to extend that time limit."

Article 7 deals with the settlement. If terms of settlement are agreed, the parties (with the assistance of the mediator if desired) are to draw up a settlement agreement setting out the terms. By signing this agreement *"the parties agree to be bound by its terms"*.

Article 9 states that, unless the parties have agreed otherwise *"and notwithstanding the mediation, the parties may initiate or continue any arbitration or judicial proceedings in respect of the dispute which is the subject of the mediation"*.

Article 10 deals with confidentiality and privacy.

v) The China Council for the Promotion of International Trade / China Chamber of International Commerce

The Conciliation Rules of the CCPIT / CCOIC were formulated *"with a view to settling by means of conciliation (mediation) disputes arising from the fields of economy, trade, maritime business, etc, so as to promote the development of international and domestic economic exchanges"*.

The Conciliation Centres of CCPIT / CCOIC accept cases in accordance with a Conciliation Agreement. Conciliation is to be conducted *"on the basis of ascertaining facts, distinguishing right from wrong and determining liabilities while respecting the terms of the contract, abiding by the law, following international practice and adhering to the principle of being just, fair and reasonable in order to bring about mutual understanding and neutral concession between the parties and help the parties to reach an amicable settlement agreement thereof "* (Articles 1, 3 and 5).

The party applying for conciliation must submit a written Application for Conciliation that is to include the facts of the case, evidential materials and the claim. The Applicant is to appoint, or authorise the Conciliation Centre to appoint, a conciliator from the Centre's Panel of Conciliators (Article 9).

If the Application for Conciliation and the annexed documents are found to be in order, the Centre forwards a copy to the Respondent. The Respondent is to confirm his/her agreement to the conciliation within 30 days and is to appoint, or authorise the Centre to appoint, one conciliator from the Panel. Failing confirmation of agreement, the conciliation proposal is deemed to have been rejected (Articles 10 and 11).

The conciliators may conduct the conciliation in the manner they deem appropriate. Experts may be invited to participate and assist in the conciliation. If the parties reach an amicable settlement they are to affix their signatures to an agreement. The conciliators are then to prepare a written Conciliation Statement in accordance with the terms of that agreement. The Statement is to be signed by the conciliators and sealed by the Conciliation Centre (Articles 14-16).

The conciliation proceedings are to terminate in any one of the following circumstances set out in Article 17:

1 the conciliation is successful and a Conciliation Statement is signed and sealed;
2 the conciliators consider that a successful conciliation is impossible;
3 the parties (or one of them) declares in writing to the conciliators that the proceedings are to be terminated.

Supplementary Provisions provide that the conciliators may meet or communicate with the parties in the manner they think appropriate. Where one party gives information and requests that such information be kept confidential, this is to be respected. The parties are to cooperate in good faith with the conciliators. If the conciliation fails, the parties are not to invoke any statements, views, opinions or proposals in any subsequent arbitration proceedings or litigation proceedings (Articles 18, 19, 20 and 22).

Article 21 provides that *"if conciliation fails, the conciliators may be appointed by one of the parties as arbitrators in the subsequent arbitration proceedings, unless such appointment is opposed by the other parties"*.

The idea of a conciliator in an unsuccessful conciliation going on to sit as arbitrator in the same dispute – a dispute in which confidential information may have been given to the conciliator in the caucus sessions – may be difficult for many lawyers to accept. An even more difficult issue may be whether an arbitrator can switch to acting as conciliator / mediator (possibly receiving information in confidence in the caucus sessions) and then switch back again to acting as arbitrator if the conciliation fails.

However, the concept of conciliation and arbitration operating together is one with which the Chinese are perfectly happy. And they have considerable experience of conciliation. Further, the idea has obvious practical benefits – and in any event the parties have the final say as the arbitration will only take place with the former conciliator acting as arbitrator provided all parties agree.

It is interesting to note that the Mediation Institute of the Stockholm Chamber of Commerce – considered next – has almost the same provision in its Mediation Rules. So does the UNCITRAL Model Conciliation Law – but not the UNCITRAL Conciliation Rules. Those Rules, enacted some 20 years before the Model Law, provide in Article 19 that:

"The parties and the conciliator undertake that the conciliator will not act as an arbitrator or as a representative or counsel of a party in any arbitral or judicial proceedings in respect of a dispute that is the subject of the conciliation proceedings. The parties also undertake that they will not present the conciliator as a witness in any such proceedings."

vi) The Mediation Institute of the Stockholm Chamber of Commerce

The SCC Mediation Institute was established in 1999 to assist in the settlement of domestic and international disputes in accordance with the SCC Mediation Rules. The Mediation Institute is part of the SCC's Arbitration Institute.

Article 1 states that the Mediator must be impartial and independent, and may not act as arbitrator in any future arbitration relating to the subject matter of the dispute, unless the parties otherwise agree (a similar provision to that in the CCPIT / CCOIC Conciliation Rules). A potential Mediator is to disclose any circumstances likely to give rise to *"justifiable doubts as to his impartiality and independence"* (Article 2).

Confidentiality, on the part of the parties and the Institute, is dealt with in Article 3. In particular *"A party may not introduce as evidence in any judicial or arbitration proceeding any views expressed or statements made in the course of the Mediation. A party may not involve as witness in any judicial or arbitration proceeding the Mediator or any expert that has participated in the Mediation."*

The mediation process is initiated by a Request for Mediation, which is to include a summary of the dispute. Where one party only submits the Request, the Institute is to communicate the Request of the other party and enquire whether or not that party agrees to participate in the mediation.

Articles 6 and 7 deal with the appointment and removal of mediators.

Article 10 deals with the proceedings before the mediator:

"(1) Giving consideration to the wishes of the parties, the Mediator shall determine the conduct of the Mediation, with a view for reaching an expeditious and efficient resolution of the dispute.

(2) Each party shall be given sufficient opportunity to present its case.

(3) Where the Mediator believes that the dispute between the parties is not likely to be resolved through mediation, the Mediator may propose other means of resolving the dispute, for the consideration of the parties."

Unless otherwise agreed, the mediation is to be terminated within two months of the date of being referred to the Mediator (Artivle 11(1)). Otherwise, the mediation is to be terminated:

"(2)(i) by a settlement agreement between the parties,

(ii) by a declaration of the Mediator to the parties and the SCC Mediation Institute, to the effect that further efforts of Mediation are unlikely to lead to the resolution of the dispute, or

(iii) by a written request from a party to the Mediator that the Mediation shall be terminated.

(3) Upon the termination of the Mediation, the Mediator shall notify the SCC Mediation Institute."

Article 12 provides: *"Upon reaching a settlement agreement the parties may, subject to the approval of the Mediator, agree to appoint the Mediator as an Arbitrator and request him to confirm the settlement agreement in an arbitral award."*

That provision would seem to have the New York Convention in mind. An agreement between the parties reached as a result of a mediation process would not fall within the Convention, which applies only to the recognition and enforcement of *arbitral* awards (Article I of the New York Convention).

Many of the institutional arbitration Rules provide that, where a settlement is reached during the course of the arbitral process, the terms of the settlement may be made the subject of an arbitral award, thus probably ensuring that the settlement agreement becomes enforceable as a New York Convention arbitration award. Here, the Stockholm Mediation Institute appears to be going a stage further by providing that a settlement in a *mediation* can be made the subject of an *arbitral* award.

vii) The Netherlands Arbitration Institute: Minitrials

Introduction

The difference between Minitrial and mediation / conciliation lies in the make-up of the tribunal. The Minitrial tribunal comprises representatives of the parties together with a 'neutral'.

It may be useful to look first at some definitions in the CPR Minitrial rules. The Commentary on the CPR Institute for Dispute Resolution Minitrial procedure describes the 'management representatives' and the 'Neutral Adviser '. Referring to the former, the Commentary states that:

> *"The negotiations are more likely to succeed if the negotiators have not been directly involved in the dispute and therefore do not feel a need to defend past actions. The settlement may well entail a new business deal in which neither party loses. The more senior the management representatives, the greater the range of options they are likely to perceive for a constructive solution. In some circumstances negotiations will be more productive if more than one representative of each party participates. The prospects for success of the process are likely to be enhanced if the management representatives are evenly matched and command the respect of the other party. Therefore, the parties should consult on the selection of their management representatives."*

Referring to the Neutral Adviser the Commentary suggests that:

> *"A highly qualified Neutral Adviser, in whose impartiality and judgment the parties have confidence, can significantly enhance the prospects for success. It may well be*

desirable to select as the Neutral Adviser a respected former judge, senior lawyer or legal scholar with a thorough knowledge of the applicable law and the ability to facilitate the conduct of the process including, if necessary, mediation between the parties. Such a person can give the executives educated, objective views on the legal issues and on the likely outcome of a lawsuit or arbitration. The Neutral Adviser could also be a person experienced in the field to which the dispute relates.

"With the concurrence of the executives, the Neutral Adviser can also play a mediating role in their negotiations and make settlement proposals. If need be, CPR can assist in the selection of a Neutral Adviser. The parties have the option of dispensing with a Neutral Adviser."

The NAI Minitrial Rules

In the case of the NAI Minitrial Rules, the references are to a "Minitrial Board". The Third Section of Rules in Article 7 states that the Minitrial Board shall preferably consist of three members, namely a mediator and *"a director of each of the parties. If there are more than two parties and neither the applicants nor the respondents can agree on the appointment of a single director, each party shall nominate one director as a member of the Minitrial Board."* The 'director' is defined as a representative of a party having authority to reach a settlement in relation to the existing dispute between the parties.

"International minitrial proceedings" are defined in Article 1 as proceedings in which *"at the moment of commencement, at least one of the parties is domiciled, has its seat or, in absence thereof, its actual residence outside the Netherlands"*.

Article 5 deals with the commencement of proceedings by the filing by the applicant of a request that is to include a description of the dispute and of the claim, together with, if possible *"the name of the director who is appointed by the applicant in accordance with article 7 (2) as a member of the Minitrial Board..."*.

The respondent is to file a 'short answer' that similarly, if possible, is to contain the name of a director appointed by the respondent as a member of the Minitrial Board. The Mediator, who is chairman of the Minitrial Board and who is to conduct the proceedings, is to be appointed by the parties acting jointly (failing which he/she will be appointed by the NAI).

When the Minitrial Board has been appointed, the parties are to serve written submissions. They are to send a *"memorial elaborating their points of view"*, which should be accompanied by the documentary evidence relied on.

The Mediator, in consultation with the other members of the Minitrial Board, is to determine the date of a meeting at which the parties are to be given the opportunity to elaborate on their contentions orally. The Mediator *"may ask questions of the representatives of the parties during the hearing with a view to clarifying any issues. The Mediator may also have private and, if thought appropriate, separate discussions with the directors representing each of the parties with a view to clarifying any observations they may have about the issues."*

Following the meeting *"the Minitrial Board shall meet with the intention of achieving a settlement to the dispute. The Mediator, if he thinks it appropriate, may see members of the Minitrial Board, together or separately, in order to try to facilitate settlement negotiations and subject to the maintenance of strict confidentiality in respect of communications received from each party separately."*

If a settlement is not reached, the Mediator can indicate to the Board *"the outcome that he would expect from a trial or arbitration of the dispute or the manner in which the dispute, in his opinion, can be resolved. In particular, the Mediator may at his discretion provide a non-binding written opinion as to the likely outcome of the case on trial or arbitration and, if he considers it helpful to do so, may propose settlement terms to the other members of the Minitrial Board. In such event a second settlement meeting between the Mediator and the other members of the Minitrial Board shall be held within 14 days."*

A settlement reached shall be recorded in a written agreement by the Minitrial Board.

Article 11 (7) makes clear the wide discretion vested in the Mediator: *"In the exercise of his functions and duties as described above, the Mediator shall in the exercise of his judgement as to how best to facilitate a settlement be at liberty to do all things which he considers appropriate to that end. The Mediator shall have therefore the widest possible discretion in the conduct of any hearing and any subsequent discussions with and between the parties."*

Article 12 states that a settlement can be recorded in an arbitral award.

Article 20(1) deals with confidentiality and Article 20(2) states that, unless the parties have agreed otherwise, the Mediator shall not act as judge, arbitrator, legal counsel or adviser in any court or arbitration proceedings relating to the dispute.

viii) The World Intellectual Property Organization

Introduction

WIPO states that ADR offers several advantages for the resolution of intellectual property disputes. In particular, mediation

> *"... is an attractive option for parties that place a premium on the preservation or enhancement of their relationship, seek to maintain control over the dispute settlement process, value confidentiality, or want to reach a speedy settlement without damage to their reputations.*
>
> *"Parties to contracts or relationships involving the exploitation of intellectual property often share these goals when a dispute arises. Common examples of such contracts include patent, know how and trademark licenses, franchises, computer contracts, multimedia contracts, distribution contracts, joint ventures, research and development contracts, technology-sensitive employment contracts, mergers and acquisitions where intellectual property assets assume importance, sports marketing agreements, and publishing, music and film contracts."*[100]

100 http://arbiter.wipo.int/mediation/why-mediation.html.

The WIPO Mediation Rules

The WIPO Mediation Rules comprise 15 Sections and 27 Articles.

Article 1 concerns 'Abbreviated Expressions'; Article 2 deals with Scope of Application of the Rules; and Articles 3-5 cover Commencement of the Mediation. The Appointment of the Mediator is dealt with in Articles 6 and 7, and Representation of the Parties and Participation in Meetings in Article 8. The Conduct of the Mediation and the Role of the Mediator are covered in Articles 9 to 13.

The parties are to cooperate in good faith with the mediator. The mediator is free to meet and to communicate separately with a party *"on the clear understanding that information given at such meetings and in such communications shall not be disclosed to the other party without the express authorization of the party giving the information"*.

The mediator is to establish a timetable for the submission by each party to the mediator and to the other party of *"a statement summarizing the background of the dispute, the party's interests and contentions in relation to the dispute and the present status of the dispute, together with such other information and materials as the party considers necessary for the purposes of the mediation and, in particular, to enable the issues in dispute to be identified"*.

The role of the mediator is to *"promote the settlement of the issues in dispute between the parties in any manner that the mediator believes to be appropriate"*. But he or she *"shall have no authority to impose a settlement on the parties"*.

The WIPO Rules contain interesting provisions in Article 13 that allow the mediator to make proposals for the resolution of the dispute by means other than mediation, including expert determination and arbitration – and that includes arbitration in which the mediator is to act as arbitrator.

> *"Where the mediator believes that any issues in dispute between the parties are not susceptible to resolution through mediation, the mediator may propose, for the consideration of the parties, procedures or means for resolving those issues which the mediator considers are most likely, having regard to the circumstances of the dispute and any business relationship between the parties, to lead to the most efficient, least costly and most productive settlement of those issues.*
>
> *"In particular, the mediator may so propose:*
>
> *(i) an expert determination of one or more particular issues;*
>
> *(ii) arbitration;*
>
> *(iii) the submission of last offers of settlement by each party and, in the absence of a settlement through mediation, arbitration conducted on the basis of those last offers pursuant to an arbitral procedure in which the mission of the arbitral tribunal is confined to determining which of the last offers shall prevail; or*
>
> *(iv) arbitration in which the mediator will, with the express consent of the parties, act as sole arbitrator, it being understood that the mediator may, in the arbitral proceedings, take into account information received during the mediation."*

Compare that with the provisions in Article 21 of the CCPIT / CCOIC Rules and Article 1 of the Stockholm Rules (see above).

The remaining Articles deal with confidentiality, termination, fees deposits and costs, the exclusion of liability, the suspension of running of limitation period under the Statute of Limitations, and waiver of defamation: *"The parties and, by accepting appointment, the mediator agree that any statements or comments, whether written or oral, made or used by them or their representatives in preparation for or in the course of the mediation shall not be relied upon to found or maintain any action for defamation, libel, slander or any related complaint, and this Article may be pleaded as a bar to any such action."*[101]

ix) Other Organisations at the International Dispute Resolution Centre

The International Dispute Resolution Centre (IDRC) in Fleet Street, London was set up specifically as a venue providing dispute resolution facilities. It is not only where the LCIA is based but has also been the home of two dispute resolution organisations: the Centre for Effective Dispute Resolution (CEDR) and the City Disputes Panel (CDP).[102]

The IDRC is supported by the major bodies in London concerned with dispute resolution. Support for the Centre has also come from the Corporation of London. The IDRC has 34 rooms, of which 16 are suitable for arbitrations or meetings of various sizes, with 18 designed as retiring rooms.

The Centre for Effective Dispute Resolution

CEDR's mission is to encourage and develop mediation *"and other cost-effective dispute resolution and prevention techniques in commercial and public-sector disputes"*. It is *"an independent non-profit organisation supported by multinational business and leading professional bodies"*.

City Disputes Panel

CDP describes itself as a leading provider of UK mediation services *"and tailored ADR solutions"*.

> *"Our mediators provide expert facilitation skills that offer tangible benefits and genuine alternatives to litigation.*
>
> *"One of our key aims is to promote the use and benefits of ADR in business throughout the UK and internationally.*
>
> *"Our approach is tailor-made and inherently flexible, bringing together the optimum combination of process with people who have the experience to ensure that dispute resolution is achieved efficiently, to the satisfaction of all parties."*

---

101 http://arbiter.wipo.int/mediation/rules/index.html.

102 The CDP has recently moved to Bloomsbury Square, the London HQ of the Chartered Institute of Arbitrators. Further information on the three organisations referred to in this Section can be found on their websites: www.idrc.co.uk, www.cedr.co.uk and www.citydisputespanel.org.

4) United Nations Commission on International Trade Law (UNCITRAL)

This section looks again at UNCITRAL, this time at the Model Conciliation Law and the UNCITRAL Conciliation Rules.

i) Resolution of the UN General Assembly

In January 2003 the General Assembly of the United Nations adopted a resolution on the Model Law on International Commercial Conciliation. This stated that the General Assembly recognised the value for international trade law of methods of settling commercial disputes *"in which the parties in dispute request a third person or persons to assist them in their attempt to settle the dispute amicably"* and noted that such dispute settlement methods *"referred to by expressions such as conciliation and mediation and expressions of similar import, are increasingly used in international and domestic commercial practice as an alternative to litigation"*.

The General Assembly considered that the use of such dispute settlement methods *"results in significant benefits, such as reducing the instances where a dispute leads to the termination of a commercial relationship, facilitating the administration of international transactions by commercial parties and producing savings in the administration of justice by States"*.

The General Assembly was convinced that *"the establishment of model legislation on these methods that is acceptable to States with different legal, social and economic systems would contribute to the development of harmonious international economic relations"* and noted the completion and adoption by UNCITRAL of the Model Law on International Commercial Conciliation.

ii) UNCITRAL Model Law on International Commercial Conciliation

Article 1 of the Model Law deals with scope of application and contains definitions. As mentioned earlier, it is interesting to note that the Model Law treats the terms 'mediation' and 'conciliation' as having the same meaning. Article 1 defines conciliation as *"a process, whether referred to by the expression conciliation, mediation or an expression of similar import, whereby parties request a third person or persons ('the conciliator') to assist them in their attempt to reach an amicable settlement of their dispute arising out of or relating to a contractual or other legal relationship. The conciliator does not have the authority to impose upon the parties a solution to the dispute."*

The Article also states that a conciliation is international if:

"(a) The parties to an agreement to conciliate have, at the time of the conclusion of that agreement, their places of business in different States; or

(b) The State in which the parties have their places of business is different from either:

(i) The State in which a substantial part of the obligations of the commercial relationship is to be performed; or

(ii) The State with which the subject matter of the dispute is most closely connected."

However, the Article states that the Law also applies to a commercial conciliation where the parties agree that the conciliation is international or where they agree to the applicability of the Conciliation Law.

Article 2 states that, in the interpretation of the Law, regard is to be had to "*its international origin and to the need to promote uniformity in its application and the observance of good faith*".

Articles 4 and 5 deal with the commencement of the conciliation proceedings and the number and appointment of conciliators (one, unless the parties agree otherwise). The parties may seek the assistance of an institution, which should have regard to such considerations as are likely to secure *"the appointment of an independent and impartial conciliator and, where appropriate, shall take into account the advisability of appointing a conciliator of the nationality other than the nationality of the parties"*.

Article 6 contains the vital provisions dealing with the conduct of the conciliation. It states that the parties are free to agree *"by reference to a set of rules or otherwise"* on the manner in which the conciliation is to be conducted. Failing such agreement, the conciliator may conduct the conciliation proceedings in such manner as he or she considers appropriate *"taking into account the circumstances of the case, any wishes that the parties may express and the need for a speedy settlement of the dispute. In any case, in conducting the proceedings, the conciliator shall seek to maintain fair treatment of the parties and, in so doing, shall take into account the circumstances of the case."* The conciliator is entitled at any stage to make proposals for a settlement of the dispute.

Articles 7 to 10 contain provisions dealing with communications between the conciliator and the parties; disclosure of information; confidentiality; and the admissibility of evidence in other proceedings:

> *"A party to the conciliation proceedings, the conciliator and any third person, including those involved in the administration of the conciliation proceedings, shall not in arbitral, judicial or similar proceedings rely on, introduce as evidence or give testimony or evidence regarding any of the following:*
>
> *(a) An invitation by a party to engage in conciliation proceedings or the fact that a party was willing to participate in conciliation proceedings;*
>
> *(b) Views expressed or suggestions made by a party in the conciliation in respect of a possible settlement of the dispute;*
>
> *(c) Statements or admissions made by a party in the course of the conciliation proceedings;*
>
> *(d) Proposals made by the conciliator;*
>
> *(e) The fact that a party had indicated its willingness to accept a proposal for settlement made by the conciliator;*
>
> *(f) A document prepared solely for purposes of the conciliation proceedings."*

The conciliation proceedings terminate in four circumstances: at the conclusion of a settlement agreement; by a declaration of the conciliator that further efforts to conciliate are no longer justified; by a declaration of the parties that the proceedings are terminated; or by a declaration of one party to the other party or parties to the same effect (Article 11).

Article 12 deals with a situation that many find difficult, and that was referred to above: Can a conciliator go on to act as arbitrator in the same dispute? Article 12 states that, unless otherwise agreed by the parties, the conciliator *"shall not act as an arbitrator in respect of a dispute that was or is the subject of the conciliation proceedings or in respect of another dispute that has arisen from the same contract or legal relationship or any related contract or legal relationship"*. As mentioned earlier, the UNCITRAL Conciliation Rules, pre-dating the Conciliation Law by some 20 years, do not permit the conciliator to go on to act as arbitrator either (under Article 19 of the Rules, see below).

Article 13 deals with the significant question of the stay of litigation or arbitration where parties have agreed to conciliate: *"Where the parties have agreed to conciliate and have expressly undertaken not to initiate during a specified period of time or until a specified event has occurred arbitral or judicial proceedings with respect to an existing or future dispute, such an undertaking shall be given effect by the arbitral tribunal or the court until the terms of the undertaking have been complied with, except to the extent necessary for a party, in its opinion, to preserve its rights. Initiation of such proceedings is not of itself to be regarded as a waiver of the agreement to conciliate or as a termination of the conciliation proceedings."*

Finally, Article 14 deals with the enforceability of any settlement reached during the course of the conciliation process, leaving it open to enacting States how such enforcement is to take place: *"If the parties conclude an agreement settling a dispute, that settlement agreement is binding and enforceable... [the enacting State may insert a description of the method of enforcing settlement agreements or refer to provisions governing such enforcement]."*

iii) UNCITRAL Conciliation Rules

The UNCITRAL Conciliation Rules were adopted by the UN General Assembly in December 1980. The General Assembly stated its conviction that *"the establishment of conciliation rules that are acceptable in countries with different legal, social and economic systems would significantly contribute to the development of harmonious international economic relations"*.

The Model Conciliation Clause provides:

> *"Where, in the event of a dispute arising out of or relating to this contract, the parties wish to seek an amicable settlement of that dispute by conciliation, the conciliation shall take place in accordance with the UNCITRAL Conciliation Rules as at present in force."*

The Rules contain 20 Articles, which are broadly along the lines of the provisions of the Model Conciliation Law:

Article 1: Application of the Rules

Article 2: Commencement of conciliation proceedings

Article 3: Number of conciliators

Article 4: Appointment of conciliators

Article 5: Submission of statements to conciliators

Article 6: Representation and assistance

Article 7: Role of the conciliator:

"(1) The conciliator assists the parties in an independent and impartial manner in their attempt to reach an amicable settlement of their dispute.

(2) The conciliator will be guided by principles of objectivity, fairness and justice, giving consideration to, among other things, the rights and obligations of the parties, the usages of the trade concerned and the circumstances surrounding the dispute, including any previous business practices between the parties.

(3) The conciliator may conduct the conciliation proceedings in such a manner as he considers appropriate, taking into account the circumstances of the case, the wishes the parties may express, including any request by a party that the conciliator hear oral statements, and the need for a speedy settlement of the dispute.

(4) The conciliator may, at any stage of the conciliation proceedings, make proposals for a settlement of the dispute. Such proposals need not be in writing and need not be accompanied by a statement of the reasons therefor."

Article 8: Administrative assistance

Article 9: Communication between conciliator and parties

Article 10: Disclosure of information

Article 11: Co-operation of parties with conciliator

Article 12: Suggestions by parties for settlement of dispute:

"Each party may, on his own initiative or at the invitation of the conciliator, submit to the conciliator suggestions for the settlement of the dispute."

Article 13: Settlement agreement:

"(1) When it appears to the conciliator that there exist elements of a settlement which would be acceptable to the parties, he formulates the terms of a possible settlement and submits them to the parties for their observations. After receiving the observations of the parties, the conciliator may reformulate the terms of a possible settlement in the light of such observations.

(2) If the parties reach agreement on a settlement of the dispute, they draw up and sign a written settlement agreement. If requested by the parties, the conciliator draws up, or assists the parties in drawing up, the settlement agreement.

(3) The parties by signing the settlement agreement put an end to the dispute and are bound by the agreement."

Article 14: Confidentiality

Article15: Termination of conciliation proceedings

Article 16: Resort to arbitral or judicial proceedings

Article 17: Costs

Article 18: Deposits

Article 19: Role of conciliator in other proceedings (referred to earlier)

"The parties and the conciliator undertake that the conciliator will not act as an arbitrator or as a representative or counsel of a party in any arbitral or judicial proceedings in respect of a dispute that is the subject of the conciliation proceedings...."

Article 20: Admissibility of evidence in other proceedings

5) ADR in Action

An example of mediation in action is provided by a case that came before the City Disputes Panel (CDP). The ADR tribunal was chaired by Lord Browne-Wilkinson, a former senior Law Lord.

In an article published in *The Times* on 20 September 2004, Lord Browne-Wilkinson described the situation:

> *"A multiparty action brought by 300 claimants against a well-known City institution was recently concluded successfully by the City Disputes Panel. The resolution of the disputes took less than 18 months from beginning to end and was achieved at a fraction of the cost of litigating through the courts."*

The dispute in question related to the collapse of a foreign exchange business that maintained accounts with various high-street banks and whose *modus operandi* was to *"bulk up smaller orders and take a turn on the rate benefits, thereby offering consumers a better rate than the high-street and at the same time making a profit for themselves"*. When the business failed, many of its clients lost substantial sums. The deposits were held in client accounts in euros, US dollars, and so on. More than 500 potential claimants were identified.

CDP was appointed to establish a scheme for the review and determination of the claims. Lord Browne-Wilkinson was asked to be chairman of the review board: *"From the judicial point of view the advantages of dealing with a large number of claims in what was effectively one managed mass arbitration were speed and having the expertise required to resolve these disputes available within the tribunal."*

There were points of law to be resolved and a hearing was held, which lasted three days. Once those points of law had been decided, and the tribunal had written its judgement, *"the rest was largely resolved by agreement. There were perhaps 30 cases that needed to be adjudicated individually on the facts, but they took very little time – just over a day."*

Lord Browne-Wilkinson said that the most difficult part of the process was persuading claimants to join the scheme. But had the matter been litigated through the courts *"such litigation would have taken many years and cost millions of pounds"*.

One of the keys to the success of the scheme, and indeed to resolving other claims, was the efficiency of a multidisciplinary tribunal model: *"Contrast the weeks of expert evidence you might normally expect a court to hear in a case such as this, with having the expertise within the tribunal. The experts sitting on the tribunal, in this case an accountant and a banker, can educate the lawyer as you go along. This is extremely valuable."*

Lord Browne-Wilkinson concluded his article in *The Times* by saying that *"having spent years in court reading the papers for a case, only to be told at the last minute that the parties have come to terms, I am persuaded that it ought to be possible to convince people that alternative dispute resolution is something worth trying first."*

This is no doubt a view that Antonio Piazza would endorse.

6) International ADR – Future Developments

Nearly 20 years ago the distinguished international practitioners and authors, Alan Redfern and Martin Hunter, in the first edition of their leading work *Law and Practice of International Commercial Arbitration,* questioned

> *"... whether or not ADR, or any particular form of ADR, will ultimately be exported from the USA in the sense of developing into a system for resolving international trade disputes, where the outcome may have to be enforced against the reluctant loser by the courts of a foreign country, remains to be seen. In the short term, at least, for the practitioner who regards the New York Convention as an essential element for the resolution of disputes in international trade, it seems unlikely that ADR methods which fall short of the type of process required for enforcement under the New York Convention will hold much attraction. International commercial arbitration, which produces a legally binding decision which is enforceable internationally, is to be preferred."*[103]

Their view was expressed to be in the short term. Now, some 20 years later, ADR has developed considerably. The view that it has a role to play in dispute resolution – a role that offers a viable and cost-effective alternative to litigation and arbitration – has spread from the United States to other countries around the world. Most of the major international commercial arbitral bodies provide various types of ADR processes such as mediation / conciliation. The United Nations, through the work of UNCITRAL, has also adopted a Model Law on Conciliation.

Picking up again the Redfern and Hunter line, a settlement reached through mediation / conciliation – which may not even be enforceable in a domestic context, let alone in an international context – clearly cannot be compared with an arbitral award enforceable under the New York Convention. However, the Mediation Institute of the SCC may have come up with a solution in Article 12 of their Mediation Rules. This provides that the parties may request the mediator to assume the role of arbitrator and then to make an arbitral award in the terms of the settlement agreement.

International arbitration and international mediation / conciliation are clearly two different animals. But what ADR in an international context does seem to be able to offer, through organisations like UNCITRAL and the major international commercial arbitral institutions, is the possibility of resolving international disputes before they reach the stage of a full-scale international commercial arbitration battle. One particular example is the use of ADR as a filter process aimed at resolving disputes at an early stage: Only if the ADR process fails does the dispute then proceed to arbitration.

The use of ADR in its various forms, particularly mediation / conciliation, must surely increase both in the domestic sphere and internationally. It has too much to offer for it to fail.

103 Sweet and Maxwell, 1986.

20 Expert Determination

1) Introduction

Expert determination is the fourth method of dispute resolution considered in the field of international commercial dispute resolution. It is very different from the three other forms of dispute resolution considered so far in this part of the Manual: litigation, arbitration and ADR in its various forms.

Using experts to determine technical or valuation matters has been the practice in England for hundreds of years. The parties agree to instruct a third party to determine a specific matter. Expert determination operates in a fairly narrow field. For example, it is used in the petroleum industry for equity redetermination and for the resolution of specific matters identified in the relevant contract.

This chapter compares expert determination and arbitration; discusses two reported cases dealing with expert determination; and considers some of the institutions offering expert determination facilities

2) Expert Determination and Arbitration

Although it may be difficult at times to distinguish between expert determination and arbitration, the differences between the two are significant.

Arbitration in England is governed by the provisions of the 1996 Arbitration Act.[104] Due process is very much part and parcel of the arbitral process. Leaving aside documents-only arbitrations, the parties will in all probability present their case to the arbitral tribunal and the decision of that tribunal is based on the evidence and submissions put forward by the parties and their professional advisers. The arbitral tribunal must, in arriving at its decision, apply the relevant law.

On the other hand, there are no statutory provisions governing expert determination. 'Due process' may be conspicuously absent, as the parties may not necessarily present their case or submit evidence. The expert is appointed to obtain the benefits of his/her expert opinion, which will be used to arrive at the determination. Very often the matters to be decided will involve the expert in a valuation exercise.

The assistance of the courts is available to aid the arbitral process. For example, under the English Arbitration Act the court can appoint arbitrators. There is no such provision in relation to experts. Similarly, the courts can assist the arbitral tribunal by enforcing peremptory awards of that tribunal, by securing the attendance of witnesses and by making orders in relation to the taking of evidence, the preservation of evidence and the

1 The provisions of the English Arbitration Act – the ways in which that Act supports the arbitral process in both the domestic and international spheres – were considered in Chapter 16.

making of orders relating to any property that is the subject matter of the proceedings: for example, in relation to the preservation and custody of such property. The court also has powers to grant interim injunctions and appoint receivers in support of the arbitral proceedings. An arbitral award can be challenged on the grounds of 'serious irregularity', and there is a limited right of appeal in relation to points of law.

Such safeguards do not apply in the case of expert determination. Any challenge to the determination of an expert can only be made on fairly limited grounds relating, for example, to fraud or collusion, or to an allegation that the expert had departed from his or her instructions to a material extent.

But perhaps one of the most significant differences between expert determination and arbitration lies in the area of enforcement. On the domestic level, an arbitral award is normally enforced through the national courts. That is the case in England, where an award is enforceable as if it were a judgment of the court. No such assistance is available in relation to the determination of an expert. Such determination is enforceable – if it is enforceable at all – purely as a matter of contract.

The problem of enforcement on the international level is perhaps even more significant. The determination of an expert is not an arbitral award and therefore cannot be enforced under the New York Convention.

3) Reported Cases Dealing with Expert Determination

It may now be helpful to see the approach that the courts have taken to expert determination. The following examples are taken from decisions of the English courts, both of which concern the petroleum industry.

Shell (UK) Limited v Enterprise Oil PLC: Commercial Court [105]

The claimants and the defendants were involved in the exploration and production of hydrocarbons from reservoirs in the North Sea. The parties' respective ownership interests in the oilfields were reflected in their participation in the proceeds (and the costs) of exploration and production in given proportions. These proportions were to be redetermined three times during the life of the agreement. Matters that could not be agreed by the parties were to be referred to an agreed expert.

During the course of the second redetermination, the defendants contended that the expert determination was of no contractual effect and that the parties were therefore not bound by it. The contention was that, for mapping the contours of strata of rock under the seabed, the expert had used a computer package other than the one that had been contractually agreed to.

Mr Justice Lloyd said that the law concerning the status of a decision by an expert and possible challenges to it had been stated in the decision in *Jones v Sherwood Computer Services PLC* [1992] 1 WLR 277. In that case it had been held that if a mistake was made

105 [1999] 2 Lloyd's Reports 456.

by an expert who had departed from his/her instructions in a material respect, the conclusions of that expert were not binding. Whether an expert had departed from his/her instructions in a material respect depended on the materiality of the error. That had to be considered according to the potential effect on the result and/or the process.

In this case, the judge determined that it would be unfair for Enterprise to be held subject to the findings of a programme that had not been agreed to in the contract.

Veba Oil Supply and Trading GmbH v Petrotrade Inc: Commercial Court[106]

The defendants sold 25,000 tonnes of gasoil to the claimants. Clause 10 of the contract provided that the quantity and quality of the cargo was to be determined by a mutually agreed independent inspector at the loading installation (Antwerp) in the manner customary at such installation and that *"such determination shall be final and binding for both parties save for fraud or manifest error"*.

Clause 3 of the contract dealt with quantity. Clause 4 provided *"products / quality: Gasoil meeting the following guaranteed specifications: test limit method Density at 15 deg. C + 0.876 KG/L max ASTM. D 1298."*

Celeb Brett were appointed as the inspectors. They produced a report that determined the density at 0.8750 kg/1. The claimants sold on to the Lebanese Ministry of Oil. On arrival, the density was found to exceed the contractual maximum. The claimants sought damages. They submitted that the determination was not final and binding on them because the method used for testing the product was ASTM D 4052 rather than D 1298 as specified under the contract.

The defendants applied for summary judgment dismissing the claim brought against them. They argued that there had not been a material departure by the inspector and that the test used was more accurate and was widely used for calculating the density of gasoil.

The application for summary judgment was dismissed by Mr Justice Morison. He said that the parties *"had only agreed to be bound by a determination of quantity and quality which, using the test prescribed, complied with the contractual specification. The fact that the method used was more modern or more accurate is not to the point.... As I read the decided cases, a contractual stipulation as to an expert determination must be observed."*

Later, the judge said: *"it is not the business of the Court to weigh the importance of the stipulation in the contract. If the requirement to use the method specified in Clause 4 was contractual that is the end of the matter, whether or not the Court thinks it was important or would have made a difference.... The position is, I think, that it is no business of the Court to inquire why the buyers asked for this particular test.... In my view, this approach has recently been approved by the Court of Appeal in Bouygues UK Limited v Dahl Jensen UK Limited [unreported] July 31 2000 and is consistent with what Mr Justice Lightman said in British Shipbuilders v VSEL Consortium Plc [1971] 1 Lloyd's Rep 106."*

106 [2001] 2 Lloyd's Reports 731.

In that case Mr Justice Lightman had stated that the Court may set aside the decision of an expert who *"goes outside his remit e.g. by determining a different question from that remitted to him or if his determination fails to comply with any conditions which the agreement requires him to comply with in making his determination"*.

4) Some Institutions Offering Expert Determination

Examples are given of just three organisations providing expert determination services.

i) The International Chamber of Commerce

The ICC's International Centre for Expertise offers a range of services, in addition to providing a set of Rules for use in the field of expertise.[107]

The International Centre for Expertise was founded some 30 years ago, and has since then

> *"... built up unique access to experts in every conceivable subject relevant to business operations. It casts its net wide to find the expert most likely to propose the best solution. Ability to deliver the right expert is vital. Equally important are ICC's Rules for Expertise, to which parties may refer in their contracts or at a later stage in their relationship. The rules, updated for 2003, provide the basis for ICC expertise. Parties can request that the Centre propose an expert, appoint an expert or administer the expertise proceedings.*
>
> *"To make the right choice, the Centre relies on its own extensive contacts, a standing committee – whose members are themselves experts – and a network of more than 90 ICC national committees, all able to call on experts in their own countries.*
>
> *"ICC expertise can cover technical, financial or contractual issues. It may be requested by one or several parties to a contract or before a deal has been struck. Expertise provided through the Centre can assist amicable settlement of a dispute or resolve a mere difference of opinion. It may do no more than remove uncertainty about a set of facts. If the parties wish, the findings can be binding. ICC expertise may also be used during litigation or arbitration."*

The ICC Rules for Expertise are in five sections:

Section I: general principles

Section II: proposal of experts

Section III: appointment of experts

Section IV: administration of expertise proceedings

Section V: miscellaneous

Article 1 of the Rules sets out the three types of services available: the proposal of experts, the appointment of experts and the administration of expertise proceedings.

4 www.iccexpertise.org.

In the case of administered proceedings, the Rules describe the role of the Expert. After consulting with the parties the Expert is to set out his/her 'mission' in a document, which is to include a list of the issues to be dealt with in the Expert's Report. The Expert's main task is to set out in that Report his/her findings, after having given the parties the opportunity to be heard and/or to make written submissions.

ICC expertise can, for example, be used when parties want to resolve a difference of opinion or remove uncertainty about a set of facts. If the parties in an expertise proceeding so wish, the expert's findings can be binding. Recourse to ICC expertise can also be made during litigation or arbitration, by either one of the parties, the judge or an arbitral tribunal.

The proposal is free if it is made at the request of an arbitral tribunal acting under the ICC Rules of Arbitration

The International Centre for Expertise also administers the ICC's Rules for Documentary Credit Dispute Resolution Expertise (DOCDEX), which are considered in the next Part.

ii) The London Court of International Arbitration

Expert determination is one of the dispute resolution services offered by the LCIA. The LCIA is *"happy to discuss with parties and their advisers other tailor-made dispute-resolution services. For example, where an appointing authority is required, where there is provision for expert determination of a dispute, or for the appointment of an adjudicator, or for the establishment of a standing dispute-review panel."*

iii) The Chartered Institute of Arbitrators

The Chartered Institute operates an ad hoc scheme under which the President of the Institute will make an appointment for expert determination.

5) Conclusions

There is no limit to the areas in which litigation can operate.

The field of operation of international arbitration, and to a lesser extent ADR in an international context, is very wide.

Expert determination, on the other hand, has a fairly restricted field of operation. Nevertheless, it has an important role to play in the field of international commercial dispute settlement, as is indicated by the two petroleum cases decided by the English courts.

Part V: The Electronic Era

"Our belief that cyberspace would not be a harmonious place was based on a very simple observation. Cyberspace seemed to us to be too active, too entrepreneurial, too competitive, and too lucrative a place for it not to have many conflicts. Even in 1996 it was apparent that cyberspace involved too many people applying their creative energies and imaginations in new ways for there not to be a need for processes to settle disputes. Cyberspace was a place where the number of transactions could only grow, and we thought, where transactions and relationships go, disputes will follow.

"Our assumption that the Internet might become a kind of 'dispute resolution space' and serve as a vehicle for resolving disputes was also based on a rather simple observation. This was that cyberspace was a place where powerful tools were being developed for communicating, storing, and processing information. We knew that these activities were also at the heart of dispute resolution. As capabilities for working with information and managing information online improved, we thought that opportunities for directing these capabilities at dispute resolution would also improve."

Ethan Katsh and Janet Rifkin[108]

108 Ethan Katsh and Janet Rifkin, *Online Dispute Resolution: Resolving Conflicts in Cyberspace*, Jossey-Bass, San Francisco, 2001, p 3.

21 Introduction

This part of the Manual looks at what may be broadly described as 'online dispute resolution' (ODR) in two areas: international trade and intellectual property.

The specific area of international trade to be considered is documentary credits (or letters of credit), which have been described as the life-blood of commerce. The International Chamber of Commerce (ICC) operates a system designed to resolve disputes concerning documentary credits speedily and cost-effectively: the Documentary Credit Dispute Resolution Expertise (DOCDEX) system, which was mentioned briefly in the previous chapter.

The specific area of intellectual property to be considered is domain name disputes. The United Nations World Intellectual Property Organization (WIPO) has instituted a system to deal with the problem of what is commonly referred to as 'cybersquatting': the abusive registration of Internet domain names.

There are a number of differences between the dispute resolution systems considered here and the systems dealt with in the earlier Parts of the Manual:

- The first and most obvious difference is that the communication systems they rely on can broadly be described as 'electronic'. The ICC DOCDEX system requires communications to be by way of *"teletransmission or other expeditious means"*. The WIPO system requires communications to the *"by telecopy or facsimile transmission... by electronic mail (e-mail)... or where both parties agree, through the Center's Internet-based case filing and administration system"*.
- The second difference relates to hearings. In complex international arbitration cases, hearings are inevitable. In the case of the DOCDEX system a hearing is ruled out completely. In the case of the WIPO domain name system a hearing can only take place in exceptional circumstances – and then only at the discretion of the WIPO Domain Name Panel.
- A third distinguishing feature of the two systems is the speed with which a decision is to be delivered. In the case of DOCDEX the draft decision is to be ready within 30 days of the panel – the Appointed Experts – obtaining the information and documents that they require. In the case of a WIPO panel the decision is to be available within 14 days of the appointment of that panel.

These factors – primarily electronic communications, no hearings and speedy panel decisions – enable both the DOCDEX and WIPO systems to achieve their twin aims of being low cost and able to resolve disputes quickly.

The use of the Internet in commercial dispute resolution is a comparatively recent development. In an article published in 1999, this writer raised the question of whether electronic commerce would lead to the development of dispute resolution processes that make use of the Internet:[109]

---

109 Anthony Connerty, 'Electronic Commerce: A United Kingdom View', *E- Commerce: Special Issue of International Company and Commercial Law Review*, Sweet and Maxwell, 1999.

> *"Could the costly and time-consuming processes involving physical arbitration hearings be replaced by on-line electronic dispute resolution processes? Will we see the emergence of the cyber arbitrator?*
>
> *"The ICC may already have shown the way to resolve cross-border disputes swiftly and cost effectively without the necessity for physical meetings. In October 1997 the ICC published the DOCDEX Rules: the 'Rules for Documentary Credit Dispute Resolution Expertise'. The system is made available through the ICC's International Centre for Expertise in Paris.... Three 'appointed experts' are to draft a decision which is to be submitted to the Centre within 30 days. That decision is based on documents only. The Rules state that the parties may not seek an oral hearing in front of the appointed experts....*
>
> *"In all probability the three experts will be from three different countries. There is no requirement in the DOCDEX Rules that they should physically meet. The communications between the experts for the purpose of arriving at their decision can therefore be by telephone, fax or e-mail. The way is obviously open for on-line communication between the experts."*

The writer then went on to consider a system that was then being proposed by WIPO:

> *"The World Intellectual Property Organization is one of a number of specialised agencies operated by the United Nations. For some time WIPO has been working on an on-line dispute resolution system aimed at dealing with domain name disputes. Draft Rules issued in 1997 contain provisions dealing with hearings. These were defined as including telephone or video conferencing and the 'simultaneous, authenticated exchange of electronic communications on the same channel in a manner that enables all Parties authorised to use the channel to receive any communications sent and to send communications.'*
>
> *"Although intended specifically to deal with domain name disputes the draft Rules could be adopted to deal with on-line electronic commerce disputes generally.*
>
> *"Perhaps the WIPO Center in Geneva and the ICC's International Centre for Expertise in Paris are showing the way towards a dispute resolution process which can be used to resolve electronic commerce disputes on an on-line basis without the necessity for physical meetings."*

Both the ICC and WIPO systems are now operating.

The emergence of ODR will be looked at in Chapter 22, after which the DOCDEX and WIPO systems will be considered in Chapters 23 and 24. Chapter 25 considers the possible future development of ODR.

22 The Emergence of Online Dispute Resolution

1) Electronic Commerce

In the introduction to the 1999 article on electronic commerce referred to in the last Chapter, this writer stated that:

> *"For the past few years the emergence and development of the Internet has made changes to the life of millions of people worldwide. The rate of development is extraordinary. Even today, no one can predict with certainty where the Internet will take us. One of the areas where the Internet has had a particular impact is commerce. Cross-border trading can take place on the Internet virtually without regard to national boundaries. The problems which this raises for politicians, lawyers and legislators are immense....*
>
> *"Broadly speaking, there are two types of business being transacted on the Internet: that between business and consumer and that between business and business.... Many consumers in the United Kingdom are now becoming used to shopping on the Internet: not just supermarket shopping, but shopping in increasingly sophisticated areas.... If the increasing consumer business on the Internet in Britain follows the trend in America, the rate of growth will be staggering. The estimated business-to-consumer trading in America, presently put at $8 billion, is reckoned to increase to $108 billion over the next five years. But this is small beer compared with business-to-business trading. The American forecasts for inter-company trading put the present figure at $43 billion, increasing to $1.3 trillion in 2003....*
>
> *"Business on the Internet – electronic commerce – will not simply present opportunities and challenges to businessmen: cybertrade presents challenges and opportunities to lawyers, legislators, governments and international bodies concerned with international trade."*[110]

The article then went on to consider problems likely to be created in relation to trading on the Internet:

- formation of a contract;
- digital signatures, encryption and authentication;
- electronic payment;
- intellectual property rights;
- governing law and jurisdiction;
- dispute resolution.

It is the last of these topics – dispute resolution – that will now be considered: specifically, online dispute resolution (ODR).

110 *Supra.*

2) Online Dispute Resolution

ODR may be defined as a dispute resolution process that operates entirely by electronic means, without the need for the parties in dispute to meet physically. The actual dispute resolution procedures used may include some of the types of alternative dispute resolution (ADR) systems considered in Part IV of the Manual.[111]

ODR has been developing not only in the commercial field, but also internationally through organisations such as the United Nations.

i) Commercial Developments: eBay and Square Trade

The Internet auction organisation, eBay, has instituted a system for resolving disputes online that operates in conjunction with SquareTrade. eBay says that online dispute resolution is a *"new, unbiased method that can help you resolve disputes that may arise involving eBay transactions. SquareTrade, eBay's preferred dispute resolution provider, offers two services: a free web-based forum which allows users to attempt to resolve their differences on their own or, if necessary, the use of a professional mediator."*

According to eBay, the benefits of the system are that *"All eBay buyers and sellers can use this online dispute resolution service. It's free to file a complaint. SquareTrade will contact and encourage the other party to respond to your case. You can then try and settle your dispute through SquareTrade's free Web-based process and patent-pending technology. A significant number of complaints are directly resolved in this way. Because we believe this service helps make eBay a better place to trade, you can request the assistance of a professional mediator for $15 (eBay will subsidize the rest of the cost)."*

To file a complaint, an online form is to be completed in which details of the complaints are to be entered: *"SquareTrade will send a notification email to the other party who can then respond to you. Your complaint and the other party's response will appear in a secure area on the SquareTrade Web site. Only you, the other party and the mediator (if you choose to involve one) will be granted access. Disputes are often successfully settled with this independent resolution method.... If you'd like, you can also use a SquareTrade mediator for $15 to guide you through the Web-based process. The mediator works to understand both points of view and to help develop a fair, agreeable settlement. If a resolution can't be reached, the mediator will recommend a solution based on principles of fairness and good conduct."*

SquareTrade's ODR service is said to have *"a proven track record of resolving disputes, having handled over 1 million disputes in areas ranging from online auctions to traditional home purchases. SquareTrade uses a worldwide network of over 250 professional mediators, and is advised by experts in the fields of consumer protection, cyberlaw, and dispute resolution.... SquareTrade was founded in 1999 to provide a way for people to transact online with peace of mind. Since then, SquareTrade has rapidly grown to become the world's leading online dispute resolution service. The SquareTrade Seal Program has become the most recognizable symbol of trust, attracting several thousand new members*

111 A useful work in this comparatively new area is Etan Katsh and Janet Rifkin, *Online Dispute Resolution: Resolving Conflicts in Cyberspace*, Jossey-Bass, 2001.

each month.... SquareTrade was recognized with the '2002 Outstanding Practical Achievement Award' by the prestigious CPR Institute for Dispute Resolution. The World Economic Forum selected SquareTrade as one of the top 100 Technology Pioneers of 2001 and 2002. SquareTrade has acted as a key presenter to the Federal Trade Commission, the European Union and the United Nations Economic Commission for Europe on the issue of global online consumer protection. SquareTrade is a privately held company funded by top tier investors...."

ii) ***International developments: the United Nations***

A Forum on Online Dispute Resolution was organised in June 2002 under the auspices of the United Nations Economic Commission for Europe (UNECE). UNECE explained:

> *"Numerous discussions have taken place on Online Dispute Resolution (ODR), and several international fora on the subject matter have been organized over the last few years. The objective of this Forum, the first of its kind in the UN, is to take stock of accumulated knowledge and expertise in this area, and to prepare an inventory of the work that has been undertaken or is currently underway in international organizations.*
>
> *"The Forum is to analyze the current development process of ODR from both Alternative Dispute Resolution (ADR) and increasing interface with new Information and Communications Technology (ICT). By focusing on major existing ODR activities at the regional and global level, it aims at understanding the current state of technology and its likely future directions.*
>
> *"Overall six expert panels on technical, economic and legal issues will be held during one and half day meeting, bringing together regional and international experts who will discuss the major issues and set the venue for further work in this field...*
>
> *"The Forum will also seek to find the ways and means of expanding benefits of ODR to developing and transition economies in order to contribute to reducing digital divide. Finally, it will set out the future directions of ODR in technical, financial and legal terms.*
>
> *"Confirmed speakers include the representatives from the European Commission, US Federal Trade Commission, the business communities, academic institutions and major international organizations, OECD, WIPO, UNCITRAL, CEFACT, ICC, UNCTAD, among others..."*

In late 2002 one of those organisations, the United Nations Centre for Trade Facilitation and Electronic Business (UN/CEFACT) produced a Draft Recommendation on ODR. The Introduction stated that:

> *"The increasing activity on the internet in both the Business-to-Business (B2B) and the Business-to-Consumer (B2C) sectors inevitably results in a growing number of conflicts in the electronic business environment.*
>
> *"Characteristics of transactions on the internet are the absence of concrete obstacles making it easy for parties to create legally binding contracts involving participants in different jurisdictions. This is coupled with the dematerialisation of the medium of message exchange and, thus, contract conclusion. Parties negotiating on the internet are able to attempt to achieve consensus by a mouse-click. Click-wrap and click-through contracts are already widespread. This new way of communication and contracting has raised the need for special dispute resolution mechanisms.*

Consequently, rapid, adequate and inexpensive instruments for conflict resolution, as an alternative to national litigation, need to be in place in order to create confidence and trust in electronic business. Because of the specificity of the electronic business environment, these alternative methods for dispute resolution are also increasingly being carried out also by electronic means. Many virtual forums for dispute resolution already offer services on the internet thus making Online Dispute Resolution (ODR) a reality. This, however, raises issues concerning the compatibility of ODR with the contemporary national and international legal frameworks and the appropriate regulation of ODR."

The Draft Recommendation concluded:

"The United Nations Centre for Trade Facilitation and Electronic Business (UN/CEFACT) agrees to recommend that:

1 *Governments should promote and facilitate the development of Online Alternative Dispute Resolution in both the business-to-business and business-to-consumer sectors. In particular, Governments should refrain from adopting any rules hindering ODR in their future legislation, such as accreditation requirements for dispute resolution providers. The promotion and implementation of ODR can be done especially in combination with self-regulatory instruments for electronic business such as codes of conduct and trust-mark schemes.*

2 *Governments should ensure that, in case of disagreement between a service provider and the recipient of the service in the information society, their legislation encourages and facilitates the use of out-of-court schemes, available under national law, for dispute settlement, including appropriate electronic means so as to support the development of international trade.*

3 *Governments, national, international and non-governmental organizations developing ODR should encourage the bodies responsible for out-of-court settlement (in particular of consumer disputes) to operate in a way which provides adequate procedural guarantees for the parties concerned.*

4 *Governments should encourage bodies responsible for out-of-court dispute settlement to inform all relevant institutions of the significant decisions they take regarding information society services and to transmit any other information on the practices, usages or customs relating to electronic commerce."*[112]

Possible future development in ODR is considered in Chapter 25.

112 The Draft Recommendation of UN/CEFACT can be viewed at www.e-arbitration-t.com/papersadr/Legal_Group_UNCEFACT_ODR.doc.

23 The ICC DOCDEX System

1) Introduction

DOCDEX, standing for Documentary Credit Dispute Resolution Expertise, is a rapid, cost-effective system intended to resolve disputes involving International Chamber of Commerce (ICC) rules on documentary credits. Originally introduced in 1997, it is a private, expert-based and (unless otherwise agreed) non-binding alternative to international litigation and arbitration. The ICC says that DOCDEX has been used by practitioners worldwide who need quick decisions on outstanding conflicts.

The original DOCDEX system dealt with two of the ICC's sets of Rules: the Uniform Customs and Practice for Documentary Credits (UCP 500) and the Uniform Rules for Bank-to Bank Reimbursements under Documentary Credits (URR 525). Since then, the Rules have been revised, expanding the DOCDEX process to encompass two other sets of ICC Rules: the Uniform Rules on Collections (URC 525) and the Uniform Rules for Demand Guarantees (URDG 458).[113]

The ICC says that:

"The purpose of an expertise under the DOCDEX Rules is to enable a panel of three independent, experienced documentary instruments experts, appointed by the ICC International Centre for Expertise, to issue an opinion and/or recommendation on any given dispute for a fair and rapid resolution of a dispute. There are no hearings, the decision is not binding and not intended to conform with the legal requirements of an arbitral award. The ICC urges banks to respect DOCDEX Decisions on a voluntary basis. If the parties wish to increase the enforceability of DOCDEX Decisions, they may specify in advance that the DOCDEX Decision will be legally binding between them....

"All the parties are given the opportunity to participate in the DOCDEX proceedings. However, the DOCDEX panel issues an opinion regardless of whether or not the Respondent agrees to participate.

"The DOCDEX Experts' Panel remains anonymous. All communication between Experts and parties passes through the Centre; there are no hearings. The Experts are chosen from a list maintained by the ICC Commission on Banking Technique and Practice.

"The Chair of the Experts' Panel has to issue an opinion to the Centre within 30 days following receipt of the relevant documents. The Experts' decision is examined by the Technical Adviser of the Banking Commission, who ascertains that their decision is in line with the applicable ICC Rules and their interpretation by the Banking Commission.

"The Experts' decision is issued by the Centre as a DOCDEX Decision. It is issued in English (unless the Appointed Experts decide otherwise), and is to include a summary of the representations made and a determination of the issues and the decisions taken with 'succinctly stated reasons'. The Decision is deemed to be made in Paris on the date it is issued.

113 See www.iccdocdex.org.

"The DOCDEX Rules provide that the ICC may publish any DOCDEX Decision provided that the identities of the parties to the dispute are not disclosed. DOCDEX Decisions have already been published in DC Insight."

Decisions are also published in the collection of ICC decisions from the Commission on Banking Technique and Practice.[114]

2) The DOCDEX Rules

Article 1

Article 1.1 explains the scope of the DOCDEX dispute resolution service; as noted above, this relates to disputes under the various ICC rules. The Article states that the objective of the service *"is to provide an independent, impartial and prompt expert decision (DOCDEX Decision) on how the dispute should be resolved on the basis of the terms and conditions of the documentary credit, the collection instruction, or the demand guarantee and the applicable ICC Rules, be it the UCP, the URR, the URC or the URDG (ICC Rules)."*

References for the various publications – and copies of these publications – can be obtained from the ICC.

Article 1.3 deals with the appointment of the Experts' Panel:

> *"When a dispute is submitted to the Centre in accordance with these rules, the Centre shall appoint three experts from a list of experts maintained by the Banking Commission. These three experts (Appointed Experts) shall make a decision which, after consultation with the Technical Adviser of the Banking Commission, shall be issued by the Centre as a DOCDEX Decision in accordance with these rules. The DOCDEX Decision is not intended to conform with any legal requirements of an arbitration award."*

Article 1.4 provides that, unless otherwise agreed, a DOCDEX Decision is not binding on the parties. Article 1.5 states that in the DOCDEX procedure, communication with the Centre *"shall be conducted exclusively in writing, i.e. by communication received in a form that provides a complete record thereof, via teletransmission or other expeditious means"*.

Article 2

The Initiator of the process is to apply for a DOCDEX Decision by the submission of a Request: *"The Initiator may be one of the parties to the dispute applying individually, or more or all parties to the dispute submitting jointly a single Request."* Article 2 states that the Request must be concise and is to set out all necessary information, including:

> *"2.2.1 full name and address of the Initiator, clearly stating such Initiator's function(s) in connection with the documentary credit, the collection, or the demand guarantee, and*

114 Decisions taken over a seven-year period have been collected in a single volume: ICC, *DOCDEX Decisions 1997-2003*, International Chamber of Commerce, 2004.

2.2.2 *full name and address of any other party to the dispute (Respondent), clearly stating such Respondent's function(s) in connection with the documentary credit, the collection, or the demand guarantee, where the Request is not submitted jointly by all parties to the dispute, and*

2.2.3 *a statement of the Initiator formally requesting a DOCDEX Decision in accordance with the ICC DOCDEX Rules, ICC Publication No.811, and*

2.2.4 *a summary of the dispute and of the Initiator's claims, clearly identifying all issues related to the documentary credit, the collection, or the demand guarantee and the applicable ICC Rules to be determined, and*

2.2.5 *copies of the documentary credit, the collection instruction, or the demand guarantee in dispute, all amendments thereto, and all documents deemed necessary to establish the relevant circumstances, and*

2.2.6 *a statement by the Initiator that a copy of such Request, including all documents annexed thereto, has been sent to each Respondent named in the Request...."*

Article 3

Provisions relating to any Answer to be submitted by the Respondent are set out in Article 3:

"3.1 *The Respondent may submit an Answer to the Initiator's Request. The Respondent may be one or more of the parties to the dispute named in the Request as Respondent, each submitting an individual Answer or submitting jointly a single Answer. The Answer must be received by the Centre within the period stipulated in the Centre's Acknowledgement of the Request (see Article 5). The Answer, including all documents annexed thereto, shall be supplied to the Centre in Paris, France, in four copies.*

3.2 *An Answer shall be concise and contain all necessary information clearly presented, in particular the following:*

3.2.1 *name and address of the Initiator, and*

3.2.2 *date of the relevant Request, and*

3.2.3 *a statement of the Respondent formally requesting a DOCDEX Decision in accordance with the ICC DOCDEX Rules, ICC Publication No. 811, and*

3.2.4 *a summary of the Respondent's claims, clearly referring to all issues related to the documentary credit, the collection, or the demand guarantee and the applicable ICC Rules to be determined, and*

3.2.5 *copies of all additional documents deemed necessary to establish the relevant circumstances, and*

3.2.6 *a statement of the Respondent that a copy of such Answer, including all documents annexed thereto, has been sent in writing to the Initiator and to the other Respondent named in the Request.*

3.3 *If the Respondent does not provide a statement pursuant to Article 3.2.3, then the final DOCDEX Decision will not be made available to him."*

Article 4

Article 4 contains provisions dealing with the Request, Answers and Supplements (defined in the Article). All three are final as received, and the Centre may ask the Initiator and Respondent *"by way of an Invitation, to submit specific supplementary information, including copies of documents, relevant to the DOCDEX Decision (Supplement).... The Supplement shall be concise and contain all necessary information clearly presented and include copies of relevant documents."*

Article 5

Provisions relating to the acknowledgement of the receipt of Requests, Answers and Supplements, together with provisions relating to time limits, are set out in Article 5.

Article 6

Article 6 deals with the appointment of Appointed Experts:

> "6.1 *The Banking Commission will maintain internal lists of experts having profound experience and knowledge of the applicable ICC Rules.*
>
> 6.2 *Upon receipt of a Request, the Centre shall appoint three independent experts from the list. Each Appointed Expert shall declare his independence of the parties indicated in the Request. The Centre shall designate one of the three Appointed Experts to act as their Chair.*
>
> 6.3 *An Appointed Expert shall at all times keep strictly confidential all information and documents related to any DOCDEX case."*

This Article also contains provisions for the replacement of an Appointed Expert who is unable to carry out his/her functions.

Article 7

Article 7 deals with the procedure to be followed by the Appointed Experts, and contains the significant provision that the parties are not entitled to seek an oral hearing before those Experts. The Article also contains the 30-day time limit for production of a draft decision:

> "7.1 *The Centre shall submit to the Appointed Experts the Request, Answer(s) and Supplement(s) received in connection therewith.*
>
> 7.2 *The Appointed Experts shall render their decision impartially and exclusively on the basis of the Request, Answer(s) and Supplement(s) thereto, and the documentary credit and the UCP and/or URR, or the collection and the URC, or the demand guarantee and the URDG.*
>
> 7.3 *Where it is deemed necessary by the Appointed Experts, their Chair may ask the Centre to invite the Initiator and Respondent, pursuant to Article 4 of these rules, to provide additional information and/or copies of documents.*
>
> 7.4 *Within 30 days after they have received all information and documents deemed by them to be necessary and appropriate to the issues to be determined, and provided that the Additional Fee as mentioned in Article 10.1 is paid, the*

Appointed Experts shall draft a decision and their Chair shall submit the decision to the Centre.

7.5 Neither the Initiator nor the Respondent shall

- *seek an oral hearing in front of the Appointed Experts,*
- *request ICC to reveal the name of any Appointed Expert,*
- *seek to have an Appointed Expert or officer of the Banking Commission called as witness, expert or any similar function to an arbitral tribunal or a court of law hearing the dispute in connection with which such Appointed Expert or officer of the Banking Commission participated by rendering a DOCDEX Decision."*

Article 8

Provisions relating to the DOCDEX Decision are set out in Article 8. The Article provides that the draft decision of the Appointed Experts is to be considered by the Technical Adviser of the ICC's Banking Commission.

These provisions are, to a limited extent, similar to the *"scrutiny of the award"* provisions contained in the ICC Arbitration Rules. Article 8 states that, on receipt of the decision of the Appointed Experts *"... the Centre shall consult with the Technical Adviser of the Banking Commission or his nominated delegate, to ascertain that the DOCDEX Decision will be in line with the applicable ICC Rules and their interpretation by the Banking Commission. Amendments suggested by the Technical Adviser (or his delegate) shall be subject to the consent of the majority of the Appointed Experts."*

The DOCDEX Decision is to contain a summary of the representations relevant to the issues, together with a determination of those issues and the decisions taken *"with succinctly stated reasons"*. The Decision is deemed to be made at Paris and on the date of its issue by the Centre.

Article 9

Article 9 provides that the ICC may publish any DOCDEX Decision *"provided always the identities of the parties to the dispute are not disclosed"*.

Articles 10 and 11

Article 10 deals with costs. Article 11 contains general provisions relating to confidentiality and liability.

3) DOCDEX Decisions

Background: problems in the banking industry

Before looking at some decisions under the DOCDEX Rules, it may be useful to consider the kind of problems that had arisen in the banking world in relation to documentary credits, which problems had persuaded the ICC of the need to deal with the difficulties being created. These largely came about because some banks were refusing to pay letters of credit on the grounds of alleged 'discrepancies'.

One of the essential elements of the documentary credit system is the autonomy of the letter of credit. The letter of credit contract is separate from the sale contract or 'underlying contract', and banks must pay it regardless of disputes concerning the underlying contract. The goods may have been lost at sea or the purchaser may have complaints regarding defects in the goods, but the bank must pay. If traders cannot rely on the obligation of banks to honour documentary credits then the system of international trade will be put at risk.

Charles del Busto of the ICC's Commission on Banking Technique and Practice explained that:

> *"As most participants in international trade know, there have been serious problems with certain banks as to the application, interpretation and adherence to the UCP. In addition, there is great concern at what appears to be avoidance by certain banks of their duty to honour their irrevocable and independent undertakings under their Documentary Credits.*
>
> *"The rejection of documents presented under these Documentary Credits is based on 'alleged' discrepancies and is due in part either to misinterpretation, misapplication of the UCP or to the 'fabrication' of discrepancies with the sole intent to delay payment or to justify non-payment of the bank's irrevocable obligation. To any party involved in Documentary Credits, this practice is destructive.*
>
> *"We all recognise that the Documentary Credit is part of the lifeblood of international commerce. If this practice of avoiding or delaying payment were to become widespread, the Documentary Credit would lose it into integrity, independence and thereby its raison d'etre...."*

The discrepancies of which Charles del Busto spoke may arise, for instance, in connection with shipping documents. Suppose there is a contract for the sale of 10,000 tons of US citrus pulp pellets by a German company to a Dutch company, delivery to be c.i.f. Rotterdam. The sale contract provides for payment by letter of credit. The shipping documents specified in the letter of credit include a commercial invoice, an insurance certificate and a certificate of origin. The spelling of a name on the commercial invoice differs slightly from the spelling in the documentary credit and the issuing bank refuses to pay. Is it entitled to do so? Is there a 'discrepancy' that justifies the issuing bank refusing payment?

Such a problem arose in the case of *Hing Yip Hing Fat Co. Ltd v Daiwa Bank Ltd.*[115] The credit application was made by Cheergoal Industries Ltd. However, the presenting bank presented the letter of credit on a document that showed the drawee as Cheergoal Industrial Ltd. The case was heard by Mr Justice Kaplan, who said that the reference to "Industrial" was an obvious typographical error that should cause no confusion and could not be relied on as a discrepancy.

It is this type of case that might well be referred to a DOCDEX Panel.

115 [1991] 2 HKLR 35.

Examples of DOCDEX decisions

As noted above, the ICC publishes DOCDEX decisions but without names or any references that might identify the parties.

Bill of Lading and Shipping Company Certificate

In this first case, the Initiator / Applicant for the DOCDEX decision was a bank in Europe and the Respondent to the application was a Middle Eastern bank.

The Middle Eastern bank was the Issuing Bank under the Documentary Credit. It had refused documents on various grounds, one of which was that the Shipping Company Certificate indicated that the vessel in question had sailed on 18 April 1998 whereas the Bill of Lading (i.e. loading) date was 14 April 1998.

The Shipping Company Certificate stated "SLD 18.04.1998". The Issuing Bank translated that into 'sailing date'. That date was not stated in the Documentary Credit or in the Bill of Lading, which contained an issuing date and a 'Shipped on Board' date. Evidently the abbreviation 'SLD' is not commonly known, even in the transport industry.

Although banks are not expected to have a specific knowledge regarding goods or shipping and related abbreviations, it is nevertheless known to be common practice that goods are loaded on a ship over a period of several days, and that shipping companies nevertheless issue Bills of Lading for a specific date of loading. Therefore the issuing and /or loaded onboard date might not actually be the date of 'sailing'.

The DOCDEX Panel said that there was therefore no inconsistency between the shipping company certificates indicating "SLD 18.04.1998" and the Bill of Lading giving the date of shipment as 14 April 1998. The Panel's decision was that the Issuing Bank had no reason to refuse payment under the Documentary Credit.

Commercial invoice

The second DOCDEX case considered involved a dispute concerning a commercial invoice. Article 37 (c) of the UCP requires that the description of the goods in the commercial invoice must correspond with the description in the Documentary Credit.

The Initiator was a confirming bank and the Respondent was the issuing bank. The Documentary Credit issued by the Respondent and confirmed by the Initiator included in the Description of Goods field the trade term "ex-works USA".

The credit was issued to cover the transport from Sacramento, USA by vessel to Mersin Free Zone, Turkey. The credit was subsequently amended to read simply "ex-works" and the invoice was amended to read "ex-warehouse Mersin Free Zone – Turkey".

The Panel held that this was acceptable. 'Ex-works USA' had meant, among other things, that the price quoted was for delivery of goods at the disposal of the buyer at a named place in the United States. The new wording in the invoice "ex-works Mersin Free Zone – Turkey " merely added to the required term 'ex-works' in the amended Documentary Credit some additional information, which information was not forbidden by the letter of credit.

24 The WIPO Domain Name Dispute Resolution System

The World Intellectual Property Organization (WIPO) has already been considered in relation to arbitration and mediation in earlier chapters of the Manual. Here, a closer look is taken at WIPO and its specialist system relating to domain names.

1) Introduction

WIPO is an international organisation *"dedicated to promoting the use and protection of works of the human spirit. These works – intellectual property – are expanding the bounds of science and technology and enriching the world of the arts. Through its work, WIPO plays an important role in enhancing the quality and enjoyment of life, as well as creating real wealth for nations."*

WIPO, which has its headquarters in Geneva, Switzerland, is one of the 16 specialised agencies of the United Nations. It administers 23 international treaties dealing with different aspects of intellectual property protection and has 180 nations – over 90 per cent of the world's countries – as member States.

There are more than 900 WIPO staff, who are drawn from around the world. The tasks carried out by WIPO in relation to the protection of intellectual property rights include *"administering international treaties, assisting governments, organizations and the private sector, monitoring developments in the field and harmonizing and simplifying relevant rules and practices. In all that it does, the key words are relevance, efficiency, communication and international cooperation."*

In the view of WIPO, there is a vital need for

> *"... quick and inexpensive ways of settling commercial disputes involving intellectual property rights, and providing private parties with an alternative to often lengthy and costly court proceedings. This need has increased in recent years with the growing importance of international trade. WIPO's Arbitration and Mediation Center helps to meet those needs for companies and individuals anywhere in the world. The Center maintains an extensive list of specialized mediators or arbitrators from over 100 countries, who conduct dispute resolution procedures according to rules made available by WIPO. The procedures may take place in any country, in any language, and under any law, allowing a great deal of flexibility. Indeed, because they are cost-effective, the WIPO procedures are particularly interesting for companies that are unable or unwilling to enter into expensive or protracted litigation, especially at the international level. The subject matter of disputes resolved by means of WIPO procedures has included both contractual (e.g. patent and software licenses, trademark coexistence agreements, distribution agreements for pharmaceutical products and research and development agreements) and non-contractual disputes (e.g. patent infringement)."*

Turning to the specific problem of 'cybersquatting', WIPO states that the Center *"is the leading dispute resolution service provider for challenges related to abusive registration and use of Internet domain names, commonly known as 'cybersquatting'. In 2003, the Center received 5,722 cases under the Uniform Domain Name Dispute Resolution Policy (UDRP) and similar procedures, involving parties from 116 countries. In addition, some 15,510 domain name cases were decided under special procedures. The Center provides this service both for the generic top-level domains, such as .com, .net, .org, .info, and for certain country-code domains. Trademark owners can file complaints using model documents made available on the Center's website. The entire procedure is conducted on-line, resulting in enforceable decisions within two months."*

The Center's IT case facilities allow the parties involved *"to communicate via the Internet without being physically present in the same place, greatly reducing the time and cost of reaching a settlement. Using such expertise, the Center also assists in the design of tailor-made dispute avoidance and resolution procedures upon demand, for example in the area of information technology."*

In addition to dealing with the abusive use of trademark rights in domain names, WIPO also deals with other types of cybersquatting, including the use of personal names, international non-proprietary names for pharmaceutical substances and the names of intergovernmental organisations.

Full details of WIPO's services are available on its website.[116]

2) The Policy and Rules

There are three matters to be considered when looking at the Domain Name Dispute Resolution system operated by WIPO:

i) the Internet Corporation for Assigned Names and Numbers (ICANN) Uniform Domain Name Dispute Resolution Policy (UDRP): the ICANN Policy;

ii) the ICANN Rules for UDRP; and

iii) the WIPO Supplemental Rules for UDRP.

Before looking at the Policy and the two sets of Rules, however, it may be useful to describe briefly how the WIPO system works.

The process is aimed at the problem of 'cybersquatting': the registration of a domain name similar to an established corporation's well-known trademark, often with the intention of either selling the domain name to the corporation at an excessive price or of disrupting that corporation's business. One of the great benefits of the scheme is that the system of registering domain names incorporates within itself a dispute resolution procedure.

Under that procedure a Complainant must show:

1 that the domain name registered is identical or confusingly similar to a trademark or service mark in which the Complainant has rights;

116 www.arbiter.wipo.int.

2 that the Respondent who registered the domain name has no rights or legitimate interest in that name; and

3 that the name was registered and is being used in bad faith.

Where a complaint made under the WIPO system is upheld, the WIPO Panel may either order the cancellation of the domain name or order the transfer of that domain name to the Complainant.

i) The ICANN UDRP Policy

The UDRP Policy sets out the legal framework for the resolution of disputes between a domain name registrant and a third party in relation to the abusive registration and use of an Internet domain name. At its meetings in August 1999 in Santiago, Chile, the ICANN Board of Directors adopted the UDRP Policy, based largely on the recommendations of a WIPO Report. All ICANN-accredited registrars who are authorised to register names in the .com, .net, .org, .biz, .info and .name generic top level domains (gTLDs) have adopted the UDRP Policy and have agreed to abide by it. Any person or entity wishing to register a domain name in the gTLDs and country code top level domains (ccTLDs) is required to consent to the terms and conditions of the UDRP Policy, which contains a dispute resolution procedure and the machinery to enforce its decisions.

The Notes to the Policy state that it is between the registrar and its customer (the domain-name holder or registrant) and therefore the policy uses 'we' and 'our' to refer to the registrar and 'you' and 'your' to refer to the domain-name holder.

Paragraph 1

Paragraph 1 of the Policy states that the Policy is incorporated by reference:

> *"into your Registration Agreement, and sets forth the terms and conditions in connection with a dispute between you and any party other than us (the registrar) over the registration and use of an Internet domain name registered by you. Proceedings under Paragraph 4 of this Policy will be conducted according to the Rules for Uniform Domain Name Dispute Resolution Policy (the 'Rules of Procedure')... and the selected administrative-dispute-resolution service provider's supplemental rules."*

Paragraph 2

Paragraph 2 deals with representations. By applying to register a domain name, the applicant represents that:

> *"(a) the statements that you made in your Registration Agreement are complete and accurate;*
>
> *(b) to your knowledge, the registration of the domain name will not infringe upon or otherwise violate the rights of any third party;*
>
> *(c) you are not registering the domain name for an unlawful purpose; and*
>
> *(d) you will not knowingly use the domain name in violation of any applicable laws or regulations. It is your responsibility to determine whether your domain name registration infringes or violates someone else's rights."*

Paragraph 3

The circumstances in which cancellations, transfers and changes will be made are set out in Paragraph 3 and include:

> "b. *our receipt of an order from a court or arbitral tribunal, in each case of competent jurisdiction, requiring such action; and/or*
>
> c. *our receipt of a decision of an Administrative Panel requiring such action in any administrative proceeding to which you were a party and which was conducted under this Policy or a later version of this Policy adopted by ICANN."*

Paragraph 4

Paragraph 4 is at the heart of the Domain Name Dispute Resolution process. It deals with the three elements mentioned above that are essential in a cybersquatting case and contains the remedies.

Paragraph 4 (a) sets out the type of disputes in relation to which the domain name holder is required to submit to a *"mandatory administrative proceeding"* before one of the *"administrative-dispute-resolution service providers"*:

> *"a. Applicable Disputes. You are required to submit to a mandatory administrative proceeding in the event that a third party (a 'complainant') asserts to the applicable Provider, in compliance with the Rules of Procedure, that*
>
> *(i) your domain name is identical or confusingly similar to a trademark or service mark in which the complainant has rights; and*
>
> *(ii) you have no rights or legitimate interests in respect of the domain name; and*
>
> *(iii) your domain name has been registered and is being used in bad faith.*
>
> *In the administrative proceeding, the complainant must prove that each of these three elements are present."*

The burden of proving each of the three elements is therefore on the Complainant.

Evidence of the 'registration and use in bad faith' element of Paragraph 4 (a) (iii) is indicated in Paragraph 4 (b):

> *"For the purposes of Paragraph 4 (a) (iii) the following circumstances, in particular but without limitation, if found by the Panel to be present, shall be evidence of the registration and use of a domain name in bad faith:*
>
> *(i) circumstances indicating that you have registered or you have acquired the domain name primarily for the purpose of selling, renting, or otherwise transferring the domain name registration to the complainant who is the owner of the trademark or service mark or to a competitor of that complainant, for valuable consideration in excess of your documented out-of-pocket costs directly related to the domain name; or*
>
> *(ii) you have registered the domain name in order to prevent the owner of the trademark or service mark from reflecting the mark in a corresponding domain name, provided that you have engaged in a pattern of such conduct; or*
>
> *(iii) you have registered the domain name primarily for the purpose of disrupting the business of a competitor; or*

(iv) by using the domain name, you have intentionally attempted to attract, for commercial gain, Internet users to your web site or other on-line location, by creating a likelihood of confusion with the complainant's mark as to the source, sponsorship, affiliation, or endorsement of your web site or location or of a product or service on your web site or location."

Paragraph (4) (c) sets out how the domain-name holder can demonstrate the Paragraph 4 (a) (ii) element of rights or legitimate interests:

"... Any of the following circumstances, in particular but without limitation, if found by the Panel to be proved based on its evaluation of all evidence presented, shall demonstrate your rights or legitimate interests to the domain name for purposes of Paragraph 4 (a) (ii):

(i) before any notice to you of the dispute, your use of, or demonstrable preparations to use, the domain name or a name corresponding to the domain name in connection with a bona fide offering of goods or services; or

(ii) you (as an individual, business, or other organization) have been commonly known by the domain name, even if you have acquired no trademark or service mark rights; or

(iii) you are making a legitimate noncommercial or fair use of the domain name, without intent for commercial gain to misleadingly divert consumers or to tarnish the trademark or service mark at issue."

Paragraph 4 (d) deals with selection of a Provider and 4 (e) with the initiation of proceedings: *"The Rules of Procedure state the process for initiating and conducting a proceeding and for appointing the panel that will decide the dispute (the 'Administrative Panel')."*

Paragraph 4 (f) contains provisions dealing with consolidation.

The important provisions relating to remedies are contained in Paragraph 4 (i): *"the remedies available to a complainant pursuant to any proceeding before an Administrative Panel shall be limited to requiring the cancellation of your domain name or the transfer of your domain name registration to the complainant."*

Paragraphs 5 and 6

Paragraph 5 deals with other disputes and litigation concerning the domain name that do not involve the registrar, and Paragraph 6 states that the registrar will not participate in any dispute between the domain name holder and any other party.

Paragraphs 7 and 8

Paragraphs 7 and 8 deal with the status of the domain name. The registrar will not cancel, transfer, activate, deactivate or otherwise change the status of any domain name registration save in accordance with the Paragraph 3 provisions dealing with cancellations and transfers (Paragraph 7). Paragraph 8 covers the transfer of a domain name to another holder or to another registrar during a dispute.

Paragraph 9

Paragraph 9 deals with modifications to the Policy: the registrar may modify the Policy at any time, but only with the permission of ICANN.

ii) The ICANN Rules

In October 1999 the ICANN Board adopted a set of Rules for UDRP. These Rules set out the procedures and other requirements for each stage of the dispute resolution administrative procedure. The procedure is administered by dispute resolution service providers accredited by ICANN, one of which is the WIPO Arbitration and Mediation Center.

Rule 1

Rule 1 sets out a series of definitions, which include:

- *Complainant:* the party initiating a complaint concerning a domain-name registration.
- *Respondent:* the holder of a domain-name registration against which the complaint is initiated.
- *Panel:* an administrative panel appointed by a Provider.
- *Provider:* a dispute-resolution service provider, approved by ICANN.
- *Registrar:* the entity with which the Respondent registered the domain name that is the subject of a complaint.
- *Registration Agreement:* the agreement between a Registrar and a domain-name holder (which agreement will incorporate by reference the UDRP Policy).
- *Reverse Domain Name Hijacking:* means "using the Policy in bad faith to attempt to deprive a registered domain-name holder of a domain name".
- *Mutual Jurisdiction:* means " a court jurisdiction at the location of either (a) the principal office of the Registrar... or (b) the domain-name holder's address as shown for the registration of the domain name in Registrar's Whois[117] database at the time the complaint is submitted to the Provider."

Rule 2

This Rule deals with Communications.

Rules 3 and 4

Rules 3 and 4 concern the Complaint, which initiates the proceedings. Rule 3 states that it is to be submitted in hardcopy and in electronic form. The Complaint is to:

- state whether the Complainant elects to have the dispute decided by a single-member or a three-member Panel (and if three, providing three names that may be drawn from an ICANN-approved Providers' list);
- specify the domain name in question;

117 Whois (or WHOIS) is an Internet utility through which information can be obtained about the ownership of domain names.

- specify the trademark or service mark on which the complaint is based;
- describe the grounds in the Policy that are relied on: i.e. the three elements of Paragraph 4 (a) of the Policy (identical or confusingly similar / no rights or legitimate interests / bad faith);
- specify the remedies sought;
- annex any documentary or other evidence, including a copy of the Policy applicable to the domain name(s) in dispute and any trademark or service mark registration on which the complaint relies.

Notification of the Complaint by the Provider to the Respondent is dealt with in Rule 4.

Rule 5

Rule 5 deals with the Response form. The Response is to:

- respond specifically to the Complaint;
- deal with the constitution of the panel;
- annex any documentary or other evidence.

Rule 6

This Rule deals with the appointment of the panel. There will be a single Panellist unless the Complainant or the Respondent has elected for a three-member panel.

Rule 7

Impartiality and independence is dealt with in Rule 7: *"A Panelist shall be impartial and independent and shall have, before accepting appointment, disclosed to the Provider any circumstances giving rise to justifiable doubt as to the Panelist's impartiality or independence. If, at any stage during the administrative proceeding, new circumstances arise that could give rise to justifiable doubt as to the impartiality or independence of the Panelist, that Panelist shall promptly disclose such circumstances to the Provider. In such event, the Provider shall have the discretion to appoint a substitute Panelist."*

Rules 8 and 9

Rules 8 and 9 deal with communications between the parties and the Panel and the transmission of the file to the Panel.

Rule 10

The general powers of the Panel are set out in Rule 10. The Panel is to conduct the administrative proceedings in such manner as it considers appropriate, but in accordance with the Policy and Rules. The Panel is to ensure that *"the Parties are treated with equality and that each Party is given a fair opportunity to present its case"*. The administrative proceeding is to take place with due expedition. It is for the Panel to determine the admissibility, relevance, materiality and weight of the evidence. The Panel has the power to consolidate multiple domain name disputes.

Rule 11

Rule 11 states that the language of the administrative proceeding is the language of the Registration Agreement, but with power given to the Panel to determine otherwise.

Rule 12

Under Rule 12, the Panel may request further statements or documents from the parties.

Rule 13

Rule 13 contains provisions that are essential to the speed and cost-effectiveness of online dispute resolution:

> *"There shall be no in-person hearings (including hearings by teleconference, videoconference, and web conference), unless the Panel determines, in its sole discretion and as an exceptional matter, that such a hearing is necessary for deciding the complaint."*

Rules 14 and 15

Default provisions are set out in Rule 14. The Panel is to decide a complaint on the basis of *"the statements and documents submitted and in accordance with the Policy, these Rules and any rules and principles of law that it deems applicable"*.

The decision of the panel is to be forwarded to the Provider within 14 days of the appointment of the Panel. The decision is to be in writing and to set out the reasons on which is based. In the case of a three-member panel the decision is by majority. Dissenting opinions are to accompany the majority decision. If the Panel finds that the complaint was brought in bad faith *"for example in an attempt at Reverse Domain Name Hijacking or was brought primarily to harass the domain-name holder, the Panel shall declare in its decision that the complaint was brought in bad faith and constitutes an abuse of the administrative proceeding"* (Rule 15).

Rules 16 and 17

Rule 16 deals with the communication of the decision and Rule 17 with settlement or other grounds for termination. Where legal proceedings are initiated prior to or during an administrative proceeding, the Panel has a discretion whether to suspend or terminate the administrative proceeding or to proceed to a decision.

Rules 19, 20 and 21

These Rules deal with fees, exclusion of liability and amendments to the Rules.

iii) The WIPO Supplemental Rules [level 3]

There are 12 WIPO Supplemental Rules containing the machinery for dealing with a WIPO domain name dispute complaint. Rule 1 states that the Supplemental Rules are to be read in conjunction with the ICANN Rules and Rule 2 provides that terms used in the Supplemental Rules have the same meaning as in the ICANN Rules.

Communications are dealt with in Rule 3 and the submission of a Complaint in Rule 4. Rule 5 deals with Formalities Compliance Review. The WIPO Center is to review the Complaint for compliance with the formal requirements of the Policy, the ICANN Rules and the WIPO Supplemental Rules.

A Case Administrator is to be appointed – a member of the Center's staff who will deal with administrative matters (Rule 6). The procedure for the appointment of panellists, and the Presiding Panellist where a three-member panel is requested is set out in Rule 7. Candidates appointed are required to submit a declaration of independence and impartiality (Rule 8)

Rule 9 deals with fees and Rule 10 with word limits: 5,000 words for the Complaint and the Response but no limit for the Panel decision.

Rules 11 and 12 deal with amendments and exclusion of liability.

3) WIPO Decisions

The WIPO Domain Name Dispute Resolution service has operated with considerable success. Since the UDRP went into effect in December 1999, WIPO's Arbitration and Mediation Center has handled over 8,350 disputes, involving parties from 127 countries and covering some 16,000 domain names.[118]

A total of 1,456 cybersquatting cases were filed with the WIPO Center in 2005, a 20 per cent increase as compared to 2004. This increase represents the highest number of cybersquatting cases handled by the Center since 2001.

The pattern of many of the cases involves the abusive registration of a domain name with the intention of benefiting financially, usually by offering to sell a domain name that is identical to or similar to a well-known trademark or service mark. Alternatively, the abusive registration may be aimed at the disruption of a well-established corporation or other business organisation.

One example of a WIPO Decision relates to an oil company: *Statoil ASA v Magne Espelund,* where the domain names statoil-gas.com and statoilgas.com were in dispute (see Box 11).

---

118 The WIPO Center's online index of WIPO UDRP Decisions (http://arbiter.wipo.int/cgi-bin/domains/search/legalindex) allows for an extensive search on legal and procedural issues under the UDRP.

Box 11: Administrative Panel Decision in *Statoil ASA v Magne Espelund*

1. The Parties

The Complainant was Statoil ASA of Sweden, represented by Cogent IPC AB of Sweden. The Respondent was Magne Espelund of Norway.

2. The Domain Names and Registrar

The disputed domain names were statoil-gas.com and statoilgas.com. The domain names at issue were registered with Capital Networks Pty Ltd dba.

3. Procedural History

The Complaint was filed with the WIPO Arbitration and Mediation Center on 10 February 2003. On 12 February 2003, the Center emailed a request to Capital Networks Pty Ltd dba TotalNIC.net for registrar verification in connection with the domain names at issue. On date of registrar verification, Capital Networks Pty Ltd. dba TotalNIC.net emailed its verification response confirming that the Respondent was listed as the registrant and providing the contact details for the administrative, billing and technical contact. The Center verified that the Complaint satisfied the formal requirements of the UDRP, the ICANN Rules and the WIPO Supplemental Rules.

The Center formally notified the Respondent of the Complaint and the proceedings commenced on 4 March 2003. In accordance with the Rules, the due date for Response was 24 March 2003. The Respondent did not submit any response. Accordingly, the Center notified the Respondent's default on 25 March 2003.

The Center appointed Peter G Nitter as the Sole Panellist on 4 April 2003.

4. Factual background

The Complainant is an oil and gas company founded in 1972, with thousands of employees in 25 countries, and is among the leading suppliers of gas to the European market. Statoil complained that the domain names were virtually identical to its trademark 'STATOIL'. The addition of the suffix 'gas' strengthened the impression that the domain names belonged to the Complainant and were therefore confusingly similar. The Respondent did not reply to Statoil's contentions.

5. Decision

The Panel found (i) that the Respondent had no rights or legitimate interest in the contested domain names; (ii) that the domain name were confusingly similar; and (iii) that there was evidence that there had been offers to sell the domain names to the Complainant for an amount considerably in excess of the Respondent's out-of-pocket costs. This indicated bad faith. The Panel ordered that the domain names be transferred to the Complainant.

Source: The WIPO Internet report of the case (No. D2003-0097): http://arbiter.wipo.int/domains/decisions/html/2003/d2003-0097.html.

Another example, the case of *PepsiCo, Inc. v Henry Chan,* shows the potential dangers of cybersquatting to long-established businesses and their trademarks (see Box 12). The case also shows that cybersquatting is itself a large-scale business.

In all a total of 10 domain names were registered by the Respondent. The Complainant was the owner of the 'PEPSI' and 'MOUNTAIN DEW' trademarks marks and other trademarks and domain names incorporating those two marks. The Claimant contended that the Respondent had registered some 25,000 domain names.

Box 12: Administrative Panel Decision in *PepsiCo, Inc. v Henry Chan*

1. The Parties

The Complainant was PepsiCo, Inc., New York, USA. The Respondent was Henry Chan of Nassau, Bahamas.

2. The Domain Names and Registrar

The Domain Names in dispute were set out in the Complaint of 15 January 2004. At that stage these comprised the following: thepepsichart.com, pepsimiusic.com, pepsiearena.com, pepsisweep.com, pepsinfl.com, pepsicoliseum.com and montaindew.com. All the domain names were registered with iHoldings.comInc.d/b/a dotregistrar.com.

A further disputed domain name was added by amendment to the Amended Complaint of 5 February 2004, namely pepsicollection.com. That domain name was registered with the same registrar. Two further disputed domain names were added by re-amendment to the Re-Amended Complaint dated 25 March 2004, namely pepsicareer.com and pepsidownloads.com. Again, those domain names were registered with the same registrar.

3. Procedural History

The Complaint and annexes were filed with the Center on 16 January 2004. On 19 March 2004, the Center appointed Anthony R Connerty as Sole Panellist. No Response was filed by the Respondent.

4. Factual Background

The Complainant is the owner of the PEPSI and MOUNTAIN DEW marks and other trademarks and domain name incorporating those two marks. The Complainant said that for more than a century the PEPSI-COLA name and mark (and its shortened version, PEPSI) have been continuously used. The Complainant's brands of soft drinks are currently sold in most countries of the world, including the Bahamas.

Recognition of the significance of the PEPSI mark was indicated by two earlier WIPO cases that were relied on in this respect by the Complainant: PepsiCo, Inc., v Diabetes Home Care, Inc, WIPO Case No. D 2001 -0174 ("one of the world's most famous" marks) and *PepsiCo, Inc. v "null"* aka Alexander Zhavoronkov, WIPO Case No.D 2002 -0562 (a "universally recognised" mark).

The PEPSI mark was first used in North Carolina in 1898. The PEPSI brand has been valued at over US$11 billion. The Complainant owns over 100 registrations in the

USA of the PEPSI mark and variants and has at least a dozen PEPSI-variant marks registered in the Bahamas. The Complainants' expenditure on global advertising since 1991 on the PEPSI mark has exceeded US$200 million a year.

The MOUNTAIN DEW name was first registered by the Hartman Beverage Company of Knoxville, Tennessee and was subsequently acquired by PepsiCo, Inc. in 1964. It has since been marketed continuously for almost 40 years. By the mid-1980s, the sale of Mountain Dew products in countries outside the United States exceeded 9,450 million cases. One valuation puts Mountain Dew as the fourth most valuable brand in the United States.

Numerous Internet domain names for active websites based on the PEPSI and MOUNTAIN DEW marks have been continuously owned and used by the Complainant.

Confusingly Similar

The Complainant submitted that the disputed domain names were nearly identical or confusingly similar to the PEPSI mark, and the addition of common terms such as 'chart', 'collection', 'career' and 'download' was of no relevance.

The Complainant relied on a number of previous WIPO decisions in support of its contention:

- *Sony Kabushiki Kaisha v Kil Inja,* WIPO Case No. D 2000-1409 (addition of descriptive word to a world-famous mark does not detract from the overall impression of the famous mark),
- *America Online, Inc v Chris Hoffman,* WIPO Case No. D 2001-1184 (use of short phrases with a well-known mark is still confusingly similar),
- *Chernow Communications, Inc. v Jonathan D Kimball,* WIPO Case No. D 2001-0119 ("... the use or absence of punctuation marks, such as hyphens, does not alter the fact that a name is identical to a mark").

In relation to the use of misspelled variations of the PEPSI and MOUNTAIN DEW marks, the Complainant relied on one of the 'typo-squatting' or 'typo-piracy' cases: *Ultimate Electronics, Inc v Phayze, Inc,* WIPO Case No. D 2002-085.

Further, the Complainant argued that the unique character of the Pepsi and Mountain Dew marks would lead consumers to readily believe that the Domain Names were related to the Complainant.

Registered and Used in Bad Faith

The Complainant contended that the Respondent's bad faith registration and use was established by the fact that the Respondent was using the domain names to divert web traffic to search engines and linking portals that provided links to websites used for gambling, music and movie downloads and tickets for sporting events, none of which were related to the Complainant. These offered a revenue programme that paid domain name owners for diverted traffic 50 per cent of all revenues generated from searches, pop-ups, exit pop-ups and the like.

In addition, the Complainant relied on the Respondent's "pattern of registering domain names containing the trademark and names of third parties and then using those domain names to direct web traffic to websites from which he derives financial benefit".

The Complainant stated that the Respondent had been found to have registered and used domain names in bad faith by at least five administrative panels. The Complainant referred to a number of WIPO and National Arbitration Forum (NAF) cases in which the Respondent had registered domain names (including 'typo' domain names) so as to direct web traffic to websites from which he derived a financial benefit.

Next, the Complainant relied on the fact that the Respondent owned in excess of 25,000 domain names, many of which were based on third party names and marks, including a number of 'typo' domain names. Examples included newharrypotter.com, disneycredit.com, citibankdirect.com and saksfifthavenue.com.

Bad faith was also demonstrated, the Complainant said, by the Respondent's pattern of using multiple addresses for his domain name registrations, including addresses in Hong Kong and the Bahamas.

5. Decision

The Panel ordered that the 10 domain names be transferred to PepsiCo.

Source: The WIPO Internet report of the case (No. D2004-0033): http://arbiter.wipo.int/domains/decisions/html/2004/d2004-0033.html.

The victims of cybersquatting are not only international commercial corporations. Individuals have also been the targets. One example is the film actress Julia Roberts. In the case of *Julia Fiona Roberts v Russell Boyd,* the Respondent put the domain name in question up for auction on the commercial website eBay. This case is an example of a three-member WIPO Administrative Panel (see Box 13).

Box 13: Administrative Panel Decision in *Julia Fiona Roberts v Russell Boyd*

1. The Parties

The Claimant was Julia Fiona Roberts, a United States citizen. The Respondent was Russell Boyd, a United States citizen.

2. The Domain Name and Registrar

The domain name at issue was juliaroberts.com. The registrar was Network Solutions, Inc. (the 'Registrar'), USA.

3. Procedural History

The Center received the Complaint on 25 March 2000. Having verified that the Complaint satisfied the formal requirements of the Policy, the Rules and the

Supplemental Rules, the Center on 29 March 2000 sent the Respondent a notification of the administrative proceeding together with copies of the Complaint.

In correspondence with the Center, the Respondent requested and was granted an extension of time to file his Response. On 8 May 2000, the Center received the Response. On 18 May 2000 the Center notified the parties of the appointment of a three-member Administrative Panel consisting of Mr Richard W Page as the Presiding Panellist, Ms Sally M Abel as Complainant's party-appointed panellist and Mr James Bridgeman as Respondent's party-appointed panellist.

On 8 and 9 May 2000, Complainant tendered a Reply by fax and email. The acceptance of a Reply is subject to the discretion of the Panel. The Panel met by telephone conference call on 25 May 2000 and decided not to accept or consider Complainant's Reply.

4. Factual Background

The Complainant, Julia Fiona Roberts, is a famous motion picture actress. She has appeared in numerous movies including *Erin Brockovich, Notting Hill, Runaway Bride, My Best Friend's Wedding, Everyone Says I Love You, The Pelican Brief, The Player, Hook, Sleeping With the Enemy, Flatliners* and *Pretty Woman*. She has earned two Academy Award nominations.

Respondent registered the subject domain name on 9 November 1998. As of 24 March 2000, the website www.juliaroberts.com featured a photograph of a woman named 'Sari Locker'. The Respondent had placed the domain name up for auction on the commercial auction website, eBay, specifically at http://cgi.ebay.com/aw-cgi/eBayISAPI.dll?ViewItem&item=285891617.

The Respondent had also registered over 50 other domain names, including some incorporating other movie stars names, for example, madeleinestowe.com and alpacino.com, and a famous Russian gymnast's name: elenaprodunova.com. Respondent listed his email address as mickjagger@home.com. Respondent was offered US$2,550 in the eBay auction for the domain name registration.

Bad Faith

Paragraph 4 of the Policy provides that evidence of bad faith registration and use includes circumstances showing:

(ii) you have registered the domain name in order to prevent the owner of the trademark or service mark from reflecting the mark in a corresponding domain name, provided that you have engaged in a pattern of such conduct.

The Respondent admitted that he had registered other domain names including several famous movie and sports stars. Such actions necessarily prevented Complainant from using the disputed domain name and demonstrated a pattern of such conduct. Therefore, the Panel found that Respondent had registered and used the domain name juliaroberts.com in bad faith and that the requirement of the Policy paragraph 4 (a) (iii) was satisfied.

In addition, the Respondent had placed the domain name up for auction on the commercial website eBay. When considered in conjunction with the pattern of registrations described above, the Panel found that such action constituted additional evidence of bad faith.

5. Decision

The Administrative Panel's decision was (a) that the domain name juliaroberts.com was identical to Complainant's common law trademark in her name 'Julia Roberts,' (b) that Respondent had no rights or legitimate interest in the domain name and (c) that Respondent registered and used the domain name in bad faith. Therefore the Panel ordered that the domain name juliaroberts.com be transferred to Complainant Julia Fiona Roberts.

Source: The WIPO Internet report of the case (No. D2000-0210): ttp://arbiter.wipo.int/domains/decisions/html/2000/d2000-0210.html.

This brief look at some of the Decisions illustrates the nature of the WIPO process. The number of such Decisions since the start of the Scheme shows the very considerable success of the WIPO Domain Name system.

25 Future Development of Online Dispute Resolution

The future of online dispute resolution (ODR) – or online alternative dispute resolution, as the United Nations Centre for Trade Facilitation and Electronic Business (UN/CEFACT) describes it – seems assured in a world where cyber trade and cyber commerce increase day by day. The interest and involvement of the UN establishes the importance of ODR.

If proof were needed of the inevitable increase in the use of ODR, it can be found in the success of consumer online dispute resolution systems such as that operated by SquareTrade on behalf of eBay. Further proof can be seen in the more complex areas of international trade and international intellectual property, through the success of the DOCDEX system of the International Chamber of Commerce (ICC) and the Domain Name Dispute Resolution system of the World Intellectual Property Organization (WIPO).

Moreover, in November 2005 the ICC launched NetCase, a platform for the conduct of ICC arbitrations in an online environment. NetCase enables all participants in an arbitration to keep in touch 24 hours a day from any computer in the world through a secure website hosted by ICC. Correspondence and documents are posted on the site rather than sent by the traditional methods of courier, post or fax.[119]

The day of the cyber arbitrator – or the cyber online dispute resolver – has arrived.

119 Details can be obtained from www.iccwbo.org/iccfaja/index.html.

Part VI: Epilogue

"What is the argument on the other side? Only this, that no case has been found in which it has been done before. That argument does not appeal to me in the least. If we never do anything which has not been done before, we shall never get anywhere. The law will stand still whilst the rest of the world goes on: and that will be bad for both."

Lord Justice Denning[120]

120 *Packer v Packer* [1954] P 15 at 22. Quoted by Lord Denning, Master of the Rolls, in *The Discipline of Law*, Butterworths, 1979.

26 Summary – and a Look into the Future

1) Five Topics

This Manual has tried to give an overview of five topics in the field of international dispute settlement:

1 **Supranational disputes** where one or more of the parties is likely to be a State. The areas chosen were those that it is hoped will be of particular interest to Commonwealth countries: territorial disputes, maritime delimitation disputes and investor-State disputes.

2 **Supranational dispute resolution bodies** dealing with such disputes. Four were chosen, again in the hope that they will be of particular interest to Commonwealth governments: the International Court of Justice (ICJ), the Permanent Court of Arbitration (PCA), the International Tribunal for the Law of the Sea (ITLOS) and the World Bank's International Centre for Settlement of Investment Disputes (ICSID Centre).

The dispute settlement methods considered in relation to supranational disputes – and the international dispute settlement bodies dealing with such disputes – were litigation, arbitration and mediation / conciliation.

3 **Dispute resolution in the area of international trade and commerce.** Here, four methods of dispute resolution were considered: litigation: but this time in the national rather than the international sphere; arbitration; various forms of alternative dispute resolution (ADR) – in particular, mediation / conciliation; and expert determination.

4 **Institutions and other bodies concerned with dispute resolution in international trade and commerce.** The international commercial arbitral institutions looked at included the International Chamber of Commerce (ICC), the London Court of International Arbitration (LCIA) and the American Arbitration Association (AAA). In addition, organisations concerned with international trade and commerce, in particular the United Nations, were also considered.

In an attempt to 'put some meat on the bones', various topics were illustrated by reference to decisions of the supranational dispute resolution bodies as well as to decisions of national courts, particularly in relation to the vitally important New York Convention and the UN Commission on International Trade Law (UNCITRAL) Model Law.

5 **Online dispute resolution.** After looking at commercial user developments in the form of eBay and SquareTrade, two particular areas were chosen – again in the hope that Commonwealth countries would find them useful. These are of great significance in the fields of international trade and commerce and international intellectual property: documentary credits and domain name disputes. The specific systems considered were the ICC's DOCDEX scheme and the Domain Name Dispute Resolution system of the World Intellectual Property Organization (WIPO).

The point was made early on in this book that the topics that the Manual has tried to cover are vast, and that any one of them would justify a learned work. The Manual has sought to do no more than give an overview of the various subjects and to highlight matters of particular importance. In that respect, it has indicated sources such as classic textbooks by learned academics and lawyers where detailed information can be obtained.

2) What Does the Future Hold? World Trade and Globalisation: the UN and the ICC

In the chapter dealing with the ICJ, the point was made that the number of disputes coming before the Court has increased in the last 15 years and that it is now resorted to by States from all corners of the world. These include many Commonwealth countries: Australia, Botswana, Cameroon, Canada, India, Namibia, Nauru, New Zealand, Nigeria, Pakistan, Singapore, South Africa and Uganda.

Both the United Nations and the ICC have made it clear that world trade needs to expand. The increase in the use of the ICJ – and of the other courts and tribunals considered in the Manual – seems likely to continue as world trade increases.

The United Nations

In September 2000 the UN Millennium Declaration was adopted by 190 Heads of State and Government and passed unanimously by the members of the UN General Assembly. It grew out of a number of international development goals set in 1996 and reaffirmed the commitment of UN members to achieving significant, measurable improvements in people's lives.

Millennium Development Goal 8 is concerned with *"contributing to and upholding an open, equitable, rules based, predictable, and non-discriminatory multilateral trading system… [which] is also an important instrument for achieving other Goals."* [121]

At the request of UN Secretary-General Kofi Annan, the UN Millennium Project has identified practical strategies to eradicate poverty by scaling up investments in infrastructure and human capital. These strategies are described in the UN Millennium Project's Report *Investing in Development: A Practical Plan to Achieve the Millennium Development Goals.*[122]

Various task forces have identified the interventions and policy measures needed to achieve each of the Goals. In *Trade for Development*, the Task Force on Trade makes a strong case for a multilateral trading system that is more supportive of economic growth and poverty alleviation in developing countries. Trade expansion, it noted, is critical for the achievement of the UN Goals:

> *"Openness to trade is associated with higher incomes and better economic performance. While there are differences of view about the magnitude and strength*

121 UN Millennium Project Task Force on Trade, *Trade for Development*, Earthscan, 2005. See www.unmillenniumproject.org/reports/tf_trade.htm.

122 Available at www.unmillenniumproject.org/reports/index.htm.

of this relationship, the general direction of effect is not in doubt: no closed or isolated economy has performed better than those integrated into the world economy. Openness to trade gives firms and households access to world markets for goods, services, and knowledge – lowering prices, increasing the quality and variety of consumption goods, and fostering specialization of economic activity in areas where countries have a comparative advantage. Trade generates more investment and fosters higher knowledge. Trade is important for generating the positive externalities that are associated with learning through the diffusion and absorption of technology."

The Task Force also makes the following important points:

> *"The transparency requirements of the trading system not only facilitate trade but help to promote good governance of trade policy by requiring countries to make information on trade-related policies publicly available – and hence contribute to global good governance.*
>
> *"The trading system provides for the settlement of trade disputes in an orderly process of negotiation and adjudication, rather than by sheer weight of economic or trade power alone."*

That latter statement perhaps summarises the areas that this Manual has tried to cover: systems and tribunals whose aim – through litigation, arbitration or ADR – is the fair and orderly resolution of international disputes in the areas of trade and commerce, intellectual property and investment.

The International Chamber of Commerce

The ICC has produced a Report – *Standing up for the Global Economy* – that looks at the importance of world trade from the perspective of businesses.[123]

In the Preface to the Report, the Secretary-General of the ICC, Maria Livanos Cattaui, says that companies *"are in a unique position to observe and help shape today's global economy. They are at the heart of international trade and investment, engaging in business across borders and linking economies together into a more interconnected world."*

The purpose of the Report *"is to provide a business perspective on some of the main issues and concerns raised by globalization. Is it pushing governments to the sidelines? Is it a threat to jobs? Is it helping to overcome poverty, or creating more? How can the changes arising from globalization be managed?"*

The Secretary General says that globalisation *"has already brought unprecedented improvements in material welfare to billions of people. The evidence suggests that the global economy of today offers an unparalleled opportunity to raise living standards across the world. That disparities between rich and poor are still too big is undeniable. But those who sincerely want to alleviate the poverty of millions in the developing world should focus on practical ways to harness the potential of globalization instead of making globalization a scapegoat."*

---

123 The Report can be viewed at: www.iccwbo.org/home/statements_rules/statements/2004/Globalization%20paper%2004.

Ms Livanos Cattaui goes on to say that there are two key elements in the Report that she wishes to highlight as *"promising avenues in the quest for a more inclusive global economy: the vast potential for increased South-South trade and the key importance of good governance. A more open world economy and more effective governments are by no means contradictory goals."*

The Report stresses the importance of openness to foreign trade and investment, and the need for *"a sufficiently comprehensive, transparent and non-discriminatory legal framework to operate modern commercial operations (including company law, bankruptcy law, competition law, protection of property rights including intellectual property), and free access to an impartial judicial system to redress wrongs and settle disputes".*

Again, these are points that this Manual has tried to make.

3) The Need for a Fair Legal Framework

Both the United Nations, operating on an inter-governmental level, and the ICC, concerned with the international business community, make the point that a fair legal framework is vital to the development of world trade. The Task Force on Trade emphasises that: *"The creation of an enabling environment for markets to develop requires the rule of law (both an appropriate set of laws, in particular for protecting property rights and resolving contractual disputes, and the fair and effective enforcement of those laws), as well as investment in the basic infrastructure that underpins the whole economy (energy, roads, water, and telecommunications, as well as health and education) ...."*

The Task Force also states that:

> *"Economically sound and legally fair multilateral rules protect the weaker players from the protectionism of the strong and help to create a more level playing field for trade – say, for example, by banning export subsidies in industrial sectors (more easily or massively used by rich countries) or 'voluntary' export restraints (more easily imposed on others by large economies).*
>
> *"The most favored nation (MFN) principle protects smaller players by preventing larger players from carving up world markets among them. MFN spreads the benefits of deals made between major players to all members of the trading system. It also prevents countries from using trade to punish or reward individual countries for political reasons.*
>
> *"Sound rules give predictability to world trade, enabling necessary investments to be made by traders and investors.*
>
> *"Sound multilateral rules reinforce domestic reform efforts and provide a means of locking in reforms and undermining pressures for policy reversal by powerful vested interests. As certain interests have more influence in politics than value in economics, the domestic political process will sometimes choose import protection even when it does not serve the national economic interest – hence the value of international obligations in the making of national trade policy."*

In the Preface to *Standing up for the Global Economy*, the Secretary-General of the ICC echoes this point. She says that, more than ever *"globalization requires the enforcement of the rule of law, the encouragement of innovation, the development of efficient infrastructure, the improvement of education and social programmes, and greater political and economic stability in order for countries to seize all the opportunities that the world economy can offer"*.

A fair legal framework, operating in the context of international tribunals, is vital to the harmonious operation of international trade and commerce, and to the settlement of disputes in those areas. Harmonious international relations are also vital in the other areas considered in the Manual: land and maritime boundary disputes and investor-State disputes.

In dealing with the five chosen topics in the field of international dispute settlement, the Manual has attempted to cover systems and tribunals whose aim – through litigation, arbitration or ADR – is the fair and orderly resolution of supranational disputes and international commercial disputes. In doing so it has sought to take a view from within the Commonwealth, looking at the world beyond the Commonwealth.

List of Cases and Arbitral Awards

Decisions of National Courts

Australia

Esso/BHP v Plowman [1995] 128 ALR 391

China

Food Industries Planning and Servicing Ltd (Switzerland) v *China Hua Yang Technology and Trade Corporation* [1997] Beijing No 1 People's Intermediate Court

France

Hilmarton (UK), Appellant v Omnium (France), Appellee [1994] Decision No. 484, Cour de Cassation, First Civil Chamber

Hong Kong

Hing Yip Hing Fat Co Ltd v Daiwa Bank Ltd [1991] 2 HKLR 35

United Kingdom

Adams v Cape Industries [1990] 2 WLR 657

BHP Billiton Petroleum and others v Dalmine SpA [2003] EWCA Civ 170, [2003] BLR 271

Bouygues UK Limited v Dahl Jensen UK Limited [unreported decision of the Court of Appeal] 31 July 2000

British Shipbuilders v VSEL Consortium Plc [1971] 1 Lloyd's Rep 106

Channel Tunnel Group Limited v Balfour Beattie Construction Limited [1993] 2 WLR 262 HL

Jones v Sherwood Computer Services Plc [1992] 1 WLR 277

Lemenda Trading Co Ltd v African Middle East Petroleum Co [1998] 1 QB 448

Minmetals Germany GMBH v Ferco Steel Ltd [1999] 1 All ER (Comm) 315

Omnium de Traitement et de Valorisation SA v Hilmarton Ltd [1999] 2 Lloyd's Rep 222

Shell (UK) Limited v Enterprise Oil Plc [1999] 2 Lloyd's Rep 456

Soleimany v Soleimany [1998] 3 WLR 811

Veba Oil Supply and Trading GmbH v Petrotrade Inc [2001] 2 Lloyd's Rep 731

Westacre Investments Inc v (1) Jugoimport-SDRP Holding Co Ltd (2) Beogradska Banka DD [1999] EWCA Civ 1401, [2000] QB 288, [1999] 3 WLR 811, [1999] 2 Lloyd's Rep 65

United States

Bridas Corporation and Others v Government of Turkmenistan and Others, and State Concern Turkmenneft [2003] No. 02-20929, US Court of Appeals 5th Cir (9 September 2003)

Bridas S.A.P.I.C. v Government of Turkmenistan, No. 04-20842, 2006 WL 1046963 at *1 (5th Cir 21 April 2006) www.ca5.uscourts.gov/opinions/pub/04/04-20842-CV0.wpd.pdf

Garrity v Lyle Stuart [1976] 40 NY2d 354

Clout

Canada: *Europcar Italia S.p.A v Alba Tours International Inc* [1997] OJ No. 133, 23 OTC 376 (Gen. Div.) http://interarb.com/clout/clout366.htm

Bermuda: *Skandia International Insurance Company and Mercantile & General Reinsurance Company, and others v Al Amana Insurance* [1995] 4 Re LR 63 http://interarb.com/clout/clout127.htm

Decisions of International Tribunals

International Court of Justice (ICJ)

Application of the Convention on the Prevention and Punishment of the Crime of Genocide (*Bosnia and Herzegovina v Serbia and Montenegro)* ongoing ICJ www.icj-cij.org/icjwww/idocket/ibhy/ibhyframe.htm as at 11 May 2006

Armed Activities on the Territory of the Congo (Democratic Republic of the Congo v Uganda) [2005] ICJ General List No 116 (19 December 2005) www.icj-cij.org/icjwww/idocket/ico/icoframe.htm

Asylum Case (Columbia v Peru) [1950] ICJ Rep 266 www.icj-cij.org/icjwww/idecisions/ isummaries/icpsummary501120.htm

Case Concerning the Frontier Dispute (Burkino Faso / Republic of Mali) [1986] ICJ General List No 69 ICJ 2 (22 December 1986), [1986] ICJ Rep. 554 www.icj-cij.org/icjwww/icases/iHVM/ihvm_iorders/ihvm_iorder_19870409.pdf

Case Concerning the Temple of Preah Vihear, Merits [1962] ICJ Judgement (15 June 1962), [1962] ICJ Reps 6 www.icj-cij.org/icjwww/idecisions/isummaries/ictsummary620615.htm

Certain Criminal Proceedings in France (Republic of the Congo v France) Judgement pending; latest press release at www.icj-cij.org/icjwww/idocket/icof/icofframe.htm

Clipperton Island Case [1932] 26 AJIL 390

Croatia v Serbia and Montenegro latest developments at www.icj-cij.org/icjwww/idocket/iybh/iybhframe.htm

Eastern Greenland Case: Denmark v Norway [1932] reported at [1933] PCIJ Rep. Ser. A/B No 53 www.icj-cij.org/cijwww/cdecisions/ccpij/serie_AB/AB_53/01_Groenland_Oriental_Arret.pdf and www.icj-cij.org/icjwww/icases/igjm/igjm_ijudgments/igjm_ijudgment_19930614.pdf

Gulf of Maine (USA v Canada) [1984] ICJ Reps 246, 23 ILM 1197 www.icj-cij.org/icjwww/icases/icigm/icigm_ijudgment/icigm_ijudgment_19841012.pdf

Land, Island and Maritime Frontier Dispute (El Salvador / Honduras: Nicaragua intervening) [1992] Judgement of ICJ (11 September 1992), [1992] ICJ Rep. 351 www.icj-cij.org/icjwww/icases/ish/ish_ijudgments/ish_ijudgment_19920911.pdf

Maritime Delimitation in the Black Sea (Romania v Ukraine) [2004] General List No 132, ICJ (19 November 2004), latest press release at www.icj-cij.org/icjwww/idocket/iru/iruframe.htm

Minquiers and Ecrehos (France / United Kingdom), Merits [1953] Judgement, ICJ (17 November 1953), [1953] ICJ Reps.47 www.icj-cij.org/icjwww/idecisions/isummaries/ifuksummary531117.htm

North Sea Continental Shelf Cases [1969] ICJ Rep 3 www.icj-cij.org/icjwww/idecisions/isummaries/icssummary690220.htm

Oil Platforms Case (Islamic Republic of Iran v United States of America) [2003] ICJ Judgement (6 November 2003) www.icj-cij.org/icjwww/idocket/iop/iopjudgment/iop_ijudgment_20031106.PDF

Western Sahara [1975] Advisory Opinion, ICJ (16 October 1975), [1975] ICJ Reps 12 www.icj-cij.org/icjwww/idecisions/isummaries/isasummary751016.htm

International Tribunal for the Law of the Sea (ITLOS) [124]

"Camouco" Case (Panama v France), Prompt Release [2000] ITLOS Case No 5 (7 February 2000)

Case concerning Land Reclamation by Singapore in and around the Straits of Johor (Malaysia v Singapore), Provisional Measures [2003] ITLOS Case No 12 (8 October 2003)

124 All the cases listed under ITLOS can be found at www.itlos.org/start2_en.html.

Case concerning the Conservation and Sustainable Exploitation of Swordfish Stocks in the South-Eastern Pacific Ocean (Chile / European Community) [2000] ITLOS Case No 7 (20 December 2000)

"Chaisiri Reefer 2" Case (Panama v Yemen), Prompt Release [2001] ITLOS Case No 9, order of 6 July 2001 and order of 13 July 2001

"Grand Prince" Case (Belize v France), Prompt Release [2001] ITLOS Case No 8 (20 April 2001)

"Juno Trader" Case (Saint Vincent and the Grenadines v Guinea-Bissau), Prompt Release [2004] ITLOS Case No 13 (18 December 2004)

"Monte Confurco" Case (Seychelles v France), Prompt Release [2000] ITLOS Case No 6 (18 December 2000)

MOX Plant Case (Ireland v United Kingdom), Provisional Measures [2001] ITLOS Case No 10 (3 December 2001)

M/V "Saiga" Case (Saint Vincent and the Grenadines v Guinea), Prompt Release [1997] ITLOS Case No 1 (4 December 1997)

M/V "Saiga" (No. 2) Case (Saint Vincent and the Grenadines v Guinea), Merits [1999] ITLOS Case No 2 (1 July 1999)

Southern Bluefin Tuna Cases (New Zealand v Japan; Australia v Japan), Provisional Measures [1999] ITLOS Case Nos 3 and 4 (27 August 1999)

"Volga" Case (Russian Federation v Australia), Prompt Release [2002] ITLOS Case No 11 (23 December 2002)

Permanent Court of International Justice (PCIJ)

Chorzow Factory Case [1928] PCIJ Ser A No 17 www.icj-cij.org/cijwww/cdecisions/ccpij/serie_A/A_17/54_Usine_de_Chorzow_Fond_Arret.pdf

International Awards

International Centre for the Settlement of Investment Disputes (ICSID)

SGS Société Générale de Surveillance S.A. v Islamic Republic of Pakistan [2003] ICSID Case No. ARB/01/13 6 August 2003 www.worldbank.org/icsid/cases/SGS-decision.pdf

SGS Société Générale de Surveillance S.A. v Republic of the Philippines [2004] ICSID Case No. ARB/02/6 29 January 2004
www.worldbank.org/icsid/cases/SGSvPhil-declaration.pdf

Compaña de Aguas del Aconquija S.A. and Vivendi Universal v Argentine Republic [2001] 40 ILM 426; ICSID Case No. ARB/97/3 (21 November 2000)
www.worldbank.org/icsid/cases/ada_AwardoftheTribunal.pdf

Permanent Court of Arbitration (PCA)

Bank for International Settlements [2003] Final Award of Tribunal (19 September 2003)
www.pca-cpa.org/ENGLISH/RPC/BIS/EFA.pdf

Barbados / Trinidad – Arbitration pending
www.pca-cpa.org/ENGLISH/RPC/#Barbados/Trinidad%20and%20Tobago

Belgium / Netherlands ("Iron Rhine Arbitration") [2005] Award of Arbitral Tribunal (24 May 2005) www.pca-cpa.org/ENGLISH/RPC/BENL/BE-NL%20Award%20240505.pdf corrected award of 24 May 2005 www.pca-cpa.org/ENGLISH/RPC/BENL/BE-NL%20Award%20corrected%20200905.pdf

Eritrea-Ethiopia Boundary Commission – Arbitration pending
www.pca-cpa.org/ENGLISH/RPC/#Eritrea-Ethiopia%20Boundary%20Commission

Eritrea-Ethiopia Claims Commission – Arbitration pending
www.pca-cpa.org/ENGLISH/RPC/#Eritrea-Ethiopia%20Claims%20Commission

Government of the State of Eritrea and the Government of the Republic of Yemen [1996] Arbitration Agreement, PCA (3 October 1996)
www.pca-cpa.org/PDF/EY%20Phase%20I.PDF

Guyana / Suriname – Arbitration pending
www.pca-cpa.org/ENGLISH/RPC/#Guyana/Suriname

Ireland v United Kingdom – Arbitration pending
www.pca-cpa.org/ENGLISH/RPC/OSPAR/OSPAR%20final%20award%20revised.pdf

Island of Palmas (US v Netherlands) [1928] 2 RIAA 829
www.pca-cpa.org/ENGLISH/RPC/EY/2ch1ER-YE.htm

Larsen / Hawaiian Kingdom [2001] Arbitral Award, PCA (5 February 2001)
www.pca-cpa.org/PDF/LHKAward.pdf

Malaysia / Singapore [2005] Settlement Agreement, PCA (1 September 2005) Award on Agreed Terms of 1 September 2005
www.pca-cpa.org/ENGLISH/RPC/MASI%20Award.pdf

Netherlands / France [2004] Final Award, PCA (12 March 2004), Final Award of 19 September 2003 www.pca-cpa.org/ENGLISH/RPC/BIS/EFA.pdf

Saluka Investments B.V. v Czech Republic – Arbitration pending; press release of 22 March 2006
www.pca-cpa.org/ENGLISH/RPC/SAL-CZ%20Press%20release%20220306.pdf

Telekom Malaysia Berhad / Government of Ghana [2005] Award of the Arbitral Tribunal, PCA (24 May 2005); very brief description with names of arbitrators www.pca-cpa.org/ ENGLISH/RPC/#A%20Malaysian%20company%20and%20an%20African%20government

World Intellectual Property Organization (WIPO)

America Online, Inc v Chris Hoffman [2001] WIPO Case No. D2001-1184 (19 November 2001) http://arbiter.wipo.int/domains/decisions/html/2001/d2001-1184.html

Chernow Communications, Inc. v Jonathan D Kimball [2000] WIPO Case No. D2000-0119 (18 May 2000) http://arbiter.wipo.int/domains/decisions/html/2000/d2000-0119.html

Julia Fiona Roberts v Russell Boyd [2000] WIPO Case No. D2000-0210 (29 May 2000) http://arbiter.wipo.int/domains/decisions/html/2000/d2000-0210.html

PepsiCo, Inc v Diabetes Home Care, Inc [2001] WIPO Case No. D2001-0174 (28 March 2001) http://arbiter.wipo.int/domains/decisions/html/2001/d2001-0174.html

PepsiCo, Inc v Henry Chan [2004] WIPO Case No. D2004-0033 (20 April 2004) http://arbiter.wipo.int/domains/decisions/html/2004/d2004-0033.html

PepsiCo, Inc v "null" aka Alexander Zhavoronkov [2002] WIPO Case No. D2002-0562 (30 July 2002) http://arbiter.wipo.int/domains/decisions/html/2002/d2002-0562.html

Sony Kabushiki Kaisha v Kil Inja [2000] WIPO Case No. D2000-1409 (9 December 2000) http://arbiter.wipo.int/domains/decisions/html/2000/d2000-1409.html

Statoil ASA v Magne Espelund [2003] WIPO Case No. D2003-0097 (5 May 2003) http://arbiter.wipo.int/domains/decisions/html/2003/d2003-0097.html

Ultimate Electronics, Inc v Phayze, Inc [2002] WIPO Case No. D2002-0851 (3 November 2002) http://arbiter.wipo.int/domains/decisions/html/2002/d2002-0851.html

ad hoc

Eureko B.V. v Poland [2005] Partial Award and Dissenting Opinion (19 August 2005) http://ita.law.uvic.ca/documents/Eureko-PartialAwardandDissentingOpinion.pdf

List of Websites

American Arbitration Association: New York, USA – www.adr.org

American Arbitration Association's International Centre for Dispute Resolution: Dublin, Ireland – www.icdr.org

Arbitration Institute of the Stockholm Chamber of Commerce: Stockholm, Sweden – www.sccinstitute.com

Chartered Institute of Arbitrators: London, UK – www.arbitrators.org

China International Economic Trade Arbitration Commission: Beijing, People's Republic of China – www.cietac.org.cn

CPR Institute for Dispute Resolution: New York, USA – www.cpradr.org

International Chamber of Commerce: Paris, France – www.iccwbo.org

International Centre for Settlement of Investment Disputes: Washington DC, USA – www.worldbank.org/icsid

International Court of Justice: The Hague, The Netherlands – www.icj-cij.org

International Dispute Resolution Centre: London, UK – www.idrc.co.uk

International Tribunal on the Law of the Sea: Hamburg, Germany – www.itlos.org

London Court of International Arbitration: London, UK – www.lcia-arbitration.com

Netherlands Arbitration Institute: Rotterdam, The Netherlands – www.nai-nl.org

Permanent Court of Arbitration: The Hague, The Netherlands – www.pca-cpa.org

SCC Mediation Institute – the Mediation Institute of the Stockholm Chamber of Commerce: Stockholm, Sweden – www.sccinstitute.com

United Nations: New York, USA – www.un.org

United Nations Commission on International Trade Law: Vienna, Austria – www.uncitral.org

World Intellectual Property Organization: Geneva, Switzerland – www.arbiter.wipo.int

Index

About the Author

Anthony Connerty is an English barrister in practice in Chambers in London, Birmingham and Leeds. He is also a consultant to French and Italian law firms in Paris and Milan. He has appeared in most English courts. His areas of practice include international trade and business law: contractual disputes; sale and carriage of goods; oil contracts; documentary credits; conflict of laws; jurisdiction disputes, etc.

Mr Connerty acts as counsel and sits as arbitrator in both domestic and international arbitrations – International Chamber of Commerce (ICC), London Court of International Arbitration (LCIA), American Arbitration Association (AAA) and ad hoc (including arbitration under the UNCITRAL Rules) – in claims involving hundreds of millions of US dollars. He has a particular interest in oil and gas. He is a long-time member of the Energy Institute (formerly the Institute of Petroleum) and has spoken at meetings organised in Shanghai and Qatar by the World Petroleum Congress (now the World Petroleum Council). He also has a great interest in China and is one of the few UK members of the China International Economic and Trade Arbitration Commission (CIETAC) in Beijing.

In addition, Mr Connerty is a Chartered Arbitrator, a Fellow of the Chartered Institute of Arbitrators, a Fellow of the Hong Kong Institute of Arbitrators, and a panel member of various international arbitration bodies including, as well as CIETAC, the Hong Kong International Arbitration Centre, the UN's World Intellectual Property Organization (WIPO), the Cairo Regional Centre for International Commercial Arbitration, the American Arbitration Association's International Panel, the Lagos Regional Centre for International Commercial Arbitration and the Energy Arbitrator's List. He is a Centre for Effective Dispute Resolution (CEDR)-accredited mediator and acts as counsel and as mediator in commercial mediations. He has lectured on arbitration and other dispute resolution processes in Britain, Europe, Africa, the Middle East and Asia. In May 2005 Mr Connerty spoke on domestic and international arbitration and acted as sole arbitrator at a mock international commercial arbitration at the Lagos Regional Centre for International Commercial Arbitration in which leading members of the Nigerian Bar participated.

Mr Connerty was the Chairman of the Organising Committee for a two-day Conference on Dispute Resolution in the Oil and Gas Industries, which was held at the Guildhall in the City of London in 2004. The Keynote Speaker was HRH The Duke of Kent.

Mr Connerty's articles on international dispute resolution – with an emphasis on oil and gas – have been published in various journals worldwide. Some of his articles on China have been translated into Mandarin.

anthonyconnerty@lambchambers.co.uk
anthonyconnerty@arc-chambers.com
www.arc-chambers.com

Kolibri 360 GmbH
Ferdinand-Jühlke-Straße 7
99095 Erfurt, Deutschland
produktsicherheit@kolibri360.de